10-3   Pa

Symbiosis in Parent–Offspring Interactions

Symbiosis in Parent–Offspring Interactions

Edited by
LEONARD A. ROSENBLUM
Downstate Medical Center
Brooklyn, New York

and
HOWARD MOLTZ
The University of Chicago
Chicago, Illinois

PLENUM PRESS • NEW YORK AND LONDON

Library of Congress Cataloging in Publication Data

Main entry under title:

Symbiosis in parent–offspring interactions.

   Includes bibliographical references and index.
   1. Mother and child — Addresses, essays, lectures. I. Rosenblum, Leonard A. II.
Moltz, Howard. [DNLM: 1. Object attachment — Congresses. 2. Parent–child rela-
tions — Congresses. WS 105.5.F2 S986 1982]
BF723.M55S95 1983   155.4'18   83-13671
ISBN 0-306-41410-4

The cover design incorporates medieval symbols from *The Book
of Signs,* by Rudolf Koch. They represent man, woman, pro-
creation, pregnancy, childbirth, and the united family. They are
used with the permission of Dover Publications, New York,
New York.

Cover design by Gary G. Schwartz and Josephine Wan

©1983 Plenum Press, New York
A Division of Plenum Publishing Corporation
233 Spring Street, New York, N.Y. 10013

Printed in the United States of America

Contributors

JEFFREY R. ALBERTS • Department of Psychology, Indiana University, Bloomington, Indiana

CHRISTOPHER L. COE • Department of Psychiatry and Behavioral Sciences, Stanford University School of Medicine, Stanford, California

BENNET G. GALEF, JR. • Department of Psychology, McMaster University, Hamilton, Ontario, Canada

DAVID J. GUBERNICK • Department of Psychology, Indiana University, Bloomington, Indiana

MYRON A. HOFER • Departments of Psychiatry and Neuroscience, Albert Einstein College of Medicine at Montefiore Hospital and Medical Center, The Bronx, New York

THERESA M. LEE • Committee on Biopsychology, The University of Chicago, Chicago, Illinois

SEYMOUR LEVINE • Department of Psychiatry and Behavioral Sciences, Stanford University School of Medicine, Stanford, California

DENNIS W. LINCOLN • M.R.C. Reproductive Biology Unit, Centre for Reproductive Biology, Edinburgh, Scotland

CAROL ZANDER MALATESTA • The Graduate Faculty, New School for Social Research, New York, New York

HOWARD MOLTZ • Committee on Biopsychology, The University of Chicago, Chicago, Illinois

LEONARD A. ROSENBLUM • Department of Psychiatry and Primate Behavior Laboratory, State University of New York, Downstate Medical Center, Brooklyn, New York

GARY G. SCHWARTZ • Department of Psychiatry and Primate Behavior Laboratory, State University of New York, Downstate Medical Center, Brooklyn, New York

RAE SILVER • Department of Psychology, Barnard College, Columbia University, New York, New York

DEL THIESSEN • Department of Psychology, The University of Texas at Austin, Austin, Texas

SANDRA G. WIENER • Department of Psychiatry and Behavioral Sciences, Stanford University School of Medicine, Stanford, California

ALAN R. WIESENFELD • Department of Psychology, Livingston College, Rutgers University, New Brunswick, New Jersey

Preface

As part of the preparation of the materials for this volume, the contributors attended a conference designed to explore the basic concept of symbiosis and its applicability to the study of parents and their offspring. Each participant was asked to focus not on the parental behavior of various species, but on parent and offspring as a symbiotic unit. The presentations were informal and the discussions intense. The chapters that follow were written many months after the conference and reflect the authors' efforts to integrate the comments and criticisms of their colleagues. Out of this amalgam, the present volume was shaped. We wish to thank the National Institute of Mental Health for supporting the conference (Grant MH 36276) and the University of Chicago for hosting it. The editors would also like to acknowledge the contributions of Dr. M. Lewis and Dr. J. Reinisch, who provided additional perspectives on the discussions held at the meeting. Special thanks are due Gary Schwartz for his thoughtful assistance throughout the course of this project. Lu Ann Homza has provided invaluable secretarial help.

Leonard A. Rosenblum
Howard Moltz

Contents

1. A Conceptual Framework for the Study of Parent–Young Symbiosis   1
   Howard Moltz and Leonard A. Rosenblum

2. Reciprocity and Resource Exchange: A Symbiotic Model of
   Parent–Offspring Relations   7
   Jeffrey R. Alberts and David J. Gubernick

3. The Coordinate Roles of Mother and Young in Establishing and
   Maintaining Pheromonal Symbiosis in the Rat   45
   Howard Moltz and Theresa M. Lee

4. The Mother–Infant Interaction as a Regulator of Infant
   Physiology and Behavior   61
   Myron A. Hofer

5. Physiological Mechanisms Governing the Transfer of Milk from
   Mother to Young   77
   Dennis W. Lincoln

6. The Thermoenergetics of Communication and Social Interactions
   among Mongolian Gerbils   113
   Del Thiessen

7. Biparental Care: Hormonal and Nonhormonal Control
   Mechanisms   145
   Rae Silver

8. Assessing Caregiver Sensitivity to Infants: Toward a
   Multidimensional Approach   173

   Alan R. Wiesenfeld and Carol Zander Malatesta

9. Psychoendocrine Responses of Mother and Infant Monkeys to
   Disturbance and Separation   189

   Christopher L. Coe, Sandra G. Wiener, and Seymour Levine

10. Allometric Influences on Primate Mothers and Infants   215

    Gary G. Schwartz and Leonard A. Rosenblum

11. Costs and Benefits of Mammalian Reproduction   249

    Bennett G. Galef, Jr.

Index   279

A Conceptual Framework for the Study of Parent–Young Symbiosis

HOWARD MOLTZ and LEONARD A. ROSENBLUM

In 1879, the German botanist, Anton De Bary coined the term *symbiosis* in recognition of the fact that dissimilar organisms often enter into close physical associations. Although broadly defined, the concept was narrowly applied. Most often, the associations referred to were parasitic and the organisms studied were from widely different taxa. Today, the term *symbiosis* is used more broadly; it includes commensal and mutual as well as parasitic relationships. In other words, one symbiote may benefit without disadvantage to the other (commensal symbiosis) or indeed both may benefit (mutual symbiosis). More-over, we now recognize that members of the same species, physically dissimilar only with respect to gender or developmental status, may also enter into relationships properly called symbiotic.

A significant example of a symbiotic relationship between conspecifics is that between parent and young. Yet, here, the concept of symbiosis has been applied almost exclusively in its older and narrower sense, the association being considered parasitic. That symbiosis may not be exclusively parasitic—that the mother, for example, may benefit from the association—has rarely been considered. Of course, in an obvious sense, she does benefit: it is through the survival of her offspring that she achieves a measure of intergenerational representation. Thus, the parent–offspring symbiosis may be viewed as an association that has evolved in the interest of genetic continuity, an adaptation that promotes the fitness of each member.

HOWARD MOLTZ • Committee on Biopsychology, The University of Chicago, Chicago, Illinois 60637.   *LEONARD A. ROSENBLUM* • Department of Psychiatry and Primate Behavior Laboratory, State University of New York, Downstate Medical Center, Brooklyn, New York 11203.

Parents and offspring, of course, are not genetically identical, and so they have divergent needs across their respective lifetimes. This potential conflict notwithstanding, it is our view that their relationship is not simply an "arms race" (Dawkins & Krebs, 1979). Indeed, we suggest that the members of the unit most often interact in a complementary rather than a competitive fashion. This complementarity we take to be the result of selection; in other words, we regard the parent–young symbiosis as having evolved toward a relationship that is most economical for the unit as a whole. It is assumed, furthermore, that such overall economy maximally enhances the fitness of the individual partners as well. By this formulation, we do not deny that parent–offspring conflict exists; rather, we emphasize the the unit reflects an integrative effort at adaptation. Of course, many increments to fitness that result from the success of the symbiotic unit do not emerge until long after the symbiotic union has been dissolved. These are ultimate benefits, important but removed in time.

What we want to focus on at present are proximate benefits and prox- imate costs, the advantages and disadvantages that accrue to both parent and young during the most interactive phase of their relationship. We shall be concerned, therefore, with the short-term phenotypic consequences of the parent–young symbiosis, rather than the long-term genotypic effects.

Parents and young interact in a variety of ways, and each interaction carries cost or benefits that may be the same or different for the two partners. Moreover, even when their behavior is complementary, the physiological effects of the interaction may be quite dissimilar. For example, the rat mother consumes the feces of her young, and the young consume the feces of their mother. In the mother, there is a change in the microfloral profile of the gut and an alteration in the metabolism of selected liver steroids; in the young, there is an increase in deoxycholic acid and the promotion of brain myelin. For the young, there are distinct benefits; for the mother, there appears to be neither proximate benefit nor proximate cost (see Chapter 3). Obviously, the symbiotic relationship between parent and young is complex, certainly too complex to be characterized simply as *parasitic, commensal,* or *mutual.* It is not that these terms are without meaning; it is that they have been applied too broadly. We propose instead a conceptual framework that focuses not on the symbiotic relationship as a whole, but on the individual interactions consti- tuting that relationship. And of each interaction we ask, "What are the consequences for both parent and young?"

Our emphasis on consequences reflects two assumptions. The first is that natural selection has shaped the symbiotic relationship to maximize the fitness of both parent and young. The second is that selection has operated on functionally distinct exchanges. Based on these assumptions, we believe that an appropriate unit of study is the interaction itself. Accordingly, our framework considers particular exchanges between parent and young and classifies each in terms of *what* is being exchanged and of what *effects* the exchange is exerting.

But what, in fact, is meant by the "interaction as the unit of analysis"? Both the temporal span across which one views the interaction and the level of analysis undertaken will shape the characterization of the exchange under study. The period of time during which the parent–offspring interaction is viewed may vary, and the duration of our observation directly influences our assessment of the form and consequences of the interaction. Parental actions may have imperceptible consequences for the infant in the immediate present, but important consequences may be discernible when a wider time frame is adopted. For example, parental singing in the presence of the fledgling sparrow does not have manifest consequences for song acquisition until many months have passed.

Similarly, depending on the level of analysis, the consequences of an interaction may be detected or may escape notice entirely. Thus, behavioral observations of a rat litter may reveal active suckling behavior on the part of the pups, but little response in the sleeping mother. Neuroendocrine analysis, on the other hand, would uncover the complex chain of neural and hormonal events that leads to the letdown of milk in the sleeping mother (see Chapter 5). This does not mean that one level of analysis is superior to another, only that each approach makes its own contribution to our understanding of the symbiotic exchange.

This example of the nursing litter reflects still another dimension of our proposed framework: there may be a considerable difference in what each partner furnishes the other in the exchange. Thus, the suckling infant provides sustained negative pressure on the teat, and the mother, after an interval, ejects milk into the pup's mouth. Likewise, the specific cry of a human baby produces sudden changes in the cardiac activity of the mother. These changes are accompanied by caregiving behavior, which in turn alters the baby's physiological state (see Chapter 8). We see that a partner's contribution to an exchange may be informational rather than physical. On the other hand, what each partner contributes to the exchange need not differ except perhaps in quantity. The infant primate clings to the ventrum of the mother, draws heat, and thus reduces its own thermogenic requirements; the mother in turn, may utilize the clinging infant as a heat sink to cool her own body (see Chapter 10). The rat mother provides her litter with fluid in the form of milk. The pups, in turn, provide the mother with fluid in the form of urine—which she avidly ingests (see Chapter 2). These thermal and fluid exchanges mutually benefit both parent and offspring. Certainly, this is not always the case. As a dramatic example, the cannabalized rodent "sacrifices" its own survival for the presumptive proximate benefit of the mother. More subtly, the human infant pays an immunological cost when bottle-fed, while the mother avoids the energetic and metabolic demands of lactation. We can define a symbiotic interaction as any bilateral exchange of commodities or signals between parents and offspring determined at any level of analysis, across any delimited temporal interval.

In recognition of the diversity of these interactions, we propose the following descriptive categories. It is our intention that these categories be used conjointly in classifying any exchange:

1. *Synchrony-asynchrony.* The consequences of any exchange may emerge at the same time or at different times for the two partners.
2. *Homomorphy-heteromorphy.* What is exchanged may be the same or different for the two partners.
3. *Isovalency-contravalency.* The consequences of any exchange carry a valence (beneficial, neutral, or detrimental) that may be the same or different for the two partners.

As an example of how these categories might be applied, consider the following set of exchanges between a monkey mother and her infant: (1) a 3-week-old infant crawls several feet from its attendant mother; (2) approached suddenly by another member of the group, the infant screeches; (3) the mother rushes to the infant and retrieves it to her ventrum; (4) the infant clings, then begins rooting for the nipple; (5) reaching the nipple, the infant begins nursing; (6) five minutes later, the mother, with her infant still nursing, is approached and then groomed by two females in the group.

Assuming that only behavioral observations were made, how might we characterize the exchanges recorded here?

A. *Infant screeches—mother retrieves:* With the two events close together in time, with one member providing a vocal cue and the other physical support, and with the infant benefiting at no apparent cost or benefit to the mother, we would classify this a *synchronous, heteromorphic,* and *contravalent* exchange.

B. *Mother retrieves—mother is groomed by others:* Since these two events are separate in time and the mother, in offering physical support to the infant signals her maternal status to conspecifics, we would classify this as an *asynchronous, heteromorphic, isovalent* exchange.

Had we carried out selected physiological measurements (EKG's, for example) in parallel with our behavioral observations, additional exchanges would have come into view:

A. *Infant screeches—mother retrieves:* The infant screech is accompanied by a rapid increase in cardiac activity, first in the infant and then in its mother. Retrieval rapidly attenuates this response in both partners. From the perspective of cardiovascular stress, both partners benefit; but this benefit to the mother is the product of a contribution to the exchange that is decidedly different from that provided by the infant. Viewed at this level, the exchange would be described as *synchronous, heteromorphic,* and *isovalent.* The same exchange viewed above entirely from a behavioral perspective was judged *contravalent* because of its presumed benefit to the infant with neither cost nor benefit to the mother.

A conceptual framework, if it is to do more than merely pigeon-hole a particular set of phenomena, must reach beyond itself. It must prompt the user to look where he or she might not have looked. It must point to relationships that might otherwise have excaped notice. Since our conceptual framework is not restricted in time nor anchored to a particular species, and since it is as relevant to a behavioral as to a physiological level of analysis, it can be widely applied. It allows us to take phenotypically different forms of exchange and look at each under the same conceptual rubric. This, of course, is an elemental step in the development of any science. Having taken that step, we can then undertake the task of seeking lawful relationships among symbiotic interactions both within and between species. We offer the present classificatory scheme as a modest beginning, and we welcome both the critical judgments and the constructive contributions of our colleagues.

References

De Bary, A. *Die Erscheinung der Symbiose.* Strassburg; Karl J. Trubner, 1879.
Dawkins, R., & Krebs, J.R. Arms races between and within species. *Proceedings of the Royal Society of London,* 1979, *205,* 489–511.

Reciprocity and Resource Exchange

A Symbiotic Model of Parent–Offspring Relations

JEFFREY R. ALBERTS and DAVID J. GUBERNICK

Introduction

The concept, metaphor, model, or reality of "symbiosis in parent–young interactions" poses a delightful intellectual and empirical challenge. This chapter represents a preliminary exploration of a symbiotic model of parent–offspring relations. Our purpose is to examine whether, how, to what extent, and with what outcomes the relations of parents and offspring are, indeed, symbiotic. We will attempt to establish a psychobiological framework for our model of symbiosis in parent–young relations. This framework is based on both biological and psychological concepts of symbiosis. However, we rely primarily on the biological model, because biologists have grappled with conceptual and empirical problems relating to symbiosis for more than a century. There is much to be learned from their experience.

First, we review some ways in which the term *symbiosis* has been used in biology and in psychology. We then draw on these notions to place parent–infant relations first in a context of "reciprocal relations" and then in a parallel framework of "resource exchange," both of which bear on the overall

JEFFREY R. ALBERTS and DAVID J. GUBERNICK • Department of Psychology, Indiana University, Bloomington, Indiana 47405. Preparation of this chapter and some of the research reported herein were supported by research Grant MH 28355 and Research Scientist Development Award MH 00222 both from the National Institutes of Mental Health to Jeffrey R. Alberts, and by grant BNS-81-09656 from the National Science Foundation to Jeffrey R. Alberts and David J. Gubernick. The authors gratefully acknowledge this support.

concept of symbiotic relationships. In the final section of the chapter, we consider parent–offspring relations in a framework that addresses the questions and issues that constitute a "psychobiology of intimate associations" and then use symbiosis as a model of parent–offspring relations.

The Meaning of Symbiosis

Biological

About a century ago, in a paper delivered to a group of naturalists and physicians, Heinrich Anton De Bary (1879) introduced the term *symbiosis* (from the Greek, *meaning* "living together"). *Symbiosis* was proffered by De Bary as a *general term* that includes all instances and degrees of relationships that involve the "living together of unlike organisms." (For a terminological tour de force on this topic, see Hertig, Taliaferro, & Schwartz, 1937.) The types of associations between dissimilar organisms explicitly embraced by De Bary's term included *parasitism* (associations in which there is overt and damaging exploitation of one associate by the other); *mutualism* (associations that involve mutual benefit); and *commensalism* (associations in which one member benefits nutritionally from the other without harming it).

Over the years, it became increasingly common for biologists to use the term *symbiosis* in reference to associations of mutual benefit. Hertig *et al.* (1937) suggested that the use of *symbiosis* in its "restricted" sense (denoting *mutualism*) derived from the appeal of numerous stunning examples of mutualism that had become prominent in the literature, as well as from some erroneous interpretations of earlier work. Still more recently, there has been a trend toward using *symbiosis* in its original, "general" sense, partly in recognition of the futility of devising systems of nonoverlapping categories that can incorporate the full range of the interindividual associations found in nature (Henry, 1966; Starr, 1975; Whitfield, 1979). The various uses of *symbiosis* have generated considerable confusion and debate among association biologists. It is clear that there is no single accurate or correct meaning of *symbiosis*, even within the diciplines of biology.

The following "hybrid" definition represents the common, albeit imprecise, criteria that appear in contemporary biological usage: Symbiotic relationships connote some degree of physical closeness, which often involves the sharing of some resources, as well as the integration of behavioral and/or physiological activities. Symbiotes are usually members of two dissimilar species. The mutual benefits enjoyed by each participant, when they exist, are not necessarily assumed to be equal; the emphasis is usually on some type of interdependence, often metabolic.

Psychoanalytic

Symbiosis is also an important and respected concept within the psychoanalytic literature. Margaret Mahler and her associates (Mahler & Furer, 1960; Mahler, Pine & Bergman, 1975) applied the term *symbiosis* to a crucial stage in child development. Their definition of the term differs in many important ways from the original biological definition, but there are fundamental commonalities between the two that are directly relevant to our purpose in this chapter.

In its psychoanalytic sence, the word *symbiosis* denotes a state of psychological "undifferentiation," an inferred and hypothetical stage of early "intrapsychic" development, during which the human infant does not distinguish itself from the mother or from its physical environment.

The symbiotic phase of child development (which can span postnatal months 2–7) is characterized by close physical contact between the infant and the mother. General cutaneous contact and the stimulation derived from nursing are considered the crucial experiential components of this phase. The normal symbiotic phase provides the undifferentiated infant with a secure emotional base from which to experience and interpret the world. With this security, the infant can proceed through the process of "individuation," which results in the emergent ability to distinguish the "I" from the "not-I" (Mahler *et al.*, 1975).

Mahler's emphasis was primarily on the infant and its development, but she explicitly recognized the existence and functional value of the stimulation received by the mother during the symbiotic phase. The concept of parental stimulation by offspring is an important consideration that we discuss later. The psychological metaphors of mother–young symbiosis have spawned several divergent lines of inquiry and analysis. Research by Bowlby (1969) and by Ainsworth (1973), for example, has made important contributions to our appreciation of the mechanics and the functional outcomes of mother–infant interactions. Their behavioral (and to some extent biological) variation of the analytic theme provides a valuable indication that the idea of symbiosis can be applied productively to parent–young relationships.

The psychoanalytic concept of symbiosis shares with the biological use of the term: (1) a denoted intimacy of association involving proximity, contact interaction, and some mutualistic use of resources, and (2) recognition of a functional bond that satisfies some "need(s)" of the participants (cf. Mahler *et al.*, 1975, pp. 43–44). The *differences* between the two uses of the term, however, are enormous. The analytic term is expressly mentalistic. The biological meaning describes patterns of interactions on physical levels. In their purest forms, the two "meanings" or uses of *symbiosis* appear nonconvergent.

Symbiosis for Psychobiologists

One of the challenges of psychobiology, however, is to integrate and to synthesize approaches, methods, concepts, and data from separate sources into a unified view. An implicit assumption underlies this approach, namely, that the biology of behavior is simultaneously organized on multiple levels. Psychobiological concerns, therefore, include both "proximate" and "ultimate" causes of behavior, and they lead investigators to evaluate the organismic, environmental, and phylogenetic factors that mediate, shape, and determine the behavior of organisms.

Which facets of symbiotic relations are pertinent to psychobiologists interested in parent–offspring relations? For our purposes, symbiosis is the existence of interdependent and mutually beneficial relations between individuals with dissimilar characteristics. Most "biological" examples of symbiosis involve individuals from two different species, but the behavior, anatomy, and physiology of adult mammals are as dissimilar from those of their neonatal counterparts as are the differences between symbiotic species. So, we can apply symbiotic concepts intraspecifically (to parents and offspring) and still honor the original spirit of the term.

Among the common hallmarks of (biological) symbiotic relations are processes of *close integration* and *mutual benefit,* which usually involve a degree of *metabolic interdependence.* Can we find such processes, real or parallel, in mother–infant systems? Clearly, the physical proximity of parents and infants is one way in which the developmental dyad fulfills at lease some of the biological criteria. But what about the notion of mutualism?

It is common for adult humans to recognize and even to extol the contributions of time, goods, and services made by parents to their offspring. Indeed, embodied in the concept of "parental investment" is an underlying belief in a fundamentally *unidirectional flow of resources* from parent to offspring, usually at some cost to the parent.

In contrast to the traditional unidirectional view of parent–infant relations, a symbiotic model implies a *bidirectional* resource flow. In recent years, our awareness of offspring effects on parents has been heightened (see, for example, Harper, 1981; Lewis & Rosenblum, 1965). This relatively new awareness validates our plan to explore a symbiotic model of parent–offspring relations. Our focus in this chapter is on the proximate causes of behavior (as opposed to evolutionary ones) and other immediate avenues of interaction between parents and offspring. We ask, therefore, about the reciprocal nature of parent–young relations and about the commodities and cues transmitted and received by parents and offspring. What is exchanged, and to what extent is the flow of commodities and cues bidirectional? If these exchanges exist, do they conform to the criteria of symbiotic relations? What are the consequences of the exchange in terms of the regulation of parent–offspring relations?

Reciprocity in Parent–Offspring Interactions

As a first step in our analysis, we shall discuss the kinds of perspectives that reveal reciprocities between parents and offspring. These perspectives alert us to the different types of reciprocal relations that exist on separate, but interconnected, levels of organization. We shall consider the maternal behavior cycle of the Norway rat in relation to offspring development as an exemplar of our approach.

Perspectives and Levels

To integrate the processes of offspring's behavioral development and parental behavior, it is necessary to apply two perspectives simultaneously. One is a *developmental* perspective, a view through time of the dynamic changes in the behavioral profiles of the offspring and of the parents. The second perspective is a *dyadic* view: the behaviors of the offspring and the parent are separable, but by virtue of their interaction, the behavior of one is indecipherable when isolated from the other.

We use the term *developmental dyad* to refer to the parent–offspring association. Implicit in this term is an understanding that the organization of the dyad as an entity changes over time as each participant undergoes developmental change. The overall organization of the dyad and the interaction of its components reflect the *synchrony* that often exists in dyadic relations. Rosenblatt and Lehrman (1963) provided some of the most incisive and lucid analyses of developmental dyads, and they made seminal contributions to current methodological and conceptual approaches, particularly in studies of nonhuman species.

The conceptualization of developmental synchrony was seminal because it stimulated further investigations into the complexities of dyadic control in parent–offspring relations. As will be discussed below, it is known that the states and activities of each member of the dyad are, in part, reciprocally regulated by stimuli presented by the other member. Dyadic controls and interactions exist at numerous levels of organization (e.g., behavioral and physiological) and are evident within different time frames (ranging in length from seconds to weeks). When closely coupled bidirectionality exists in specific reciprocal relations, the resultant loops can synchronize dyadic events. Thus, the source of order, organization, timing, and control of developmental synchrony is not completely endogenous within each part of the dyad. Some control of the one is to be found with the other. This is the concept of *reciprocity* or *reciprocal relations* in developmental dyads. Awareness of such reciprocal processes is fundamental to our appreciation of the dynamic relations between parents and offspring. Reciprocity is also one of the primary features of symbiotic relationships (see above).

Reciprocities between parents and offspring can be identified on both behavioral and physiological levels. The channels of reciprocity that operate in parent–infant dyads can cross between levels of organization. Thus, the behavior of the infant can alter the *physiology* of the mother and vice versa. Interindividual synchronization between behavior and physiology, elucidated by Lehrman (1965; see also Silver, this volume) for breeding pairs of ring doves, also applies to developmental dyads.

We consider here some examples of reciprocal relations in the mother–litter dyad that involve both behavior and physiology and then proceed to a more detailed discussion of resource exchange as a parallel system of reciprocity. An enormous spectrum of intricate and intimate "connections" forms within an interacting dyad when behavior and physiology are interwoven. Nevertheless, important functional relations between parents and infants can be subtle, and they require special empirical analyses. Interindividual connections between parents and offspring have been called "hidden regulatory processes" by Hofer (1978). He used the term to emphasize our relative naiveté in these realms and, also, our general reluctance to recognize the causal link between "internal" physiological events and "external" behavioral stimuli.

Maternal Behavior Cycle in Relation to Offspring Development

The mother–litter dyad in the Norway rat (*Rattus norvegicus*) provides useful data for our consideration of symbiotic relations between parents and offspring. Numerous reviews exist that detail virtually all aspects of the maternal behavior cycle in the rat (Rosenblatt, 1969; Rosenblatt & Lehrman, 1963; Rosenblatt & Siegel, 1981; Weisner & Sheard, 1933) and the development of the pups (Altman & Sudarshan, 1975; Bolles & Woods, 1964; Small, 1899). We shall therefore illustrate a few major points and then discuss the issues relevant to the present analysis.

Maternal behavior in the rat is usually made up of four definable activities: nest building, licking the pups, nursing, and transport (see Figure 1). Associated with each activity is a resource flow that can be viewed as a commodity exchange in a symbiotic framework.

Figure 2 depicts the general pattern of results that has been found repeatedly in quantitative studies of maternal behavior and maternal

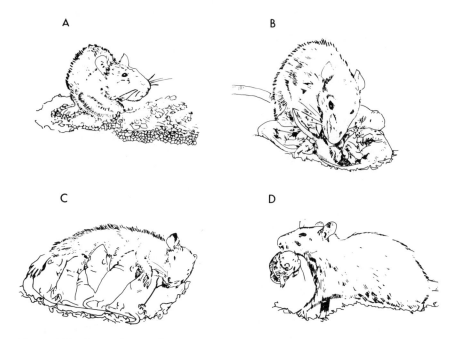

Figure 1. The four major maternal activities of rats: A. nest building; B. licking; C. nursing; D. carrying.

"responsiveness." The amount of time spent in each category of maternal behavior, the vigor of the behavior, and the dam's readiness to perform such behavior surge around the time of birth, are maintained at high levels for the first week or so, and then gradually wane.

Figure 3 is a general overview of rat pup development and emphasizes the rapidity and the drama of the ontogenetic changes packed into the three weeks from birth to weaning. Born in a litter of 6–12 pups, the infants are transformed from glabrous, blind and deaf, squirming neonates into furry, highly social, and versatile young mammals.

Rosenblatt and Lehrman (1963; see also Rosenblatt, 1965) carefully observed and documented the exquisite adaptive relationships that exist at each postnatal stage between the quantity and quality of maternal activities and the needs and abilities of the offspring. If we compare the cycle of maternal behavior (Figure 2) with the profile of pup development (Figure 3), we can begin to appreciate the adaptive "fit" of the two developmental processes. As the offspring manifest increasing sensorimotor capacities, relative thermal independence, and a more complex social repertoire, the dam's behavior is appropriately attenuated and redirected.

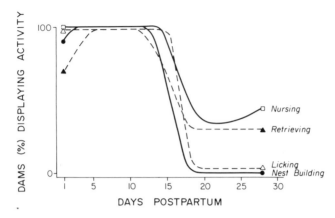

Figure 2. Generalized pattern of maternal activities during the lactational cycle.

Reciprocities Affecting Approach and Contact Behavior

Initially, rat pups cannot actively approach the mother and establish contact. Stimuli from the dam serve as cues for approach when the pups become mobile and as cues for cohesion when they are in proximity. Nevertheless, mother–young contact is not controlled solely by the dam. The litter as a whole, and the pups individually, present stimuli that can attract the mother (see below) and can control the dam's presence in the nest. Mother–young reunions are a reciprocal dance of approach and contact. A variety of pup cues attract and guide the behavior of the mother.

Acoustic Cues

Rat pups emit high-frequency vocalizations (30–40 kHz) under a number of circumstances. These "ultrasonic" cries are highly audible to the mother and may either call her to the litter or alert her to an infant isolated from the nest (Bell, 1974).

Chemical Cues

Chemical cues are often important attractants within developmental dyads. It is not always possible to dissociate odor and taste stimuli as they are presented in complex, natural situations, so we will for the present merely refer to these as chemical cues. Chemical cues from pups determine the amount of genital licking contact they receive from the mother (Moore & Morelli, 1979). Male rat pups are licked more than female pups. Males possess a urinary stimulus that acts as an attractant. Production of this attractant begins within the first few days after birth and is presumably linked to early testicular function.

Mother rats, in turn, present a variety of chemical cues that attract the pups and that operate on the pups' behavior minutes after birth. Blass and his associates have suggested that chemical cues common to both amniotic fluid and the saliva of lactating rats are behaviorally attractive to infant rats (Blass & Teicher, 1980; Pedersen & Blass, 1981; Teicher & Blass, 1976). Saliva deposited on the nipples during the mother's self-licking can guide the newborn to the appropriate stimuli (nipples) in its new, extrauterine environment (Pedersen & Blass, 1981). Dimethyl disulfide has been tentatively identified as a constituent of amniotic fluid and saliva that functions as a stimulus for nipple attachment.

Fecal (Leon, 1974), urinary (Galef & Muskus, 1979; Nyakas & Endroczi, 1970), and other residual odors (Galef & Muskus, 1979) deposited by rat dams and other conspecific adults attract rat pups. One of the most thoroughly analyzed cases of olfactory attraction is the pup's response to the anal excreta of lactating rats. The soft, volatile anal excreta of mother rats, emitted in large quantities during lactation when their food intake is extraordinarily great (Fleming, 1976a), have been found to guide approaches by pups in a special airstream device (Leon, 1974; Leon & Moltz, 1971). Interestingly, the mother rat does not emit behaviorally significant amounts of this attractant until about Day 14 of lactation—the age at which rat pups first become behaviorally responsive to this cue. Leon and Moltz (1971, 1972) documented this remark-

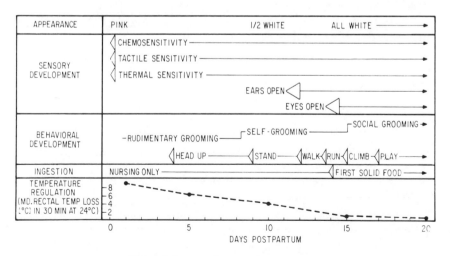

Figure 3. Pattern of rat pup development.

able instance of developmental synchrony between stimulus emission and behavioral responsivity in a classic set of experiments. Cessation of maternal production of the attractant coincides with the age at which pups' responsivity wanes—around Day 28 postpartum. In fact, stimuli from the growing, maturing pups terminate the dam's production of the attractant (Moltz & Leon, 1973; Moltz, Leidahl & Rowland, 1974; Moltz & Lee, this volume).

Thermotactile Cues

Most mammals, young and adult, are strongly attracted to warm stimuli, and this tendency is usually augmented by "comfortable" tactile cues. Rat pups approach and maintain contact (i.e., huddle) with virtually any animate or inanimate object that is warm (Alberts, 1978a; Alberts & Brunjes, 1978; Cosnier, 1965; see also Rosenblatt, 1976). Adult rats display a similar propensity (Latane, Joy, Meltzer, & Lubell, 1972). The body heat and general tactile cues of the mother represent powerful stimuli for the establishment and maintenance of contact by the pups (Alberts, 1978a). For about the first two weeks of life, thermal cues seem to be the most salient for contact behavior in rats (Alberts & Brunjes, 1978). Even at older ages, when olfactory cues are more salient, thermal cues do not diminish in overall attractiveness (Alberts & Brunjes, 1978). Jeddi (1979) has suggested that thermotactile cues are of great importance to human neonates. He posited that the mother's breasts are, in effect, attractive zones of heat surrounded by a challenging region of relative cold. According to Jeddi's view, the infant is equipped to channel its behavior at such warm zones and, by doing so, provides itself with rewards.

Offspring also represent sources of heat to the mother, and to each other in species that bear multiple young.

Reciprocities between Behavior and Physiology

Behavioral Regulation

The chain of events comprising the "act" of nursing in the rat involves a melange of reciprocal interactions. When the mother reunites with the litter in the nest, there is a bidirectional barrage of thermal, olfactory, and tactile stimulation. For instance, maternal licking of the pups provides tactile stimulation, cools the pups by evaporation (Barnett & Walker, 1974), and may release the visceral (internal) stimuli that accompany voiding (Capek & Jelinek, 1956). The pups, aroused and activated by the dam, follow chemical and tactile cues on the mother's ventrum that lead to her nipples. The pups exert rhythmic stimulation by sucking and simultaneously kneading the region around the nipples with their forepaws. Pup stimulation induces sleep or a sleeplike state in the dam (Lincoln, Hentzen, Hin, van der Schoot, Clarke & Summerlee, 1980; Voloschin & Tramezzani, 1979). While the dam is in this behaviorally quiescent condition, characterized by high-amplitude, low-frequency electroencephalographic patterns, the stimulation derived from suckling summates in the paraventricular nucleus of the dam's hypothalamus and activates a pulsatile release of oxytocin from the posterior pituitary body. The hormone quickly reaches the densely vascularized mammary region, where it reduces contractions of the myoepithelial cells around the mammary tissue and thereby ejects the milk from the lumina of the mammary glands into the pups' mouths. The milk stimulus, in turn, elicits a dramatic "extension reflex" in the pups (Lincoln, this volume). The sequence is repeated every 4–10 min for the duration of the nursing bout (Lincoln, Hill, & Wakerly, 1973).

The physiological effects of maternal presence and of mother's milk eventually produce profound quiescence in the pups. Most of the pups' sucking time may be spent in sleep or in sleeplike states, characterized by high-amplitude, low-frequency EEG patterns (Shair, Brake, & Hofer, 1980).

Behaviorally, and on a relatively broad scale, the suckling relationship between litter and mother involves reciprocally synchronized alternation of activation and quiescence. The pups are initially aroused by the dam. The activate pups then directs their activities at the mother, and, as they attach to nipples and suckle, the dam settles. Maternal quiescence is a permissive condition for milk delivery, as well as a stimulus that eventually produces quiescence in the pups.

Autonomic Regulation

Physiologically, the suckling relationship also has numerous reciprocal consequences. Maternal stimuli maintain an autonomic state in rat pups. Hofer (1970) removed dams from the maternal nest and found a 40% reduction in heart rate and respiration in 2-week-old pups. This cardiorespiratory depression was prevented when the pups were provisioned with appropriate amounts of milk (Hofer, 1973). Similarly, it has been independently suggested that autonomic stress reactions can be reversed or attenuated by normal, nest-typical olfactory cues (Campbell & Raskin, 1978; Conely & Bell, 1978; Compton, Koch, & Arnold, 1977).

Endocrine Regulation

Smotherman, Wiener, Mendoza, & Levine (1976) have proposed that pup cues, specifically tactile stimulation provided by suckling, create a state of adrenocortical responsiveness that "buffers" the lactating female from normal stress responses. The degree to which adrenocortical responses are reset depends on the quantity of suckling stimulation the dam receives. Svare (1981) has described a parallel system of suckling stimulation regulating the maternal aggression of mice.

Suckling stimulation affects the release of maternal pituitary hormones, which have profound effects on the mother's physiology and behavior and the course of the maternal cycle. During the normal course of lactation, mother rats nearly triple their premating levels of food intake (Cole & Hart, 1938; Ota & Yokoyama, 1967) in order to meet the nutritive demands of a growing litter (see the section below on "Nutritive Resources"). Fleming (1976a) showed that milk production by the mother is not totally responsible for the maintenance of lactational hyperphagia. Rat mothers that received injections of ergocornine (a drug that inhibits prolactin secretion and hence blocks lactation) or direct galactophore ligation continued to show maternal behavior and significant (though attenuated) hyperphagia if they received suckling stimulation from pups. Leon (1974) reported that the inverse manipulation, an injection of prolactin, induced hyperphagia in females. Grosvenor (1965) has shown that teat stimulation acts to release both prolaction and oxytocin from the rat pituitary (cf. Lincoln, this volume). The act of nursing not only involves reciprocal behavioral and physiological interactions and consequences for mother and offspring but also provides a pathway for resource exchange.

Maturation Regulation

Another reciprocal system in parent–offspring relations in rodents involves the regulation of sexual maturation rate. This is an especially interesting example because it involves male participation. The rate of sexual maturation in young mice can be significantly accelerated or retarded by exposure to adult conspecific urine. The direction and magnitude of the modulatory effect is determined by the gender and the reproductive status of the urine "donor." Female mouse pups, that were exposed to the urine of adult males reach reproductive maturity 8 days early, an acceleration of about 30% relative to control mice (Vanderbergh, 1967, 1973). The urine of adult *female* mice retards the rate of female sexual maturation relative to controls (Drickamer, 1977).

These data thus provide an example of how adult stimuli can regulate the hormonal status of the offspring. The litter's regulation of female hormonal status and the parents' ability to modulate the endocrine development affecting sexual maturation and gender differentiation (Moore & Morelli, 1979; Vandenbergh, 1973; Ward, 1972) complete a reciprocal loop of hormonal regulation between parents and offspring.

Resource Exchange in Parent–Offspring Relations

Symbiotic relations, as we have presented them, involve a *close integration* of the participants that may be of some *mutual benefit*. There is often a degree of *metabolic interdependence* that includes the *sharing of some resource*. In the previous section we presented one aspect of our symbiotic model of parent–offspring relations; the close integration and reciprocal nature of mother–infant interactions.

The notion that resources are transferred and exchanged between members of a symbiotic partnership is also central to our model of parent–offspring relations. In this section, we examine the resources or commodities that are transferred and exchanged between mothers and infants and the extent of metabolic interdependence. These commodities include nutritive, thermal, and mechanical resources, water, and electrolytes. In the final section of this chapter, we integrate these two concepts of reciprocity of interactions and resource exchange and then provide a "psychobiology of intimate associations."

Nutritive Resources

Milk initially provides almost all the dietary needs of the young for maintenance, growth, and heat production. But to meet the nutritional needs of the developing young and the metabolic demands imposed by lactation, mothers increase their food and water intake and their selection of specific nutrients, rather than depleting their own body reserves.

For example, average daily food consumption may increase from 15 g to 60 g over the first 25 days of lactation (Brody, 1945; Redman & Sweney, 1976; Stolc, Knopp, & Stolcova, 1966). Females with large litters ingest more food than females with smaller litters (Fleming, 1976b; Kumaresan, Anderson, & Turner, 1967; Ota & Yokoyama, 1967). This lactational hyperphagia represents a 180%–250% increase over the food intake of nonreproductive females and is controlled in part by the suckling stimulation provided by the young (Cotes & Cross, 1954; Fleming, 1976a). As a result, lactating females may consume from 50 to 250 kcal/day over the first three weeks postpartum, depending on the caloric value of their diet (Brody, 1945; Kennedy, 1957; Stolc *et al.,* 1966).

Furthermore, lactating females elevate their consumption of specific nutrients (Richter & Barelare, 1938). Some of these nutrients appear to affect mainly the volume of milk produced, while others, such as calcium, fats, vitamins, and minerals, primarily affect the composition of milk and therefore what is transferred to the young (see Nelson & Evans, 1961, for fuller discussion).

Milk secretion also dramatically alters the water balance of lactating

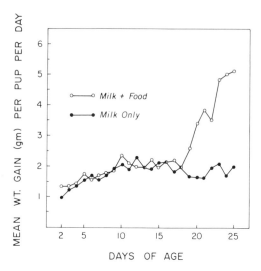

Figure 4. Growth rate of rat pups maintained on food and maternal milk (normally weaned) or milk only (delayed weaning).

females (see below) and necessitates enhanced water consumption. Water intake increases during lactation by 100%–200% (Nelson & Evans, 1961; Richter & Barelare, 1938).

These resources are eventually transformed into milk, which is then passed to the young. Milk production reaches a maximum on Days 15–16 postpartum, then gradually declines and terminates by Days 28–30 (Babicky, Ostadalova, Parizek, Kolar, & Bibr, 1970). The amount of milk produced by a female with a litter of eight pups may increase from 10 ml on Day 2 to 50 ml on Day 15 (Brody, 1945; Hanwell & Linzell, 1972; Stolc *et al.*, 1966). Litter size affects milk yield but not the time of maximum milk production or of milk termination (Babicky, Ostadalova, Parizek, Kolar, & Bibr, 1973).

Neonatal rats depend solely on maternal milk for nutrients and water throughout the first two weeks postpartum (Babicky *et al.*, 1970; Babicky, Pavlik, Parizek, Ostadalova, & Kolar, 1972). The calories provided in milk are sufficient to meet the energetic demands of the growing young during that time, that is, 35–40 kcal/day/100 g body weight (Brody, 1945; Hahn & Koldovsky, 1966). Estimates of the energetic output of milk vary, depending on the assumed caloric content of milk, for example, 1.63 kcal/g (Stolc *et al.*, 1966); 1.7 kcal/g (Hahn & Koldovsky, 1966); or 2.3 kcal/g (Brody, 1945). Reported calorific values of milk for a female with a litter of eight range from 10–15 kcal on Day 1 to 65–80 kcal on Day 15 to 80–115 kcal on Day 21 postpartum (Brody, 1945; Stolc *el al.*, 1966), resulting in a total of 500–1400 kcal of milk produced over the first three weeks of lactation.

However, since the milk supply diminishes after Day 15 (Babicky *et al.*, 1970) and becomes calorically less dense (Keen, Lonnerdal, Clegg, & Hurley, 1981; see below), and mothers increasingly avoid the nursing attempts of their young (Rosenblatt, 1965), rat pups must meet their energy requirements by ingesting other sources of food and water. That a continued supply of maternal milk is not alone sufficient to maintain normal growth is illustrated in Figure 4, which presents the growth of pups maintained only on milk (delayed weaning) or a mixed diet of milk, solid food, and water (normal weaning). The increased growth rate of the normally weaned pups between Days 18 and Day 25 coincides with their increasing consumption of food and water during that time.

In summary, lactation is the mother's way of transforming nutritive resources that the young cannot gather and process into a form that they can digest and utilize (Pond, 1978). Thus, milk secretion can be viewed as the continuation of a flow of resources originating in the external environment and passing through the mother on the way to the pups. However, as discussed below, the flow of milk resources is not always so unidirectional.

Exchange of Milk Components

A commodity may be transferred in only one direction, from mother to young, while other resources are mutually exchanged. A resource that flows in only one direction can still have important consequences for the continued integration and elaboration of mother–infant interactions. The production and transfer of milk, or more accurately milk constituents, nicely illustrates the unidirectional and bidirectional flow of resources.

Water is the major constituent of the milk of most species (Ling, Kon, & Porter, 1961; Jenness, 1974). Mammary gland secretions may have evolved as a means of providing water to the young, especially the young of terrestrial vertebrates (Chadwick, 1977). For some time after birth the mother's milk is the *only source* of water and electrolytes for the developing young. Thus, the production of milk is an important feature in the water and salt regulation of mothers and young. It is the transfer of water and electrolytes between mother and young that provides us with a fascinating example of bidirectional resource exchange and mutual interdependence and benefit.

Rats' milk is nearly 73% water (Luckey, Mende, & Pleasants, 1954) and provides the only substantial source of water for rat pups until Days 17–18 postpartum, when pups first drink water (Babicky *et al.*, 1972). The amount of milk (and water) produced and transferred to the pups gradually increases, reaching a maximum on Days 15–16 postpartum, and then slowly declines and ceases by Days 28–30 (Babicky *et al.*, 1970). The amount of water transferred to the young can be considerable. For example, at Day 10 postpartum, a female with a litter of eight pups produces 42–48 ml of milk (Friedman &

Bruno, 1976; Hanwell & Linzell, 1972), which contains 31–35 ml of water. This water loss represents 30%–35% of the female's total daily water intake (Friedman, Bruno, & Alberts, 1981) and imposes a severe drain on the female's body fluid balance. All is not lost, however, for mothers recover this water in a simple, yet elegant, fashion—by ingesting pup urine.

Mothers lick their pups' anogenital regions and consume pup urine during the suckling period (Rosenblatt & Lehrman, 1963). Over a 24-hour period, a litter of eight 10-day-old pups produces 23 ml of urine (Friedman, 1979), nearly all of which is consumed by the mother (Friedman & Bruno, 1976; Friedman et al., 1981). By licking pup urine, the mothers reclaim 65%–70% of the fluids they had previously transferred to their young.

Mothers can use pup urine and water interchangeably as a source of fluid. When the consumption of urine is prevented by urethral ligation of pups, lactating females increase their water intake by approximately the same amount (18 ml) that they would have normally ingested of pup urine (Friedman et al., 1981). Females deprived of water increase the anogenital licking of pups and presumably consume more urine (Friedman et al., 1981). Urine consumption is thus an important means of water conservation for lactating females (cf. also Baverstock & Green, 1975).

Urine consumption also helps maintain the female's body fluid homeostasis. Females deprived of water and pup urine (urethras ligated) for 24 hr on Day 10 postpartum sustained an intracellular dehydration similar to that of mothers deprived of water only (Friedman et al., 1981). However, the mothers deprived of both water and urine were twice as hypovolemic as the water-deprived females, a result indicating that the consumption of pup urine helps primarily to preserve the extracellular fluid balance.

Mothers deprived of both water and urine ingested more isotonic saline during a 4-hr session than water-deprived females, although both consumed equal amounts of water. This enhanced saline intake may reflect their response to a greater plasma volume deficit, or it may reflect, in part, the well-known salt appetite of lactating rats (Richter & Barelare, 1938).

This salt appetite is of some interest, since pup urine contains sodium, potassium, and chloride, which are transferred to the pup in the mother's milk (Ling et al., 1961). Pup urine is hypotonic for the first 2½ weeks postnatally (Falk, 1955; Friedman, 1979). Lactating rats prefer hypotonic 0.08-M saline solution to water during the first two weeks after birth, as shown in Figure 9. The anogenital licking of pups by mothers may therefore be modulated, in part, by the female's appetite for salt. The extent to which urine consumption helps regulate maternal electrolyte concentrations is as yet undetermined.

While pups help regulate the water conservation and fluid homeostasis of their mothers, mothers also help modulate the water metabolism of their young. Not only does the female provide water in the form of milk, but by licking the anogenital area of her pups, she provides exteroceptive stimulation, which induces the kidneys to produce and excrete more urine (Capek & Jelinek, 1956). And since rat pups do not spontaneously micturate until Days 15–18, they must depend on their mothers' licking in order to micturate reflexively (Capek & Jelinek, 1956). This reflex is of further importance because the neonatal rats' kidneys may be deficient in detecting the presence of excess water or rapidly increasing urine output until the third week postpartum (Falk, 1955).

Another fascinating example of resource exchange and the subtle regulation of mother–infant functioning in rats is iodine and thyroxine uptake and secretion in milk. During lactation, there is a marked increase in iodine uptake by the mammary glands and a concomitant decrease in maternal thyroidal iodine uptake and serum thyroxine (Iino & Greer, 1961; Lorscheider & Reineke, 1971). Although the concentration of iodine in milk remains about the same (180 ± 75 ng/ml), the amount of iodine transferred to the young increases as the amount of secreted milk increases, reaching a peak around Days 14–16 postpartum (Stolc et al., 1966). In addition to the iodine that the mothers lose through milk production, they also excrete substantial amounts of iodine/thyroxine in feces and urine. The percentage of a dose of radioactively labeled iodine (I^{131}) excreted by lactating females on Day 14 postpartum was 10% in milk, 10% in urine, and 30% in feces (Grosvenor, 1962). Lactating females increase their dietary intake of iodine, but in an amount that appears to be somewhat less than what is lost (Nelson & Evans, 1961; Stolc et al., 1966). The predicted iodine deficiency is not realized, however, partly because of the maternal consumption of pup urine and the reclamation of the iodine lost in the milk (Samel, Caputa, & Struharova, 1963), and possibly also by mothers' ingesting their own feces.

In addition to the recycling of iodine, the thyroxine secreted in milk regulates the thyroid functioning of suckling pups by suppressing both the iodine uptake of the thyroids and the serum thyroxine levels (Strbak, Macho, Knopp, & Struharova, 1974). For example, when milk thyroxine is withdrawn from pups, through either premature weaning (Macho, Strbak, & Strazovcova, 1970) or thyroidectomy of the mothers (Strbak et al., 1974), the pups' thyroids increase in iodine uptake and the production of thyroxine. The normal suppression of pup thyroid activity that occurs from about Days 2–20 postpartum (Samel, 1968) corresponds to the increased iodine and thyroxine intake by pups during that time (Stolc et al., 1966), while increased thyroid activity parallels decreased iodine–thyroxine consumption. An intriguing potential source of maternal thyroxine/iodine for pups is maternal feces (Grosvenor, 1962), which pups start to ingest about Day 15 postpartum (Galef, 1979). The importance of coprophagia as a means of procuring thyroxine or regulating pup thyroid functioning remains unexplored.

Transfer of Milk Components

The flow of milk's nutritive components, unlike water and electrolytes, is unidirectional. The composition of rats' milk changes considerably with advancing lactation (Keen *et al.*, 1981; Luckey *et al.*, 1954). The gradual transition to solid food also involves an additional change in diet (Hahn & Koldovsky, 1966). As a result, the nutritive intake of the pup changes markedly during the suckling period. Pups also exhibit behavioral and physiological changes that parallel the changing diet composition, in another illustration of the synchrony between mother and young.

The major nutritive components of milk are fats, proteins, and carbohydrates (cf. Ling *et al.*, 1961; Jenness, 1974). Rat milk is relatively high in fats (10%–15%) and low in carbohydrates (3%) throughout lactation (Keen *et al.*, 1981; Luckey *et al.*, 1954). The transition to a solid food diet incorporates a change in the ratio of fat to carbohydrate intake (i.e., higher in carbohydrate, lower in fat) and modifications in digestive physiology. Pups utilize milk lipids to meet almost all of their energy requirements during the first three weeks, and they show large increases in body fat stores as a result of the fat transferred in milk (Hahn & Koldovsky, 1966; Spray & Widdowson, 1950). Milk protein increases steadily from 8% to 12% during the first three weeks, then declines (Keen *et al.*, 1981), and is utilized mostly for growth during the suckling period, rather than as a source of energy (Hahn & Koldovsky, 1966).

The carbohydate reserves of the rat pup are rapidly depleted during the suckling period and are barely maintained by milk carbohydrates (Hahn & Koldosvky, 1966). The predominant and characteristic carbohydrate of milk is lactose, a disaccharide, which is split into its constituent monosaccharides by the intestinal enzyme lactase (β-galactosidase) (Doell & Kretchmer, 1962; Kretchmer, 1972). Lactose increases from 2% to 4% over the first two weeks, then declines to less than 1% by Day 25 (Keen *et al.*, 1981; Luckey *et al.*, 1954). Changes in lactase activity roughly parallel those of lactose. Lactase activity remains elevated until Days 20–21, when there is an abrupt decrease in activity to the low adult levels (Alvarez & Sas, 1961; Doell & Kretchmer, 1962; Rubino, Zimbalatti, & Auricchio, 1964). Without lactase, lactose cannot be utilized and produces gastrointestinal distress (McCracken, 1971). This lactase deficiency and the consequent lactose intolerance may be a means of affecting the rate and time of weaning (Lieberman & Lieberman, 1978). The decline in lactase activity coincides with the transition to solid food, the increased activity of other carbohydrate enzymes (e.g., maltase and sucrase; Rubino *et al.*, 1964); increased glucose absorption; and increased dietary carbohydrate intake (Hahn & Koldovsky, 1966).

Young mammals are susceptible to the invasion of pathogenic agents since infants cannot produce antibodies for some time after birth (Lovell &

Rees, 1961). However, mothers transmit antibodies to their young, providing them with a form of "instant" protection (Solomon, 1971). In rats, some transfer of immunity from mother to young occurs *in utero*, but most passive transfer occurs postnatally (Brambell, 1970; Culbertson, 1938). Maternal immunoglobulins (glycoproteins), derived from blood serum or locally synthesized in the mammary glands (Brambell, 1970; Lascelles, 1977), are transmitted to the young in colostrum and in later milk (Butler, 1974; Lascelles, 1977; Solomon, 1971). Maternal antibodies in colostrum (e.g., IgG) are passed rapidly to the pup's circulation through the walls of the small intestines, while local enteric immunity is established (Barlow, Santulli, Heird, Pitt, Blanc, & Schullinger, 1974). Suckling rats continue to absorb antibodies selectively from immune milk for up to 18 days postnatally, after which this absorptive ability declines and is lost by Day 21, even though maternal antibodies are still available in the milk (Halliday, 1955, 1956, 1959). This decline in the transmission of passive immunity from mother to young coincides with the increasing ability of the pups to actively synthesize their own antibodies (Brambell, 1970) and with a transition to a solid food diet and changes in intestinal enzyme activity (Halliday, 1959). The transmission of such passive immunity to *Trypanosoma, Salmonella, Rickettsiae, Toxoplasma,* and *Brucella,* among others, has been demonstrated (see Brambell, 1970, for further examples).

Although the nutritive components of milk flow in only one direction from mother to young, such transfers help regulate the development of the young and the nature of mother–infant interactions. Mothers increase their food and water intake in response to their young. These nutriments are transformed by the mother into a form the young can utilize. However, the increasing energy demands of the young in the face of a decreasing milk supply that is also becoming calorically less dense necessitate the intake of solid food and water. This consumption of alternate resources results in a change in diet composition. The pup's digestive physiology correspondingly changes with alterations in its diet. Moreover, there are parallel changes in the behavioral interactions between mothers and their young and the development of the offspring (see the section above on "Maternal Behavior Cycle in Relation to Offspring Development").

Thermal Resources

The developing rat pup and the parturient dam both have distinct thermal characteristics that are relevant to the causality and the ecology of their interactions. Thermal balance within and between infants and mothers is an important aspect of the physiology and the psychology of the mother–offspring relationship. Thermal energy is exchanged between the dam and the offspring and is an important regulatory aspect of the dyad. Small, immature mammals are thermally fragile and generally depend on external sources of heat for optimal thermal homeostasis. Calories not used by the pups for body temperature regulation represent energy that can be channeled into the processes of growth and development. In contrast to the infants, the mothers generally have a surfeit of metabolic heat, partly because of stimulation from the offspring.

The normal conditions associated with pregnancy and lactation establish in the dam a unique energetic state in which she generates large quantities of metabolic heat. To maintain thermal homeostasis, rat dams augment heat loss by increasing self-licking, particularly along their well-vascularized, thinly furred nipple lines (Roth & Rosenblatt, 1967, 1968), and by exposing their extended ventral surface for heat dissipation (Wilson & Stricker, 1979). The body-temperature set-point is raised so that the dam can function at higher "basal" temperature, which helps to compensate for increased heat production (Thoman, Wetzel, & Levine, 1968; Wilson & Stricker, 1979).

Numerous morphological and physiological factors make the process of body temperature regulation in the infant rat different from that in the adult. Relative to its size, the infant produces less and loses more body heat than the adult (Taylor, 1960). Thermogenesis by shivering is absent in the infant, and the limits of metabolic heat production are below those of the adults. Heat loss is rapid in the pup for a number of reasons. Infants lack insulative fur and subcutaneous fat. They cannot control heat loss by regulatilng vascular blood flow (Hull, 1973). With small body size comes a relatively enormous heat-losing surface area, and this is one of the greatest physical obstacles to heat balance for small organisms. The problem of thermoregulation is solved in part by the presence of the dam in the nest and her transfer of heat to the litter. The dam's presence in the nest is in turn modulated by a thermal exchange with the litter. The duration of nest bouts declines progressively during the first two postpartum weeks (see the section above on "Reciprocity in Parent-Offspring Interactions"), in terms of both the total time spent with the pups each day and the average length of each visitation by the mother (Grota & Ader, 1969; Plaut, 1974). Leon, Crosskerry, and Smith (1978) systematically examined the relationship of maternal body temperature to nesting time (i.e., time spent in contact with the litter) during the lactational cycle. They presented a parsimonious model that accounts for the observed patterns of nest bout duration (Crosskerry, Smith, Leon, & Mitchell, 1976).

Direct recordings of maternal temperature suggested that nest bouts are terminated when the dam becomes hyperthermic. Increasing heat dissipation from the dam by shaving her fur, lowering the ambient termperature, or cooling the litter increased nest bout duration. Conversely, the time spent with pups was decreased in dams by manipulations that retarded the dissipation of maternal heat: shortening the dam's tail, raising the ambient temperature, and warming the litter. Suppression of prolactin and adrenocortical hormones (secretions that are normally stimulated by the litter) both reduced the normal chronic elevation of maternal body temperature and disrupted the progressive decline in nest bout duration. Maturational factors in the pups that affect the rate of body temperature in the mother were concluded to be the determinants of nest bout duration. More recently, however, Woodside and Leon (1980) have suggested, with empirical support, that the control of nest bout duration is based on the mother's self-regulation of her body temperature, and that dams do not monitor or directly regulate the temperature of the pups. The model clearly focuses on the singular role of the dam and her temperature.

However, the observation that the litter aggregate, or huddle, contracts when the dam leaves the nest and expands when the dam returns (Addison & Alberts, 1980) and that nest temperature and pup temperature are maintained within 2–4°C (Leon *et al.*, 1978; Addison & Alberts, 1980) suggests a more active exchange and maintenance of thermal balance between mother and litter.

The huddle itself is also a major factor in the thermal balance of the developing rat (Alberts, 1978b; Cosnier, 1965). The rat pup reduces its exposed surface area by huddling and thus decreases its surface–volume ratio, conferring the allometric advantages of larger size (see Schwartz & Rosenblum, this volume, for a discussion of scaling and thermoregulation). Alberts (1978b) measured metabolic rate (oxygen consumption) in rat pups alone or in huddles. Huddling reduced metabolic expenditure by as much as 40%, a fact suggesting that huddling is used by pups to conserve metabolic energy. This regulatory interpretation is further supported by an analysis of the behavioral mechanics of huddling. Alberts (1978b) found, for instance, that litters of rat pups display "group regulatory behavior" whereby they increase and decrease the total area size of the huddle as a function of ambient temperature. Huddles were small and compact at low ambient temperatures and were large and dispersed at warm temperatures. The outlines shown along the lines in Figure 5 depict the kinds of area changes represented by the data. Each line shows the average huddle size for a single group of four littermates, tested at one of three different ages.

Not only does huddle size change in response to temperature but pups within the huddle itself systematically and regularly exchange positions (see Figure 6), further enhancing thermoregulation (Alberts, 1978b). The alterations in huddle size and the flow of bodies within the huddle indicate that litters of pups function as a behavioral and metabolic unit, creating and controlling the physical conditions that augment their thermal and metabolic efficiency.

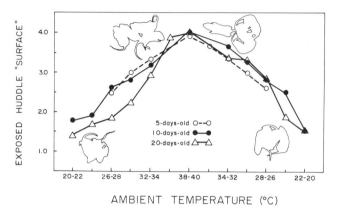

Figure 5. Changes in huddle size as a function of ambient temperature.

When the mother returns to the nest, the huddle expands. It is possible, although not yet confirmed, that the dam uses the litter as a heat "sink." The small, rapidly cooling pups can serve as a highly conductive mass into which the dam can pass some of her excess body heat. Our preliminary data are suggestive. After one hour on a thermocline (an apparatus that provides a calibrated gradient of surface temperatures), lactating rats prefer to stay in cooler temperatures than do virgin females (see Figure 7).

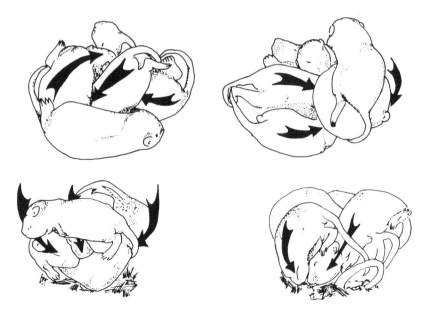

Figure 6. The active flow of pups in a huddle. (Adapted from Alberts, 1978b.)

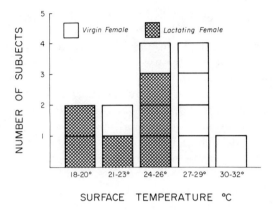

Figure 7. Temperature preferences of lactating and virgin females on a thermocline.

Thermal interactions in mother–young relations are not unique to rats or to rodents; they are characteristic of mammals in general (e.g., Hull, 1973). Despite their relatively large size, human infants are susceptible to thermal challenges similar to those discussed earlier. In general, human infants are protected from heat loss by swaddling and with insulative clothing, but Phillips (1974) has found that heat transfer from direct cutaneous contact with the mother is sufficient to block decreases in body temperature seen in otherwise unprotected infants.

Mechanical Resources

Because of their extremely limited and specialized motor abilities, young altricial infants are generally incapable of prolonged or efficient movement. The transport of offspring by parents is the common solution to this problem, and theoretically, the energy savings enjoyed by the infants is considerable. The energy cost of transport to the parent is an important question about which little is known. Many grazing species, of course, bear precocial young that are equipped shortly after birth with the strength and the coordination to follow the parents or the herd. Rats and most other altricial species establish nests in which the young remain while the mother or parents forage. Nevertheless, the Norway rat, like many altricial animals, displays a species-typical pattern of transport. It is not easy to posit an avenue by which the young provide a form of mechanical energy in direct exchange for that provided by the parents. However, offspring often display stereotyped postures or compensatory adjustments that clearly reduce the energy cost of transport for the adult.

Rat pups, for example, are equipped with a reflexlike reaction to tactile stimulation around the dorsal scapular region. Gripping the skin of these areas, as a rat dam would do with her teeth in transporting her young, elicits a reflex tucking of the tail and retraction of the legs, as shown in Figure 8 (see also Figure 1D). Brewster and Leon (1980) have examined the ontogeny of this response and found that the response subsides in the infant before transport behavior subsides in females.

Many other rodent species display transport as a feature of maternal behavior. In several species of deermice (*Peromyscus*), the young are also transported while they are attached to the mother's nipples (King, 1963).

Transport is quite a ubiquitous feature of parental behavior throughout the animal world. The female scorpion carries as many as 20 young on her back. Male seahorses carry their young in brood pouches (Cloudsley-Thompson, 1960). Some bats regularly transport their young in flight (Bradbury, 1977). A mother sea otter (*Enhydra lutris nereis*) carries her infant on her chest while holding it with her forepaws and swimming on her back (Fisher, 1940).

Figure 8. The transport response of rat pups, a compensatory response to being carried (see also Figure 1D).

Primates of all taxonomic families carry their young. In most species, the offspring cling to the mother's belly or back in a species-typical orientation (Devore, 1963; Hediger, 1955). The infant may be transported for extensive periods of time during the day and for months thereafter. The newborn gorilla is supported by the mother's arm (Schaller, 1963). Similarly, human infants and children receive arm and hand support during transport (Rheingold & Keene, 1965). Other primates, however, that bear altricial young and nest in trees (e.g., *Galago* spp.) transport their young orally, with compensatory responses by the young to being carried (Sauer, 1967).

Symbiosis as a Model of Parent–Offspring Relations

Metaphors of Mother Love

Metaphors play an important role in the thinking and the writing of natural scientists, engineers, and poets alike. The use of figurative language, analogies, and models to explain or clarify one process in terms of another is a valid and valuable approach to examining the world (Hinde, 1960; Lakoff & Johnson, 1980).

In the present chapter, we have used symbiosis as a metaphor in exploring parent–offspring relations. We found that the functional organization of the mother–litter association in *R. norvegicus* can be viewed within the framework of a symbiotic model. The application of symbiotic concepts to parent–infant relations raises new and lively questions that might otherwise have gone unasked and unexplored. To the extent that these new questions yield answers that enhance our understanding of parent–offspring relations, the enterprise is successful.

It is possible to discern ways in which parent–offspring relations are symbiotic in both the most "general" and the most "restricted" senses of the term (see the discussion above of the definitions of *symbiosis*). For instance, in its most general sense (cf. De Bary, 1979), symbiosis encompasses relationships that involve parasitism, commensalism, and mutualism (as defined earlier, p. 8). The analogy of the suckling infant as a parasite has been beautifully elaborated by Galef (1981), who, in another essay in the present volume, has also argued that for most female mammals, the "costs" of reproduction are negligible, a view that supports an analogy of commensalism. Our efforts, in the present chapter, were to explore the implications of symbiosis in its more mutualistic sense, and this approach also proved useful as a heuristic for the analysis of developmental dyads.

It is inappropriate to ask which of these metaphors is "true," or even the most accurate. Unlike a hypothesis, the validity of a metaphor is *not* testable (i.e., falsifiable). We seek to benefit from metaphors through clarified communication, and by deriving inspiration for new perspectives and novel hypotheses.

The "metaphors of mother love" (*viz.*, the various symbiotic views of parent–offspring relations) can be used to help clarify the structure and function of dyadic interactions. Our treatment of symbiosis in parent–offspring relations was organized around two concepts: reciprocity and resource exchange. There is a historical precedent for such organization. The concept of reciprocal relations derives primarily from behavioral analyses, such as those illuminating the dyadic interactions of mothers and infants, and the regulation of behavioral synchrony in rat mothers and their pups. The concept of resource exchange is borrowed from biological traditions, in which the passage between organisms of physical or physiological entities is quantified and is often described in an "economic" framework.

Distinctions fade between reciprocity and resource exchange when viewed in a framework of symbiotic metaphors. Resource exchange appears to be one form of the expression of reciprocal interaction. The *concepts* of behavioral reciprocity and resource exchanges are not completely separable. We should, however, distinguish between these *concepts* and the more singular *process* by which various kinds of commodities move between individuals. The metaphors of symbiosis, as we have reviewed them, help us to see the surprising variety of commodities that are real and important in parent–offspring relations. In the next section, we consider these commodities and the problems of estimating their value in the process of reciprocal exchange.

Commodities of Reciprocal Exchange

Classes of Commodities

The units or commodities that flow between members of a developmental dyad can be initially divided into metabolic and nonmetabolic units. Metabolic commodities are familiar entities: nutritive, thermal, and mechanical energy, water, and electrolytes, as well as antibodies of the immune systems and intestinal bacteria that facilitate the use of nutrients.

To account for the full range of interactions that constitutes parent–offspring reciprocity, the symbiotic model must include commodities of exchange other than traditional metabolic units. At this juncture, symbiosis becomes, for psychobiologists, an exciting conceptual enterprise. There was a safety in the realm of familiar commodities: milliliters of water, calories of energy, milliequivalents of solute, etc. We must, however, expand our view to incorporate levels of exchange that are somewhat less obvious, but not less real. It is essential to recognize the importance and power of nonphysiological stimuli as regulators of both physiological processes and behavior. This recognition is at the heart of our "psychobiological" account of symbiosis in parent–offspring interactions. Such nonmetabolic commodities include specific and general forms of stimulation, such as those derived from tactile, auditory, visual, and olfactory cues. These stimuli can be validly regarded as commodities in a symbiotic framework, because their effects can establish and coordinate synchrony, reciprocity, and interdependent relations.

Levels of Exchange

Instances in which an exchange involves a single metabolic commodity, A, that cycles between the mother and the litter are particularly amenable to a symbiotic model because the degree of equity established between the participants can be evaluated along a single, common dimension. For example, on Day 10 postpartum, a litter of rat pups derives about 30 ml of water from the mother, via her milk. By licking the pups and consuming their urine, the dam reclaims a volume of water equal to about 70% of the amount originally passed to the pups (Friedman *et al.*, 1981; see the section above on "Resource Exchange").

Reciprocal relations also exist in which Commodity A is exchanged for a *different* commodity, B. With different commodities flowing between participants, it is more difficult, particularly in the short run, to estimate the relative value of the cost–benefit ratio derived from the exchange. Moreover, because reciprocal relations occur continuously and simultaneously within and across different "levels of organization" (behavior $\rightleftarrows$ behavior; behavior $\rightleftarrows$ physiology), there can be exchanges of metabolic commodities for nonmetabolic commodities, and vice versa. Finally, one commodity, A, can be exchanged for several different commodities, B and C. For example, when a mother nurses her offspring she is acting simultaneously on them at several levels: she provides nutrients, electrolytes, and water; antibodies innoculate the infants' gut; and a contribution of thermal energy is made. Each point at which stimuli from one participant impinges on the other is a potential site for reciprocal interaction. As an ongoing part of the nursing interaction, the offspring reciprocate and make their contributions. At some stages, excess metabolic heat from the mother is accepted, water and electrolytes are released back to the dam, and tactile and olfactory stimulation are provided. Tactile stimulation by the pups, provided during episodes of both nutritive and nonnutritive suckling, help to regulate hormonal titers in the mother, which allow her to perform the extraordinary metabolic feats required to control simultaneously her own homeostatic processes and those of the biomass of offspring. The same tactile stimulation from the pups regulates more immediate events in the mother, by stimulating the release of milk (see the section above on "Reciprocities between Behavior and Physiology").

Cues of Commodities

In the exchange of primary metabolic resources such as nutritive or thermal energy, the resources themselves often serve as the stimuli toward which behavior is directed. In addition, dyadic interactions are also regulated by previously neutral cues that become, by an experience-dependent process, "token stimuli" and affect the behaivor and physiology of the receiver as though some primary physical cue were in operation. For example, it is usually asserted that nipple stimulation is the stimulus for oxytocin release and milk letdown, but there is also evidence that over the course of the lactational period, the sight or sound of the offspring can elicit milk ejection and concomitant changes in mammary blood supply (Vuorenkoski, Wasz-Hockert, Koivisto, & Lind, 1969). It is commonly assumed that there are experience-dependent processes that render sights, sounds, or odors behaviorally and physiologically effective commodities, but, with few exceptions, these have not been analyzed.

The Value of Commodities

Commodities of symbiotic exchange have measurable "value" to the organisms that use and respond to them. Problems of scaling these values notwithstanding (see the section above on "Classes of Commodities"), it appears that the functional values of both metabolic and nonmetabolic commodities as perceived by symbiotes are dynamic, not fixed or static. For example, rats normally prefer salty tastes. Pregnant and lactating rats, however, are reported to display a dramatically enhanced sodium preference (Richter & Barelare, 1938). Dams voluntarily consumed 3% (.5-M) solutions of NaCl that nonreproductive rats found aversive. Recent work in our laboratory has extended these findings. We presented lactating and nonreproductive female rats with a choice of a dilute, .08-M saline solution and water. Nonreproductive rats were essentially indifferent and consumed nearly equal amounts of dilute saline and water. Lactating dams, however, appeared supersensitive and displayed a significant preference for the .08-M saline solution (Figure 9).

The observation of Richter and Barelare (1938), that the dam's sodium preference returned to baseline upon weaning, suggests that the enhanced value to the mother of NaCl was linked to the presence of the pups. One fascinating implication of this idea is that stimulation of the dam by the litter may increase the mother's sodium appetite and thereby enhance the attractiveness (value) of pup urine, which is salty. In effect, then, the pups may enhance their own attractiveness by interacting with the mother and thereby regulating the amount of maternal attention they receive.

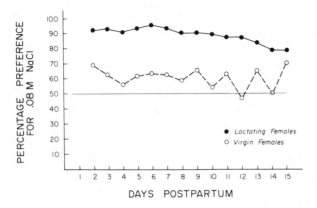

Figure 9. Preference of lactating and virgin females for a .08-M saline solution over water in a two-choice test.

Demonstrations that arbitrary cues can acquire biobehavioral signifi-cance (Alberts, 1981) have important implications for the development over time of complex reciprocal relations. Arbitrary odors become attractive and reinforcing if rat pups experience those odors on the fur of a maternally active rat (Alberts, 1981; Galef & Kaner, 1980). If the arbitrary odor is simply experienced for an equivalent amount of time, odor preferences either do not develop or are very short-lived. Alberts (1981) has reported that the odor preferences that guide filial contact behavior (huddling) in rat pups are derived specifically from thermotactile interactions in the nest. The nutritive rewards and the reinforcing value of nursing do not influence the development of the olfactory preferences that guide huddling. On the other hand, several researchers have found that the nutritive rewards of milk and the nonnutritive reinforcement of suckling stimulation can shape other aspects of pup behavior (Brake, 1981; Kenny & Blass, 1977). Thus, through normal reciprocal inter-actions, stimuli can acquire a reinforcing value that further enhances the stability, intensity, or breadth of interaction that comprises the symbiotic relationship itself.

A Psychobiology of "Intimate Associations"

Aspects of the mother–litter dyad in the Norway rat satisfy both the traditional biological and the psychological criteria for symbiotic association. In terms of the biological criteria: (1) the participants interact in close physical proximity; (2) there is active, bidirectional exchange of metabolic commodi-ties, such as water, electrolytes, and thermal energy; (3) the resource exchange contributes to the participants' homeostasis and creates mutual metabolic interdependency; and (4) they share the same nest resource, which is a strategy of symbionts called *inquilinism* (Whitfield, 1979).

In addition, the maintenance of close physical contact between the rat mother and her young, the attraction each has for the other, and the evidence that infants separated from the mother show both acute and long-term behavioral and physiological disruptions provide a clear parallel to the meaning of symbiosis as it has evolved as a metaphor of psychological development (cf. Mahler *et al.*, 1975).

To answer some of the "psychobiological" questions posed at the beginning of this chapter, we should again make explicit our definition of *symbiosis*. The broad implications of a psychobiological analysis are best served by a relatively "general" use of the term. Smyth (1976), a contemporary proponent of the generalist view, has introduced the term "intimate association" to characterize the types of interindividual relations that exist in nature. The term *intimate association* is especially appropriate in describing parent–infant relations. The organization of developmental dyads is not static. With each stage, the nature and the balance of relations between the participants can change considerably. Smyth's term emphasizes closeness and a sense of unity without specifying a particular kind or constancy of order in dyadic relations.

A psychobiology of intimate associations, as we propose to construct it, is primarily concerned with the early postnatal phase, during which the offspring and parent(s) reside in close physical proximity and the nursing relationship is in operation. Intimacy implies proximity and reciprocity. In this context, resource exchange, when it occurs, is seen as one form of reciprocity.

The parent–infant dyad is a multileveled arena in which reciprocal relations are conducted. Reciprocity involves behavior, physiology, and metabolic goods. The connectedness, or "oneness," implied by symbiotic metaphors is realized in a variety of ways within the parent–infant dyad. The application of symbiotic concepts, as we have framed them, to parent–offspring relations is a new enterprise, and it is much too early to make judgments about its overall merit. Nonetheless, we are sufficiently impressed with the fruits of these early labors to discuss a preliminary and admittedly speculative model of parent–offspring relations based on perspectives inspired by the use of symbiotic metaphors. It is a "psychobiology of intimate associations."

Reciprocal relations between mother and infant start before birth, probably as soon as implantation. But the events most germane to our analysis start shortly before birth. It is in the late stages of pregnancy that the female begins to show clear changes in "maternal responsiveness." The preparturient rat displays a marked change in her pattern of self-licking. The female redistributes her self-licking and concentrates her attentions on her nipple line and anogenital regions (Roth & Rosenblatt, 1967). Self-licking of the genitals decreases when the females have the opportunity to ingest extra salt, suggesting that the enhanced sodium appetite characteristic of pregnancy might mediate potentiated self-licking (Steinberg & Bindra, 1962). When nipple and genital self-stimulation is blocked by fitting wide rubber collars on pregnant rats, mammary development is reduced by 50%, as measured by lubuloalveolar weight and secretory activity (Roth & Rosenblatt, 1968). It is likely that the hormonal profile of pregnancy, which is triggered partly by the fetuses, mediates the dam's self-licking and hence prepares her mammary apparatus for suckling. Grosvenor and Turner (1960) have made a similar suggestion concerning the onset of lactation in late pregnancy, which coincides with the release of prolactin from the pituitary gland, an event that they attributed to stimulation provided by fetal distention of the uterus (cf. Rosenblatt & Siegel, 1981).

The event of birth marks a major transition in mother–young interactions because the mother and offspring no longer occupy the same space at the same time. Postpartum interactions thus have the special quality of active unity that requires a primary state of separateness. Although reciprocal relations clearly exist between fetus and mother, the reciprocal repertoire enters a new realm at birth, when the juxtaposition of bodies increases the quantity of the qualities of the interactive sites.

There appears to be a distinct set of reciprocal interactions in the early neonatal period. Early neonatal interactions appear to consist largely, though not exclusively, of interactions that involve *resource exchange*. Primary metabolic resources seem to play the dominant role. The "balance" between mother and offspring during this early neonatal stage of intimate association would seem to be tipped toward the dam. Nutritive energy, water, electrolytes, antibodies, and thermal energy appear to stream out from the dam to the pups, which, in turn, direct tactile stimulation and auditory and visual cues back to the dam. The pups may also serve as an efficient heat sink at these early ages, relieving the dam of excess metabolic heat. Nevertheless, we can already anticipate and appreciate that this is not a static relationship and that major changes are on the immediate horizon.

Even in the early neonatal phase, the litter is not a passive recipient of energy and attention. The pups play an active role by providing stimulation to the mother. By so doing, the pups actively participate in *providing for themselves.* They do this in several ways. Pup stimulation has numerous effects on the dam, including the release of prolactin, which maintains the mammary activity necessary for nursing; increased metabolic rate and hyperphagia in the dam, which leads to the conversion of food energy into a form of nutritive resource (milk) that is utilizable by the pup; and establishing a firm state of maternal responsiveness in the dam. Insofar as the milk, electrolytes, water, and heat derived from the mother are resources collected, converted, and delivered because of maternal conditions induced and maintained by the offspring, we can see that in the early association of mother and offspring, the pups use the mother as a *medium* rather than as a *source*.

The interindividual flow of primary metabolic resources stands out as a dominant dimension of early mother–offspring relations. Nevertheless, there are other important parallel events that also help determine the developmental elaboration of parent–offspring relations. The stimulation (experiences) concomitant with acts of resource exchange can function in several ways that shape the performance of both the parents and the offspring in their dyadic interactions.

Stimulation concomitant with resource exchanges can regulate future resource availability and thus maintain or synchronize the supply-and-demand features of dyadic interactions. For instance, suckling stimulation (independent from the withdrawal of milk) promotes and maintains high levels of lactogenesis and therefore regulates the subsequent availability of the milk resource (see the section above on "Nutritive Resources"). Similarly, the tactile stimulation that releases the micturition reflex of young pups not only is the stimulus that delivers water and electrolytes to the dam but has also been implicated in the facilitation of urine formation by the pups (see the section on "Nutritive Resources"). Licking the pups thus has both immediate and future benefits for the dam.

Exchange-concomitant stimulation, as we view it, generally involves the tactile, visual, auditory, and olfactory correlates of interactions in which primary resources such as heat, water and nutrients are exchanged. As we noted erlier, it is possible for cues, such as odors or visual arrays, to acquire the power of a primary physiological stimulus and thus enter into the active orchestration of dyadic interactions. Research from our laboratory on the formation of the olfactory preferences of rat pups provides examples of how primary resource exchange involving the conduction of thermal energy from mother to pups induces specific olfactory preferences for odors that are experienced in temporal contiguity with such heat transfer (Alberts, 1981). Within the first two weeks or so of life, these odors become the cue that attracts pups to other rats and brings them into contact with sources of heat, nutrition, social interactions, and, eventually, reproductive opportunities (Alberts & Brunjes, 1978).

Viewing the mother–litter dyad as a symbiotic unit thus provides a novel perspective on sources of stimulation and potential interrelations. It is possible that quite complex relationships can be established and maintained through relatively simple and direct acts of reciprocity and resource exchange. The concept of symbiosis deserves careful consideration in the context of parent–offspring relationships.

ACKNOWLEDGMENTS

Jeffrey Alberts was a Visiting Scholar at the University of Colorado at Boulder during the early phases of preparation of this work. Discussions there with colleagues and friends, such as Inge Bretherton, Dave Chiszar, Mertice Clark, Jeff Galef, Gene Gollin, Jerry Rudy, and Louise Silvern were important and influential. We also thank Sheryl L. Mobley and Nancy Jean Layman for typing the manuscript.

References

Addison, K. S., & Alberts, J. R. *Patterns of mother–litter interaction in a semi-natural habitat.* Paper presented at the Annual Meeting of the International Society for Developmental Psychobiology, Cincinnati, 1980.

Ainsworth, M. D. S. The development of infant–mother attachment. In B. M. Caldwell & H. N. Ricciuti (Eds.), *Review of child development research* (Vol. 3). Chicago: University of Chicago Press, 1973, pp. 1–94.

Alberts, J. R. Huddling by rat pups: Multisensory control of contact behavior. *Journal of Comparative and Physiological Psychology,* 1978, *92,* 220–230. (a).

Alberts, J. R. Huddling by rat pups: Group behavioral mechanisms of temperature regulation and energy conservation. *Journals of Comparative and Physiological Psychology,* 1978, *92,* 231–240. (b)

Alberts, J. R. Ontogeny of olfaction: Reciprocal roles of sensation and behavior in the development of perception. In R. N. Aslin, J. R. Alberts, & M. R. Petersen (Eds.), *Development of perception: Psychological perspectives* (Vol. 1). New York: Academic Press, 1981.

Alberts, J. R., & Brunjes, P. C. Ontogeny of thermal and olfactory determinants of huddling in the rat. *Journal of Comparative and Physiological Psychology,* 1978, *92,* 897–906.

Altman, J., & Sudarshan, K. Postnatal development of locomotion in the laboratory rat. *Animal Behaviour,* 1975, *23,* 896–920.

Alvarez, A., & Sas, J. B-Galactosidase changes in the developing intestinal tract of the rat. *Nature,* 1961, *190,* 826–827.

Babicky, A., Ostadalova, J., Parizek, J., Kolar, J., & Bibr, B. Use of radioisotope techniques for determining the weaning period in experimental animals. *Physiologia Bohemoslovenca,* 1970, *19,* 457–467.

Babicky, A., Pavlik, L., Parizek, I., Ostadalova, I., & Kolar, J. Determination of the onset of spontaneous water intake in infant rats. *Physiologia Bohemoslovenca,* 1972, *21,* 467–471.

Babicky, A., Ostadalova, I., Parizek, J., Kolar, J., & Bibr, B. Onset and duration of the physiological weaning period for infant rats reared in nests of different sizes. *Physiologia Bohemoslovenca,* 1973, *22,* 449–456.

Barlow, B., Santulli, T. V., Heird, W. C., Pitt, J., Blanc, W. A., & Schullinger, J. N. An experimental study of acute neonatal enterocolitis—The importance of breast milk. *Journal of Pediatric Surgery,* 1974, *9,* 587–594.

Barnett, S. A., & Walker, K. Z. Early stimulation, parental behavior, and the temperature of infant mice. *Developmental Psychobiology,* 1974, *7,* 563–577.

Baverstock, P., & Green, B. Water recycling in lactation. *Science,* 1975, *187,* 657–658.

Bell, R. W. Ultrasounds in small rodents: Arousal-produced and arousal-producing. *Developmental Psychobiology,* 1974, *7,* 39–42.

Blass, E. M., & Teicher, M. H. Suckling. *Science,* 1980, *210,* 15–22.

Bolles, R. C., & Woods, P. J. The ontogeny of behaviour in the albino rat. *Animal Behaviour,* 1964, *12,* 427

Brake, S. Suckling rats learn a preference for a novel olfactory stimulus paired with milk delivery. *Science,* 1981, *211,* 506–507.

Bowlby, J. *Attachment and loss, Vol. 1: Attachment.* New York: Basic Books, 1969.

Bradbury, J. W. Social organization and communication. In W. A. Wimsatt (Ed.), *Biology of bats* (Vol. 3). New York: Academic Press, 1977, pp. 1–72.

Brambell, F. W. R. *The transmisison of passive immunity from mother to young: Frontiers of biology* (Vol. 18). Amsterdam: North-Holland, 1970.

Brewster, J., & Leon, M. Facilitation of maternal transport by Norway rat pups. *Journal of Comparative and Physiological Psychology*, 1980, *94*, 80–88.

Brody, S. *Bioenergetics and growth*. New York: Rheinhold, 1945.

Butler, J. E. Immunoglobulins of the mammary secretions. In B. L. Larson & V. R. Smith (Eds.), *Lactation* (Vol. 3). New York: Academic Press, 1974, p. 217–255.

Campbell, B. A., & Raskin, L. A. Ontogeny of behavioral arousal: The role of environmental stimuli. *Journal of Comparative and Physiological Psychology*, 1978, *92*, 176–184.

Capek, K., & Jelinek, J. The development of the control of water metabolism I. The excretion of urine by young rats. *Physiologia Bohemoslovenca*, 1956, *5*, 91–96.

Chadwick, A. Comparison of milk-like secretions found in non-mammals. *Symposia of the Zoological Society of London*, 1977, *41*, 341–358.

Cloudsley-Thompson, J. L. *Animal behaviour*. London: Oliver and Boyd, 1960.

Cole, H., & Hart, G. Effect of pregnancy and lactation on growth in the rat. *American Journal of Physiology*, 1938, *123*, 589–597.

Compton, R. P., Koch, M. D., & Arnold, W. J. Effect of maternal odor on the cardiac rate of maternally separated infant rats. *Physiology and Behavior*, 1977, *18*, 769–773.

Conely, L., & Bell, R. W. Neonatal ultrasounds elicited by odor cues. *Developmental Psychobiology*, 1978, *11*, 193–197

Cosnier, J. *Le comportement du rate d'elevage*. Unpublished doctoral dissertation, University of Lyon, France, 1965.

Cotes, P. M., & Cross, B. A. Influence of suckling on food intake and growth of adult female rats. *Journal of Endocrinology*, 1954, *10*, 363–367.

Crosskerry, P. G., Smith, G. K., Leon, L. N., & Mitchell, E. A. An inexpensive system for continuously recording maternal behavior in the laboratory rat. *Physiology and Behavior*, 1976, 16, 223–225.

Culbertson, J. T. Natural transmission of immunity against *Trypanosoma lewisi* from mother rats to their offspring. *Journal of Parasitology*, 1938, *24* 65–82.

De Bary, H. A. *Die Erscheinung der Symbiose*. Strassburg: Karl J. Trubner, 1879.

DeVore, I. Mother–infant relations in free-ranging baboons. In H. L. Rheingold (Ed.), *Maternal behavior in mammals*. New York: Wiley, 1963, pp. 305–335.

Doell, R. G., & Kretchmer, N. Studies of small intestine during development: I. Distribution and activity of B-galactosidase. *Biochemical Biophysics Acta*, 1962, *62*, 353–362.

Drickamer, L. C. Delay of sexual maturation in female house mice by exposure to grouped females or urine from grouped females. *Journal of Reproduction and Fertility*, 1977, *51*, 77–81.

Falk, G. Maturation of renal function in infant rats. *American Journal of Physiology*, 1955, *181*, 157–170.

Fisher, E. M. Early life of a sea otter pup. *Journal of Mammalogy*, 1940, *21*, 132–137.

Fleming, A. S. Control of food intake in the lactating rat: Role of suckling and hormones. *Physiology and Behavior*, 1976, *17*, 841–848. (a)

Fleming, A. S. Ovarian influences on food intake and body weight regulation in lactating rats. *Physiology and Behavior*, 1976, *17*, 969–978. (b)

Friedman, M. I. Effects of milk consumption and deprivation on body fluids of suckling rats. *Physiology and Behavior*, 1979, *23*, 1029–1033.

Friedman, M. I., & Bruno, J. P. Exchange of water during lactation. *Science*, 1976, *197*, 409–410.

Friedman, M. I., Bruno, J. P., & Alberts, J. R. Physiological and behavioral consequences in rats of water recycling during lactation. *Journal of Comparative and Physiological Psychology*, 1981, *95*, 26–35.

Galef, B. G., Jr. Investigation of the functions of coprophagy in juvenile rats. *Journal of Comparative and Physiological Psychology*, 1979, *93*, 295–305.

Galef, B. G., Jr. The ecology of weaning: Parasitism and the achievement of independence by altricial mammals. In D. J. Gubernick & P. H. Klopfer (Eds.), *Parental care in mammals*. New York: Plenum Press, 1981, pp. 211–241.

Galef, B. G., Jr., & Kaner, H. C. Establishment and maintenance of preference for natural and artificial olfactory stimuli in juvenile rats. *Journal of Comparative and Physiological Psychology,* 1980, *94,* 588–595.

Galef, B. G., Jr., & Muskus, P. A. Olfactory mediation of mother-young contact in Long-Evans rats. *Journal of Comparative and Physiological Psychology,* 1979, *93,* 708–716.

Grosvenor, C. E. Thyroxine excretion in lactating rats. *Endocrinology,* 1962, *70,* 75–78.

Grosvenor, C. E. Evidence that exteroceptive stimuli can release prolactin from the pituitary gland of the lactating rat. *Endocrinology,* 1965, *76,* 340–342.

Grosvenor, C. E., & Turner, C. W. Release and restoration of pituitary lactogen in response to nursing stimuli in lactating rats. *Endocrinology,* 1960, *66,* 90–96.

Grota, L. J., & Ader, R. Continuous recording of maternal behavior in *Rattus norvegicus. Animal Behaviour,* 1969, *17,* 722–729.

Hahn, P., & Koldovsky, O. *Utilization of nutrients during postnatal development.* Oxford: Pergamon Press, 1966.

Halliday, R. The absorption of antibodies from immune sera by the gut of the young rat. *Proceedings of the Royal Society,* 1955, *143,* 408–413.

Halliday, R. The termination of the capacity of young rats to absorb antibody from the milk. *Proceedings of the Royal Society,* 1956, *145,* 179–185.

Halliday, R. The effect of steroid hormones on the absorption of antibody by the young rat. *Journal of Endocrinology,* 1959, *18,* 56–66.

Hanwell, A., & Linzell, J. L. A simple technique for measuring the rate of milk secretion in the rat. *Comparative Biochemistry and Physiology,* 1972, *43A,* 259–270.

Harper, L. V. Offspring effects upon parents. In D. J. Gubernick & P. H. Klopfer (Eds.), *Parental care in mammals.* New York: Plenum Press, 1981, pp. 117–168.

Hediger, H. *Studies of the psychology and behavior of captive animals in zoos and circuses* (G. Sircom, trans.). New York: Criterion Books, 1955.

Henry, S. M. (Ed.). Foreword in *Symbiosis* (Vol. 1). New York: Academic Press, 1966.

Hertig, M., Taliaferro, W. H., & Schwartz, B. The terms symbiosis, symbiont and symbiote. *Journal of Parasitology,* 1937, *23,* 326–329.

Hinde, R. A. Energy models of motivation. *Symposia of the Society for Experimental Biology,* 1960, *14,* 199–213.

Hofer, M. A. Physiological responses of infant rats to separation from their mothers. *Science,* 1970, *168,* 871–873.

Hofer, M. A. The role of nutrition in the physiological and behavioral effects of early maternal separation on infant rats. *Psychosomatic Medicine,* 1973, *35,* 350–359.

Hofer, M. A. Hidden regulatory processes in early social relationships. In P. P. G. Batesone & P. H. Klopfer (Eds.), *Perspectives in ethology* (Vol. 3). New York: Plenum Press, 1978, pp. 135–163.

Hull, D. Thermoregulation in young mammals. In C. G. Whittow (Ed.), *Comparative Physiology of Thermoregulation* (Vol. 3). New York: Academic Press, 1973.

Iino, S., & Greer, M. A. Thyroid function in the rat during pregnancy and lactation. *Endocrinology,* 1961, *68,* 253–262.

Jeddi, E. Ontogenesis of thermal comfort: Its role in affective development. In J. Duvand & J. Raynaud (Eds.), *Thermal comfort: Physiological and psychological bases.* Paris: Institute National de la Santé et de la Recherche Médicale, 1979.

Jenness, R. The composition of milk. In B. L. Larson & V. R. Smith (Eds.), *Lactation* (Vol. 3). New York: Academic Press, 1974, pp. 3–107.

Keen, C. L., Lonnerdal, B., Clegg, M., & Hurley, L. S. Developmental changes in composition of rat milk: Trace elements, minerals, protein, carbohydrate and fat. *Journal of Nutrition,* 1981, *111,* 226–230.

Kennedy, G. C. The development with age of hypothalamic restraint upon the appetite of the rat. *Journal of Endocrinology,* 1957, *16,* 9–17.

Kenny, J. T., & Blass, E. M. Suckling as incentive to instrumental learning in preweanling rats. *Science*, 1977, *196*, 898–899.

King, J. A. Maternal behavior in *Peromyscus*. In H. L. Rheingold (Ed.), *Maternal behavior in mammals*. New York: Wiley, 1963, pp. 58–94.

Kretchmer, N. Lactose and lactase. *Scientific American*, 1972, *227*, 71–78.

Kumaresan, P., Anderson, R. R., & Turner, C. W. Effect of litter size upon milk yield and litter weight gains in rats. *Proceedings Society Experimental Biology Medicine*, 1967, *126*, 41–45.

Lakoff, G., & Johnson, M. *Metaphors we live by*. Chicago: University of Chicago Press, 1980.

Lascelles, A. K. Role of the mammary gland and milk in immunology. *Symposia of the Zoological Society of London*, 1977, *41*, 160–241.

Latane, B., Joy, V., Meltzer, J., & Lubell, B. Stimulus determinants of social attraction in rats. *Journal of Comparative and Physiological Psychology*, 1972, *79*, 13–21.

Lehrman, D. S. Interaction between internal and external environments in the regulation of the reproductive cycle of the ring dove. In F. A. Beach (Ed.), *Sex and behavior*. New York: Wiley, 1965, pp. 355–380.

Leon, M. Maternal pheromone. *Physiology and Behavior*, 1974, *13*, 441–443.

Leon, M., & Moltz, H. Maternal pheromone: Discrimination by pre-weanling rats. *Physiology and Behavior*, 1971, *7*, 265–267.

Leon, M., & Moltz, H. The development of the pheromonal bond in the albino rat. *Physiology and Behavior*, 1972, *8*, 683–686.

Leon, M., Crosskerry, P. G., & Smith, G. K. Thermal control of mother-young contact in rats. *Physiology and Behavior*, 1978, *21*, 793–811.

Lewis, M., & Rosenblum, L. A. (Eds.), *The effect of the infant on its caregiver*. New York: Wiley, 1965.

Lieberman, M., & Lieberman, D. Lactase deficiency: A genetic mechanism which regulates the time of weaning. *American Naturalist*, 1978, *112*, 625–627.

Lincoln, D. W., Hill, A., & Wakerly, J. B. The milk-ejection reflex of the rat: An intermittent function not abolished by surgical levels of anesthesia. *Journal of Endrocrinology*, 1973, *57*, 459–476.

Lincoln, D. W., Hentzen, K., Hin, T., van der Schoot, P., Clarke, G., & Summerlee, A. J. S. Sleep: A prerequisite for reflex milk ejection in the rat. *Experimental Brain Research*, 1980, *38*, 151–162.

Ling, E. R., Kon, S. K., & Porter, J. W. G. The composition of milk and the nutritive value of its components. In S. K. Kon & A. T. Cowie (Eds.), *Milk: The mammary gland and its secretion* (Vol. 2). New York: Academic Press, 1961, pp. 195–263.

Lorscheider, F. L., & Reineke, E. P. The influence of lactational intenstiy and exogenous prolactin on serum thyroxine levels in the rat. *Proceedings of the Society of Experimental Biology and Medicine*, 1971, *138*, 1116–1118.

Lovell, R., & Rees, T. A. Immunological aspects of colostrum. In S. K. Kon & A. T. Cowie (Eds.), *Milk: The mammary gland and its secretion* (Vol. 2). New York: Academic Press, 1961, pp. 363–381.

Luckey, T. S., Mende, T. J., & Pleasants, J. The physical and chemical characterization of rat's milk. *Journal of Nutrition*, 1954, *54*, 345–359.

Macho, L., Strbak, V., & Strazovcova, A. Thyroid function in prematurely weaned rats. *Physiologia Bohemoslovenca*, 1970, *19*, 77–82.

Mahler, M. S., & Furer, M. Observations on research regarding the "symbiotic syndrome" of infantile psychosis. *Psychoanalytical Quarterly*, 1960, *29*, 317–327.

Mahler, M. S., Pine, F., & Bergman, A. *The psychological birth of the human infant*. New York: Basic Books, 1975.

McCracken, R. D. Lactase deficiency: An example of dietary evolution. *Current Anthropology*, 1971, *12*, 479–517.

Moltz, H., & Leon, M. Stimulus control of the maternal pheromone in the lactating rat. *Physiology and Behavior*, 1973, *10*, 69–71.

Moltz, H., Leidahl, L., & Rowland, D. Prolongation of pheromonal emission in the maternal rat. *Physiology and Behavior*, 1974, *12*, 409–412.

Moore, C. L., & Morelli, G. A. Mother rats interact differently with male and female offspring. *Journal of Comparative and Physiological Psychology*, 1979, *93*, 677–684.

Nelson, M. N., & Evans, H. M. Dietary requirements for lactation in the rat and other laboratory animals. In S. K. Kon & A. T. Cowie (Eds.), *Milk: The mammary gland and its secretion* (Vol. 2). New York: Academic Press, 1961, pp. 137–191.

Nyakas, C., & Endroczi, E. Olfaction guided approaching behavior of infantile pups to the mother in a maze box. *Acta Physiologica Academia Scientiarum Hungaricae*, 1970, *38*, 59–65.

Ota, K., & Yokoyama, A. Body weight and food consumption of lactating rats nursing various sizes of litters. *Journal of Endocrinology*, 1967, *38*, 263–268.

Pedersen, P. E., & Blass, E. M. Olfactory control over suckling in albino rats. In R. N. Aslin, J. R. Alberts, & M. R. Petersen (Eds.), *Development of perception: Psychobiological perspectives* (Vol. 1). New York: Academic Press, 1981, pp. 359–382.

Phillips, C. R. N. Neonatal heat loss in heated crib vs. mothers' arms. *Journal of Obstetric, Gynecologic, and Neonatal Nursing*, 1974, *3*, 11–15.

Plaut, S. M. Adult-litter relations in rats reared in single and dual-chambered cages. *Developmental Psychobiology*, 1974, *7*, 111–120.

Pond, C. M. The significance of lactation in the evolution of mammals. *Evolution*, 1978, *31*, 177–199.

Redman, R. S., & Sweney, L. R. Changes in diet and patterns of feeding activity of developing rats. *Journal of Nutrition*, 1976, *106*, 615–626.

Rheingold, H. L., & Keene, G. C. Transport of the human young. In B. M. Foss (Ed.), *Determinants of infant behaviour* (Vol. 3). London: Methuen, 1965, pp. 87–110.

Richter, C. P., & Barelare, B. Nutritional requirements of pregnant and lactating rats studied by the self-selection method. *Endocrinology*, 1938, *23*, 15–24.

Rosenblatt, J. S. The basis of synchrony in the behavioral interaction between the mother and her offspring in the laboratory rat. In B. M. Foss (Ed.), *Determinants of infant behaviour* (Vol. 3). New York: Wiley, 1965, pp. 3–41.

Rosenblatt, J. S. The development of maternal responsiveness in the rat. *American Journal of Orthopsychiatry*, 1969, *39*, 36–56.

Rosenblatt, J. S. The basis of early responses to the mother, siblings and the home and nest in altrical young of selected species of subprimate mammals. In R. A. Hinde & P. P. G. Bateson (Eds.), *Growing points in ethology*. New York: Cambridge University Press, 1976, pp. 345–386.

Rosenblatt, J. S., & Lehrman, D. S. Maternal behavior of the laboratory rat. In H. L. Rheingold (Ed.), *Maternal behavior in mammals*. New York: Wiley, 1963, pp. 8–57.

Rosenblatt, J. S., & Siegel, H. I. Factors governing the onset and maintenance of maternal behavior among nonprimate mammals: The role of hormonal and nonhormonal factors. In D. J. Gubernick & P. H. Klopfer (Eds.), *Parental care in mammals*. New York: Plenum Press, 1981, pp. 14–76.

Roth, L. L., & Rosenblatt, J. S. Changes in self-licking during pregnancy in the rat. *Journal of Comparative and Physiological Psychology*, 1967, *63*, 397–400.

Roth, L. L., & Rosenblatt, J. S. Self-licking and mammary development during pregnancy in the rat. *Journal of Endocrinology*, 1968, *42*, 363–378.

Rubino, A., Zimbalatti, F., & Auricchio, S. Intestinal disaccharidase activities in adult and suckling rats. *Biochimica et Biophysica Acta*, 1964, *92*, 305–311.

Samel, M. Thyroid function during postnatal development in the rat. *General and Comparative Endocrinology*, 1968, *10*, 229–234.

Samel, M., Caputa, A., & Struharova, L. Extra-uterine re-circulation of iodine-131 from the young to mother in rats. *Nature*, 1963, *198*, 489.

Sauer, E. G. F. Mother-infant relationship in galagos and the oral child-transport among primates. *Folia Primatologia,* 1967, *7,* 127–149.

Schaller, G. B. *The mountain gorilla, ecology and behavior.* Chicago: University of Chicago Press, 1963.

Shair, H. N., Brake, S. C., & Hofer, M. A. *Sucking and arousal states during normal nursing in the young rat.* Paper presented at the International Society for Developmental Psychobiology, Cincinnati, 1980.

Small, W. Notes on the psychic development of the albino rat. *American Journal of Psychology,* 1899, *11,* 80–100.

Smotherman, W. P., Wiener, S. G., Mendoza, S. P., & Levine, S. Pituitary-adrenal responsiveness of rat mothers to noxious stimuli and stimuli produced by pups. In *Breast-feeding and the mother,* Ciba Foundation Symposium 45. Amsterdam: Elsevier, 1976, pp. 5–22.

Smyth, J. D. *Introduction to animal parasitology* (2nd ed.). London: Hodder and Stoughton, 1976.

Solomon, J. B. *Foetal and neonatal immunology.* Amsterdam: North-Holland, 1971.

Spray, C. M., & Widdowson, E. M. The effect of growth and development on the composition of mammals. *British Journal of Nutrition,* 1950, *4,* 332–353.

Starr, M. P. A generalized scheme for classifying organismic associations. *Symposia Society Experimental Biology,* 1975, *29,* 1–20.

Steinberg, J., & Bindra, D. Effects of pregnancy and salt intake on genital licking. *Journal of Comparative and Physiological Psychology,* 1962, *55,* 103–106.

Stolc, V., Knopp, J., & Stolcova, E. Iodine, solid diet, water and milk intake by lactating rats and their offsprings. *Physiologia Bohemoslovenca,* 1966, *15,* 219–225.

Strbak V., Macho, L., Knopp, J., & Struharova, E. Thyroxine content in mother milk and regulation of thyroid function of suckling rats. *Endocrinologia Experimentalis,* 1974, *8,* 59–69.

Svare, B. B. Maternal aggression in mammals. In D. J. Gubernick & P. H. Klopfer (Eds.), *Parental care in mammals.* New York: Plenum Press, 1981, pp. 179–210.

Taylor, P. M. Oxygen consumption in new-born rats. *Journal of Physiology* (London), 1960, *154,* 153–168.

Teicher, M., & Blass, E. M. Suckling in newborn rats: Eliminated by nipple lavage, reinstated by pup saliva. *Science,* 1976, *193,* 422–425.

Thoman, E. B., Wetzel, A., & Levine, S. Lactation prevents disruption of temperature regulation and suppresses adrenocortical activity in rats. *Communications in Behavioral Biology,* 1968, (A)2, 165–171.

Vandenbergh, J. G. Effect of the presence of a male on the sexual maturation of female mice. *Endocrinology,* 1967, *81,* 345–349.

Vandenbergh, J. G. Acceleration and inhibition of puberty in female mice by pheromones. *Journal of Reproduction and Fertility,* 1973, *19,* 411–419.

Voloschin, L. M., & Tramezzani, J. H. Milk ejection reflex linked to slow wave sleep in nursing rats. *Endocrinology,* 1979, *105,* 1202–1207.

Vuorenkoski, V., Wasz-Hockert, O., Koivisto, E., & Lind, J. The effect of cry stimulus on the temperature of the lactating breast of primipara: A thermographic study. *Experientia,* 1969, *25,* 1286–1287.

Ward, I. L. Prenatal stress feminizes and demasculinizes the behavior of males. *Science,* 1972, *175,* 82–84.

Weisner, B. P., & Sheard, N. M. *Maternal behaviour in the rat.* London: Oliver and Boyd, 1933.

Whitfield, P. J. *The biology of parasitism: An introduction to the study of associating organisms.* London: Edward Arnold, 1979.

Wilson, N. E., & Stricker, E. M. Thermal homeostasis in pregnant rats during heat stress. *Journal of Comparative and Physiological Psychology,* 1979, *93,* 585–594.

Woodside, B., & Leon, M. Thermoendocrine influences on maternal nesting behavior in rats. *Journal of Comparative and Physiological Psychology,* 1980, *94,* 41–60.

CHAPTER 3

The Coordinate Roles of Mother and Young in Establishing and Maintaining Pheromonal Symbiosis in the Rat

HOWARD MOLTZ and THERESA M. LEE

In the rat, a new olfactory-based association emerges between mother and young at about 14 days postpartum. The mother begins to excrete a pheromone in her feces that strongly attracts the young. Both the pheromone and the young's responsiveness to it remain in evidence only about two weeks—a relatively brief time even in the life span of the rat. But although obviously short-lived, this pheromonal bond, as it has been called, serves important developmental ends, some of which have come to light recently in our laboratory. What we want to deal with first, however, are not the adaptive advantages that accrue to the young in responding to the pheromone, but how the pheromonal relationship comes to be formed.

The key word in the present conference is of course *symbiosis*. As we all know, there are three kinds of symbiotic relationships: mutual, commensal, and parasitic. We shall be talking about a commensal and possibly a mutual symbiosis. The pheromonal bond advantages the young and seems to do no harm to the mother (commensal), or it may even advantage the mother insofar as the survival of the young enhances her chances of gene representation (mutual). But whether commensal or mutual, rat mother and young establish a special kind of chemically based relationship, certainly symbiotic, and perhaps all the more dramatic for its short life.

HOWARD MOLTZ and THERESA M. LEE • Committee on Biopsychology, The University of Chicago, Chicago, Illinois 60637. The research carried out in the laboratory of Howard Moltz was supported by NIH Grant HD-06872 and by Biomedical Research Support Grant PHS 5 SO7RR07029.

Perhaps the mother is programmed to emit the pheromone 14 days after parturition and the young are programmed to respond beginning 14 days after birth. Such "programming" can be invoked as well to explain why pheromonal emission most often stops at 27 days postpartum, and why the young charcteristically lose interest in the attractant at 27 days of age. In other words, mother and young may be behaving independently, and their behavior may be so synchronized by selection as to need no further modulation. As it turns out, the two programs are not independent. Their synchrony requires an ongoing dialogue—a behavioral, chemical, and endocrine dialogue between mother and young. If the vocabulary is wrong, the pheromonal bond fails. To extend the metaphor, our aim is to discuss how the young speak to the mother, how the mother answers, and how, out of this interchange, an olfactory-based association is established.

Prolactin and the Young

It is well known that prolactin is elevated at the time of parturition and that it remains elevated for the first 14 days postpartum (Amenomori, Chen, & Meites, 1970; Marinari & Moltz, 1978), provided, of course, that there are pups available for suckling. If the pups are removed, the hormone drops quickly to basal levels and the estrous cycle returns (Grosvenor, Mainweg, & Mena, 1970; Mena, Pacecho, Whitworth, and Grosvenor, 1980). Since prolactin is so prominent during lactation, we asked whether this peptide might be involved in the synthesis of the attractant. Accordingly, we attempted to block prolactin release in lactating females by using the dopamine agonist ergocornine hydrogen maleate (Leon & Moltz, 1972). Other lactating females were either ovariectomized, adrenalectomized, or, in some case, subjected to the combined operation. Only the ergocornine-injected mothers stopped emitting the pheromone, even though they continued to behave maternally. That simultaneous injections of the hormone blocked the inhibitory action of the drug made it all the more likely that prolactin is involved in pheromonal emission.

Subsequently, Leon (1974) and Kilpatrick and Moltz (1982) showed that prolactin injections alone elicited the pheromone in otherwise non-pheromone-emitting virgin females. We had the opening lines of pheromonal discourse. The pups suckle, their suckling sustains the postpartum rise of prolactin, and the hormone somehow changes the feces of the mother to attract the young. We speculated that whatever the nature of this fecal change, it might remain in evidence as long as prolactin remained high.

It is well known (e.g., Bruce, 1961; Nicoll & Meites, 1959) that rats continue to lactate for an inordinately long time if there are young pups available for suckling. In other words, high serum levels of prolactin persist when a mother's own litter is replaced shortly before weaning by a younger litter, and such a substitution is continued serially, foster litter after foster litter. Under these conditions, the mother often lactates for more than 100 days, long past the usual postpartum period. She also continues to emit the pheromone (Moltz, Leidahl, & Rowland, 1974).

At this point, we wondered whether nulliparous females that behave maternally when housed continuously with young pups would also emit the pheromone. If they did, then we would expect prolactin to be elevated in such females even though they were neither lactating nor being suckled. Although suckling, of course, promotes the discharge of prolactin from the adenohypophysis, perhaps the pups typically release the hormone through other channels as well, channels that do not involve nipple stimulation. There is no doubt that nulliparous females emit a pherome that strongly attracts young (Leidahl & Moltz, 1975, 1977). But they do so only if they behave maternally. If a nullipara is housed with young but fails to build a nest, to retrieve and to crouch in a nursing posture, she fails to emit an attractant. That the attractant of the maternally behaving nulliparous females is probably the same as that of the maternally behaving lactating female is attested by several facts: (1) the lactating female and the nulliparous female carry the pheromone in their feces (Leidahl & Moltz, 1977); (2) the young respond equally to the excreta of both (Leidahl & Moltz, 1975, 1977); (3) each female begins to emit the pheromone 14 days after the start of maternal behavior and ceases emission at approximately 27 days (Leidahl & Moltz, 1975); (4) for pheromonal onset to occur, both females must have pups that advance commensurately in age, so that on Day 2 of the maternal episode, they are caring for two-day-old pups, on Day 3, for 3-day-old pups, etc. (Leidahl & Moltz, 1977); and finally, (5) both females exhibit elevated levels of prolactin throughout the two-week period immediately preceding release of the attractant (Amenomori et al., 1970; Marinari & Moltz, 1978). This last shared characteristic is particularly important since pheromonal emission, as already suggested, is thought to require an increase of prolactin in blood. For such an increase to occur and for the pheromone to appear, it is obvious that suckling is not necessary. The female's prolactin response is evidently attuned to a variety of pup stimuli, as the pheromone itself seems to be.

A select number of male rats also behave maternally when kept in association with young, and they do so in a manner virtually indistinguishable from that of maternally behaving females (Weisner & Sheard, 1933). Obviously, the question is whether such males also emit the pheromone. They do not, not even when castrated and injected daily with prolactin (Leidahl & Moltz, 1975; Moltz & Leidahl, 1977). Why males fail to show the attractant, first in response to pups and then in response to the hormone when repeatedly administered, provided a clue to the identity of the pheromone. It also revealed another channel through which the pups communicate with the mother.

First, as to what the pheromone might be. We knew from the work of Leon (1974) that the pheromone is synthesized in the cecum and is not the product of some anal gland. Consequently, we thought that since bile from the liver is discharged directly into the gut (the rat does not have a gall bladder) and affects cecal chemistry, the pheromone might reflect an alteration in bile composition. If it did, then drawing bile from a pheromone-emitting female and injecting such bile into the cecum of a male should induce pheromonal emission in the male. This was exactly what happened, as Moltz and Leidahl (1977) discovered. Males receiving intracecal injections of bile from pheromone-emitting females came to emit the pheromone, while those receiving injections under the same regimen, but from non-pheromone-emitting females, failed to do so. For the first group of males, we apparently provided a biliary "additive" necessary for pheromonal synthesis. We belive that the additive is cholic acid. In other words, our hypothesis is that an increase in cholic acid underlies the pheromone and that what elevates the output of cholic acid is the uptake of prolactin at the liver.

The major organic constituents of bile are the bile acids, which constitute over 50% of the solid components. Cholic and chenodeoxycholic acid, the primary bile acids, are synthesized in the liver and enter the small intestine, where, at the terminal ileum, they are largely reabsorbed into the enterohepatic circulation. The fraction that escapes into the cecum is transformed by indigenous microflora into a variety of compounds. Among such compounds are the secondary bile acids, deoxycholic and lithocholic acid.

The general bile picture of male and female is of course similar: both synthesize cholic and chenodeoxycholic acid as primary bile acids and deoxycholic and lithocholic acid as secondary bile acids. However, there is a sex-related difference in liver functioning that we think affects the biliary concentration of cholic acid and thereby the appearance of the pheromone (Kelly, Posner, Tsushima, & Friesen, 1974).

From the work of Posner and his colleagues (Posner, Kelly, & Friesen, 1974, 1975; Posner, Kelly, Shiu, & Friesen, 1974), and from the more recent work of Manni, Chambers, and Pearson (1978), we know that prolactin induces its own receptors at the liver, which is to say that the liver responds to an increase in circulating prolactin by forming additional binding sites to take up the peptide. There is, however, a male–female difference in liver responsiveness, the female liver showing a substantially greater capacity to form new prolactin receptors than the male liver (Costlow, Buschow, & McGuire, 1975; Kelly *et al.,* 1974). The result, of course, is that with more prolactin receptors, the female liver recognizes more of the peptide than the male liver and so takes up more. We suspect that this hepatic difference becomes magnified during maternal behavior, when prolactin levels are significantly elevated. Specifically, our contention is that the male liver continues to bind relatively little of the peptide, while the female liver binds a great deal more than it would otherwise have bound. As a result, we believe that the female liver comes to synthesize cholic acid in greater than normal amounts, enabling a critical fraction of this bile steroid to show up in the cecum. That the male liver, as we have said, characteristically forms fewer hepatic prolactin receptors than the female liver—and so presumably experiences little or no change in the output of cholic acid—would explain why the male, although capable of releasing the pheromone in response to injected bile, cannot do so endogenously. The question of how this prolactin sensitivity becomes gender-related was the subject of a recent experiment in our laboratory (Kilpatrick & Moltz, 1982).

It is well known that a number of drugs and steroids are metabolized by the liver along different biosynthetic pathways in the male and the female (Denef & deMoor, 1973; Gustafsson & Stenberg, 1976). This sexual differentiation occurs perinatally and is due to the presence or absence, respectively, of testicular secretions. Our suggestion is that the capacity of the liver to recognize prolactin is also programmed perinatally, in other words, that the presence of androgen early in the development of the male decreases the prolactin sensitivity of his liver, so that thereafter he fails to from as many hepatic binding sites to the hormone as the female and consqently fails to show the requisite increase in cholic acid. We castrated males prior to 2 hr of age and injected females with testosterone propionate within 3 days of age. As shown in Table 1, only those animals spared exposure to androgen during the immediate postpartum period gave evidence of the pheromone when injected

Table 1. Percent and Choices of Test Young[a,b]

Neonatal manipulation	Neonatally manipulated animal	Nulliparous female or no response	Significance[c]
Castrated males	69.4	30.6	<.05
Sham-castrated males	61.1	38.8	>.05
Testosterone-injected females	47.2	52.8	>.05
Oil-injected females	77.8	22.2	<.05

[a] From Kilpatrick and Moltz (1982).
[b] Each neonatally manipulated animal was injected with prolactin as an adult and was paired with a nontreated nulliparous female.
[c] Chi square.

with prolactin as adults. It is very much to the point that their biliary output of cholic acid was elevated as well.

All this is not to say, however, that cholic acid is the pheromone. Cholic acid is a steroid carrying a high molecular weight, making it a compound that has low volatility at room temperature. Rather, we think of cholic acid as the precursor of the pheromone, converted to the pheromone by the action of selected bacteria in the cecum.

As a precursor, of course, we would expect cholic acid to be heightened in bile during the time of pheromonal emission. Kilpatrick, Bolt, and Moltz (1980b) showed that it characteristically is. They drew bile from postpartum rats that had been lactating for either 5, 12, 21, or 30 days. These postpartum days were chosen to provide a bile-acid profile for animals known to be non-pheromone-emitting (5 days); pre-pheromone-emitting (12 days); pheromone-emitting (21 days), and post-pheromone-emitting (30 days). The bile thus drawn was analyzed enzymatically after chromatographic separation to quantitate cholic, chenodeoxycholic, and deoxycholic acid. Only cholic acid reached a peak level in bile that was tied specifically to the appearance of the pheromone.

A subsequent study by Kilpatrick, Bolt, and Moltz (1980a) underscored the importance of cholic acid in pheromonal emission. In both rats and humans, it is possible to augment the biliary concentration of a particular bile acid simply through the ingestion of that bile acid. Accordingly, these researchers fed non-pheromone-emitting virgin females either cholic, deoxycholic, or chenodeoxycholic acid. The aim, of course, was to determine whether cholic acid—and cholic acid alone—promotes pheromonal release. The data left no doubt that it does. Only females fed cholic acid showed evidence of the pheromone, as Table 2 illustrates.

The hypothesis that we now have concering the pheromone pictures a sequence of events that begins with the elevation of prolactin in the blood, followed by an increase in the uptake of the hormone at the liver, leading in turn to an elevation of cholic acid in the bile and then to the conversion of this

Table 2. Choice Behavior of 16- to 21-Day-Old-Young[a]

Group	Bile-acid-supplemented female	No response	Non-supplemented female	N	Significance
Cholic diet[b]	32	2	12	48	$p < .05$
Chenodeoxycholic diet	21	12	21	54	NS
Deoxycholic diet	19	11	12	42	NS
Postcholic diet[b]	21	3	24	48	NS

[a] From Kilpatrick, Bolt, and Moltz (1980a).
[b] Differs significantly from each other ($\chi^2 = 10.26; p < .01$).

steroid in the cecum. We believe the final result to be a unique product: an as-yet-unidentified derivative of cholic acid that is highly volatile and serves to attract the young to the feces of the mother (Moltz & Lee, 1981).

But there is a problem in connection with this hypothesis that the present discussion has not yet faced. The problem has to do with prolactin itself. Pheromonal emission, as we have shown, requires high levels of the hormone, which the pups, of course, typically promote. And yet the pups sustain such levels for only about 12 days. In other words, although the mother continues to behave maternally, the blood levels of prolactin start to decrease. The point is that this decrease begins with the appearance of the pheromone and continues for the remainder of the pheromonal period. Since the pheromone is emitted during a time of falling prolactin levels, how can it be prolactin-dependent?

The answer emerged when we measured the concentration of prolactin in liver as well as the concentration of prolactin in the blood (Lee, Lee, & Moltz, 1983). We confirmed that blood prolactin is elevated during the first 12 days of the maternal episode and then decreases progressively. What was new was that the concentration of prolactin in hepatic cytosol ran a near-opposite course to that in blood. Prolactin in the liver was significantly higher during the period of pheromonal emission than during the period preceding pheromonal emission, as illustrated in Figure 1.

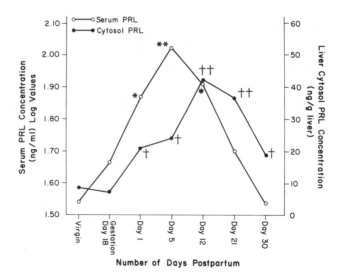

Figure 1. Prolactin in blood and in liver cytosol of virgin, pregnant, and lactating rats. ††, **: Significantly greater than all other cytosol PRL concentrations and serum concentrations; †, *: Significantly greater than virgin and pregnant cytosol PRL concentrations and serum concentrations.

It is evident that the pups, through suckling and other stimulus channels, sustain high blood levels of prolactin only through the first half of the maternal episode. Nonetheless, their role is important, since the elevation of prolactin in blood, however, short-lived, has the effect of heightening the concentration of prolactin in hepatic cytosol. This heightened concentration, in turn, probably increases the activity of selected enzyme systems in the liver (as, for example, those involved in the hydroxylation of cholesterol). It is not difficult to picture such enzymatic changes as raising the output of cholic acid, since we know that biliary cholic acid, like liver prolactin, reaches peak values during the time of pheromonal emission (Kilpatrick *et al.*, 1980). Cholic acid, of course, is thought to be the immediate precursor of the pheromone, the bile component transformed in the cecum to attract young.

But even at this point, the sequence is incomplete. Another step remains to be elucidated. It turns out that preweanling pups not only promote prolactin release, they govern the metabolic conversion of cholic acid to produce the pheromone.

The Young and the Conversion of Cholic Acid

It is puzzling that for pheromonal emission to occur a female, whether nulliparous or lactating, must have pups that advance commensurately in age so that on Day 2 of the maternal episode, she is caring for 2-day-old pups, on Day 3, for 3-day-old pups, etc. When, through litter substitution, she is kept with pups of constant age—1–3 days old, for example—she fails to show evidence of the attractant.

Perhaps a clue can be found if we ask not why the pups must advance in age, but why the mother typically emits the pheromone when her pups become 14 days old. What is there about 14-day-old pups that influences the appearance of the attractant?

At 14 days, rat young typically begin to consume solid food as a supplement to their diet of maternal milk. This change alters the chemistry of their feces (Lee & Moltz, 1980). Specifically, when maternal milk is consumed as an exclusive food source, the growth of *Lactobacillus* and *Bifidobacterium* is promoted in the gut (Pitt, Barlow, & Neired, 1977; Smith, William, & Crabb, 1961). These bacteria render the gut highly acidic through their synthesis of lactic and acetic acid. But at 14 days, when the same young begin to consume milk and solid food, gut acidity is reduced because of a decrease in *Lactobacillus-Bifidobacterium* relative to weakly acid-producing bacteria such as *Escherichia coli* (Lee & Moltz, 1980). Perhaps it is this reduction in the fecal acidity of the young that influences the mother, possibly by lowering the acidity of her own gut. In turn, such an increase in maternal pH may "lift" from acidic suppression the cecal bacteria that the mother needs to metabolize cholic acid to produce the pheromone.

As already mentioned, our hypothesis states that cholic acid is not the pheromone but a precursor of the pheromone, transformed by the enzymatic action of cecal bacteria. *Clostridia* and *Streptococci* are among the microorganisms that convert cholic acid to a variety of steroidal and nonsteroidal compounds (Dickenson, Gustafsson, & Norman, 1971; Lifshitz, Wapner, Wehman, Diaz-Bensussen, & Pergolizzi, 1978). Since the growth of these bacteria is inhibited when the gut is acidic and is facilitated when the gut is either neutral or alkaline, it should be possible to affect the metabolism of cholic acid, and hence the appearance of the pheromone, by manipulating the acid–base balance of the maternal intestine.

As an integral part of the care she provides, the maternally behaving female licks her young, particularly their perineal region, inducing them to defecate. She characteristically ingests a large part of the feces she promotes. We recently discovered (Lee & Moltz, 1980) that as the pH of this material changes, so does the pH of the mother's own intestine. Thus, when her pups are consuming a diet of milk alone, which makes their feces acidic, the gut of the mother becomes acidic. And when her pups begin to consume a mixed diet of milk and solid food, and their feces correspondingly increase in pH, so too does the pH of the mother's gut.

Taking advantage of the fact that the acidity–alkalinity profile of the mother's gut mirrors that of her pup's feces, we manipulated the kind of pup feces that the mother had available for ingestion. As anticipated, when these feces were highly acidic, pheromonal emission was inhibited; when they were reduced in acidity, pheromonal emission occurred earlier than usual, that is on Day 10 postpartum rather than on Day 14 postpartum. Finally, to underscore the relation between the pH of the mother's gut and her release of the pheromone, we added trace amounts of acetic acid to the drinking water. Females that otherwise would have emitted the pheromone failed to do so. The conclusion that the young use their feces to "speak" to the mother, to "tell" her when to emit the attractant, seems inescapable.

What the Mother Probably Gives the Pups in Return

Young between the ages of 14 and 27 days not only approach pheromone-containing feces, they consume such feces. We established this by feeding lactating females a dye called eosin 7, which colors anal excreta but leaves milk unaffected (Kilpatrick, 1981). Examining the content of the pup's gut revealed that maternal feces are first ingested at 14 days of age, and that by about 27 days, such ingestion decreases dramatically. Using the same dye, we also established that pups 14–27 days old preferentially ingest pheromone-containing feces over non-pheromone-containing feces (Kilpatrick, Lee, & Moltz, 1983). The possible adaptive value of this age-related preference prompts the question of what developmental challenges the 14- to 27-day-old pup might be meeting. Why, at just this age, does it typically respond to the pheromone and avidly consume pheromone-containing feces?

At 14 days, rat young begin to ingest solid food, and we know from our research that the ingestion of solid food escalates the bacterial challenge to the infantile gut (Lee & Moltz, 1980). It increases the population of potentially pathogenic *E. coli* relative to such protective microorganisms as *Lactobacillus-Bifidobacterium*. By about 30 days, the rat develops an important defense against *E. coli*.

Beginning at approximately 15 days of age, rat young show a sharp increase in the depostion of brain myelin. The rate of deposition remains high until 30 days. Thereafter, it slows, never again to show the same pace. Although myelination probably continues throughout the life of the rat, the period from 15 to 30 days of age is a special period of brain development.

But what has the gut to do with the brain? We think the relationship lies in the fact that the development of enteric immunocompetence and the deposition of central myelin share a common need: the need for bile acids. We know from our own research (Kilpatrick, 1981; Kilpatrick, Lee, & Moltz, 1983), as well as from the research of Barth, Zaumsell, and Klinger (1977), that rat pups present an immature bile profile. Cholic acid, for example, does not reach adult levels until 24 days of age, and deoxycholic acid not until 28 days, as illustrated in Figure 2. We know also from data obtained in our laboratory that the output of deoxycholic acid, but not that of either cholic or chenodeoxycholic acid, is heightened in maternal feces during the period of pheromonal emission (Kilpatrick, Lee, & Moltz, 1983). In brief, we are suggesting that in approaching the pheromone, rat young are behaving adaptively. They are responding to an attractant that leads them to consume maternal feces and thereby receive from the mother deoxycholic acid. This "gift" is a recognized by-product of cholic acid, and the pheromone, of course, is believed to be a derivative of the same steroid.

Consider first the vulnerability of the immature gut and the role of deoxycholic acid in guarding against gastrointestinal infection. Necrotizing enterocolitis (NEC) is an enteric disease that largely affects the very young. Both in the rat pup and in the human infant, it has the following symptomatology: gaseous abdominal distention, delayed gastric emptying, intestinal bleeding, and, in the terminal stages, perforation of the ileum and the colon resulting in sepsis and death. There is convincing evidence that deoxycholic acid offers protection against NEC: (1) when the endotoxin of *E. coli* was extracted with phenol and treated with sodium deoxycholate, the toxic units

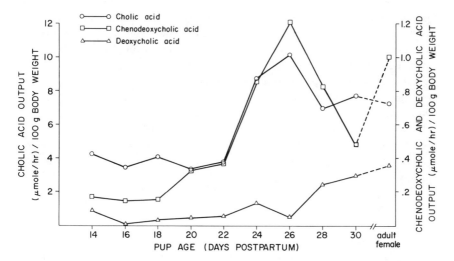

Figure 2. The development of the bile-acid profile of the rat. (From Kilpatrick, Lee, & Moltz, 1983.)

were split into smaller, nonpyrogenic structural elements (Rudback, Anacker, Haskins, Johnson, Mil, & Ribi, 1966); (2) when the endotoxin was incubated with sodium deoxycholate and administered parenterally, no pathological effects were seen; whereas without prior incubation, overwhelming sepsis occurred (Bertok, 1977; Kocsar, Bertok, & Varteresg, 1969); and (3) when the *E. coli* endotoxin was administered orally to intact rats in dosages 500–3,000 times the parenterally lethal dose, the animal remained asymptomatic; however, when the bile duct was cannulated to prevent bile from reaching the gastrointestinal tract, oral administration rapidly resulted in death (Berczi, Bertok, Bainther, & Veress, 1968; Bertok, 1977).

Perhaps even more compelling than the research just cited is a study carried out recently in our laboratory involving pups that were both stressed and denied access to maternal feces (Lee & Moltz, unpublished data = a). Stress is an important parameter in the etiology of NEC (Barlow & Santulli, 1975; Barlow, Santulli, Heird, Pitt, Blanc, & Schullinger, 1974; Pitt, Barlow, & Heird, 1977). When a mammal is stressed, blood is reflexively shunted away from the mesenteric vascular bed to the heart and the brain. This reflexive redistribution of blood produces ischemia in the gut wall, making the mucosa of the gut susceptible to bacterial adherence and subsequent bacterial invasion (McNeish, Felming, Turner, & Evans, 1975; Touloukian, Posch, & Spencer, 1972). Under conditions of stress, we would expect rat young deprived of maternal feces (and so the protection of deoxycholic acid) to show a high mortality, succumbing specifically to NEC. To test this expectation, we subjected pups daily for 5 min to temperatures of 0°F when they were between the ages of 14 and 21 days. Those prevented from consuming maternal feces (a "cup" was fitted to the anus of the mother) suffered a mortality of more than 30%. That they probably died of NEC was suggested by diarrhea, abdominal swelling, and blood in the stool. In contrast, pups similarly treated and of comparable weight, but given deoxycholic acid in their diet, showed a mortality as low as that of control animals. Moreover, they presented none of the symptoms of NEC. Figure 3 pictures the tail cup and illustrates the disparity in size between a pup reared by a tail-cupped mother and one reared by a control mother.

We mentioned a second adaptive advantage possibly linked to the pheromone and to the consumption of maternal feces. This has to do with the role of bile acids in the absorption of fat from the gut and the involvement of such fat in the deposition of brain myelin.

Myelin, of course, has a large lipid component. The pup garners fatty acids for its myelin first from the milk it consumes and then from the solid food it begins to eat at about Day 14. From milk, it draws fatty acids of short-chain length, and from solid food, fatty acids of long-chain length. This difference is important because chain length determines the absorbability of fat from the gut. For example, the fat globules of rat milk, having short carbon chains (C_4 to C_{10}), are readily hydrolyzed and pass easily from the gut into the systemic circulation. In contrast, the fats contained in solid food (for example, in Purina Chow) are triglycerides of C_{18} to C_{28}. It is these long-chain fatty acids that predominate in the lipid fraction of myelin, and to gain enetry into the blood and reach the brain, they must be acted on by bile in the gut. The first step is emulsification by bile acids to "prepare" the C_{18} to C_{28} material for hydrolysis by pancreatic lipase. The free fatty acids and the 2-monoglycerides thus produced by the lipolytic action of lipase are then solubilized by bile acids to penetrate the gut wall. Resynthesis occurs within the enterocytes of the gut wall, so that what enters the systemic circulation and reaches the brain are triglycerides, which, although largely different in molecular structure from those initially ingested, are once again of long-chain length. The point is that bile acids are critical in moving certain types of fats out of the gut for use centrally in myelination.

The rat pup, as already mentioned, lacks the bile-acid capabilities of the adult, and it is not until 30 days that it presents a mature bile picture. However, between 15 and 30 days, the maximum rate of myelin deposition occurs, probably demanding in this unique stage of development a full-scale bile-acid complement. The pup does not have such a complement. We are suggesting that its response to the pheromone compensates for the deficiency.

If the deoxycholic acid contained in maternal feces is essential for brain myelination, then one would expect that pups denied access to maternal feces

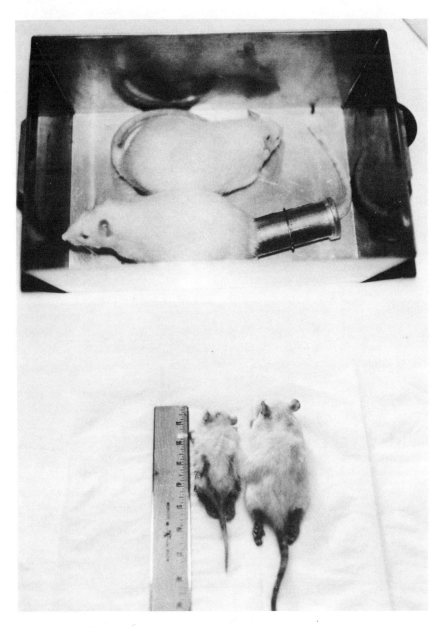

Figure 3. A tail-cupped mother, a control mother, and their respective young.

would show selected neurobehavioral deficits. Such pups, in fact, do (Lee & Moltz, 1983a). Those reared by mothers fitted with the anal cup mentioned above proved deficient in a variety of developmental tests involving reflex, motor, and sensory abilities. They also had significantly smaller brains than control pups. The next step, of course, is to look at blood lipids and central myelin to determine whether the deficit expected from our experimental rearing procedure can be prevented by feeding deoxycholic acid.

In conclusion, we want to emphasize that the pheromone is not an artifact of cage rearing. We have placed several rats together in a seminatural environment and found that the mothers emitted the attractant and that the pups responded to it (Lee & Moltz, 1983b). Indeed, in such an environment, the pheromonal bond was even more evident than among animals conventionally housed. This finding gives us confidence that the dialogue we have discussed occurs in nature, providing the pups with an adaptive edge, and the mother with an increased chance of being represented in the gene pool. The establishment and maintenance of this symbiotic relationship is summarized in Figure 4.

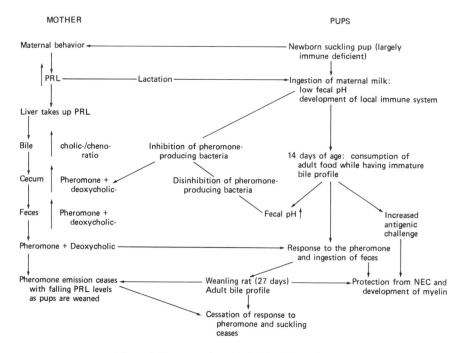

Figure 4. Pheromonal symbiosis of mother and young.

References

Amenomori, Y., Chen, C. L., & Meites, J. Serum prolactin levels in rats during different reproductive states. *Endocrinology*, 1970, *86*, 506–510.

Barlow, B., & Santulli, T. V. Importance of multiple episodes of hypoxia or cold stress on the development of enterocolitis in an animal model. *Surgery*, 1975, *5*, 687–690.

Barlow, B., Santulli, V., Heird, W. C., Pitt, J., Blanc, W. A. & Schullinger, J. N. An experimental study of acute neonatal enterocolitis—the importance of breast milk. *Journal of Pediatric Surgery*, 1974, *9* 587–594.

Barth, A., Zaumsell, & Klinger, W. Gallenflusse und Gallensaureausschedung bei mannlichen Wisterraten (Jena) verschedienen Alters. *Zeitschrift Versuchstierk,* 1977, *19*, 26–35.

Berczi, Il., Bertok, L., Bainther, K., Jr., & Veress, B. Failure of oral *Escherichia coli* endotoxin to induce either specific tolerance or toxic symptoms in rats. *Journal of Pathology and Bacteriology*, 1968, *96*, 481–486.

Bertok, L. Physico-chemical defense of vertebrate organisms: The role of bile acids in defense against bacterial endotoxins. *Perspectives in Biology and Medicine*, 1977, *21*, 70–76.

Bruce, H. M. Observations on the suckling stimulus and lactation in the rat. *Journal of Reproduction and Fertility*, 1961, *2*, 17–34.

Costlow, M. E., Buschow, R. A., & McGuire, W. L. Prolactin stimulation of prolactin receptors in rat liver. *Life Science,* 1975, *17*, 1457–1466.

Denef, C., & deMoor, P. Sexual differentiation of enzymes induced by testosterone at birth and expressed at puberty even in the absence of gonads or adrenals. In M. Kirkelstein, A. Koppler, P. Jungblut, & C. Conti (Eds.), *Research on steroids* (Vol. 15). Rome: Societa Edifice Universo, 1973, pp. 245–248.

Dickenson, A. B., Gustafsson, B. E., & Norman, A. Determination of bile acid conversion potencies of intestinal bacteria by screening in vitro and subsequent establishment in germ-free rats. *Acta Pathologica et Microbiologica Scandinavica*, 1971, *79*, 691–698.

Grosvenor, C. E., Mainweg, H., & Mena, F. A study of factors involved in the development of the enteroceptive release of prolactin in the lactating rat. *Hormones and Behavior*, 1970, *1*, 111–120.

Gustafsson, J. A., & Stenberg, A. Specificity of neonatal, androgen-induced imprinting of hepatic steroid metabolism in rats. *Science*, 1976, *191*, 203–204.

Kelly, P. A., Posner, B. J., Tsushima, T., & Friesen, H. G. Studies of insulin, growth hormone and prolactin binding: Ontogenesis, effects of sex and pregnancy. *Endocrinology*, 1974, *95*, 532–539.

Kilpatrick, S. J. *Emission of the maternal pheromone in the rat: Mechanism and function.* Doctoral Dissertation, University of Chicago, 1981.

Kilpatrick, S. J., & Moltz, H. Manipulation of testosterone in the neonatal rat and pheromal emission in the adult. *Physiology and Behavior*, 1982, *28*, 53–56.

Kilpatrick, S. J., Lee, T. C., & Moltz, H. The maternal pherome of the rat: Testing some assumptions underlying a hypothesis. *Physiology and Behavior*, 1983, *30*, 539–543.

Kilpatrick, S. J., Bolt, M., & Moltz, H. Induction of the maternal pheromone by cholic acid in the virgin rat. *Physiology and Behavior*, 1980, *25*, 31–34. (a)

Kilpatrick, S. J., Bolt, M., & Moltz, H. The maternal pheromone and bile acids in the lactating rat. *Pharmacology, Biochemistry and Behavior*, 1980, *12*, 555–558. (b)

Kocsar, L. T., Bertok, L., & Varteresg, V. Effects of bile acids on the intestinal absorption of endotoxin in rats. *Journal of Bacteriology*, 1969, *100*, 220–223.

Lee, T. M., & Moltz, H. How rat young govern the release of a maternal pheromone. *Physiology and Behavior*, 1980, *24*, 983–989.

Lee, T. M. & Moltz, H. The importance of maternal feces for pup development in the rat. Unpublished data, 1983. (a)

Lee, T. M. & Moltz, H. The maternal pheromone of the rat in a semi-natural environment. Unpublished data, 1983. (b)

Lee, T. C., Lee, C., & Moltz, H. Prolactin in liver cytosol and pheromal emission in the rat. *Physiology and Behavior*, 1982, *28*, 631–633.

Leidahl, L. C., & Moltz, H. Emission of the maternal pheromone in the nulliparous female and failure of emission in the adult male. *Physiology and Behavior*, 1975, *14*, 421–424.

Leidahl, L. C., & Moltz, H. Emission of the maternal pheromone in nulliparous and lactating females. *Physiology and Behavior*, 1977, *18*, 399–402.

Leon, M. Maternal pheromone. *Physiology and Behavior*, 1974, *13*, 441–453.

Leon, M., & Moltz, H. Endocrine control of the maternal pheromone in the postpartum female rate. *Physiology and Behavior*, 1972, *10*, 65–67.

Lifshitz, F., Wapner, R. A., Wehman, H. J., Diaz-Bensussen, S., & Pergolizzi, R. The effects of small intestinal colonization by fecal and colonic bacteria on intestinal function in rats. *Journal of Nutrition*, 1978, *108*, 1913–1923.

Manni, A., Chambers, M. J., & Pearson, O. H. Prolactin induces its own receptors in rat liver. *Endocrinology*, 1978, *103*, 2168–2171.

Marinari, K. T., & Moltz, H. Serum prolactin levels and vaginal cyclicity in concaveated and lactating female rats. *Physiology and Behavior*, 1978, *21*, 525–528.

McNeish, A. S., Felming, J., Turner, P., & Evans, N. Mucosal adherence of human enteropathogenic *Escherichia coli*. *Lancet*, 1975, *2*, 946–948.

Mena, F., Pacheco, P., Whitworth, N. S., & Grosvenor, C. E. Recent data concerning the secretion and function of oxytocin and prolactin during lactation in the rat and rabbit. *Frontiers of Hormone Research*, 1980, *6*, 217–250.

Moltz, H., & Lee, T. M. The maternal pheromone of the rat: Identity and functional significance. *Physiology and Behavior*, 1981, *26*, 301–306.

Moltz, H., & Leidahl, L. Bile, prolactin and the maternal pheromone. *Science*, 1977, *196*, 81–83.

Moltz, H., Leidahl, L., & Rowland, D. Prolongation of pheromonal emission in the maternal rat. *Physiology and Behavior*, 1974, *12*, 409–412.

Nicoll, C. S., & Meites, J. Prolongation of lactation in the rat by litter replacement. *Proceedings of the Society for Experimental Biology and Medicine*, 1959, *101*, 81–82.

Pitt, J., Barlow, B., & Heird, W. C. Protection against experimental necrotizing enterocolitis by maternal milk: I. Role of milk leukocytes. *Pediatric Research*, 1977, *11*, 906–909.

Posner, B. I., Kelly, P. A., & Friesen, H. G. Induction of a lactogenic receptor in rat liver: Influence of estrogen and the pituitary. *Proceedings of the National Academy of Sciences*, 1974, *71*, 2407–2410.

Posner, B. I., Kelly, P. A., Shiu, R. P. C., & Friesen, H. G. Studies of insulin, GH and prolactin binding: Tissue distribution, species variation and characterization (monkey, rat, guinea pig, rabbit, sheep). *Endocrinology*, 1974, *95*, 521–531.

Posner, B. I., Kelly, P. A., & Friesen, H. G. Prolactin receptors in rat liver: Possible induction by prolactin. *Science*, 1975, *188*, 57–59.

Rudback, J. A., Anacker, R. L., Haskins, W. T., Johnson, A. G., Mil, K. C. & Ribi, E. Physical aspects of reversible inactivation of endotoxin. *Annals of the New York Academy of Sciences*, 1966, *133*, 629–643.

Smith, H. W. & Crabb, W. E. The faecal bacteria flora of animals and man: Its development in the young. *Journal of Pathology and Bacteriology*, 1961, *82*, 53–66.

Touloukian, R. F., Posch, J. N., & Spencer, R. The pathogenesis of ischemic gastroenterocolitis of the neonate: Selective gut mucosal ischemia in asphyxiated neonatal piglets. *Journal of Pediatric Surgery*, 1972, *7*, 194–205.

Weisner, B. P. & Sheard, N. M. *Maternal behaviour in the rat*. Edinburgh: Oliver & Boyd, 1933.

The Mother–Infant Interaction as a Regulator of Infant Physiology and Behavior

MYRON A. HOFER

Introduction

Parents and young are held together by some aspects of their interaction and tend to be in conflict over others. Resources are exchanged, shared, exploited, and given with apparent pleasure by one to the other. In addition, there is mounting evidence that this symbiosis involves an unexpected modification of the homeostatic organization of the infant, so that the regulation of the infant's *mileu intérieur* is partially delegated to processes within the relationship with its mother. In this way, the individual homeostatic organization of the infant is partially subordinated to the organization of the symbiosis during early postnatal development. We are familiar with such a state of affairs during the intrauterine period of mammals in the form of the placental circulation, but we do not ordinarily think of the parent–young interaction serving such purposes.

The picture that emerges is of two individual homeostatic systems, linked in a superordinate organization that we may call *symbiosis*. The guiding principle of this superordinate organization appears to be the developmental trajectory of the relationship, a predictable course of changes that unfolds over time.

MYRON A. HOFER • Departments of Psychiatry and Neuroscience, Albert Einstein College of Medicine at Montefiore Hospital and Medical Center, Bronx, New York 10467. The research reported in this chapter was made possible by a Research Scientist Award and Project Grant support from the National Institutes of Mental Health.

One goal of this symbiotic relationship is, of course, its own dissolution through the establishment of the infant's individual homeostatic organization and the return of the mother to other concerns. The ultimate or evolutionary goal of symbiosis is the provision of the experiences necessary for expression of the mother's genetic potential in the offspring. The long duration of this symbiotic period in altricial mammals is thought to allow the environment to modify genetic expression in the infant through variations in the mother's contribution to the infant's developing behavioral systems.

I will present evidence that the mother–infant interaction is in a position to modify the physiological development of the offspring as well as its behavior. In this way, mother–infant symbiosis may have effects on susceptibility to bodily disease that need not act through the mediation of altered behavior, but that work directly through early alterations of the organ systems responsible for diseases later in life.

Behavior of the young is affected by the specific learning that takes place during interactions with parents. But I will give examples of how more general charcteristics of infant behavior—and, indeed, the underlying electrophysiology and neurochemistry of the infant's brain—may also be regulated by aspects of the parent–infant interaction. In this way, the regulatory nature of the symbiotic relationship may be seen to determine behavioral characteristics at the basic level of neural systems.

This chapter suggests that, hidden within observable mother–infant interactions are processes by which the mother serves as an external regulator of the infant's autonomic cardiovascular system, its brain chemistry, and the electrophysiology of its sleep–wake state organization, in addition to its behavioral responsiveness to novelty (see Figure 1).

We reached this unexpected view of the first relationship through the experimental separation of infant from parent, followed by the replacement of various modalities of interaction singly or in combination. All of the work was done on the laboratory rat at 2 weeks of postnatal age, a time when the young can first survive without their mothers. Although surviving, the young were

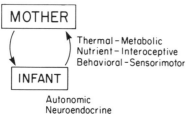

Figure 1. Schematic plan of one aspect of mother–infant symbiosis: the regulatory process by which the interaction controls the physiological and behavioral homeostasis of the infant. The three broad classes of interaction, as distinguished in this paper, are indicated in the space between the two individuals. The systems described in the four parts of this paper are listed below the infant.

found to undergo profound changes in a number of different physiological systems within their *milieu intérieur* as well as in their behavioral responsiveness.

These changes were not part of the rapid-acting psychophysiological responses of infants to isolation or maternal separation as described by Levine and Coe in this volume. Two-week-old rats, like many other young mammals, do show markedly increased vocalization, hyperactivity, and accelerated heart rate as an immediate response (within seconds) to finding themselves suddenly alone, even in their familiar home cage (Hofer & Shair, 1978). However, I deal here with slower-acting changes that take place over hours following the removal of the mother, and that occur despite the continued presence of littermates and despite a home cage environment undisturbed except for the mother's absence. These later effects of maternal separation have generally been supposed to represent the expression of a prolonged emotional response, but I believe that they are more profitably viewed within the conceptual framework I have outlined above.

Using the model in Figure 1 as a guide, we first attempted to find out whether a given response is due primarily to the withdrawal of one of the three major categories of interaction: (1) thermal; (2) nutrient; or (3) sensorimotor. We did this by systematically replacing heat, nutrients, or elements of the behavioral interaction either artificially or by altering the mother (e.g., by ligating her mammary ducts). We used these results to direct a more specific analytic investigation of the regulatory processes at work, both in terms of the precise modality and timing supplied by the mother, and in terms of the afferent and efferent pathways within the infant over which the response was mediated. Through this approach, we began to understand the nature of some of the shared homeostatic systems within the overall symbiotic organization of the early parent–young relationship in this species.

Mother's Milk as a Regulator of Her Infant's Resting Heart Rate

We tend to assume that the second major category of interaction in Figure 1 (nutrient) affects the young by supplying the metabolic substrate for growth or as a reinforcement for behavior. But as Alberts and Gubernick and Moltz have described in their chapters, what the pup and the mother ingest has other unexpected effects as well. The findings below illustrate that nutrients may also act through gastrointestinal tract interoceptors. These interoceptors provide information to the brain, which then regulates distant physiological functions, such as the resting heart rate, by adjusting the autonomic cardiovascular balance.

The developmental pattern of resting heart rates in infant rats is represented by the solid line in Figure 2. The rates were recorded from chronically

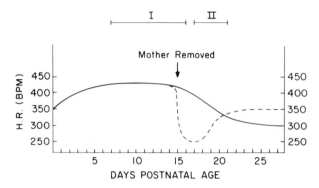

Figure 2. Schematic plan of resting heart rates in beats per min (BPM) recorded from unrestrained unanesthetized rats in their home-cage litter groups throughout early development. The solid line represents the rates of normally reared infants. The significance of the stages indicated by I and II is described in the text. The dashed line represents the resting heart rates of infants separated from their mothers but remaining in their home cage with littermates, starting at the age indicated ("Mother Removed"). The values graphed in schematic form here represent the values obtained from many infants recorded over several years of experimentation.

implanted subcutaneous electrodes by lightweight leads while freely moving infants were quiet or asleep in their home-cage nest area with their littermates. The 25 postnatal days on the graph cover the transition from a hairless, fetal-appearing newborn to an individual that resembles a small adult and is approaching puberty.

The developmental pattern records a small increase during the newborn period, a high plateau during infancy, and a marked decrease thereafter to puberty. This pattern is roughly the same for both the human and the rat. We found that the high plateau (Figure 2) was the result of high sympathetic tone, since parasympathetic blockade with methylatropine had little or no effect, whereas β-adrenergic blockade with propranolol reduced resting rates dramatically (Hofer & Reiser, 1969). The gradual decline in resting rate after 15 days of age was found to result from the maturation of vagal (parasympathetic) tone, since methylatropine given to 3-week-old pups raised resting rates back to the level of 2-week-olds (Hofer & Weiner, 1975).

If the mother is removed from the home cage, 2-week-old infants show a marked decrease in heart rate similar to that shown by the dotted line in Figure 2. Beginning 4 hr after separation, the heart rate falls rapidly, to 60% of normal by 18–24 hours. A further small decrease takes place the second day, followed by leveling off and recovery phases during the next few days. Maternally deprived pups at 20 and 24 days have significantly higher rates than normally reared infants (Hofer, 1975b).

This dramatic decrease in cardiac rate after maternal separation resulted from a fall in the normally high sympathetic drive at this age, rather than from an increase in vagal tone. The low rates of 24-hr separated pups were not fixed: a firm tail pinch would raise them briefly to preseparation levels (Hofer & Weiner, 1971).

These low heart rates were accompanied by decreased respiratory rates, and we could have concluded that these physiological changes were part of an emotional response to disruption of the attachment bond. We were concerned, however, that the infants were responding to the loss of some discrete aspect of mothering, for example, the warmth supplied by her body heat. But the pups kept at nest temperature by a thermoregulated heating pad decreased in cardiac rate to the same degree as those separated at room temperature (Hofer, 1973a). We had noticed that 14-day-old pups did not eat well from the mash and water provided for them in the mother's absence and that they lost weight consistently for the first two days. To see whether their heart rate decline was the result of starvation, we fed the pups every 4 hr for 24 hr by gastric intubation so that they all gained weight. The cardiac rates remained at the same levels as those of unfed separated pups at the end of 24 hr (Hofer, 1970). This outcome showed that the low heart rates did not result from starvation. But normally mothered pups get more milk than we were able to give them in that experiment, and a series of studies revealed that the low heart rates of 18-hr separated pups could be rapidly but transiently reversed by gastric intubation with milk (Hofer, 1971). After 4 hr, the heart rates returned to their characteristic low levels, a result explaining the lack of observable effect in our first 24-hr intubation study.

Cardiac rates began to rise within 2–3 min after milk was placed in the stomach (see Figure 3). The tachycardia produced by intragastric milk in deprived pups was dose-dependent and was not simply the result of gastric distension with a nonnutritive solution. The route of nutrient administration was crucial: sugars and amino acids given intravenously were without effect. The central nervous system mediated the response, since spinal cord section at

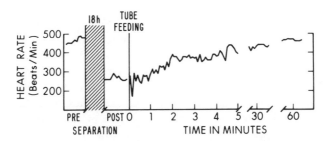

Figure 3. Heart rate recording (cardiotachometer tracing) of a 2-week-old rat pup during separation from its mother and refeeding with 1.2 ml bovine milk formula ("tube feeding").

T_1 completely prevented the intragastric milk effect (Hofer & Weiner, 1975). It was also prevented by a dose of propranalol (a β-adrenergic blocker), which had no effects on the resting rates of separated pups (Hofer, 1971).

The last two findings strongly implicated the β-adrenergic cardioaccelerator nerves that emerge from the upper thoracic spinal cord, as the efferent limb of this cardiac regulatory system. (Both thyroid and adrenal medulla were unnecessary to the response.) But how could the central nervous system "sense" the presence of nutrient in the gut? The vagal afferents were ruled out by finding that the response was unaffected by bilateral subdiaphragmatic vagotomy (Hofer & Weiner, 1975). I was able to remove the celiac ganglion and two to three sympathetic paravertebral ganglia without affecting the response, but sympathetic afferents were virtually impossible to extirpate, particularly in such a small animal. Sharma and Nasset (1962) found changes in the firing patterns of mesenteric nerves in response to infusion of different nutrients in the gut lumen and traced these neural signs as far as the caudate nucleus of the brain. This route remains a prime candidate for the afferent pathway of the milk effect on cardiac rate.

Other possible afferent routes are the gut hormones, which could be released by the nutrient, carried by the circulaton, and then sensed by the brain. However, the injections of insulin glucagon, histamine, gastrin, cholecystokinin, and secretin do not mimic the milk effect on cardiac rate in 18-hr separated pups.

Some recent unpublished work suggests a possible mechanism for the milk effect and places these cardiac changes in the context of a more widespread cardiovascular adjustment. We found that the low heart rates of deprived pups could be restored to preseparation levels by an α-adrenergic receptor blocking agent, phenoxybenzamine (PBZ), which has the effect of decreasing arterial vasoconstrictor tone. The effect was not a direct action but depended on β-adrenergic receptors, since the PBZ tachycardia was entirely prevented by propranalol. Finally, whereas a sensitive dose–response relationship was found for PBZ in separated pups, no dosage had any effect on the high cardiac rates of mothered pups.

These latest findings strongly suggest that the low heart rates of separated pups are accompanied by greatly increased α-adrenergic vasoconstrictor tone, an effect possibly mediated by baroreceptors, which maintain blood pressure near normal levels during the increased peripheral resistance. The normally fed pups, in contrast, seem to have little or no α-adrenergic vasoconstrictor tone and require high cardiac rates in order to maintain normal blood pressure. Our recent laboratory work supports this idea by demonstrating that tail cuff and direct arterial blood pressure are maintained at normal levels in deprived infants (Shear, Brunelli, & Hofer, 1983). A second kind of experimental evidence further supports this proposition: the decrease in cardiac rate with nutritional deprivation does not occur in adrenalectomized infants unless a permissive level of glucocorticoid is given (Hofer & Weiner, 1975). It was in the rat mesenteric bed that physiologists first demonstrated the absence of vasoconstriction of arterioles treated with norepinephrine unless a permissive level of glucocorticoids was also present (Zweifach, Sharr, & Black, 1953). It appears as if the adrenalectomized, separated infant cannot vasoconstrict and therefore retains its high heart rate. Most recently, we have found that sinoaortic baroreceptor denervation significantly attenuates the fall in cardiac rates after nutrient deprivation.

In summary, the nutrient levels supplied to the young rat seem to control the degree of arterial vasoconstriction and the cardiac rate through central neural integration. This process accommodates the cardiovascular system to demands for the absorption and the transport of foodstuff from the gut. If this inference is correct, the cardiac rate should be maintained without the mother's presence for prolonged periods of time when the rates are adjusted to the amount of nutrient supplied.

Figure 4 shows that this is precisely what we found (Hofer, 1973b). A correlation coefficient of .79 ($p < .01$) was found between the percentage of change in weight and the percentage of change in cardiac rate among individual infants in our series of experiments. In Figure 3, the infusion rate of .4 ml/hr produced a normal weight gain, whereas .15 ml/hr maintained weight without loss, and, of course, those not fed through their cannulas showed the expected weight loss of maternally deprived pups.

These findings have led to a view of the mother as an external physiological regulating agent controlling autonomic cardiovascular balance in her infants by the level of milk she supplies to them.

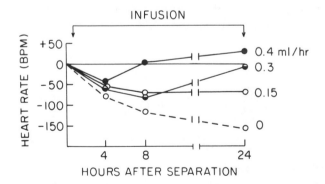

Figure 4. Changes in resting heart rates of 2-week-old rat pups separated from their mothers for 24 hr and fed milk formula continuously at different rates (see right-hand edge of figure) through previously implanted gastric cannulae. Each point represents 8–24 infants. The heart rates at the end of 24 hr for the four groups were significantly different by ANOVA ($p < .001$).

**Mother–Infant Behavioral Interaction as a Regulator
of Tissue Enzyme Levels**

One might suppose that an infant's tissue enzyme levels could be
influenced by the amount of warmth provided by the mother (particularly if
she provided too little) or by the different levels of nutrition supplied, acting
through known mechanisms of substrate and end-product feedback. But the
following example shows a surprising new way by which infant growth
processes are regulated by sensorimotor aspects of the mother–young
interaction.

Saul Schanberg and his associates at Duke University studied an enzyme,
ornithine decarboxylase (ODC), that is markedly elevated in rapidly growing
tissue, has a very short half-life, and is rate-limiting at an important step in the
synthesis of polyamines (building blocks for protein). These researchers were
troubled by the lack of consistency in ODC levels among 10-day-old rat
littermates. After some detective work, they found that the pups that were
sacrificed last after removal of the mother from the cage had the lowest levels
and that those measured first had the highest. Instead of standardizing the
interval and proceeding with the study, Schanberg and his associates focused
on the maternal separation phenomenon, using an approach based on our
cardiac rate experiments. Heat did not prevent the ODC fall, but after
separation, a short period of behavioral interaction with the mother rapidly
restored ODC levels, even after her mammary ducts were ligated to prevent
her from supplying nutrient (Butler, Suskind, & Schanberg, 1968). A passive
(anesthetized) mother was not capable of preventing the fall in ODC, even if
an anesthetic was used (urethane) that permitted periodic milk ejection and
thus fed the pups.

The researchers then looked for the hormone that might induce these
tissue enzyme changes. Adrenalectomy did not prevent the infant's ODC
response to the mother, nor did corticosterone change significantly during
separation. Growth hormone (GH), however, did fall rapidly after maternal
separation, and this fall was reversed by interaction with the mother (Kuhn,
Butler, & Schanberg, 1978). Figure 5 shows how closely ODC and GH track
together through separation and reunion. Other pituitary hormones, such as
thyroid-stimulating hormone and prolactin, did not change significantly following maternal separation. Thus, although all these hormones are capable of
inducing tissue ODC, growth hormone is the most likely mediator of the
infant's ODC response to its mother.

According to these data, it appears that some aspect of the *active* mother is
necessary; her olfactory presence, contour, and texture do not effect this
system in themselves. That tactile stimulation may be the critical modality is
suggested by recent results showing that continuous vigorous stimulation of

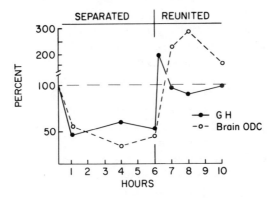

Figure 5. Plasma growth hormone and brain ornithine decarboxylase levels in rat pups after maternal separation and reunion as a percentage of the control values found in normally mothered littermates. (Graph drawn from data reported in Kuhn, Butler, & Schanberg, 1978.)

the pups' backs with a brush during the mother's absence maintains ODC levels at mothered levels, while gentler intermittent anogenital stimulation (as in her licking) does not (Evoniuk, Kuhn, & Schanberg, 1979).

This group has uncovered a novel means by which the mother rat regulates the levels of ODC in her pups' brain and other organs through the sensorimotor aspect of her interaction with them. The relevance of this finding to the human clinical phenomenon of "deprivation dwarfism" is striking. This is an example of how the mother regulates basic tissue processes within her offspring through the mediation of her behavioral interaction with them.

The Mother as a Regulator of Her Pups' Behavioral Responsiveness

The most obvious way in which the mother influences her offspring's behavior is through their attachment to her. Many species of mammal, as infants, show a set of goal-directed behaviors that maintain their proximity to their mothers: vocalization, locomotion (following), clinging, and huddling. The first two attachment behaviors are dramatically intensified immediately after separation, when vocalization and locomotion (searching) may be unremitting. Different species and ages of infants show different degrees of specificity in the object of these behaviors, and the term *attachment* is sometimes reserved for cases in which this motivational system is specifically directed toward a single individual (see Levine & Coe, this volume).

Rat pups have the set of behaviors described above, but they are directed less specifically than those of primates. At 2 weeks of age, rat pups direct their vocalization, approach, huddling, and nipple attachment behaviors according to olfactory, tactile, and thermal cues, but they do not require a specific pattern of these modalities, such as occur with specific facial recognition in primates. Likewise, rat pups show intense vocalization on isolation from mother and littermates, but this can be prevented by an artificial surrogate combining furry texture, home-cage nest smell, warmth, and a cylindrical contour (Hofer & Shair, 1980).

These are immediate responses to isolation and are most readily conceptualized in the framework of emotion and attachment theory. We have discovered a much-slower-developing alteration in behavioral responsiveness, which becomes evident only after 4–8 hr of separation and occurs even in pups left with their littermates and deprived only of their mothers (Hofer, 1975a). Litters were split, and four pups were left with the mother, the other four pups being separated with home-cage nest shavings and kept at nest temperature artifically. Then, at the end of various time intervals, different sets of litters were tested by placing the groups of four pups in a novel test box where their behaviors were observed and their overall activity level was mechanically transduced for a 10-min test period. Locomotion, rearing, self-grooming, and activity counts were all elevated in the separated pups above the levels of their mothered littermates. When a composite score was plotted over increasing time since removal of the mother, the curve in Figure 6 resulted.

This gradually developing hyperactivity in response to a novel environment took place even though the pups' body temperatures were maintained at normal levels. Our first thought was that this behavioral effect was mediated by nutrient deprivation, as we had found for cardiac rate. To our surprise, different nutrient levels infused had so systematic effect on the behavior of maternally deprived pups (Hofer, 1973b). And the provision of their mother after mammary duct ligation prevented the hyperactivity (Hofer, 1973c).

These findings let us to ask whether some aspect of the pups' behavioral interaction with their mother modulated their behavioral responsiveness, and whether the absence of this regulating effect allowed the development of hyperactivity. This was a very different approach from the standard one, which infers that separation is a stress that emotionally distrubs the animal. We reasoned that if the pups were becoming gradually more and more upset as time passed since the separation, they would become increasingly more upset if housed in a strange environment without littermates. This was not the case, as we found in a series of experiments testing both singly and in groups (Hofer, 1975a). So we returned to the less orthodox approach.

At this time, Stone and Bonnet at New York University, in collaboration with us, found that 12-day-old rat pups, separated from their mothers in a nest temperature environment for three days, accumulated dopamine and norepinephrine in their brains at a higher rate than normally reared pups (Stone, Bonnet, & Hofer, 1976). Since evidence exists that brain catecholamines may

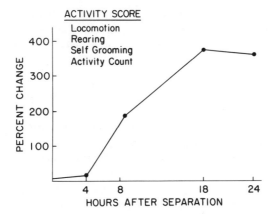

Figure 6. Activity levels of 2-week-old infant rats after various durations of maternal separation. Activity scores of normally mothered and separated littermates were composed by combining the observed counts of locomotion, rearing, and self-grooming with the output of the automated activity platform. The percentage of change at each point in time was obtained from the median percentage of difference between separated and mothered littermates, with each point representing 6 litters.

mediate generalized behavioral activity in young rats, we decided to see if drugs that prevent the accumulation of catecholamines would prevent the development of hyperactivity in separated pups. And this is precisely what we found. A small dose of reserpine, given at the time of separation, entirely prevented the development of hyperactivity during the ensuing 18 hr of maternal deprivation (Hofer, 1980). Mothered littermates showed no behavioral effects 18 hr after the same dose. Since reserpine is known to prevent the accumulation of catechol (and indole) amines at nerve terminals, we could infer that behavioral interaction with the mother normally depletes catecholamines to a moderate degree in rat pups, as did the low does of reserpine. Without interaction with the mother, catecholamines accumulate and the pups become behaviorally hyperresponsive. This "hydraulic" model needs further verification but seems an intriguing way of looking at the data.

To explore the regulating process of the mother–infant interaction in greater detail, we attempted to supply portions of the mother's sensorimotor stimulation, without other modalities, in a series of analytic experiments (Hofer, 1975a). We found that the mother's presence behind wire mesh was partially effective in preventing hyperactivity in her pups, and that this effect was blocked by making the pups anosmic with zinc sulphate. But since the maternal olfactory stimulation was not sufficient in itself, we turned to other sensory modalities. Tactile stimulation was delivered in a schedule designed to mimic the mother's periodic visits to and movements upon the litter. The more intense levels were very effective in preventing hyperactivity and, indeed, reduced activity levels below those seen in mothered pups. A periodic slowly revolving drum was also effective, whereas periodic rocking and inversion of the pups (providing primarily vestibular stimulation) was ineffective.

Thus, tactile and olfactory aspects of the mother–infant interaction, when presented alone, seemed capable of preventing infant hyperactivity. But what of the mother as a source of heat? We had found, in other experiments, that pups separated for 18 hr from their mothers, without artifically maintaining body temperature, had significantly *decreased* levels of behavior in response to the novel test box (Hofer, 1973a). And Stone (Stone *et al.*, 1976) had found that three days of room-temperature separation led to a decreased accumulation of catecholamines. It appears, then, that thermal aspects of the mother–infant interaction may also modify behavioral responsiveness and the neurochemical systems underlying it.

We hypothesize, based on these results, that the mother provides a combination of thermal, olfactory-alerting, and tactile stimulations that act together to exert a long-term control over infant behavioral responsiveness. The mother may affect behavior by regulating brain catecholaminergic systems, which mediate behavioral arousal in her infants.

The Rhythmic Pattern of Maternal Nursing Visits as a Regulator of Sleep–Wake States

Since infant brain neurochemistry and behavior seem to be regulated in part by aspects of the interaction with the mother, studying infant sleep-wake state organization could provide further insight into the workings of the mother–infant interaction.

We found that 24 hr of maternal separation in the littermate group in the home-cage nest produced consistent changes in the organization of sleep–wake states recorded electrophysiologically (Hofer, 1976). There was a marked reduction in "paradoxical" of REM sleep, an increased time spent awake, and a fragmentation of both slow-wave and REM sleep, with more frequent awakenings and shifts between states as exemplified in Figure 7. No significant changes were found in mothered pups similarly implanted and recorded on two consecutive days. These effects occurred despite nest temperature maintenance, but they were exaggerated and extended when no artificial heat was supplied. We then tried continuous nutrient infusion and the provision of the mammary-duct-ligated mother (Hofer & Shair, 1982). To our surprise, *neither* had significant ameliorating effects on the sleep–wake state disturbance. This outcome was entirely different from the case of heart rate, where the continuous infusion had been effective, or for behavioral hyperactivity, where the mammary-duct-ligated mother had been effective. One possibility was that in

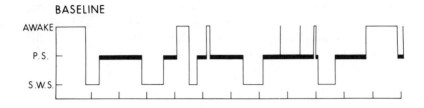

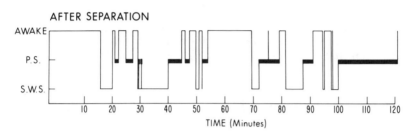

Figure 7. Sleep–wake cycles during 2-hr recordings from a 2-week-old rat pup in its home cage on baseline day and after 24 hr of maternal absence. P.S. = paradoxical sleep, or REM sleep; S.W.S. = slow-wave sleep.

this case, both nutrient and behavioral interaction were required to act in combination, in order to normalize sleep–wake organization. But before we drew this conclusion, we decided to test the idea that the rhythmic pattern of the mother's nursing cycle might be the crucial element missing in both the continuous nutrient infusion and the mammary-duct-ligated mother. For we knew, from dual cage recording studies and direct observation, that duct ligation interrupts the normal periodicity of the mother's visits to her pups for several days after the operation, resulting in long periods of constant attendance and/or many short visits.

We provided maternally deprived pups with milk by intermittent gastric infusion according to a schedule approximating that of the mother's normal nursing bouts: 15–20 min, with 40–60 min off. We supplied another group with the periodic stimulation of the slowly rotating drum, used successfully in the behavioral experiments. The result was that the periodic or rhythmic schedule of milk delivery by gastric cannula significantly attenuated the sleep distrubance, almost entirely preventing it. Periodic infusion was significantly different in its effect from continuous infusion. The periodic stimulation had an ameliorating effect that was statistically significant only when that group was compared to the pups separated without an artificial heat source (Hofer & Shair, 1982).

These results allowed us to identify another aspect of mother–infant symbiosis that exerts an important regulating effect on the infant. The rhythm and timing of the nursing interaction seem to be important in the maintenance of normal sleep–wake organization in the infant and to act primarily through some aspect of milk delivery to the infant's gastrointestinal tract. The periodic behavioral stimulation of the mother's visits may also be involved. Together, these regularly occurring events entrain the ultradian cycle of sleep–wake state organization in the infant.

Conclusion

By separating the two participants, we have found certain unexpected features of parent–infant symbiosis. Changes in (1)the infant's autonomic control of cardiac rate, (2)the levels of its brain enzyme ornithine decarboxylase, (3)its behavioral responsiveness to novelty, and (4)its sleep–wake state organization occur following separation and result from the loss of different aspects of the mother–infant interaction. The novel effect of milk on the pup's gastrointestinal interoceptors, the tactile and olfactory stimulation by the mother, her thermal input, and the rhythmicity of the maternal nursing bouts, each were found to contribute an essential part to the complex web of regulatory processes that govern the infant's physiological and behavioral homeostasis. This arrangement adds an unexpected dimension to the character of symbiosis in parent–infant interactions.

References

Butler, S. R., Suskind, M. R., & Schanberg, S. M. Maternal behavior as a regulator of polyamine biosynthesis in brain and heart of the developing rat pup. *Science*, 1968, *199*, 445–447.

Evoniuk, G. E., Kuhn, C. M., & Schanberg, S. M. The effect of tactile stimulation on serum growth hormone and tissue ornithine decarboxylase in rat pups. *Communications in Psychopharmacology*, 1979, *3*, 363–370.

Hofer, M. A. Physiological responses of infant rats to separation from their mothers. *Science*, 1970, *168*, 871–873.

Hofer, M. A. Regulation of cardiac rate by nutritional factor in young rats. *Science*, 1971, *172*, 1039–1041.

Hofer, M. A. The effects of brief maternal separations on behavior and heart rate of two week old rat pups. *Physiology and Behavior*, 1973, *10*, 423–427.

Hofer, M. A. The role of nutrition in the physiological and behavioral effects of early maternal separation in infant rats. *Psychosomatic Medicine*, 1973, *35*, 350–359. (b)

Hofer, M. A. Maternal separaton effects infant rats' behavior. *Behavioral Biology*, 1973, *9*, 629–633.

Hofer, M. A. Studies on how early maternal separation produces behavioral change in young rats. *Psychosomatic Medicine*, 1975, *37*, 245–264. (a)

Hofer, M. A. Survival and recovery of physiologic functions after early maternal separation in rats. *Physiology and Behavior*, 1975, *15*, 475–480. (b)

Hofer, M. A. The organization of sleep and wakefulness after maternal separation in young rats. *Developmental Psychobiology*, 1976, *9*, 189–206.

Hofer, M. A. Effects of reserpine and amphetamine on the development of hyperactivity in maternally deprived rat pups. *Psychosomatic Medicine*, 1980, *42*, 513–520.

Hofer, M. A., & Reiser, M. F. The development of cardiac rate regulation in preweanling rats. *Psychosomatic Medicine*, 1969, *31*, 372–388.

Hofer, M. A., & Shair, H. Ultrasonic vocalization during social interaction and isolation in 2 week old rats. *Developmental Psychobiology*, 1978, *11*, 495–504.

Hofer, M. A., & Shair, H. Sensory processes in the control of isolation-induced ultrasonic vocalization by 2 week old rats. *Journal of Comparative Physiology and Psychology*, 1980, *94*, 271–279.

Hofer, M. A., & Shair, H. Control of sleep wake states in the infant rat by features of the mother-infant relationship. *Developmental Psychobiology*, 1982, *15*, 229–243.

Hofer, M. A., & Weiner, H. The development and mechanisms of cardiorespiratory responses to maternal deprivation in rat pups. *Psychosomatic Medicine*, 1971, *33*, 353–362.

Hofer, M. A., & Weiner, H. Physiological mechanisms for cardiac control by nutritional intake after early maternal separation in the young rat. *Psychosomatic Medicine*, 1975, *37*, 8–24.

Kuhn, C. M., Butler, S. R., & Schanberg, S. M. Selective depression of serum growth hormone during maternal deprivation in rat pups. *Science*, 1978, *201*, 1034–1036.

Sharma, K. N., & Nasset, E. S. Electrical activity in mesenteric nerves after perfusion of gut lumen. *American Journal of Physiology*, 1962, *202*, 725–730.

Shear, W. K., Brunelli, S. A., & Hofer, M. A. The effects of maternal deprivation and of refeeding on the blood pressure of infant rats. *Psychosomatic Medicine*, 1983, *45*, 3–9.

Stone, E., Bonnet, K., & Hofer, M. A. Survival and development of maternally deprived rats: Role of body temperature. *Psychosomatic Medicine*, 1976, *38*, 242–249.

Zweifach, B. W., Shorr, E., & Black, M. M. The influence of the adrenal cortex on behavior of terminal vascular bed. *Annals of the New York Academy of Sciences*, 1953, *56*, 626–633.

Physiological Mechanisms Governing the Transfer of Milk from Mother to Young

DENNIS W. LINCOLN

Introduction

Breast feeding is the most overt expression of a symbiotic relationship between the mother and her offspring, insofar as the supply of milk is matched, in quality, quantity, and time with the physiological requirements set by the young. The mother has to lactate, express a desire to nurse, and eject the milk she has stored in the alveoli of her mammary glands if breast feeding is to be successful, but it is the stimulus provided by the young that is the key to the regulation of these events (Figure 1). The sucking of the nipples, besides providing the essential negative pressure for milk removal, stimulates both milk production and milk ejection by evoking the release of prolactin and oxytocin from the maternal pituitary gland. In addition, the sucking stimulus commonly inhibits either ovulation or implantation and thereby delays the arrival of subsequent offspring until the current young have reached a satisfactory state of maturity. And it is the nipple rather than the mammary gland that unites the two, transmitting sensory information to the mother and, in return, conveying milk to the young. In this chapter, attention is focused on one aspect of this relationship: the coordination of milk ejection with suckling and sucking. The control of maternal behavior and the regulation of milk production are, of course, equally important considerations, but these are mentioned here only in brief.

DENNIS W. LINCOLN ● M.R.C. Reproductive Biology Unit, Centre for Reproductive Biology, Edinburgh, Scotland EH3 9EW.

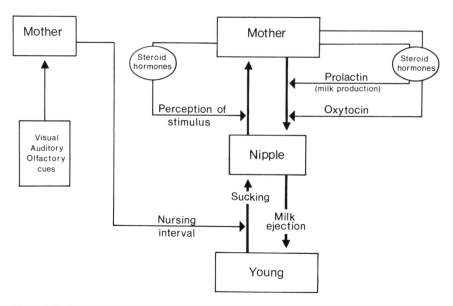

Figure 1. Pathways of interaction between mother and young in the neuroendocrine regulation of milk ejection.

The Nursing Interval

Mammals are commonly divided, when one is comparing their reproductive strategies, according to the number of young they produce and the time these young take to reach sexual maturity. In many ways, however, it is lactation and the ability to feed newborn young that are the major determinants in reproductive success. With the r-strategists, for example, the basic ploy is to feed a large litter for a relatively short period of time. The laboratory rat produces 10%–15% of its body weight/day in milk containing about 32% total solids, and when weaned at 21 days of age, the young may in total exceed the weight of their mother. The k-strategists invariably produce proportionally smaller amounts of milk, though lactation may continue for many months or even years. The domestic cow, after many generations of selection for milk production, still produces only about 1% of its body weight/day in milk, and that contains only 12% total solids. At both ends of this spectrum, however, the metabolic demands of lactation are enormous when compared with any other aspect of reproduction, and under many circumstances, these same demands set a rate-limiting step determined by the availability of an adequate food supply for the mother.

The pattern of nursing also varies enormously between species and is determined in part by the rate of milk production and the time taken to secure a food supply. The interval between one nursing episode and the next ranges from about once a day in the domestic rabbit (Zarrow, Denenberg, & Anderson, 1965) to 20 or more times in the laboratory rat (Lincoln, Hill, & Wakerley, 1973). Likewise, the total duration of nursing, defined in terms of the attachment of the young to the nipples, varies from a precise period of about 180 sec (± 5%) in the rabbit (Lincoln, 1974b) to about 18 hr/day in the rat. With the rabbit, therefore, nursing and milk ejection coincide, and the nursing interval also represents the milk ejection interval. The amount of milk transferred to the young during such a brief period of nursing is quite staggering. Rabbit pups at 10 days of age may ingest more than 25% of their body weight in milk during their daily feed; often, they are so plump after feeding that they cannot right themselves from a supine position. The rat, in contrast, displays many separate milk ejections, each lasting about 15 sec during its prolonged periods of nursing (see Figure 5); the amount of milk transferred to the young is quite small. A pup at 10 days of age obtains about 30 mg milk at each milk ejection or .2% of its body weight, but to compensate, the rat ejects milk about 80–100 times each day.

Even when the pattern of nursing is similar, different underlying strategies may be used. The red deer (*Cervus elaphus*) and the North Atlantic gray seal (*Halichoerus grypus*) make a good comparison in this respect. Both nurse about six times each day in periods of 2–6 min, but that is where the similarity ends (Bubenik, 1965; Fogden, 1971). The red deer, at least in early lactation, leaves her calf safely concealed in vegetation and returns to it at intervals. The interesting question is what brings the hind back to her calf. She roams widely in her search for food, and so the nursing interval is unlikely to be set by cues provided by the calf. One possible explanation is engorgement of the mammary gland, but this, too, seems unlikely. Findlay (1968), and Findlay and Roth (1970), in an elegant series of experiments on the rabbit, found that the desire of the doe to nurse and the duration of the nursing episode were virtually independent of the fullness of the mammary glands. In one experiment, the doe was anesthetized after several hours of separation from her young, and her mammary glands were emptied by means of an injection of exogenous oxytocin and the sucking of a foster litter; in another study, milk transfer from a doe with engorged mammary glands was prevented by sealing the teat ducts with collodion. After recovery from the anesthetic, the mothers were exposed to their own litters; in both cases, they nursed their young for about 3 min, though in neither case did the young obtain more than a nominal amount of milk. Thus, the desire to nurse and the period of nursing may relate to a maternal time-dependent mechanism, possibly located within the central nervous system. The gray seal has few equals in milk production, producing about 5 liters of milk/day of approximately 60% total solids, and the young grow from about 14 to 42 kg in the three-week period of lactation. Surprisingly, the mother does not feed during this period and remains close to her pup, either in the water or on the foreshore. Nursing occurs on demand and is initiated by the vocalization of the young. Therefore, the intervals between one nursing period and the next, and thus of milk ejection, are set in such species by factors regulating the appetite of the young.

Great differences are also apparent in the nursing behavior of women. In developed countries, it is "normal" for women to nurse their babies about six times each day in episodes lasting 10–25 min, and removing the nighttime feedings within a matter of months is common practice. Such a nursing pattern may, however, be exceedingly artificial. The !Kung tribe of Botswana and Namibia, a tribe of hunter-gatherers exhibiting features of social organization thought typical of the Pleistocene period (Lee & De Vore, 1976), display a pattern of nursing that differs markedly from that of Western (European) women. Konner and Worthman (1980) observed that !Kung women nurse their babies about four times each hour in bouts of 1.9 ± 1.3 min (Figure 2). In some respects, such a frequent pattern of sucking resembles that displayed by many nonhuman primates, although in such species, it is the young, carried clinging to the fur of the ventrum, that initiates the nursing episode. However, we must distinguish in this context between sucking for the purpose of obtaining milk and sucking associated with play and anxiety. This distinction raises the possibility that brief episodes of nursing by the !Kung women serve functions other than feeding. The milk ejection reflex in women

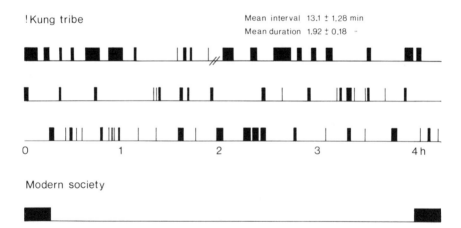

Figure 2. Patterns of breast feeding by women of the !Kung tribe from Namibia and Botswana. The periods of sucking by the babies of three women are illustrated by the length of the event bars. These data have been adapted from Konner and Worthman (1980). A typical nursing routine of women in "modern society" is provided for comparison.

has a latency of at least 30 sec after the attachment of the baby to the breast: this is the time taken for oxytocin released from the posterior pituitary to circulate to the mammary gland and promote a rise in intramammary pressure. Therefore, shorter periods of nipple attachment are unlikely to result in any transfer of milk. This need not be the case if milk is ejected in response to a nonsucking cue, and sensing milk ejection, the mother places the baby to the breast. One consequence of frequent nursing is to prolong the period of lactational amenorrhea, and so to generate a natural birth interval of over four years.

The methatherian mammals, by comparison with their eutherian counterparts discussed hitherto, have evolved exquisitively complex patterns of lactation. Marsupials at birth are almost embryonic in form: the neonate of the agile wallaby (*Macropus agilis*) weighs about .5 g at birth, or .004% of the mother's weight. After climbing into the pouch, this minute neonate attaches to one of four nipples and in so doing initiates a lactation confined to that mammary gland. For 80–100 days, the young remains continuously attached to the nipple, and as the nutritional demands of the young increase, the mammary gland continues to grow in size. At 200 days or thereabouts, the young leaves the pouch, though it continues to suck from the mammary gland on which it has been raised for a further 150 days. Mating and fertilization occur a few hours after birth, and throughout the pouch life of the previous young, a blastocyst of about 100 cells has lain dormant in the uterus (diapause). Evacuation of the pouch at 200 days triggers the activation of this blastocyst, and as a result, a new baby is born just 27 days later. This baby enters the pouch, attaches to one of the three unused nipples, and initiates a second lactation in parallel to the previous one, but over 200 days in arrears, thereby generating a case of concurrent asynchronous lactation (Figure 3) (Merchant, 1976; Lincoln & Renfree, 1981a,b). The red kangaroo (*Macropus rufus*) displays a similar pattern of double lactation (Sharman & Calaby, 1964; Sharman & Pilton, 1964). Clearly, the sucking stimulus promotes milk production in the mammary gland to which the neonate attaches. How milk ejection is organized is quite another matter. The neonate is continuously attached, while the juvenile at foot sucks only intermittently. The explanation probably lies in the differential sensitivity of the two mammary glands to oxytocin (Figure 10).

These examples illustrate the great diversity of nursing strategies in different mammals. In some species, the nursing interval is largely determined by the mother, while in others, it is determined by the appetite of the young. Likewise, the period that the young spend attached to the nipple varies from seconds to months, with one or many milk ejections occurring during each nursing episode. Clearly, the relationship of the sucking stimulus to the reflex release of oxytocin is more complex than that envisaged when the milk ejection reflex was first proposed (Cross & Harris, 1952).

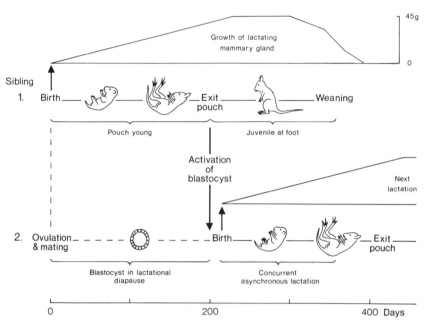

Figure 3. A diagram illustrating the sequence of events associated with the development of concurrent asynchronous lactation in the agile wallaby (*Macropus agilis*). During the pouch life of the young, the bastocyst of the next pregnancy is maintained in a state of diapause at about the 100-cell stage. Evacuation of the pouch is the trigger for that blastocyst to resume growth, and this leads to the birth of the next young 27 days later. The entry of this offspring into the pouch initiates a second lactation in parallel to the previous one, but over 200 days in arrears. The growth of the two lactating mammary glands is shown by reference to weight at autopsy.

The Sucking Stimulus

The Nipple and the Attachment of the Young

A prehensible appendage, a nipple, is essential for the effective transfer of milk, but variation in design appears to be the rule rather than the exception. The large and relatively rigid teat of the domestic cow and goat, with its large internal cistern, has prompted the most investigation because of the animals' importance in commercial milk production, although their teats' large internal asterns display little similarity to the nipples of other species. The nipples of the rat invert between one nursing episode and the next, and they terminate almost flush with the body wall. It is simple to appreciate the protective value this action affords, but it does present the pup with an additional task in that the pup has to withdraw the nipple from its recess. Sea mammals appear to have the ability to evert their nipples, but how and in response to what stimulus has not been investigated. Eversion of the nipple could relate to milk ejection triggered by the nuzzling of the pup. The mammary glands of such mammals are covered by a thick and relatively inelastic skin, and an elevation in intramammary pressure may result in the nipple's being extruded by pressure from within the gland. Alternatively, the projection of the nipple might represent a local smooth-muscle reflex. Tactile stimulation of the human nipple causes it to contract and become more erect. Internally, there may be one galactophore, as in the rat, or many, as in the human nipple. In the latter case, each galactophore drains a separate lobe of the breast and opens separately via a sphincter onto the terminal portion of the nipple.

The marsupials once again provide us with a very different design. The nipple of the agile wallaby, but only the one to which the neonate attaches, enlarges from about 6 mm in length by 2 mm in diameter at the onset of lactation to about 55 mm by 4 mm by Day 100, and it is so elastic that it can be stretched to 75 mm by 3 mm (Lincoln & Renfree, 1981a). Such great elasticity and elongation allow the young to suck from any position in the pouch and must also help to prevent the young from becoming detached during grooming or maternal locomotion. Each nipple contains some 20–30 separate galactophores, and these open separately over the terminal 3 mm of the nipple. They do not, however, possess a sphincter competent to contain the flow of milk against an elevation in intramammary pressure, and milk can leak into the pounch. Even more unusual in the mammary structure of the monotremes, the platypus (*Ornithorhynchus anatinus*) and the echidna (*Tachyglossus aculeatus*). In these species, the alveoli of the mammary glands connect to the surface of the areolar region by a multiplicity of ducts associated with hair follicles (Griffiths, Elliott, Leckie, & Schoefl, 1973).

The attachment of the young to the nipple is a matter largely overlooked in research. Only in women and occasionally in higher primates does the mother actually place the baby to the breast, though it is common for mothers of most species to assist by positioning themselves appropriately. Little is known of the cues involved, though olfactory signals probably play a major part. Anyone who attempts to apply young rat pups (Days 5–9, when their eyes are closed) to the nipples of an anesthetized mother cannot fail to notice that they make a direct line for any nipple that has just been sucked, often passing other nipples in the process. Conversely, a pup readily stops and withdraws an unsuckled nipple from its recess if the surface has been moistened with material wiped from the surface of a recently sucked nipple, a reaction that strongly suggests that the young can detect milk or some other secretion. The selection pressures are obvious in terms of survival. It is a marvel of nature how a newborn marsupial finds it way to the nipples placed deep in the pouch, but few fail to make the hazardous journey. Clearly, the precocious development of their forelimbs and olfactory bulbs is of great importance.

Sensory Receptors of the Nipple and Sensory Transmission in the Mammary Nerve

Transection of the mammary nerves or the spinal cord abolishes reflex milk ejection in the rabbit, rat, and cat, and similar effects have been produced by local anesthesia of the nipple. The nipple is richly innervated with sensory nerves when compared with other regions of the mammary gland and the overlying skin, though considerable controversy still exists regarding the nature of the sensory nerve endings (Montagna & Macpherson, 1974). Although we know little or nothing of the anatomy of the sensory receptors, it is important to discriminate between the different modalities that can be perceived. Reflex milk ejection relates to the activation of a proprioceptive input (touch and pressure) (Sala, Luther, Arbaldo & CorderoFunes, 1974). The activation of a nocioceptive input (pain) has quite the opposite effect and inhibits the reflex.

Findlay (1966), using rabbits anesthetized with urethane, recorded the electrical activity of single nerve fibers in abdominal segmental nerves and observed many units that responded with rapid adaptation to pressure applied to the nipple. Similarly, every sucking motion of a pup applied to the nipple was translated into a rhythmical barrage of information in the sensory nerve. Thus, it appears that the sucking activities of the young are relayed to the central nervous system in a very dynamic form, although to correct the record, one should add that no one has ever observed reflex milk ejection in an *anesthetized* rabbit, presumably because of the central inhibition of the reflex. The preponderance of rapidly adapting sensory receptors indicates that for maximum effect in terms of sensory transmission, the receptors require mechanical stimulation every few seconds. This requirement highlights the problem of using the phrase "the intensity of the sucking stimulus." Commonly, this term represents the sum of the sensory input derived from the number of sucking young and the period of nursing. No study has yet attempted to relate this expression to the quality of the stimulus, that is, the amount and pattern of proprioceptive stimulation applied on a second-by-second basis. Superficially, the rat pup appears to confound the issue because it rests attached to the nipple and appears simply to wait for milk ejection to occur. A detailed examination of rat pups has shown, however, that despite their somnolent appearance, they suck in short bursts every few seconds (Wakerley & Drewett, 1975). As a consequence, the sensory input they generate may be protected against habituation.

The mammary parenchyma and interlobular septa contain few sensory receptors compared with the nipple, though Findlay's (1966) recording studies from the mammary nerves of the rabbit would suggest that these receptors could provide information relating to the state of mammary engorgement and the contraction of the mammary myoepithelium at milk ejection.

On the other hand, these receptors are not sufficiently numerous to allow women to accurately localize an area of infection.

Hormonal Modulation of Nipple Sensitivity

The application of a natural sucking stimulus, let alone any experimental alternative, provides no guarantee that the stimulus will be appropriately perceived by the nervous system and result in reflex milk ejection. The sensitivity of the human breast, and in particular the nipple and the areolar region, changes dramatically during different stages of reproduction (Robinson & Short, 1977). The female breast becomes substantially more sensitive than that of the male at puberty when measured by a two-point sensory discrimination index (i.e., the minimum distance between the points of a pair of dividers that a subject can determine as separate points of contact). Sensitivity also varies during the menstrual cycle, with a peak at menstruation and a less predictable one near to the time of ovulation. Following birth, however, breast sensitivity increases markedly within 24 hr (Figure 4), and this increase could be of fundamental importance in the establishment of a milk ejection reflex. In all circumstances, an increase in breast sensitivity seems to relate to a sudden fall in the circulating levels of gonadal steroids, though exposure to high levels of hormones is a prerequisite. Which hormones are involved and whether they act centrally or peripherally have not been resolved. A word of

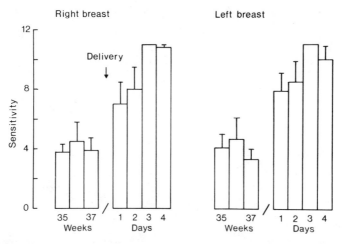

Figure 4. Changes in the tactile sensitivity of the human breast in the perinatal period. Sensitivity was measured as the minimum distance between the points of a pair of dividers that could be recognized as two points of contact. This sensitivity is expressed in arbitrary units, where high values represent increased sensory discrimination. Time is given in weeks and days before and after the delivery of the baby. These data have been adapted from Robinson and Short (1977).

caution is perhaps appropriate: these studies are evaluating cognitive perception. The milk ejection pathways from the nipples to the hypothalamus do not appear to involve higher nervous centers, though clearly higher centers can inhibit or facilitate the reflex (Tindal, 1978).

Intermittent Patterns of Milk Ejection during Prolonged Nursing

Rat pups commonly spend 30–60 min attached to the nipples during each nursing period and thereby generate what must amount to a sustained sensory stimulus. The efferent response, on the other hand (i.e., the release of oxytocin and the induction of milk ejection), operates intermittently and results in the recurrence of milk ejections every 2–10 min (Figure 5) (Lincoln *et al.*, 1973). The generation of such an intermittent pattern of milk ejection requires the sucking of at least 6 pups when the mother is anesthetized, but increasing the number of pups to 12 does not cause milk ejections to recur at shorter intervals. Neither injections of oxytocin (1 mU) nor the release of the animal's own oxytocin by electrical stimulation of the posterior pituitary results in the retiming of the endogenous pattern of milk ejection evoked by

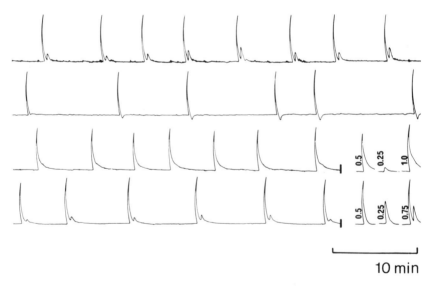

10 min

Figure 5. Recordings of intramammary pressure from four lactating rats anesthetized with xylazine (7.5 mg/kg, i.m.) and diazepam (5.0 mg/kg, i.m.). Eight to ten hungry pups were applied to the uncannulated nipples of each mother throughout these recordings. Abrupt rises in intramammary pressure, recurring every 4–10 min, represent individual milk ejections. The amplitude of these pressure waves is about 8–12 mm Hg. The lower two recordings were calibrated against bolus injections of oxytocin (mU) given into the saphenous vein.

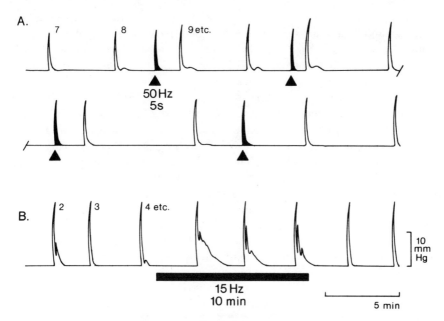

Figure 6. Failure of electrical stimulation of the posterior pituitary of the lactating rat to modify the timing of the milk ejection sequence evoked by the sucking of the young. In both recordings of intramammary pressure, the rats were anesthetized with urethane (1.1 g/kg, i.p.), and 10 hungry pups were applied to the nipples. Part A demonstrates that pulses of oxytocin released by high-frequency stimulation (50 Hz for 5 sec) failed to reset the interval between one "reflex" milk ejection and the next, although the pulses of hormone released by stimulation caused milk ejection (shown in black). Part B illustrates the same protocol with stimulation applied at 15 Hz for 10 min; this also failed to modify the sucking-induced reflex. This period of low-frequency stimulation, while not causing milk ejection, probably increased the basal level of oxytocin in the blood, and that could account for the multiple waves of contraction associated with each milk ejection elicited by the sucking of the young during this period. Sucking-induced milk ejections are numbered from the application of the pups to the nipples. These data have been adapted from Wakerley and Deversen (1975).

the sucking of the young, though both experimental manipulations introduce additional milk ejections into the natural sequence (Figure 6) (Lincoln, 1974a; Wakerley & Deverson, 1975). When a threshold number of pups has been present on the nipples for some time without evoking milk ejection, it is sometimes possible to evoke ejection within a matter of seconds by applying an additional pup or by the dilatation of a cannulated galactophore with .2 ml saline (Lincoln & Wakerley, 1975). Once triggered in this way, the neural mechanism remains refractory to further such manipulations for several minutes. Such a refractory component could account for the regular recurrence of milk ejection in the presence of what appears to be a continuous sensory stimulus. Indeed, if there were no such refractory component, the increase in intramammary pressure and the increased sucking of the pups at milk ejection would generate positive feedback, and once commenced, further milk ejections would recur every 10–15 sec (i.e., the time taken for an oxytocin pulse released from the posterior pituitary to evoke milk ejection).

Such an intermittent pattern of milk ejection as that just described for the rat has not been observed in any species other than rodents, though there is one interesting report of a woman experiencing milk ejection at regular intervals between one period of breast feeding and the next (Figure 7) (McNeilly & McNeilly, 1978). These "spontaneous" milk ejections, sensed from the draft of milk, appeared to be absent for a period after each breast feeding and declined in incidence as lactation progressed. To class such milk ejections as spontaneous is to admit that we do not understand what caused them. They were not prompted by a sucking stimulus, but there are several other alternatives. Sensory stimulation could result from clothes, movement of the breast, or engorgement with milk, given the highly sensitive state of the mammary receptors at this time. Breast movement during exercise has been reported to elevate prolactin levels in women and has been implicated in the rather common occurrence of amenorrhea in athletes (Baker, Malhur, Kirk, &

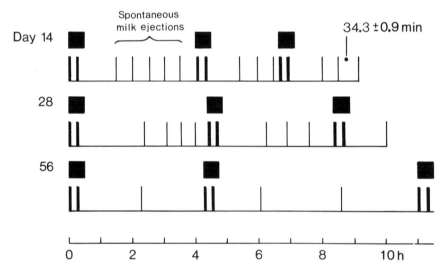

Figure 7. Occurrence of spontaneous milk ejections in a woman breast feeding twins. Each vertical event bar represents milk ejection perceived from the "draft" of the milk, while periods of breast feeding are represented by the solid blocks. The mean interval between spontaneous milk ejections was 34 ± .9 min (mean ± S.E.M.) on Day 14 of lactation; this interval appeared to increase as lactation progressed. These data have been adapted from McNeilly and McNeilly (1978).

Williamson, 1981). Alternatively, these milk ejections could also be triggered by the higher nervous system, though one need not be cognitively aware of the cues involved.

Milk Ejection during Anesthesia and Sleep

The rat, mouse, and gerbil are the only species in which milk ejection has been observed when young have been applied to the nipples of a deeply anesthetized mother. The intermittent pattern of milk ejection just discussed has been observed during anesthesia induced by such diverse agents as urethane, sodium pentobarbitone, ethyl alcohol, xylazine, and halothane, but it does not occur in the presence of opiatelike analgesics (e.g., fentanyl and etorphine). The reason that the rat ejects milk when anesthetized is rather curious and was not appreciated for several years. Rats eject milk only when asleep, and most anesthetics promote an EEG pattern akin to that of slow-wave sleep (synchronized) (Figure 8) (Lincoln, 1973; Lincoln, Hentzen, Hin, van der Schoot, Clarke, & Summerlee, 1980). Furthermore, the sucking stimulus is sleep-inducing. This is difficult to establish in an unanesthetized animal, but it can be clearly seen in a rat under urethane anesthesia. The EEG of a rat under urethane alternates between "sleep, paradoxical sleep, and arousal" (Figure 8), although the animal displays no overt sign of any change in the level of anesthesia. The application of a litter of pups eliminates these EEG changes and promotes a continuous slow-wave EEG pattern for an hour or more. Thereafter, the EEG commences to cycle back and forth, though milk ejection is confined to periods of slow-wave EEG activity (Figure 8). Such an association does not account for the regular interval between one milk ejection and the next, though it may introduce some variability into the pattern, because arousal, if it persists, results in a postponement of the next milk ejection. Likewise, any experimental manipulation that arouses the EEG of an anesthetized animal inhibits the reflex in this very nonspecific way. The situation is even more delicately balanced with the unanesthetized rat. First, the rat has to go to sleep after the attachment of the young to the nipples before milk ejection can commence, though milk ejection appears to be facilitated by the sucking stimulus. Any stimulus that provokes or maintains wakefulness (the presence of an observer) prevents milk ejection, and this is probably the reason that milk ejection in the rat had gone unobserved for so many years. Interestingly, the act of milk ejection invariably causes arousal, but this occurs about 10 sec after the neural activation associated with the release of oxytocin (see Figure 12). As a result of being aroused, the mother commonly commences to groom her young and in the process activates the micturition reflex by licking their abdomens.

In cows, sheep, rabbits, and pigs, to name only a few species, sleep is not a

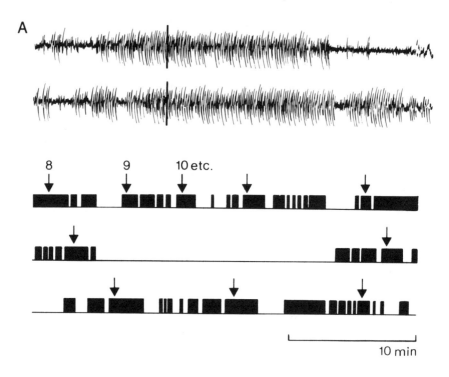

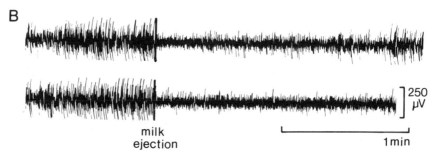

Figure 8. Evidence that reflex milk ejection in the rat is associated with "slow-wave sleep." Part A illustrates electroencephalographic activity (EEG) recorded from the frontal parts of the cerebral cortex of a rat anesthetised with urethane (1.2 g/kg, i.p.) and suckled by 10 pups. Above are shown two polygraph recordings taken to span the time of milk ejection (vertical event bar). Note that a pattern of large-amplitude slow-wave activity commenced some 10 sec or more before milk ejection and continued for about 1 min afterward. A much longer period of EEG activity is diagrammatically depicted immediately below: the solid bar represents periods of slow-wave activity, and milk ejections are indicated by the arrows and are numbered from the application of the pups to the nipple. Part B illustrates EEG activity recorded from two unanesthetized rats during the suckling of their young. Note that a large-amplitude slow-wave pattern of activity existed in the period before milk ejection (vertical event bar). At milk ejection, the EEG promptly changed to the low-amplitude pattern associated with wakefulness.

prerequisite for milk ejection (Poulain, Rodriguez, & Ellendorff, 1981). However, the rabbit and the guinea pig do enter a "trancelike" state during their brief periods of nursing and, for a time, seem quite oblivious to events around them. Such observations raise two interesting questions. Might not wakefulness be a prerequisite for milk ejection, and could that requirement not account for the failure of these species to eject milk when anesthetized? Likewise, it would be most interesting to know whether women can eject milk when asleep. Nursing at night is thought to be a major factor in determining the length of lactational amenorrhea, and it has thus been advocated that women sleep with their babies, as occurs in the !Kung tribe. Certainly, it is common for women to fall asleep when nursing, but that fact itself fails to answer the question. EEG activity has to be recorded alongside intermammary pressure, and this kind of recording has not been done.

The Mammary Contraction

The mammary glands of all mammals are largely identical in fine structure and consist of alveolar tissue within which milk is continuously secreted during lactation. An alveolar arrangement increases vastly the surface area for secretion relative to the overall size of the mammary gland, though at the same time it complicates milk removal. Small ducts generate substantial surface tension forces that oppose the movement of fluids. Thus, the negative pressure gradient applied by the sucking of the young is relatively ineffective in removing milk stored in the alveolar tissue, and that represents more than 80% of the milk in the mammary glands of most species. Only in the cow and the goat are large amounts of milk stored in cisterns directly above the teat ducts. The problem of removing alveolar milk has been overcome by investing the alveoli in a basketlike reticulum of myoepithelial cells that contracts in response to oxytocin released from the posterior pituitary. This contraction compresses each alveolus and causes the milk stored within the alveolus to be expelled through the collecting ducts and into the galactophores of the nipple, from which it can be withdrawn by the sucking of the young. One requirement for effective milk ejection is that the contraction of the myoepithelium should be synchronized throughout the mammary gland or at least within lobes of the gland: the irregular contraction of individual alveloi would be of little functional value.

One of the most informative ways of assessing milk ejection is to record the pressure from within a cannulated galactophore, because such recording measures the availability of milk at a site from which it can be withdrawn by the young. The measurement of such pressures is easier said than done, as the stress involved in the cannulation procedure tends to block, by central inhibition (see later discussion), the reflex release of oxytocin that one wishes to study. Recordings of intramammary pressure have been obtained in cows, women, and pigs, with the use of sedatives and local anesthetics, but those obtained from the rat are far more extensive simply because of the greater range of studies that can be conducted on an *animal* that will reflexly eject milk when deeply anesthetized.

The most effective and efficient way of eliciting a mammary contraction in a lactating rat is to administer a bolus intravenous injection of about 1 mU (2 ng) oxytocin; this generates a rise in pressure of about 10 mm Hg commencing after a latency of 9–11 sec (Figures 5 and 6). The injection of 2–5 mU oxytocin over 30 sec generally fails to elicit a rise in pressure, and more prolonged infusions are equally ineffective. The response to a bolus injection of hormone has a rather limited dynamic range. Injections of .2 mU or less usually produce no recordable mammary contraction, while injections of 1.5 mU and greater result in the same peak pressure (a plateau is reached). The mammary contraction also exhibits a phenomenon similar to short-term down regulation. If pulses of oxytocin are injected at intervals of 2 min or less, the response to the second and subsequent injection is substantially reduced in amplitude, presumably because of a reduction in the availability of receptors. Thus, to drive the mammary gland of the rat to maximum effect while using the minimum amount of oxytocin, one would advocate the administration of bolus injection of about 1 mU oxytocin at intervals of about 3 min, which is precisely the pattern of oxytocin that appears to be released from the posterior pituitary during the sucking of the young (Figure 5).

A series of rhythmical contractions is commonly evoked by injections or infusions of oxytocin in amounts larger than those indicated above (see Figures 6, 10, and 16). These contractions could be the result of vascular stasis during each contraction, limiting the access of oxytocin to the mammary gland, or they could reflect the inherent periodicity of the myoepithelial cells to contract when subjected to prolonged stimulation. Rhythmical contractions, not synchronized between adjacent mammary glands, are observed during engorgement of the mammary gland with milk; these contractions can be evoked by injecting fluid into cannulated glands and can be reduced by allowing excess milk to drain away. These observations suggest that such contractions are generated by the stretching of the myoepithelium of the mammary gland, though basal levels of oxytocin might well facilitate the process. As a consequence, young sucking on engorged mammary glands can obtain substantial amounts of milk in the absence of an oxytocin-induced milk ejection (Lincoln *et al.*, 1973). In a similar fashion, local mechanical stimulation might also facilitate milk removal. A brisk tap of the mammary gland of the rabbit generates a very effective rise in pressure confined to the gland in question (Cross, 1954). Calves and lambs do something rather similar, striking the udder with considerable force before attempting to suck—perhaps they have learned to capitalize on the "Cross-tap response."

Recordings of intramammary pressure during reflex milk ejection in other species have not produced such clear evidence of a pulsatile pattern of oxytocin release, save perhaps in the pig (Figure 11) (Bruhn, Ellendorff, Forsling, & Poulain, 1981). Cobo, De Bernal, Gaitan, and Quintero (1967) recorded intramammary pressure from a cannulated galactophore in the human breast while a baby was placed to suck on the opposite side. Multiple waves of pressure were observed during the 15-min nursing period, with pressure peaks at intervals of 1–2 min (Figure 9). Attempts were make by the authors to simulate these sucking-induced contractions by the subsequent infusion and/or injection of oxytocin. The most satisfactory simulation involved the administration of a bolus injection of 20–30 mU oxytocin every few minutes, though infusions of hormone (4 mU/min) produced multiple waves of contraction that were not dissimilar. One is faced, however, with a difficult problem of interpretation. In the rat, a bolus injection of physiological proportions causes a contraction of about 15-sec duration. In women, and indeed in other large species, a bolus injection of oxytocin invariably causes a mammary contraction lasting 1 min or much longer (Figure 10). Thus, pulses of oxytocin released, say, every 3 min could result in a sustained, wavelike period of mammary contractility.

Concurrent Asynchronous Lactation in Macropodid Marsupials

The mammary glands of such species as the agile wallaby (see Figure 3) can be induced to contract in the early stages of lactation to injections or infusions of oxytocin that are quite ineffective at later stages of lactation (Figure 10) (Lincoln & Renfree, 1981a). The pressures generated by these contractions are very substantial (20–60 mm Hg), and in the absence of an

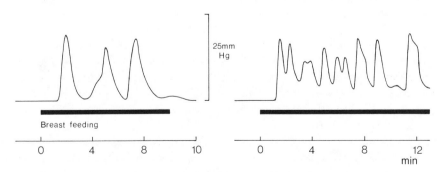

Figure 9. Two recordings from women of intramammary pressure during breast feeding. Pressure was recorded from a catheter inserted into a galactophore without anesthesia; the baby was then placed to suck on the contralateral nipple for the period indicated by the event bar. These data have been adapted from Cobo, De Bernal, Gaitan, and Quintero (1967).

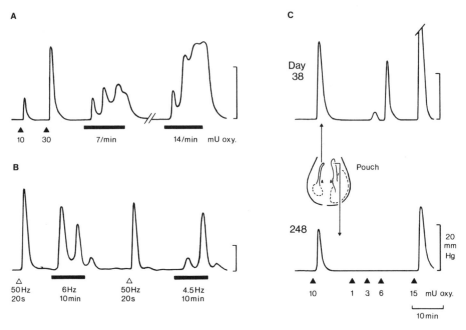

Figure 10. Recordings of intramammary pressure from the agile wallaby (*Macropus agilis*). The pouch young were removed and the mothers anesthetised with sodium pentobarbitone (given intravenously). Individual galactophores of the lactating mammary gland(s) were cannulated with a 27-gauge needle. Part A illustrates the effect on intramammary pressure of giving bolus injections and infusions of oxytocin into the external jugular vein. Part B demonstrates the effect of stimulating the pituitary stalk with a monopolar electrode inserted into the brain from a midline position between the frontal lobes of the cerebral hemispheres. Part C illustrates pressure recordings taken simultaneously from young (Day 38) and old (Day 248) lactating mammary glands in the same wallaby. These data are adapted from Lincoln and Renfree (1981 a,b).

effective teat sphincter, they could result in the milk's being "pumped" into the attached neonate. Furthermore, the exquisite sensitivity of the mammary glands in early lactation suggests that very little oxytocin need to be released from the posterior pituitary. In fact, a simple elevation in the basal level of circulating oxytocin evoked by the continuous attachment of the young to the nipple might be sufficient to induce contractions every few minutes. One could envisage, on the other hand, the juvenile which has left the pouch evoking a massive release of oxytocin when it attempted to suck at the older of the two mammary glands. A large release of oxytocin, while causing a contraction of the mammary gland in late lactation, would have very little effect on the young gland if that was already contracting, because the pressure response quickly reaches a plateau. Otherwise, the sucking of the juvenile would simply give its younger sibling an additional feed. Presumably, the decline in sensitivity to oxytocin relates to a decline in the number of oxytocin receptors or in the affinity of hormone–receptor binding. The number of receptors in the mammary gland of the rat has been measured: the number does not change markedly during lactation, although a 40-fold change is observed in the uterus in the hours surrounding parturition (Soloff, Alexandrova, & Fernstrom, 1979).

Plasma Levels of Oxytocin and Vasopressin in Relation to Milk Ejection

Long before it was fashionable to speak of the pulsatile release of pituitary hormones, Folley and his colleagues, working on the cow and goat at the National Institute for Research in Dairying at Shinfield, England, had established that the stimulus of milking or sucking caused a transient, spurt like release of oxytocin (Folley & Knaggs, 1966; Cleverley & Folley, 1970; McNeilly, 1972). Considerable variability was encountered among animals and among milking episodes in the same animal. Indeed, on about 30% of occasions, McNeilly (1972) was unable to detect a rise in the plasma level of oxytocin during the milking of some goats, while in other goats one or more episodes of release were observed during each milking period. Sucking and hand milking were equally effective in causing a release of oxytocin, but the routine associated with suckling rather than with hand milking was far more likely to lead to a "conditioned" release of oxytocin. Studies at this time also established that the sucking stimulus was selective in evoking the release of oxytocin from the posterior pituitary; there was no evidence to show a concomitant release of vasopressin (Bisset, Clark, & Haldar, 1970). This finding is of importance in two respects. Vasopressin is structurally so similar to oxytocin that it has substantial milk-ejecting activity, about 25% that of oxytocin in the rat (Berde & Boissonnas, 1968), and if released in sufficient quantities, vasopressin could evoke the changes in intramammary pressure previously discussed. It is still possible that the basal level of vasopressin may be elevated during lactation because of the increased needs for fluid retention, but any increase seems to be independent of milk ejection *per se*. The selective nature of the sucking stimulus is also of considerable experimental importance because it permits a more meaningful analysis of the neural events underlying the process of secretion.

There have been no detailed measurements of the levels of oxytocin in the plasma of rats relative to individual milk ejections (Figure 5). The task may appear quite simple. However, milk ejection in the rat is a transient event and seems to be related to the release of an oxytocin bolus. A blood sample taken over 10 sec is, in effect, an integrted sample compared with the profile to which the mammary glands are subjected. Furthermore, until this past year, all assays have demanded such large samples that their withdrawal from a rat would have evoked a vasopressin release as a result of reduced blood volume. A reasonably detailed profile has recently been obtained during the suckling of the sow, with samples taken every 15 sec (Figure 11) (Bruhn *et al.*, 1981). An abrupt rise in the plasma level of oxytocin, from 5 to 20 μU/ml, occurred in the period immediately preceding the rise in intramammary pressure at milk ejection, while the levels of lysine-vasopressin remained unchanged. Given that the half-life of oxytocin in plasma is in the range of .5–8.0 min, these studies of the sow suggest a transient release of oxytocin, perhaps lasting less than 10 sec. By contrast, recent studies of the level of oxytocin in women during breast feeding suggests a sustained period of release (Dawood, Khan-Dawood, Wahi, & Fuchs, 1981). Samples were taken every 5 min, and the mean plasma level of oxytocin was observed to rise from about 5 μU/ml before breast feeding began to about 25 μU/ml after 10 min of sucking. Of course, a progressive rise in the circulating level of oxytocin could result from multiple episodes of release, providing that the interval between each period of release is considerably shorter than the half-life of the hormone.

Oxytocin Producing Neurons

Two features of the milk ejection reflex have emerged from the foregoing discussion. The mammary glands of many species appear to respond most effectively and efficiently to bolus injections of oxytocin, while nursing in several species appears to be associated with a pulsatile or episodic pattern of oxytocin release. The sucking stimulus, on the other hand, seems poorly correlated, on a second-by-second basis, with individual episodes of oxytocin release, although it is highly selective for the release of this hormone from the posterior pituitary. The oxylocin-producing reurons of the hypothalamic magnocellular nuclei bridge the gap between the sensory input and the endocrine response. It is their pattern of electrical activity that governs hormone secretion.

Localization of Oxytocin- and Vasopressin-Producing Neurons

Oxytocin-and vasopressin-producing neurons are found in the mag-nocellular portions of the paired supraoptic and paraventricular nuclei of the hypothalamus and in scattered groups between these nuclei. Some regional localization of the two cell types within the magnocellular nuclei does exist, although the cells remain extensively intermingled (Swaab, Pool, & Nijveldt, 1975). The majority of these neurons project directly to the posterior pituitary and do not appear to branch extensively en route. On entering the posterior

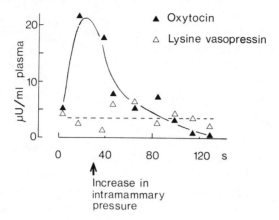

Figure 11. Measurements of oxytocin and lysine-vasopressin in the plasma of a domestic sow of the Landrace strain during milk ejection evoked by the sucking of a litter of piglets. Blood samples were taken every 15 sec during the nursing period from a catheter chronically implanted into the jugular vein. Milk ejection was "signaled" by the rapid grunting of the sow and was monitored from the rise in intramammary pressure recorded from a cannulated teat-duct. The onset of the rise in pressure at milk ejection is indicated. These data have been kindly provided by F. Ellendorff, M. L. Forsling, D. A. Poulain, and T. Bruhn from work conducted at the Institut für Tierzucht und Tierverhalten FAL, Mariensee 3057 Neustadl 1, FRG.

pituitary, the axons cross the blood–brain barrier, which could be of functional importance since factors in the circulation may modulate secretion by an action on the nerve terminals rather than on the cell body. Within the posterior pituitary, the axons display many large dilatations (or Herring bodies) and branch profusely before ending on capillaries. The Herring bodies and nerve terminals contain about 60% and 30%, respectively, of the stored oxytocin (Cross, Dyer, Dyball, Jones, Lincoln, Morris, & Pickering, 1975). This could represent the anatomical basis of the concept of readily releasable and less readily releasable pools of hormones. By means of immunohistochemistry, some oxytocin-containing nerve fibers have been traced to the brain stem and the spinal cord, most seem to arise in the parvicellular portion of the paraventricular nucleus (Sofroniew, 1980). The function of this projection is not understood.

Oxytocin Biosynthesis, Transport, and Storage

A peptide of about 20,000 molecular weight is synthetized within the endoplasmic reticulum of the magnocellular neurons. This is then transported to the Golgi apparatus, where it is packaged into membrane-bound granules of about 100–150 nm diameter (neurosecretory granules). These granules are then conveyed to the posterior pituitary at the fast rate of about 2 mm/hr, and in the process, the precursor peptide is divided by enzymes to produce a number of fragments, among which are found oxytocin (molecular weight 1,007) and the so-called oxytocin neurophysin (molecular weight 10,000) (Pickering, 1978). Oxytocin therefore represents only 5% of the precursor from which it was formed; the remainder of the peptide, which is presumably released in parallel (Legros, Raynaert, & Peeters, 1974), has no function in milk ejection.

The amount of oxytocin stored in the posterior pituitary is 100–1,000 times greater than the amount required to elicit milk ejection. The human pituitary contains 3,000–9,000 mU oxytocin (Lederis, 1961), when as little as 20 mU will evoke a milk ejection. The corresponding figures for the rat are 500 mU in the posterior pituitary and 1 mU to evoke milk ejection. Much of this store is in the Herring bodies and is probably not immediately available for release. Even so, the readily releasable pool of hormone, calculated at 5%–10%, is still large compared with that required for milk ejection and therefore is unlikely to represent a natural rate-limiting step. Furthermore, the processes of peptide biosynthesis do not have to be correlated with secretion other than over a relatively long time scale of, say, a day or more.

Electrical Activity in Oxytocin Release

Oxytocin-producing neurons, in common with other peptidergic neurons, generate action potentials as a function of the synaptic input they receive from many thousands of other neurons. The rat is the only species in which the electrical activity of oxytocin-producing neurons has been recorded during hormone release evoked by the sucking of the young (Wakerley & Lincoln, 1973; Lincoln & Wakerley, 1974, 1975; Summerlee & Lincoln, 1981). Putative oxytocinergic neurons display a slow, random pattern of background discharge with action potentials recurring at a mean rate of 0–5/sec (Figures 12 and 13). The application of the pups to the nipples cause no immediate increase in electrical activity. Dynamic second-by-second changes in firing, such as those that Findlay (1966) recorded from the mammary nerves of the rabbit, are not observed. This finding leads one to conclude that the sucking stimulus is not continuously propagated through to the oxytocin-producing cells. Perhaps this is a necessary block to transmission because it is difficult to envisage how a coordinated pattern of release could result if every sucking motion caused a small increase in the firing of the oxytocinergic neurons, although this is what we had expected at the outset. At some time after the onset of sucking, each oxytocinergic neuron displays an explosive acceleration in activity, generating 20–80 action potentials/sec for 2–4 sec (Figure 12). Milk ejection is observed 9–12 sec later, which is the time taken for oxytocin to be released, to circulate in the blood, and to promote the contraction of the

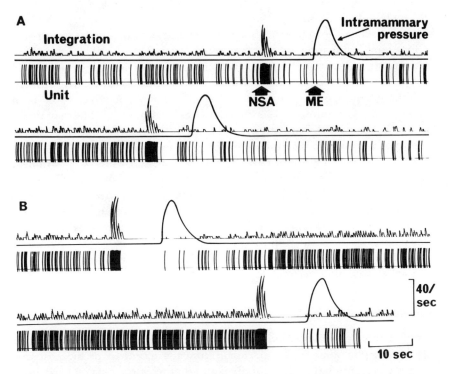

Figure 12. Polygraph recordings of the electrical activity of two supraoptic neurons in an anesthetized lactating rat during milk ejection (ME) evoked by the sucking of the young. These recordings of the action potentials of single neurons were obtained by means of glass micropipettes stereotaxically placed into the region of the supraoptic nucleus; neurons projecting to the posterior pituitary were identified by antidromic stimulation from a bipolar electrode implanted in the posterior pituitary. The position of this electrode was confirmed by stimulating at 50 Hz for 4 sec. When correctly placed, this electrode evoked oxytocin release and a rise in intramammary pressure. Each deflection of the unit trace corresponds to one action potential; an integration over .5-sec intervals is presented above the unit trace. Note that an explosive increase in electrical activity (NSA) occurred about 10 sec before milk ejection. This latency represents the time it takes for oxytocin to be released, to circulate in the blood, and to act on the myoepithelial cells of the mammary gland. The two periods of recording shown for each unit were selected to span the period of neurosecretory activation; they are not continuous. The recordings of intramammary pressure differ from those shown in Figure 5 because they are presented at a faster chart-speed. Data reproduced from Lincoln and Wakerley (1975).

myoepithelial cells of the mammary gland. There is good evidence to indicate that all the oxytocin cells are synchronously activated, although recordings are usually taken from only one cell at a time. Changes in multiunit discharge are observed during the activation of individual cells, and the latency to milk ejection is relatively constant.

These recordings of electrical activity, while providing the first definitive electrophysiological correlates for the release of a hypothalamic peptide, have given us few clues as to how the burst of electrical activity is generated. There is, for example, no apparent increase in background electrical activity as the time of activation approaches, nor is there an increase in activity associated with the vigorous sucking of the pups at milk ejection. Likewise, recruitment of hitherto unresponsive neurons or loss of responsiveness has never been observed when the number of sucking pups has been changed. The magnitude of each burst of electrical activity, rather than the interval between bursts, does appear to be related to the number of sucking pups (Figure 13). These observations could be interpreted in terms of a neural window (positioned, say, in the brain stem) that is intermittently opened as a function of both the intensity of the sucking stimulus and the interval from the previous milk ejection and that, when opened, allows information through to the magnocellular nuclei in amounts proportional to the number of sucking young. One consequence is that, within a limited range, the greater the number of pups attached to the nipples, the greater will be the amount of oxytocin released at each milk ejection.

Stimulus–Secretion Coupling

The basic premise underlying our consideration of electrical activity is that action potentials release hormone from the terminals of the posterior pituitary proportional to their number, and that release occurs by a calcium-dependent mechanism of exocytosis (Douglas, 1968; Douglas & Kagayama, 1977). Thus, the more potentials generated within the magnocellular nuclei of the hypothalamus, the greater should be the release of oxytocin from the posterior pituitary. In reality, such a linear relationship greatly underestimates the potential of the system. A process of frequency facilitation exists within the terminals whereby action potentials arriving in the terminals within 20 msec of each other (50 Hz) release 100–1,000 times as much peptide per potential as those that arrive at intervals of 1,000 msec (1 Hz). Perhaps the influx of calcium associated with the arrival of each potential becomes additive when the intervals between potentials are short, or perhaps neurosecretory granules, having moved part of the way toward the limiting membrane of the cell, are better placed for release when the second and subsequent potentials arrive. The optimal frequency of electrical stimulation of the posterior pituitary for the release of oxytocin is therefore 30–50 Hz (Harris, Manabe, & Ruf, 1969), well above the background activity of the magnocellular neurons. In Figure 14, Jean Jacques Dreifuss and I have taken the analysis one stage further. A matrix has been constructed by stimulating the posterior pituitary of a lactating rat at different frequencies and for different periods of time, and the resulting changes in intramammary pressure have been recorded. Such an analysis combines two functions: the dynamics of release and the response of

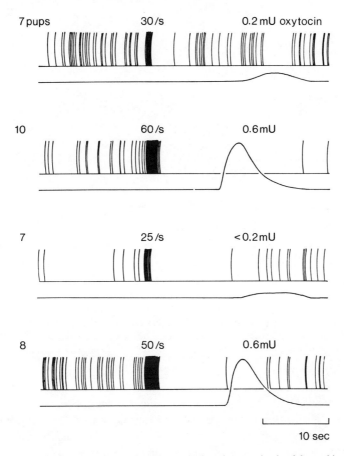

Figure 13. Evidence that the number of sucking pups (i.e., the magnitude of the sucking stimulus) governs the electrical activity of the oxytocinergic neurons of the rat, and thus the amount of oxytocin released from the posterior pituitary. Each deflection on the upper trace of the four recordings corresponds to a single action potential recorded from the same antidromically identified paraventricular neuron in a urethane-anesthetized lactating rat, and shown immediately below are the simultaneous recordings of intramammary pressure. The approximate peak frequency of discharge during the neurosecretory burst (action potentials/sec) occurring about 10–12 sec before milk ejection, as well as the approximate amount of oxytocin released from the posterior pituitary (mU), is given. The greater the number of sucking pups, the faster are the neuron discharges and the larger is the amount of oxytocin released.

the mammary gland. The amplitude of the induced mammary contractions, which is of functional significance to the sucking pup, has then been divided by the number of applied stimulation pulses to produce an index of overall efficiency. This analysis shows that the optimal parameters of electrical stimulation fall between 1.3 sec at 67 Hz and 3 sec at 30 Hz; these parameters

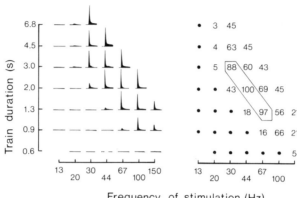

Frequency of stimulation (Hz)

Figure 14. Induction of milk ejection in the rat by electrical stimulation of the posterior pituitary: effect of stimulus frequency and train duration. The data are illustrated from one rat in which the pituitary stalk was exposed by a ventral dissection and recordings were made of intramammary pressure. Electrical stimuli were applied to the stalk for periods of .6–6.8 sec at frequencies of between 13 and 150 Hz to yield trains of 12, 18, 26, 39, 60, 89, 133, and 200 stimuli. Each stimulus consisted of a 1-msec square wave. The milk ejection responses to these different trains of stimuli are shown in the left panel. On the right, the amplitude of each milk ejection has been divided by the number of pulses applied to the pituitary stalk, and the ratio has been scaled from 0 to 100. Note that the most efficient parameters of stimulation were between 1.3 and 3.0 sec at 67 and 30 Hz, respectively (area outlined).

precisely span the explosive burst of electrical activity generated by the magnocellular neurons some 10 sec before milk ejection. In other words, by producing a synchronized burst of activity that capitalizes on the frequency facilitation process, the rat releases a pulse of oxytocin ideally matched to eliciting the most effective contraction of the mammary gland.

The posterior pituitary contains a high density of opiate-binding sites (Simantov & Snyder, 1977), β-endorphin is released in parallel with ACTH (Guillemin, Vargo, Rossier, Minick, Ling, Rivier, Vale, & Bloom, 1977), and opioid peptides and stress are associated with an inhibition of milk ejection (Haldar & Sawyer, 1978). These observations could be explained by opioid peptides, possibly released from the neurointermediate lobe, which act on the terminals of the posterior pituitary to block stimulus–secretion coupling. The intraventricular administration of morphine and long-acting enkephalin analogues to the rat blocks the oxytocin release normally evoked by direct electrical stimulation of the posterior pituitary. The effect is naloxone-reversible (Clarke, Wood, Merrick, & Lincoln, 1979). Such treatment similarly blocks oxytocin release during the sucking of the young, although the magnocellular neurons still display explosive bursts of electrical activity. It is difficult, however, to see what physiological value such a mechanism may have, because circumstances that lead to the release of endorphinlike products undoubtedly block the releae of oxytocin centrally. On the other hand, this illustrates that circulating factors may act on the terminals to modulate stimulus–secretion coupling.

Central Regulation of Oxytocin Release

The pathways of the milk ejection reflex have been traced in detail in the guina pig and the rabbit, and to a lesser extent in the rat and some ruminants (Tindal, Knaggs, & Turvey, 1967, 1969; Richard, 1970; Tindal, 1978). A large proportion of the afferent fibers run in the anterolateral parts of the spinal cord and the lateral tegmentum of the midbrain, in close association with spinothalamic fibers that convey pain, temperature, and crude tactile sensations. From the midbrain, the pathway bifurcates: one portion runs via the medial forebrain bundle to reach the magnocellular nuclei of the hypothalamus from a lateral direction, while the other branch projects forward on a more medial route. The mapping of these pathways has generated considerable controversy (Urban, Moss, & Cross, 1971; Voloschin & Dottaviano, 1976), but with the aid of hindsight, some of the difficulties can be readily appreciated. If, as we suggested earlier, a "gating mechanism" exists to integrate the signals of afferent information from the nipples, such a gate might easily filter out the obviously artificial input created by electrical stimulation. Likewise, milk ejection evoked by stimulation may not be repeatable in the short run if the gate has a refractory period of many minutes. The afferent pathways through the spinal cord and the brain stem also run in close association with nociception pathways, and the electrical stimulation of one without the other may be virtually impossible. Of course, activated pain fibers may lead to the inhibition of oxytocin release at some point further along the reflex pathway. Lesions of the ventral tegmentum of the midbrain of the rat, while not blocking milk ejection revoked by sucking, cause changes in the pattern of oxytocin release, with the frequent occurrence of double milk ejections separated by only a few seconds (Juss & Wakerley, 1981). In studies on the rabbit, in contrast, Tindal and Blake (1980) observed spontaneous milk ejections after transection of the septohippocampal inputs to the hypothalamus. Both studies suggest the existence of pathways, separate from those involved in the propagation of the sucking stimulus, that may be implicated in the timing of events.

The pharmacology of the synaptic mechanisms in reflex milk ejection has been extensively investigated. The intermittent release of oxytocin during the suckling of the rat is blocked in a dose-dependent manner by cholinoceptor antagonists of the nicotinic type (Clarke, Fall, Lincoln, & Merrick, 1978), by α-adrenoreceptor antagonists (Tribollet, Clarke, Dreifuss, & Lincoln, 1978), and by dopamine antagonists (Clarke, Lincoln, & Merrick, 1979). Various other blocking agents have been tested, to 5-HT, histamine, and GABA, but all are relatively ineffective. The converse experimental procedure of administering the appropriate agonists produces more-or-less the expected results. The intraventricular administration of either carbachol or noradrenaline causes a prolonged acceleration in the activity of oxytocinergic neurons, an acceleration that suggests that they are acting centrally in the gating mechanism previously discussed. Dopamine is particularly interesting because it causes an explosive and intermittent activation of the magnocellular neurons, not unlike that evoked by sucking. A tentative illustration of the sequence in which these synaptic mechanisms might operate is shown in Figure 15.

Anatomically, the milk ejection reflex would appear to involve solely subcortical pathways. The rat displays a sleeplike EEG pattern during suckling and therefore is probably "unaware" of the sucking stimulus at the time of magnocellular neuron activation. In other species, however, there is abundant evidence that the sucking stimulus is perceived by higher parts of the

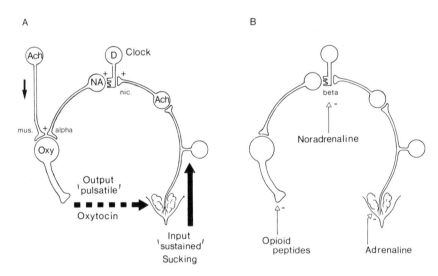

Figure 15. A schematic diagram of the synaptic mechanisms involved in the release of oxytocin in the rat. The data were compiled from studies in which the actions of a wide range of neurotransmitter antagonists and synthesis inhibitors were investigated for their ability to block or facilitate the sucking-induced release of oxytocin in lactating rats maintained under urethane anesthesia (1.2 g/kg). Part A illustrates the synaptic mechanisms promoting or facilitating oxytocin (Oxy) release. Ach, acetylcholine; D, dopamine; NA, noradrenaline; nic, nicotinic synapse; mus, muscarinic synapse; alpha, α-adrenoreceptor synapse. Part B illustrates the inhibition of the sucking-induced reflex by adrenaline, noradrenaline, and opioid peptides.

brain, and that these areas of the nervous system are capable of both inhibiting the sucking-induced reflex and of evoking the release of oxytocin independent of any sensory input from the nipples.

Central Inhibition of Milk Ejection

In 1955, Cross demonstrated that the amount of milk that rabbit pups obtained from their mother was reduced by 20%–100% when she was forcibly restrained. In most rabbits, normal milk removal was subsequently procured by the injection of 50 mU oxytocin. Failure to eject milk under these stressful conditions was clearly caused by an inability to release oxytocin, rather than by an inhibition of the mammary response to oxytocin by sympathetico-adrenal activation, as hitherto suspected. Thus, the concept of "central inhibition" was developed, and it has since received widespread support (Newton, 1961; Aulsebrook & Holland, 1969).

Central inhibition could involve the noradrenergic projection from the locus ceruleus to the hippocampus, an area of the brain involved in anxiety and the analysis of sensory information (Gray, Feldon, Rawlins, Owen, & McNaughton, 1978). There is a major noradrenergic projection from the locus ceruleus (Pickel, Segal, & Bloom, 1974), and this inhibits hippocampal neurons via β-adrenoreceptors (Bjorklund, Segal, & Stenevi, 1979). Evidence involving this projection in central inhibition is somewhat circumstantial, but it is as follows. A proportion of anesthetised rats do not eject milk in response to the sucking of their young unless given centrally active β-adrenoreceptor blocking drugs (Figure 16) (Tribollet et al., 1978), while transection of the septohippocampal connections in the rabbit results in spontaneous milk ejection (Tindal & Blake, 1980). Unfortunately, transection of the fornix, the major outflow from the hippocampus, does not alter the pattern of milk ejection in rats. Similarly, the administration of centrally active β-adrenoreceptor antagonists does not permit reflex milk ejection in anesthetized rabbits. To my knowledge, no attempt has been made to use these drugs to restore milk removal in a restrained, conscious rabbit. Inhibition of milk ejection under such circumstances is not due to opioid peptides' blocking oxytocin release from the posterior pituitary. Cross demonstrated in his early work, and I have confirmed on many occasions since, that electrical stimulation of the posterior pituitary or the pituitary stalk invariably evokes milk ejection in anesthetized animals when the sucking of the young is ineffective.

Why so many inhibitory levels of the milk ejection reflex exist remains unclear; perhaps some are simply relics of evolution that have been progressively overtaken by most sensitive control systems. The most sensitive inhibitory system in the rat (i.e., the one with the lowest threshold) is the induction of wakefulness. Perhaps it is possible to release adrenaline or opioid peptides

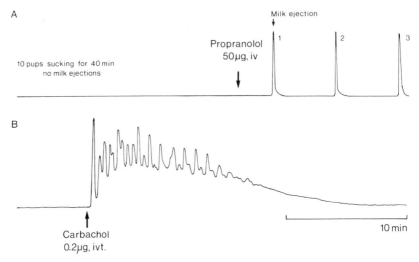

Figure 16. Two examples illustrating the central regulation of oxytocin release in the rat. A. Central inhibition. Note that this rat did not eject milk in response to the sucking of her young until given a centrally active β-adrenoreceptor blocking drug (50 μg intravenous propranolol). The observation of milk ejection following the administration of propranolol cannot be accounted for by an increase in the sensitivity of the mammary gland to oxytocin. B. Induction of oxytocin release by the intraventricular administration of .2 μg carbachol in 1 μl saline. This response, unlike that of the sucking-induced release of oxytocin, is blocked by muscarinic antagonists, such as atropine.

without creating arousal, but I think it extremely unlikely. With women, the situation is quite different, because emotional factors of even a mild nature prevent milk ejection. The rabbit, on the other hand, seems ill equipped to rely on either arousal or emotion. Indeed, a rabbit has to be severely stressed before one observes an inhibited reflex milk-ejection.

Conditioned Release of Oxytocin

Milk ejection in cattle can be evoked by a wide variety of stimuli that have nothing to do with nursing, if they are routinely applied shortly before milking commences (Borsuk, 1957; Cleverley & Folley, 1970; Cowie, Forsyth, & Hart, 1980). Evidence for other species is less convincing. There is, however, abundant evidence that women will eject milk in response to the sight or cries of their babies, or even the cries of other children (Figure 17) (Noel, Suh, & Frantz, 1974). Whether this is a conditioned reflex or a direct cognitive response is open to debate. The rat, by contrast, presents us with quite a dilemma because it ejects milk only when asleep. Sensory information is readily propagated to higher nervous centers during sleep and is subject to detailed analysis. Sleeping women express a remarkable ability to distinguish the cries of their young children from other auditory inputs. So perhaps it is not out of the question to think in terms of conditioning milk ejection in the rat, though there is no evidence that it can be done.

Milk ejection in women and cattle in response to visual, auditory, and olfactory signals, and in the absence of a sucking stimulus, implies that connections must exist between higher nervous centers and the magnocellular nuclei, although the pathways cannot be specified. A pharmacological response has been observed in rats which could relate to the activation of one of these pathways. The intraventricular injection of very small amounts of carbachol causes a profound activation of the magnocellular neurons and produces a sustained release of oxytocin (Figure 16). This response is completely blocked by atropine, whereas the same drug in a dose 200-fold larger fails to block the sucking-induced release of oxytocin (Clarke *et al.*, 1978).

The central nervous pathways involved in the sucking-induced release of prolactin from the anterior pituitary gland appear to be separate from those involved in the release of oxytocin. 5-HT, rather than noradrenaline, seems to be involved as a neurotransmitter; thus pharmacological manipulations of these transmitters, whether experimental or therapeutic, have different effects on the release of oxytocin and prolactin. The pattern of prolactin release is also different and is prolonged and sustained rather than pulsatile. Prolactin seems

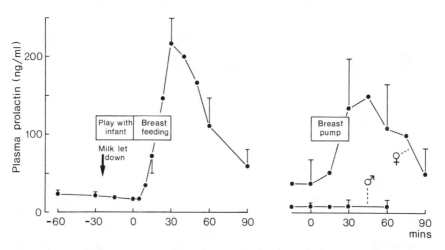

Figure 17. On the left are shown the plasma levels of prolactin of three women during anticipation of nursing and breast feeding. The levels of prolactin did not rise until the breast feeding had commenced, whereas milk ejection occurred when the mother played with her infant. The right-hand figure compares the levels of prolactin in nursing women ($n = 3$) and men ($n = 4$) during 30 min of breast pump stimulation. Data adapted from Noel, Suh, and Frantz (1974).

to be more sensitive to blockage than oxytocin, and animals may eject milk without any increased release of prolactin (Wakerley, O'Neill, & ter Haar, 1978). As a consequence, lactation itself may cease prematurely after a matter of days or weeks, despite what seems to be a normal nursing pattern. One good example of this differential control is the observation that women, in whom milk ejection has been evoked by playing with their children, do not begin to release prolactin until sucking commences (Figure 17). Presumably, there has been no selection pressure to lock the two events together. A woman can obviously relate the act of milk ejection to the feeding of her children, but she is in no immediate position to associate the release of prolactin with milk production.

Reflex Milk Ejection Redefined

The original concept of a milk ejection reflex was designed around a simple reflex arc in which the sucking of the nipples evoked, via a nervous pathway, the release of oxytocin from the posterior pituitary for the induction of milk ejection. Implicit in this concept was the notion that sensory input was tightly coupled to hormone output. This review has sought to modify this concept substantially. There are two features concerning milk ejection that appear common to all mamals. Milk is continuously secreted into the alveoli of the mammary glands, and the myoepithelial cells surrounding these alveoli, in species as diverse as the platypus and the human, contract in response to oxytocin to expel milk into the collecting ducts, cisterns, and galactophores, from which it can be withdrawn by the sucking of the young. Thus, it is the pattern of hormone release rather than the response of the mammary gland, save perhaps in some marsupials, that generates the diversity of milk ejection patterns displayed by different species. In turn, it is though the electrical activity of the oxytocin-producing neurons of the hypothalamus that this control is channeled. The major sensory input responsible for the activation of these neurons is the sucking of the nipples, but the relationship is anything but simple. The rat illustrates both the complexity and the beauty of the neural mechanisms involved. The stimulus provided by the "continuous" sucking of the pups is integrated within the brain and transformed into a pattern in which the magnocellular neurons are synchronously activated for 2–4 sec every 2–10 min to release a pulse of oxytocin perfectly matched to producing the most efficient and effective contraction of the mammary gland. Superimposed on this reflex pathway are controls from higher centers. Milk ejection in women is readily blocked by emotional factors and evoked visual or auditory cues. Reflex milk ejection still involves, therefore, the basic components originally proposed, but clearly, the nature of the sensory input and its analysis by the brain is far more complex.

To many, the key to reproductive success is the pattern of lactation; perhaps the real key is the organization of the oxytocinergic neuron.

References

Aulsebrook, L. H., & Holland, R. C. Central inhibition of oxytocin release. *American Journal of Physiology*, 1969, *216*, 830–842.

Baker, E. R., Malhur, R. S., Kirk, R. F., & Williamson, H. O. Female runners and secondary amenorrhea: Relation with age, parity, mileage and plasma hormonal and sex hormone binding globulin concentrations. *Fertility and Sterility*, 1981, *35*, 247.

Berde, B., & Boissonnas, R. A. Basic pharmacological properties of synthetic analogues and homologues of the neurohypophysial hormones. *Handbook of Experimental Pharmacology*, 1968, *23*, 802–870.

Bisset, G. W., Clark, B. J., & Haldar, J. Blood levels of oxytocin and vasopressin during suckling in the rabbit and the problem of their independent release. *Journal of Physiology (London)*, 1970, *206*, 711–722.

Bjorklund, A., Segal, M., & Stenevi, U. Functional innervation of rat hippocampus by locus coeruleus implants. *Brain Research*, 1979, *170*, 409–426.

Borsuk, V. N. Uslovnoreflektornaya regulyatsiya vývedeiya moloka iz protokov výmeni u kurov. In *Voprosy Fiziologii Sel'skokhozyaistvennykh Zhivotnikh*. Akademiya Nauk SSSR, 1957.

Bruhn, T., Ellendorff, F., Forsling, M. L., & Poulain, D. A. Neurohypophysial hormone release during natural and induced milk ejection in the sow. *Journal of Physiology (London)*, 1981, *316*, 40–41P.

Bubenik, A. B. Beitrag zur Geburtskunde und zu den Mutter-Kind-Beziehunger des Reh- (*Capreolus capreolus L.*) und Rotwildes (*Cervus elaphus L.*). *Zeitschrift für Säugetierkunde*, 1965, *30*, 65.

Clarke, G., Fall, C. H. D., Lincoln, D. W., & Merrick, P. Effects of cholinoceptor antagonists on the suckling-induced and experimentally-evoked release of oxytocin. *British Journal of Pharmacology*, 1978, *63*, 519–527.

Clarke, G., Lincoln, D. W., & Merrick, L. Dopaminergic control of oxytocin release in lactating rats. *Journal of Endocrinology*, 1979, *83*, 409–420.

Clarke, G., Wood, P., Merrick, L., & Lincoln, D. W. Opiate inhibition of peptide release from the neurohumoral terminals of hypothalamic neurons. *Nature*, 1979, *282*, 746–748.

Cleverley, J., & Folley, S. J. The blood levels of oxytocin during machine milking in cows with some observations on its half life in the circulation. *Journal of Endocrinology*, 1970, *46*, 347–361.

Cobo, E., De Bernal, M. M., Gaitan, E., & Quintero, C. A. Neurohypophyseal hormone release in the human: II. Experimental study during lactation. *American Journal of Obstetrics and Gynecology*, 1967, *97*, 519–529.

Cowie, A. T., Forsyth, I. A., & Hart, I. C. Hormonal control of lactation. *Monographs on Endocrinology 15*. Springer-Verlag: New York, 1980.

Cross, B. A. Milk ejection resulting from mechanical stimulation of mammary myoepithelium in the rabbit. *Nature*, 1954, *173*, 450.

Cross, B. A. The hypothalamus and the mechanism of sympatheticoadrenal inhibition of milk ejection. *Journal of Endocrinology*, 1955, *12*, 15–28. (a)

Cross, B. A. Neurohormonal mechanism in emotional inhibition of milk-ejection. *Journal of Endocrinology*, 1955, *12*, 29–37. (b)

Cross, B. A., & Harris, G. W. The role of the neurohypophysis in the milk-ejection reflex. *Journal of Endocrinology*, 1952, *8*, 148–161.

Cross, B. A., Dyer, R. G., Dyball, R. E. J., Jones, C. A., Lincoln, D. W., Morris, J. F., & Pickering, B. T. Endocrine neurons. *Recent Progress in Hormone Research*, 1975, *31*, 243–292.

Dawood, M. Y., Khan-Dawood, F. S., Wahi, R. S., & Fuchs, F. Oxytocin release and plasma anterior pituitary and gonadal hormones in women during lactation. *Journal of Clinical Endocrinology and Metabolism*, 1982, *52*, 678–683.

Douglas, W. W. Stimulus-secretion coupling: the concept and clues from chromaffin and other cells. *British Journal of Pharmacology*, 1968, *34*, 451–474.

Douglas, W. W., & Kagayama, M. Calcium and stimulus secretion coupling in the mast cell: stimulant and inhibitory effects of calcium-rich media on exocytosis. *Journal of Physiology (London)*, 1977, *270*, 691–703.

Findlay, A. L. R. Sensory discharges in lactating mammary glands. *Nature*, 1966, *211*, 1183–1184.

Findlay, A. L. R. The effect of teat anaesthesia on the milk-ejection reflex in the rabbit. *Journal of Endocrinology*, 1968, *40*, 127–128.

Findlay, A. L. R., & Roth, L. L. Long-term dissociation of nursing behaviour and the condition of the mammary gland in the rabbit. *Journal of Comparative Physiology and Psychology*, 1970, *72*, 341–344.

Fogden, S. C. L. Mother-young behaviour of Grey seal breeding beaches. *Journal of Zoology (London)*, 1971, *164*, 61–92.

Folley, S. J., & Knaggs, G. S. Milk-ejecting activity (oxytocin) in the external jugular vein blood of the cow, goat and sow, in relation to the stimulus of milking or suckling. *Journal of Endocrinology*, 1966, *34*, 197–214.

Gray, J. A., Feldon, J., Rawlins, J. N. P., Owen, S., & McNaughton, N. The role of the septo-hippocampal system and its noradrenergic afferents in behavioural responses to non-reward. In *Functions of the septo-hippocampal system*, Ciba Foundation Symposium 58. Amsterdam: Elsevier, 1978, pp. 275–300.

Griffiths, M. Elliott, M. A., Leckie, R. M. C., & Schoefl, G. I. Observations of the comparative anatomy and ultrastructure of mammary glands on the fatty acids of the triglycerides in platypus and echidna milk fats. *Journal of Zoology (London)*, 1973, *169*, 255–279.

Guillemin, R., Vargo, T., Rossier, J., Minick, S., Ling, N., Rivier, C., Vale, W., & Bloom, F. β-endorphin and adrenocorticotrophin are secreted concomitantly by the pituitary gland. *Science (New York)*, 1977, *197*, 1367.

Haldar, J., & Sawyer, W. H. Inhibition of oxytocin release by morphine and its analogues. *Proceedings of the Society for Experimental Biology and Medicine*, 1978, *157*, 476–478.

Harris, G. W., Manabe, Y., & Ruf, K. B. A study of the parameters of electrical stimulation of myelinated fibres in the pituitary stalk. *Journal of Physiology (London)*, 1969, *203*, 67–81.

Juss, T. S., & Wakerley, J. B. Mesencephalic areas controlling pulsatile oxytocin release in the suckled rat. *Journal of Endocrinology*, 1981, *91*, 233–244.

Konner, M., & Worthman, C. Nursing frequency, gonadal function, and birth spacing among !Kung hunter-gatherers. *Science (New York*, 1980), *207*, 788–791.

Lederis, K. Vasopressin and oxytocin in the mammalian hypothalamus. *General and Comparative Endocrinology*, 1961, *1*, 80–89.

Lee, R. B., & De Vore, I. *Kalahari hunter-gatherers*. Cambridge, Mass.: Harvard University Press, 1976.

Legros, J. J., Reynaert, R., & Peeters, G. Specific release of bovine neurophysin I during milking and suckling in the cow. *Journal of Endocrinology*, 1974, *60*, 327–332.

Lincoln, D. W. Milk ejection during alcohol anaesthesia in the rat. *Nature*, 1973, *243*, 227–229.

Lincoln, D. W. Does a mechanism of negative feedback determine the intermittent release of oxytocin during suckling. *Journal of Endocronology*, 1974, *60*, 193–194. (a)

Lincoln, D. W. Suckling, a time constant in the nursing behaviour of the rabbit. *Physiology and Behavior*, 1974, *13*, 711–714. (b)

Lincoln, D. W., & Renfree, M. B. Mammary gland growth and milk ejection in the agile wallaby, *Macropus agilis*, displaying concurrent asynchronous lactation. *Journal of Reproduction and Fertility*, 1981, *63*, 193–203. (a)

Lincoln, D. W., & Renfree, M. B. Milk ejection in a marsupial, Macropus agilis. *Nature*, 1981, *289*, 504–506. (b)

Lincoln, D. W., & Wakerley, J. B. Electrophysiological evidence for the activation of supraoptic neurosecretory cells during the release of oxytocin. *Journal of Physiology (London)*, 1974, *242*, 533–554.

Lincoln, D. W., & Wakerley, J. B. Factors governing the periodic activation of supraoptic and paraventricular neurosecretory cells during suckling in the rat. *Journal of Physiology (London)*, 1975, *250*, 443–461.

Lincoln, D. W., Hill, A., & Wakerley, J. B. The milk ejection reflex of the rat: an intermittent function not abolished by surgical levels of anaesthesia. *Journal of Endocrinology*, 1973, *57*, 459–476.

Lincoln, D. W., Hentzen, K., Hin, T., van der Schoot, P., Clarke, G., & Summerlee, A. J. S. Sleep: a prerequisite for reflex milk ejection in the rat. *Experimental Brain Research*, 1980, *38*, 151–162.

McNeilly, A. S. The blood levels of oxytocin during suckling and hand-milking in the goat with some observations on the pattern of hormone release. *Journal of Endocrinology*, 1972, *52*, 177–188.

McNeilly, A. S., & McNeilly, J. R. Spontaneous milk ejection during lactation and its possible relevance to success of breast-feeding. *British Medical Journal*, 1978, *2*, 466–468.

Merchant, J. C. Breeding biology of the agile wallaby, *Macropus agilis* (Gould) (Marsupialia: Macropodidae) in captivity. *Australian Wildlife Research*, 1976, *3*, 93–103.

Montagna, W., & MacPherson, E. E. Some neglected aspects of the anatomy of human breasts. *Journal of Investigative Dermatology*, 1974, *63*, 10–16.

Newton, M. Human lactation. In S. K. Kon & A. T. Cowie (Eds.), *Milk: The mammary gland and its secretion* (Vol. 1). New York: Academic Press, 1961, pp. 281–320.

Noel, G. L., Suh, H. K., & Frantz, A. G. Prolactin release during nursing and breast stimulation in postpartum and nonpostpartum subjects. *Journal of Clinical Endocrinology and Metabolism*, 1974, *38*, 413–423.

Pickel, V. M., Segal, M., & Bloom, F. E. A radioautoradiographic study of the efferent pathways of the nucleus locus coeruleus. *Journal of Comparative Neurology*, 1974, *89*, 317–348.

Pickering, B. T. The neurosecretory neurone: a model system for the study of secretion. *Essays in Biochemistry*, 1978, *14*, 45–81.

Poulain, D. A., Rodriguez, F., & Ellendorff, F. Sleep is not a prerequisite for the milk ejection reflex in the pig. *Experimental Brain Research*, 1981, *43*, 107–110.

Richard, Ph. An electrophysiological study in the ewe of the tracts which transmit impulses from the mammary glands to the pituitary stalk. *Journal of Endocrinology*, 1970, *47*, 37–44.

Robinson, J. E., & Short, R. V. Changes in breast sensitivity at puberty, during the menstrual cycle, and at parturition. *British Medical Journal*, 1977, *1*, 1188–1191.

Sala, N. L., Luther, R. C., Arbaldo, J. C., & Cordero-Funes, J. C. Oxytocin reproducing reflex milk ejection in lactating women. *Journal of Applied Physiology*, 1974, *36*, 154–158.

Sharman, G. B., & Calaby, J. H. Reproductive behaviour in the Red Kangaroo, *Megaleia rufa*, in captivity. *CSIRO Wildlife Research*, 1964, *9*, 58–85.

Sharman, G. B., & Pilton, P. E. The life history and reproduction of the red kangaroo, *Megaleia rufa*. *Proceedings of the Zoological Society of London*, 1964, *142*, 29–48.

Simantov, R., & Snyder, S. H. Opiate receptor binding in the pituitary gland. *Brain Research,* 1977, *124,* 178–184.

Sofroniew, M. V. Projections from vasopressin, oxytocin and neurophysin neurons to neural targets in the rat and human. *Journal of Histochemistry and Cytochemistry,* 1980, *28,* 475–478.

Soloff, M. S., Alexandrova, M., & Fernstrom, M. J. Oxytocin receptors: Triggers for parturition and lactation? *Science (New York),* 1979, *204,* 1313–1315.

Summerlee, A. J. S., & Lincoln, D. W. Electrophysiological recordings from oxytocinergic neurones during suckling in the unanaesthetized lactating rat. *Journal of Endocrinology,* 1981, *90,* 255–265.

Swaab, D. F., Pool, C. W., & Nijveldt, F. Immunofluorescence of vasopressin and oxytocin in the rat hypothalamo-neurohypophyseal system. *Journal of Neural Transmission,* 1975, *36,* 195–215.

Tindal, J. S. Central pathways in oxytocin and prolactin release. In A. Yokoyama, H. Mizuno, & H. Nagasawa (Eds.), *Physiology of mammary glands.* Baltimore: University Park Press, 1978, pp. 305–322.

Tindal, J. S., & Blake, L. A. A neural basis for central inhibition of milk ejection in the rabbit. *Journal of Endocrinology,* 1980, *86,* 525–531.

Tindal, J. S., Knaggs, G. S., & Turvey, A. The afferent path of the milk ejection reflex in the brain of the guinea pig. *Journal of Endocrinology,* 1967, *38,* 337–349.

Tindal, J. S., Knaggs, G. S., & Turvey, A. The afferent path of the milk-ejection reflex in the brain of the rabbit. *Journal of Endocrinology,* 1969, *43,* 663–671.

Tribollet, E., Clarke, G., Dreifuss, J. J., & Lincoln, D. W. The role of central adrenergic receptors in the reflex release of oxytocin. *Brain Research,* 1978, *142,* 69–84.

Urban, I., Moss, R. L., & Cross, B. A. Problems in electrical stimulation of afferent pathways for oxytocin release. *Journal of Endocrinoloy,* 1971, *51,* 347–358.

Voloschin, L. M., & Dottaviano, E. J. The channeling of natural stimuli that evoke the ejection of milk in the rat: effects of transections in the midbrain and hypothalamus. *Endocrinology,* 1976, *99,* 49–58.

Wakerley, J. B., & Deverson, B. M. Stimulation of the supraopticohypophysial tract in the rat during suckling: failure to alter the inherent periodicity of reflex oxytocin release. *Journal of Endocrinology,* 1975, *66,* 439–440.

Wakerley, J. B., & Drewett, R. F. The pattern of suckling in the infant rat during spontaneous milk-ejection. *Physiology and Behavior,* 1975, *15,* 277–281.

Wakerley, J. B., & Lincoln, D. W. The milk-ejection reflex of the rat: a 20- to 40-fold acceleration in the firing of paraventricular neurones during oxytocin release. *Journal of Endocrinology,* 1973, *57,* 477–493.

Wakerley, J. B., O'Neill, D. S., & ter Haar, M. B. Relationship between the suckling-induced release of oxytocin and prolactin in the urethane-anaesthetized lactating rat. *Journal of Endocrinology,* 1978, *76,* 493–500.

Zarrow, M. X., Denenberg, V. H., & Anderson C. O. Rabbit: Frequency of suckling in the pup. *Science (New York),* 1965, *150,* 1835–1836.

The Thermoenergetics of Communication and Social Interactions among Mongolian Gerbils

DEL THIESSEN

The Mongolian gerbil (*Meriones unguiculatus*) (Figure 1) has provided us with a behavioral window through which general biological problems can be seen. What began as studies of ventral scent marking have provoked a broader interest in the bioenergetics of communication:

> The bioenergetic needs of an organism must ultimately stipulate the structure and function of a message system. An organism runs on energy, is constructed to search out and acquire energy, judiciously guards an energy balance of debits and credits, and interestingly, uses energy to communicate needs about energy. With this in mind, it is apparent that the cellular metabolism which underlies all life processes is also the root of communication. (Thiessen, 1983)

With this more general issue of bioenergetics and behavior in mind, we focused on the relations between thermoregulation and communication in adults. Our work led us toward the exploration of mother–infant interactions, where body heat is bidirectionally transferred and where information must be exchanged. The symbiotic links between mother and infant promise to reveal a network of energy and information transfer, as well as to provide us with a better understanding of social interactions among adults.

Initial investigations with adult *Meriones unguiculatus* have uncovered correlations between communication and thermoregulation for ventral scent marking, ultrasonic emission, and Harderian gland secretion. Most informa-

DEL THIESSEN • Department of Psychology, The University of Texas at Austin, Austin, Texas 78712. The work discussed in this chapter has been generously supported for a number of years by NIMH Grant MH 14076.

Figure 1. Adult Mongolian gerbil. (Courtesy of Donald G. Robinson, Jr., Tumblebrook Farms.)

tive, thus far, has been the association between olfactory communication with Harderian secretions and thermoregulatory strategies. The Harderian system is the focus of this chapter.

The Harderian gland, with its copious secretions and implications for body temperature regulation, may become a model system for the study of energy and information exchange between adults and infants. It is perhaps during ontogeny, when thermal problems are crucial for both the infant and the parents (Alberts, 1978; Blass, Hall, & Teicher, 1979; Galef, 1976; Hofer, 1981; Leon, 1979; Moltz & Lee, 1981; Rosenblatt, 1976) that associations between communication and thermoregulation are most evident. At this stage of model development, the results are more promissory than manifest. Our first step has been to detect functions in adults and then to highlight and expand on these functions as they develop in the context of reciprocal interactions between mother and infant.

In this chapter, I briefly review the characteristics of the Harderian system in adults, outline our recent findings about infant–adult interactions,

THERMOENERGETICS OF COMMUNICATION AMONG GERBILS

and summarize our theoretical notions concerning communication and thermoregulation. The theoretical points that I wish to emphasize are that:

1. Harderian secretion and thermoregulation are intimately coupled
and stipulate the nature of the communication system.

2. Body heat integrates individual components of behavior and facilitates message transfer between adults and between infants and adults. Body
heat shares many characteristics of a hormone.

3. The ontogeny of many activities, including communication, seems
dependent on a developing hierarchy of heat-regulated neural processes. The
temperature-dependent sequence of autogrooming, which is responsible for
the release and spread of Harderian secretions, parallels the ontogenetic
development of this sequence. We refer to this adult mirror-imagery of infant
development as *sequeaction recapitulating ontogeny*.

The nature of the Harderian system and its impact on behavior and
thermoregulation are unknown in detail, so my conclusions are intended to be
more provocative than descriptive. Moreover, the ontogenetic work is still in
its infancy, and the major gaps are obvious. Finally, the theoretical notions
deliberately extend beyond the behavior that motivated them. This chapter is
meant to provide a sketch of an ongoing program of research. The details of
many of the studies discussed can be found in earlier publications (Kittrell &
Thiessen, 1981; Pendergrass & Thiessen, 1981; Randall & Thiessen, 1980;
Thiessen, 1977, 1980; Thiessen, Clancy, & Goodwin, 1976; Thiessen, Graham,
Perkins, & Marcks, 1977; Thiessen & Kittrell, 1980; Thiessen, Pendergrass, &
Harriman, 1982).

The Harderian Complex

The Harderian gland was first discovered in 1694 by Jacob Harder. He
discovered it in the deer and described it as

> a prominent gland—large, wide, conglomerated from many others, somewhat red-
> dish, unlike the rest of the glands of the eye, of a friable and soft matter, which both
> stags and does possess, and which is located in the interior orbit of the eye in a
> peculiar cavity behind the Adducens muscle. (Harder, 1694)

As a superior anatomist even for his day, he went on to describe ducts from this
gland to the anterior corner of the eye and others passing into the nasal cavity.
His original description remains unchallenged.

Since Harder's 1694 report, the gland has been studied extensively by
comparative anatomists, histologists, and biochemists, but until recently, no
definitive function had been established. Probable functions for the Mongolian gerbil have recently been reported and are described in this chapter.
They include pheromone aggregation of conspecifics (adults and infants), hair

insulation against cold and wet stress, and darkening of the pelage, which increases radiant energy absorption and body temperature. The aggregate of functions for the gland suggests close ties among social behavior, pheromone communication, and thermoregulation.

The bilaterally positioned Z-shaped Harderian glands of *Meriones unguiculatus* lie behind the eyeballs and connect to the "Harder lacrimal" canals. Paired glands of a 70-g adult male weigh approximately 350 mg. A single gland measures about 15 mm × 5 mm × 2.5 mm. Each gland apparently secretes its products into the conjunctival sac at a constant rate, to be stored until released by an autogroom. Air pressure directed at the conjunctival sac of an anesthetized animal causes an immediate discharge of the material, and several minutes must elapse before the material can be discharged again. Autogrooms have a similar periodicity.

When released, the Harderian products are discharged out the external nares and into the mouth, possibly by way of the nasal-palatine duct. India ink injected into the conjunctival sac is similarly released at the external nares and can be detected in the mouth following an autogroom. Ordinarily, the Harderian material is picked up by the paws and spread around the face, head, and body during an autogroom. The position of the glands *in situ,* their gross morphology, and the initial secretion areas spread over the body are depicted in Figure 2.

It should be kept in mind that the Harderian and lacrimal glands contribute secretions to the conjunctival sac. Therefore, other sections of this chapter refer to the duct system as the *Harder lacrimal canal.* It may also be the case that the lacrimal gland secretions affect the organism's behavioral functions.

Harderian gland secretions are primarily lipids and porphyrin pigments (Cohn, 1955; Kanwar, 1960; Woodhouse & Rhodin, 1963). Protoporphyrin is the predominant pigment in the glands of rats, mice, and gerbils, but it does not occur in the glands of the rabbit, the guinea pig, the chicken, the magpie, the turtle, or the frog (Kennedy, 1970). Protoporphyrin is responsible for the bright red fluorescence of the gland and its products when they are stimulated with long-wave ultraviolet light (Loewenthal, 1892). The fluorescent qualities appear to be characteristic of rodent species (Derrien & Turchini, 1924). Dietary proteins serve as the precursor of the porphyrin nucleus (Orten & Keller, 1946).

The significance of Harderian porphyrins is still unclear. Attempts to link the porphyrin content to cancer processes (Figge, Strong, Strong, & Shanbrom, 1942) have failed to verify any correlation (Bittner & Watson, 1946). We believe that one function is to darken the pelage and to increase the absorption of radiant energy.

Even less is known about Harderian gland lipids. In the rabbit, the major lipid has been identified as diacyl glycerol ether, a class of lipids that is

HARDERIAN COMPLEX

LATERAL VIEW   SECRETORY SPREAD

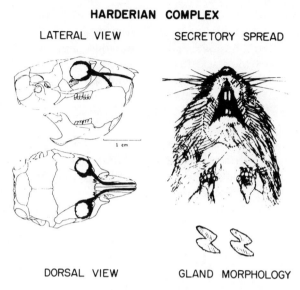

DORSAL VIEW   GLAND MORPHOLOGY

Figure 2. Drawings indicating relative position of Harderian glands, Harder lacrimal canals, and the primary points of spread of Harderian material following an autogroom. The Z-shaped Harderian glands are also indicated. The drawings are a composite of diagrams by Gulotta (1971) and Goodwin and Regnier (1981).

thought to facilitate the healing of wounds (Jost, 1974). In the mouse, the lipid secretions contain phospholipids, triglycerides, and possibly cholesterol and its esters (Cohn, 1955). In rats, the main lipid fraction appears to be a sterol ester. There have not been any recent attempts to characterize the lipid fraction of the gland, although Ronald Kagan has been attempting to do this for *Meriones unguiculatus* (1983). Earlier attempts suggest that the lipids will be species-typical.

Cellular level diversity suggests a complex evolutionary history. It is still not certain which species possess a Harderian gland, although some cataloging has been done (Kennedy, 1970). No fish examined has the gland, nor do completely aquatic amphibia. The gland is evident in all reptiles and birds and in most rodents. Among rodents, it has been described in house mice, rats, gerbils, guinea pigs, hamsters, moles, and squirrels. It also appears in dogs, sheep, and pigs. Apparently, primates do not have the gland, *or it is rudimentary*. Generally, the gland appears in species with nictitating membranes. Kennedy (1970) believes that both the Harderian and the lacrimal glands evolved in response to the need for moisture-secreting tissues for eye, mouth, and nasal passages. That may indeed have been the origin, with other uses superimposed later.

Although a great deal is known about the physiology of the Harderian gland, no one single function for this gland can be established. It has been proposed for the rabbit that the gland exists to protect the eye because of its ability to produce the antibacterial substance diacyl glycerol ether (Jost, 1974; Jost, Kühnel, & Schimassek, 1974; Kühnel, 1971). A similar function—protecting the eye from seawater—has been suggested for the duck (Fourman & Ballantyne, 1967) and the cormorant (Kennedy, 1970). Cohn (1955), however, reinforced Davis's (1929) idea that the gland serves primarily to lubricate the nictitating membrane.

In the fowl, the Harderian gland is involved in immune responses, as it contains a large number of cells resembling plasma cells and antibody-producing cells (Mueller, Sato, & Glick, 1971; Wight, Burns, Rothwell, & MacKenzie, 1971). In reptiles, the gland may serve the eye, the nose, the organ of Jacobson, and act as an accessory salivary organ (Born, 1883; Kennedy, 1970).

Several studies have focused on the possibility that the Harderian gland serves as a link in the retinal-pineal-gonadal organ chain by using its porphyrin to convert ultraviolet frequencies that are below perceptual threshold to frequencies within the visual range (Wetterberg, Geller, & Yuwiler, 1970; Wetterberg, Yuwiler, Geller, & Shapiro, 1970; Wetterberg, Yuwiler, Ulrich, Geller, & Wallace, 1970). While it is unclear whether Harderian gland porphyrins perform in the manner hypothesized (Reiter & Klein, 1971), further support for a Harderian role in the retinal-pineal chain comes from accumulated evidence that the Harderian gland produces melatonin (Cardinali & Wurtman, 1972; Bubenik, Brown, & Grota, 1976; Bubenik, Purtill, Brown, & Grota, 1978), once thought to be an exclusive product of the pineal gland. It is not yet clear, however, what role the Harderian gland melatonin might play in the retinal–pineal–reproductive-organ system. Injected melatonin, incidentally, increases the porphyrin content in rats, while melanocyte-stimulating hormone decreases the porphyrin content (Bubenik *et al.*, 1976, 1978).

More recently, the Harderian gland has been suggested as a possible source of pheromone production in the rat (Brooksbank, Wilson, & Clough, 1973; Ebling, Ebling, Randall, & Skinner, 1975a,b); the golden hamster (Payne, 1977; Payne, McGadey, Moore, & Thompson, 1976, 1977); and the Mongolian gerbil (Thiessen *et al.*, 1976; Thiessen & Rice, 1976). Payne's work with the golden hamster suggests that Harderian gland secretions could be involved in social communication as well as in sexual attraction (Payne, 1978; Payne, McGadey, Moore, & Thompson, 1976). Female Harderian extract smeared on the body of the male, for instance, appears to reduce male–male aggression.

Thus, while there is a great deal known about the Harderian gland, there are many serious gaps in our understanding. Many of the attributes are species-specific. There has been no concerted effort to characterize the gland

and its functions in any species, or to investigate its ontogeny. Most investigations focus on a single attribute. Rarely have we found more than two or three published papers by the same investigator. However, enough is now known to justify a serious study of the functional significane of the unique gland. It may turn out to be the case that the most important functions are behavioral and thermoregulatory.

Autogrooming and Harderian Secretion

During an autogroom in an adult or an adolescent, at a point where there is an intense facial scrub and a rapid eye blink, Harderian material is released at the anterior nares of the nose. The material is mixed with saliva by the paws and spread widely over the body in a rostral-caudal directon. Because of the associated protoporphyrin, the Harderian material fluoresces when stimulated with a longwave ultraviolet light. The fluorescence has a half-life of approximately two minutes, because the accompanying saliva has a degradative quality, probably involving an enzyme. Both gerbil and human saliva degrades the fluorescence *in vitro,* unless the saliva is denatured by boiling. We suspect that the intensity of fluorescence corresponds to the pheromonal intensity of the secretion, although protoporphyrin does not have pheromonal qualities apart from the remainder of the secretion (Ronald Kagan, 1983). We do not know the composition of the active fraction.

The Harderian gland is easily removed in adults or infants as young as 9 days by cutting the nictitating membrane near the conjunctival sac and pulling the gland from behind the eye with forceps. Deep nictitating membrane cuts without gland removal disrupt the connection with the Harder lacrimal canal and prevent secretion. Similarly, electrodesiccation of this area disrupts secretion by interfering with the conjunctival sac. The result of these interferences is a decrease in gland size, perhaps because of a reduced production of Harderian material, and a reduction in hair lipids. The latter effect results from the absence of lipid spread over the pelage. In any case, it is possible to prevent the secretion of Harderian lipids and pigments by gland removal, electrodesiccation, or section of the nictitating membrane.

The lipid loss on the hair can be duplicated by shampooing (Figure 3) or by allowing animals free access to a large dirt arena (Gerbil City) for a few days. Thus, it is possible to manipulate Harderian secretion and spread in a number of ways, or to allow the animals to control their own levels.

Sensory and Behavioral Control of Harderian Secretion

Gerbils, like other rodents, spend a great deal of time autogrooming and spreading Harderian material and saliva (Bolles, 1960; Thiessen, 1977).

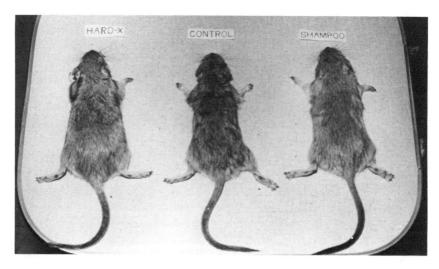

Figure 3. Visual effects of removing Harderian gland or shampooing gerbils. Both hard-X and shampooed gerbils are distinctly lighter in color and have reduced lipids and pigments (Thiessen & Kittrell, 1980).

Grooms follow exposure to novelty, high and low ambient temperatures, running in an activity wheel, eating, and social encounters involving sex or aggression. The common factor underlying all autogrooming, except that involving coat maintenance (Kittrell, 1981), seems to be an increase in body tempeature. An analysis of grooming among 43 adult males individually exposed to an open field for 10 min showed that 93% of the animals groomed once, 53% groomed twice, and only 2% groomed three times. The first groom usually occurs within 5 min (4.42 ± .33) and the second within 8 min (7.92 ± .30). Males generally groom more frequently than females (36/50 males vs. 21/50 females in a 5-min test). A typical groom sequence is pictured in Figure 4.

Our first indication that the spread of Harderian material had a pheromone function was when we observed that Harderianectomized animals appeared to be relatively indifferent to each other. Among intact male pairs, the intenstiy of the fluorescence on the face, on a 9-point scale, paralleled the number of nose-to-nose investigations following a groom (Figure 5). The mutual investigations were most intense immediately after a groom and then waned during the next 70 sec. The investigations consisted of sniffing and licking, usually by the nongrooming animals. Interestingly, too, autogrooming by one animal was often followed within a few seconds by autogrooming by the conspecific. Since this finding, Michael Goodwin and Fred Regnier at Purdue University have confirmed the synchronization of grooming patterns (1981).

Subsequent experiments strongly implicated olfactory and gustatory components. In summary, what we found was that:

1. Animals learn to inhibit bar pressing for food when Harderian extract in an airstream is followed by foot shock.

2. Animals learn to avoid food paired with Harderian material when made sick with lithium carbonate following the ingestion of food smeared with Harderian extract. This result occurred among intact gerbils and among those that were rendered anosmic with zinc sulfate.

3. Animals oriented toward visually hidden Harderian extracts, and toward Harderianectomized animals whose faces were smeared with extracts. Incidentally, the extracts induced increased autogrooming and ventral scent marking. Figure 6 gives the results of an open-field experiment in which Harderian hair extract (lipid) was placed on one side of the apparatus and a control solvent on the other. A greater-than-chance amount of time was spent on the lipid side, which was associated with a disproportionately high

Figure 4. Photographs indicating the major movements of an autogroom (Kittrell, 1981).

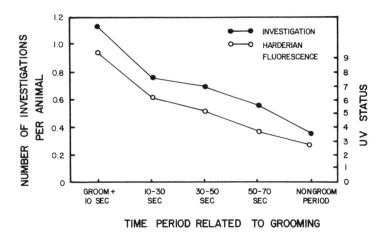

Figure 5. Relationship of time and autogrooming to the number of facial investigations by conspecifics and the spread of Harderian material on the face, as indexed by the intensity of fluorescence (UV Status) (Thiessen, 1977).

frequency of autogrooms, ventral scent marks, and defecation. Whereas about twice as much time was spent on the stimulus side, the other responses were elevated about five times over those on the nonlipid side. Clearly, Harderian material acts as an aggregating chemosignal and a trigger for other acts. As Block, Volpe, and Hayes (1980) have pointed out, saliva, which is released along with Harderian material, also attracts infants and adults. It would be informative to study the synergistic interaction of both substances in the control of social behavior.

4. Males direct their sand bathing to areas in which other males have sand-bathed. Harderianectomized males prefer sand marked by intact males, and the reverse, suggesting that Harderian material acquires meaning depending on experiential factors. Harderian material from the pelage may provide information when deposited during sand-bathing bouts.

5. Autogrooming does not generate low- or high-frequency auditory signals and so does not contribute to the mutual investigation that follows a groom. Ultrasounds can, however, evoke autogrooming, suggesting that various sensory systems are interrelated. As indicated earlier, Harderian extract elevates ventral scent marking.

6. Nose-to-nose contacts between members of a pair following an autogroom are equally high in bright or dim ambient light but do not occur at high frequencies if physical contact is prevented by a wire mesh screen (Figure 7). Thus, light does not appear to be a significant factor, although physical contact may be.

7. Finally, we have noted that Harderianectomy reduces facial inves-

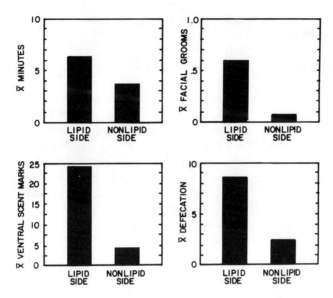

Figure 6. Open-field preference for Harderian material placed on one-half of the field during a 10-min test. The material evoked increased autogrooming, ventral scent marking, and defecation (Kittrell, 1981).

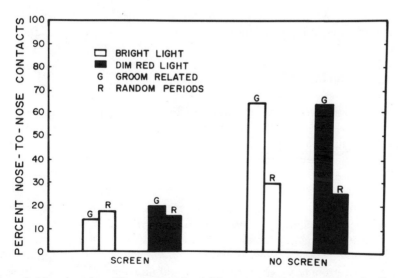

Figure 7. Mutual random (R) or groom-related (G) nose-to-nose investigations under dim red light (2–3 ft lamberts) or bright white light (40–50 ft lamberts) during a 15-min test period when paired animals were allowed to interact freely (No Screen) or were prevented from full physical contact by imposing a wire mesh screen (Screen).

tigations and aggressive behaviors between pairs and that dominant intact males autogroom more frequently than subordinate intact males.

Our results support the contention that the release of Harderian material during an autogroom acts as an aggregating pheromone. Nonolfactory stimuli, such as visual, auditory, gustatory, or tactual stimuli, are not responsible for the groom-related mutual investigation, although some stimuli (e.g., full body contact) apparently accompany the olfactory signal, whereas other stimuli (e.g. ultrasonic) can provoke autogrooming, and still other stimuli (e.g., gustation, possibly involving saliva) may supplement the information obtained from the Harderian spread.

We do not yet know the proximate trigger for autogrooming (although body temperature is certainly involved). We know little about the central control of autogrooming (Fentress, 1972; Randall, Elbin, & Swenson, 1974; Roberts, Bergquist, & Robinson, 1969; Teitelbaum & Epstein, 1962), and nothing about the role of the vomeronasal organ in the reception of the olfactory or gustatory molecules (Wysocki, 1979). We are equally blind to the social ramifications of Harderian spread. We suspect that the synchronization of grooming may also synchronize body temperature and general arousal and, in this way, assure optimal communication. Also, as Payne (1977, 1978, 1979) has demonstrated for the golden hamster, Harderian material from the opposite sex may reduce aggression and act as a sexual signal. Our results are inconclusive on these points. Current studies of thermoregulation and ontogeny are revealing the degree of complexity of the system and suggest an intimate connection between Harderian communication and thermoregulation.

Thermoregulation and Harderian Secretions

There are a number of reasons to posit a relationship between the use of Harderian secretions and thermoregulation. One of the more compelling ones is the relationship among changes in body temperature, Harderian secretion, and salivation. Increases in ambient and body temperature in several species evoke facial grooming with saliva for the purposes of evaporative cooling (Hart, 1971; Stricker, Everett, & Porter, 1968; Wilson & Stricker, 1979). Similar effects occur in the Mongolian gerbil, hinting at the connections among thermoregulation, saliva flow, and Harderian secretion. Figure 8 shows strong correlation among increases in ambient temperature, body temperature, general activity, and autogrooming in the adult gerbil. Note that the autogrooms are associated with a stabilization or a decrease in body temperature. Whenever a thermoregulatory salivary groom occurs, Harderian secretion and spread also occur. The typical pattern is for the animal to display full facial and head grooms following a .5–1.0°C increase in body temperature. With further temperature increases, there is a switch to a partial

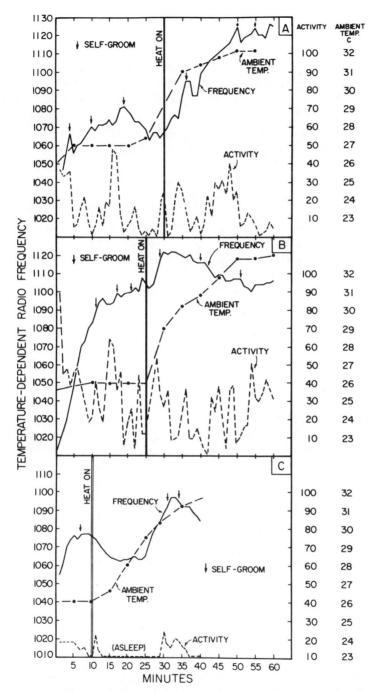

Figure 8. Relationships among ambient and body temperature, and autogrooms (↓) and general activity. Body temperature is represented by AM radio signals from implanted biotelemetry minimitters, and not absolute body temperature (Thiessen, Graham, Perkins, & Marcks, 1977).

groom, which more directly moves the saliva from the mouth to the ventral aspects of the face and body. Harderian material is simultaneously released.

Increasing body temperature can also activate facial grooming, Harderian secretion, and saliva spread. For example, animals allowed to run in an activity wheel for 3 min quickly groom when they exit from the wheel. The eating of food pellets by food-deprived animals hastens the onset of grooming. Provocative social encounters also elevate body temperature and trigger Harderian secretion and the spread of saliva. Finally, exposing animals to a cold environment increases thermogenesis and autogrooming. Long-term cold exposure, on the other hand, depresses grooming, as would be expected.

Interestingly, when animals are allowed to move over a thermal gradient, ranging from approximately 10°C to 40°C, they choose to groom and ventral scent-mark at about 28–29°C. Perhaps not coincidentally, the temperature at the interface between the ventral aspect of the body and the nest is also around 28–29°C, a fact suggesting that animals optimize their functions at this temperature. On the thermal gradient, socially naive, dominant, and subordinate males select this temperature when tested individually, but only dominant animals can control and use this region for Harderian spread, ventral scent marking, and thermoregulation. These relationships involving grooming are seen in Figure 9.

Thus, the evidence indicates that animals not only release and spread Harderian secretions during a thermoregulatory saliva spread but also seek out and defend a specific environmental temperature zone in which to conduct these activities. The preferred zone is within the gerbil's range of thermoneutrality (Kittrell, 1981; Leubbert, McGregor, & Roberts, 1979; McManus & Mele, 1969; Mele, 1972), so that the animals may be trying to reduce their energy expenditure. Perhaps by confining gerbils to this temperature range, and preventing interference from other animals, grooming would cease altogether.

Another clear indication that Harderian spread and thermoregulation are bonded is the gerbil's thermal response to a cold-wet stress after the manipulation of Harderian material on the fur. With a reduction in fur lipids of about 40% following Harderianectomy or shampooing, there is a depressed ability to withstand cold (3–5°C) and wetness. The difference in thermoregulatory ability between intact and Harderianectomized animals is illustrated in Figure 10. The *in vitro* insulating qualities of fur lipids were shown by blocking a cold-air stream with various layers of Harderian lipids. The degree of insulation was related to the thickness of the lipid layers. In a way analogous to the preen gland of certain birds (Elder, 1954; Jacob & Poltz, 1975; McKinney, 1965), gerbils spread lipids over the entire body, providing insulation against wetness and cold. Apparently, gerbils actively remove lipids and pigments from the pelage by sand bathing in order to decrease the external insulative coat. Recent unpublished data from our laboratory in-

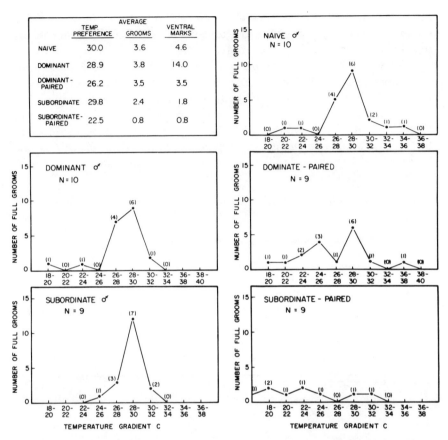

Figure 9. Responses of gerbils on a temperature gradient of 10–40°C, showing that 28–29°C is the preferred temperature for autogrooming and is the temperature zone defended by dominant males. The numbers in parentheses indicate the number of grooms at each ambient temperature (Thiessen, 1977).

dicate that animals living in the cold (5°C) for several days accumulate lipids on the pelage. Observations of this kind suggest that the primary function of the gland is thermoregulatory and that the signaling functions are ritualized and secondary (Barnett, 1981).

One additional source of data substantiates the correlation between Harderian function and thermoregulation. It involves the color change of the pelage associated with the spread of lipids and pigments (see Figure 3 for an illustration of color changes related to Harderianectomy and shampooing). As is clear in numerous species of ectotherms and birds, individuals exposed to radiant energy within the visual spectrum absorb more energy when dark in color and reflect more energy when light in color (see Ali, 1977; Burtt, 1979;

Schmidt-Nielsen, 1979, for general reviews). Thus, there may be thermal significance in the gerbil's ability to darken the fur with Harderian spread and to lighten the fur when living on sand.

Indeed, we do see a lightening of the pelage following Harderianectomy (or shampooing) and living on sand (see Figure 11), which corresponds to an increased reflectance and reduced body temperature gain under radiant exposure conditions (see Figure 12). In other words, the gerbil can adjust its thermal balance by manipulating the amounts of lipids and pigments on its fur. Grooming the Harderian material over the hair darkens the surface and increases the absorption of radiant energy, whereas sand-bathing the material off decreases the absorption of radiant energy:

> We believe that gerbils and perhaps other rodents which are normally exposed to variations in radiant energy, behaviorally regulate hair lipids and pigments by grooming and sandbathing and so adjust body temperature optimally within the context of the prevailing environment. (Thiessen *et. al.,* 1982, p. 51)

The incredible array of pheromonal and thermal influences arising from the use of Harderian material does not necessarily exhaust the possible Harderian gland functions. The gland could lubricate the eye or act as a cushion for the eyeball. It may possess antibacterial effects, and it is ideally situated and innervated for extraretinal visual reception. All of these functions have

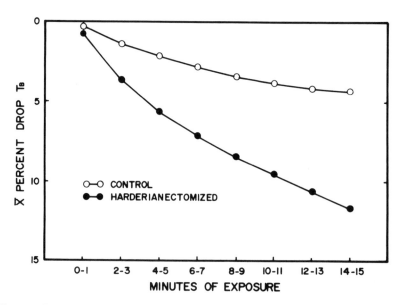

Figure 10. Body temperature (T_B) decline in Harderianectomized and control gerbils following a 1-sec ice water dip and 15 min of exposure to 3–5 °C. Shampooing out the fur lipids has a similar effect (Thiessen & Kittrell, 1980).

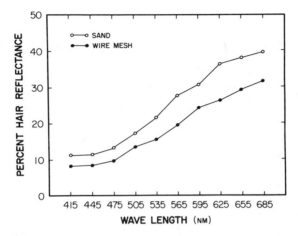

Figure 11. Reflectance of hair of animals living on sand or on wire mesh screen (Thiessen, Pendergrass, & Harriman, 1982).

been proposed at one time or another (refer to the introductory comments). Recent unpublished work by Arthur Harriman at Oklahoma State University suggests that body water may be affected during periods of water deprivation by the spread of Harderian material over the pelage. In addition, the gland could have a number of systemic effects. Jan Randall (1981) has demonstrated that the gland is a hot spot for the accumulation of the amino acid phenylalamine, uncovering the possibility that it is a gland of great metabolic capacity.

Nevertheless, we have been unable to specify any general or specific systemic effects, although other species (e.g., the hamster) show clear relations between Harderian functions and reproductive states. Even here, however, no functions can be ascribed to the gland. For examples of parameters that do not vary in *Meriones unguiculatus* as a result of Harderianectomy, refer to Table 8. Even under conditions of environmental stress, such as long-term exposure to cold or heat, or severe restrictions in water intake, Harderianectomy does not alter the animal's behavioral or physiological capacities. We still believe that the Harderian gland has a systemic role to play, but the nature of that role is not obvious. So far the data support peripheral functions involving chemocommunication and thermoregulation (Kittrell & Thiessen, 1981).

Infant Development and Parent–Infant Interactions

It is only within the past year that we have begun to explore the richness of infant development and the mediation of Harderian secretion in parent–infant interactions. Our recent investigations have focused on on-

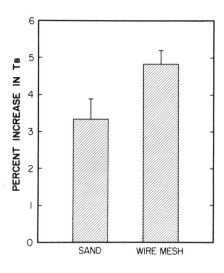

Figure 12. Average percentage increase in body temperature (T_B) for animals living on sand or on wire mesh screen. Vertical bars indicate one SE (Thiessen, Pendergrass, & Harriman, 1982).

togenetic processes that may elucidate adult chemocommunication and thermoregulation. In addition, we are investigating the relationship between the ontogenetic steps of the autogroom and the adult pattern of grooming. In a real sense, ontogeny is the paternal template of adult behavior.

There are several parallel developments in young gerbils that are of importance for an understanding of the adult's use of the Harderian gland. If one looks at the sequential development of autogrooming, one sees that the mature groom unfolds during a critical seven- or eight-day period (see Table 1). The first sign of a groom component appears on Day 10 postpartum, nasal

Table 1. Development of Autogrooming and Harderian Spread

Age in days	First groom component	Nose fluoresence	Swipe	Scrub	Partial groom	Eye blink	Eye open	Full groom
10	+							
11	+							
12	+							
13		+	+					
14		+	+					
15		+	+	+				
16		+	+	+	+			
17		+	+	+	+	?		?
18		+	+	+	+	+	+	+
19		+	+	+	+	+	+	+
20		+	+	+	+	+	+	+

Table 2. Development of Thermoregulation, Hair Growth, and Spread of Harderian
Material

Age in days	T_B °C Responses to isolation[a]	Hair growth	Number of groom components[b]
10	−.46	Sparse stubble	1
11	−.05	Soft stubble	1
12	−.12	Short hair	1
13	−.08	Short hair	2
14	−.07	Short hair	2
15	.19	Long hair	3
16	.30	Long hair	4
17	.27	Long hair	6
18	.41	Long hair	7

[a] Change in surface temperature during 5 min of isolation.
[b] Taken from Table 1.

fluorescence on Day 13, the first facial scrub on Day 15, and the first full
groom on Day 18. The frequency of occurrence of any component from Days
10 to 13 during a 15-min test is around .44, but by Days 14–16, it has increased
to approximately 2.25. After that, there is a steady increase in grooming
frequency to the adult level of approximately 3 grooms during a 15-min
period of observation.

Many other important growth events are compressed into this short span
of development. Between Days 10 and 15 of life, hair growth is essentially
complete, and the eyes open at around 18 days of age. Importantly, the
animal's abilities to thermoregulate and spread Harderian material are
coupled with hair growth (see Table 2). Thus, up to 15 days of age, body
temperature falls during short periods of isolation, but beginning at 15 days of
age, when the hair is fully formed and when the gerbil can spread Harderian
material, thermoregulatory independence is forming. Presumably, the insulation provided by hair impregnated with Harderian lipids is sufficient to
allow the gerbil substantial independence from nest, littermates, and parents.

All of these events are linked to critical changes in parent–infant interactions. At around 2 weeks of age, the offspring decrease their ultrasonic cries
for attention (DeGhett, 1974), and the parents reduce their nest-retrieval
behaviors (Ellwood, 1975; Waring & Perper, 1979); infants become fully
locomotive and begin to be attracted to maternal pheromones (Gerling &
Yahr, 1982). Overall, the ontogenetic switch is from dependent and proximate
associations between the infants and their parents to independent and distal
interactions. All of the processes involved in this switch are coadapted (see
Table 3).

During this critical time when the pups are not yet spreading Harderian

Table 3. Summary of Integrated Features of Gerbil Development Seen at about 2 Weeks of Age

Nature of developmental change	Adaptive significance
Increased hair growth	Physical insulation of body
Spread of Harderian material	Insulation of pelage with lipids
Decreased use of ultrasounds	Reduction of parental attention
Attraction toward maternal odors	Shift to distal control mechanisms
Independent locomotion	Varied

secretions, the mother is contributing her Harderian material to the offspring. For example, lipids are found on 12-day-old pups in greater amounts when the mother possesses her Harderian glands than when she does not (.0129 mg vs. .0074 mg, respectively; $t = 6.37$, $df = 29$, $p < .0001$). Moreover, lactating females tend to groom more frequently during a 5-min period (3.7 vs. 3.0), a fact suggesting that the thermoregulatory need for increased Harderian spread on the pups is compensated for by a heightened groom frequency by the mother. Conversely, the mother may facilitate her own heat loss during lactation when her body temperature is normally elevated by transferring

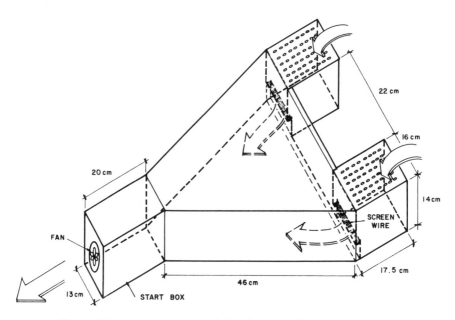

Figure 13. A two-choice apparatus designed to study olfactory preferences.

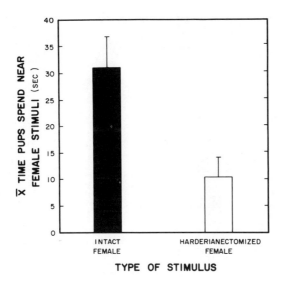

Figure 14. Olfactory preference of 14- to 19-day-old pups for intact and Harderianectomized adult females. Vertical bars represent one SE (Thiessen & Clancy, 1980).

Harderian lipids from her own body to the pups. Thus, both the infant and the mother gain by their symbiotic interaction.

The Harderian interchange between parents and offspring affects communication as well as thermoregulatory capabilities. When individual pups are placed in the two-choice olfactory apparatus pictured in Figure 13, they spend more time near an airstream containing female Harderian odors than they do near an adjacent airstream containing odors from a Harderianectomized female (see Figure 14).

Moreover, 15-day-old pups take longer to spontaneously return to the nest when both parents are Harderianectomized (see Figure 15). There is nothing to indicate that the parents are aversely affected by the loss of their glands. Measures of fertility, fecundity, gonadal integrity, body size, ventral scent marking, and parental behaviors are not affected by Harderianectomy. Therefore, the reluctance of the pups to return to a nest occupied by Harderianectomized parents appears to be due to a lack of a pheromone cue.

Unfortunately, the data do not consistently indicate that Harderian material from the mother is attractive to her offspring. On the contrary, when Harderian extract is smeared on the washed or unwashed nipples of mothers, 12-day-old pups fail to attach. The attachment latencies are seen in Table 4. Moreover, the extract is primarily aversive in a *in vitro* test where different dose levels are presented to similarly aged pups on cotton cue tips. The extract

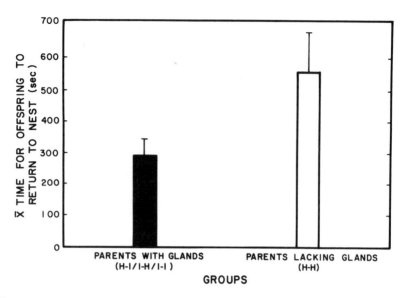

Figure 15. Average time in seconds that pups took to return to the nest when the parents lacked Harderian glands (H-H) or when both parents or at least one parent had intact Harderian glands (H-I/I-H/I-I). Vertical bars represent one SE (Thiessen & Clancy, 1980).

could contain aversive chemicals that are not ordinarily secreted by the mother. Nevertheless, preliminary tests with smears from the nose of grooming females also appear to be aversive, at least for a couple of minutes. It may be that the more volatile components are aversive, but that lingering components are attractive.

In any case, the evidence is building that the ontogeny of grooming and Harderian spread is coupled with growing independence and the need to thermoregulate outside the nest. Coinciding with this independence is a developmental switch toward the use of distal stimuli for the control of

Table 4. Nipple Attachment Latencies (Sec) for Offspring Exposed to Various Harderian Conditions[a]

Condition of nipples	Attachment latency (sec)
Unmanipulated	27.9
Washed	156.8
Washed plus Harderian extract	278.1
Unwashed plus Harderian extract	300.0

[a] Pups exposed to nipples for 5 min following 4 hr mother–infant separation.

parent–offspring interactions. Harderian material, under some circumstances, can act as an attractive substance.

The sequence of grooming and the secretion of Harderian lipids and pigments does not depend on experience, although it may be modified by extrinsic and intrinsic factors (Fentress, 1973, 1976). As seen from the data in Table 5, gerbils whose forepaws have been amputated prior to the onset of grooming do, nevertheless, engage in stereotyped phantom grooms later in life. Large amounts of Harderian secretions accumulate on the nose and the face, indicating that proprioceptive cues from the paws are not necessary for the response to occur. Without the mixing of the Harderian components with saliva, the fluorescence of the protoporphyrins lingers for extended periods. As expected, the lack of spread of Harderian materials on the pelage leaves the animal light in appearance.

The fixed action pattern of the autogroom suggests that the behavior may be relatively "hard-wired" both in its ontogeny and in its adult expression. This possibility stimulated us to look for possible relationships between the ontogenesis of the behavior and the sequence of the adult pattern.

Indeed, the rank order of adult movements in the rostral–caudal direction over the body is identical to the sequence of development (see Table 6). Movements to the face (nose and mouth) appear first, followed by grooms over the head and the ears, the flank, the ventrum, and finally the tail. Once the groom is fully developed, there may be deviations, in that the animal returns to the mouth and the nose during a sequence (presumably to obtain more saliva and Harderian material) but never jumps steps. Thus, a sequence might be face, ears, flank, face, ventrum, tail. Almost never does an animal move from face to ventrum, unless it has already moved through ears and flank. Thus, while one occasionally sees cyclical repeats, the repeats are pro-

Table 5. Phantom Grooms and Harderian Secretion

Experimental condition	Age of forepaw amputation (days)	Age of testing	Nose fluoresence prior to groom[a]	Nose fluorescence postgroom	Eye blink	Coat color
Amputation	5–10	47	3	4–6	Yes	Light
Amputation	5–10	47	3	4–6	Yes	Light
Amputation	5–10	30	3	4–6	Yes	Light
Amputation	5–10	30	3	4–6	Yes	Light
Control	5–10	47	2	3	Yes	Dark
Control	5–10	47	2	3	Yes	Dark
Control	5–10	30	1	3	Yes	Dark
Control	5–10	30	1	3	Yes	Dark
Control	5–10	30	0	3	Yes	Dark

[a] Scale: 0 = no fluorescence; 6 = high fluorescence.

Table 6. Sequeaction Recapitulates Ontogeny[a]

Body surface	Rank order of movements for adults	Age of onset (days) of movements for infants
Nose	1.00 ± .00	11.12 ± .41
Face	2.24 ± .004	14.75 ± .03
Ears	3.05 ± .003	19.50 ± .21
Flank	3.07 ± .01	19.89 ± .34
Ventrum	3.37 ± .01	26.75 ± .52
Trail	4.09 ± .02	33.75 ± .75

[a] *Sequeaction* refers to the sequence of adult movements.

gressive through the series. The gerbil may end an autogroom at any step, although it almost always involves the head and the ears.

The isomorphism between adult sequencing and ontogeny we call *sequeaction recapitulating ontogeny*. It is as if an eight-day period of development is compressed into a few critical seconds. We will make the theoretical point later that recapitulation may be typical of fixed-action patterns, can underscore the nature of the neurological substrate, and, possibly, focuses the phylogenetic progression of a response pattern on a single moment of time.

Theoretical Summary

Much of this chapter is given over to describing the nature of the Harderian system as manifested in the adult. While this is a long way from formulating rules of symbiosis between parents and offspring, it is a necessary excursion because of the novelty of the system. The gland may have been discovered by Harder in 1694, but it was only about six years ago when our investigations showed that the glandular products are excreted to the outside of the body through the Harder lacrimal canal and spread widely over the body. The greatest proportion of our efforts has been made to establish a

Table 7. Effects of Harderianectomy

Lightening of pelage
Decrease in fur lipids and pigments
Decrease in groom-induced facial investigations
Lowered resistance to cold–wet stress
Resistance to radiant energy
Decrease in fur lipids of pups of Harderianectomized mothers

Table 8. Lack of Effects from Harderianectomy

Autogroom frequency and pattern intact
No change in latency to pregnancy
No change in litter or pup number
No change in ventral scent marking or ultrasounding
No change in ventral scent gland size, testicular or seminal
    vesicle weight, or blood testosterone titer
No change in resistance to water deprivation
No change in body temperature on exposure to convective
    or conductive heat
No change in sand bathing
No change in oxygen consumption
No change in food and water consumption

relationship between the release of Harderian material and behavior. Tables 7–11 outline our findings.

Two significant points emerged. First, it became evident that the gland and its products meet all the criteria of a classic pheromone system of communication. The gland is discrete and releases species-specific molecules to the outside of the body. The volatile substances are received by conspecifics and act to trigger stereotyped behaviors of aggregation and grooming. It is perhaps the most stereotyped pheromone system seen in mammals. Second, our work quickly led us to concerns of thermoregulation. Harderian secretions are released simultaneously with saliva during a thermoregulatory groom, and they appear to be triggered by slight increases in body temperature. Moreover, the spread of Harderian lipids and pigments over the fur act to insulate the gerbil from cold and wet stresses and to alter the radiant absorption qualities of the body surface. Thus, there are at least three thermoregulatory processes operating, along with communication functions.

The rough relationship between communication and thermal events is

Table 9. Manipulations That Change Harderian Secretion

Activators of Secretion
    D-Amphetamine
    Body increases in heat and cold
    Air pressure on orbit of eye

Depression of secretion
    Deep nictitating membrane cut
    Coagulation of nictitating membrane
    Excessive ambient heat
    Excessive ambient cold

Table 10. Effects of Harderian Extracts on Behavior

Stimulates investigation
Cue for olfactory conditioning and taste aversion
Stimulates ventral scent marking
Stimulates conspecific autogrooming
Retards nipple attachment
Acts as aversive stimulus for pups

shown in Figure 16. The essential problems are to work out the details, to test the generality of the Harderian effects across species and situations, and to extend the work to the infant level.

The infant work done in our laboratory suggests that similar Harderian functions are involved, namely, communication and thermoregulation. One of the more provocative findings is that the course of development of the autogroom and the release of Harderian products is associated with increasing thermal competence and hair growth. Specifically, the use of Harderian insulating material by an infant corresponds to hair growth. Prior to that juncture, the infants appear to pirate their insulation in part from maternal Harderian secretions. In short, the developmental sequence for the use of the Harderian system corresponds to a growing need for stable thermoregulation and independence of the nest.

On a more speculative note, it appears that the ontogeny of the groom, as it shifts from simple peripheral reflexes to a more centrally organized groom sequence, corresponds to an increasing thermal regulation of neural processes. Simple peripheral reflexes are innervated at low body temperatures, but as synapses are added in more complex responses, body temperature must be higher (Prosser & Nelson, 1981). Increasing body temperature allows behaviors to increase in complexity and to shift toward a central hierarchy of control.

One other problem of growing theoretical concern is the relationship between adult behavior and ontogenesis. In the previous section, we saw that the adult autogroom went through a fairly rigid sequence of acts that reflected its ontogenetic history. This process we referred to as *sequeaction recapitulating*

Table 11. Manipulations without Effect on Harderian Secretion

Absence of salivation (e.g., atropine)
Lacrimalectomy
Mimicking proprioceptive facial stimulation
Closed or absent eyelids

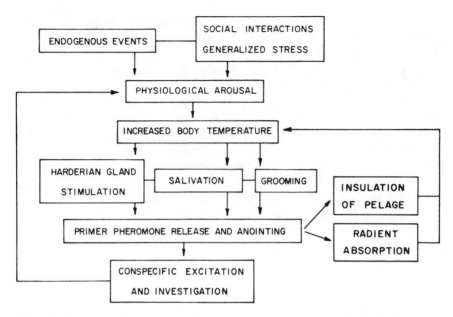

Figure 16. The relationships between chemocommunication and thermoregulation for Harderian secretions.

ontogeny, and we suggested that it may be a common occurrence for genetically programmed behaviors.

   A number of observations from various sources emphasize the reiteration of the developmental course of behavior during the display of adult performance. Zing-Yang Kuo (1967), over a wide sweep of the history of psychology, emphasized the relationships between early development and adult behaviors. One of the classic illustrations is the apparent isomorphism between pecking in the egg and pecking during posthatch activities. This work has matured with the elegant work of Gottlieb (1976) and others (see Richard, 1979, for a critique).

   Recently, Borchelt (1977) has reported sequeaction of dust-bathing development in the bobwhite (*Colinus virginianus*) and the Japanese quail (*Coturnix coturnix japonica*). Both species showed the same rank ordering of five dust-bathing components in infancy and adulthood. Richmond and Sachs (1981) have reported similar adult-ontogenetic reflectons for autogrooming in the Norway rat. This latter study is of particular interest, as the adult sequence of grooming and its ontogenetic antecedents are almost identical to those seen in the gerbil. It is of interest to note that this mirroring of early and late events is commonly known to horse breeders and equestrians (D. Stokes, July 1982).

The adult sequence of horse locomotion, beginning with the walk and progressing through the trot, canter, and gallop, mirrors the developmental sequence of these abilities. Similarly, there is a postnatal repetition of several human prenatal reflexes, such as contralateral and ipsilateral head movements, grasping sequences, and plantar reflexes (Humphrey, 1969).

There are many other response systems that seem to show recapitulation, but few have been studied from that perspective. To mention some that seem to demonstrate that relationship: locomotor behaviors among many species, swimming in vertebrates, dancing behavior in honeybees, nest building in birds and other species, and sex behavior in male mammals (Alcock, 1979). Even thermoregulation reactions, from the most primitive to the most complex, appear to recapitulate.

There is a deep-rooted theoretical issue here, because not only does adult behavior recapitulate its own formative steps; it can, as well, mirror the avenues of its evolution. If notions of recapitulation have validity (Gould, 1977), then we encounter the exciting possibility that brief sketches of behavioral sequences coded by DNA are momentary reminders of events well hidden in the fossil record.

ACKNOWLEDGMENTS

Many collaborators have contributed to this effort, including Michael Goodwin, Andrew Clancy, Melanie Kittrell, Merri Pendergrass, Meg Upchurch, Mike Graham, James Perkins, Arthur Harriman, Barbara Gregg, Jan Randall, Gaye Al-Rashid, and Sheila Marcks. I would also like to thank Robert Young, who freely gave of his statistical expertise, and Susan Martin, who typed this manuscript and in other ways furthered the work.

References

Alberts, J. R. Huddling by rat pups: Group behavioral mechanisms of temperature regulation and energy conservation. *Journal of Comparative and Physiological Psychology,* 1978, *92,*(2), 231–245.

Alcock, J. *Animal behavior: An evolutionary approach.* Sunderland, Mass.: Sinauer Associates, 1979.

Ali, M. S. *Sensory ecology.* New York: Plenum Press, 1977.

Barnett, S. A. *Modern ethology: The science of animal behavior.* New York: Oxford University Press, 1981.

Bittner, J. J., & Watson, C. J. The possible association between porphyrins and cancer in mice. *Cancer Research,* 1946, *6,* 337–343.

Blass, E. M., Hall, W. G., & Teicher, M. H. The ontogeny of suckling and ingestive behaviors. In J. M. Sprague & A. N. Epstein (Eds.), *Progress in psychobiology and physiological psychology.* New York: Academic Press, 1979, pp. 243–299.

Block, M. L., Volpe, L. C., & Hayes, M. J. Saliva as a chemical cue in the development of social behavior. *Science*, 1981, *211* (4486), 1062–1064.

Bolles, R. Grooming behavior in the rat. *Journal of Comparative and Physiological Psychology*, 1960, *53*, 306–310.

Borchelt, P. L. Development of dustbathing components in Bobwhite and Japanese quail. *Developmental Psychobiology*, 1977, *10*, 97–103.

Born, G. Die Nasenhöhlen and der Tränen-Nasengage der anmioten Wirbeltiere. *Gergenbaur's Morphologische*, 1883, *8*, 188–232.

Brooksbank, B. W. L., Wilson, D. A. A., & Clough, G. The *in-vivo* uptake of (^{3}H) androsta-4, 16-dien-3-one in tissues of the adult male rat. *Journal of Endocrinology*, 1973, *57*, i–ii.

Bubenik, G. A., Brown, G. M., & Grota, L. J. Immunohistochemical localization of melatonin in the rat Harderian gland. *Journal of Histochemistry and Cytochemistry*, 1976, *24*, 1173–1177.

Bubenik, G. A., Purtill, R. A., Brown, G. M., & Grota, L. J. Melatonin in the retina and the Harderian gland: Ontogeny diurnal variations and melatonin treatment. *Experimental Eye Research*, 1978, *27*, 323–333.

Burtt, E. H., Jr. *The behavioral significance of color*. New York: Garland STMP Press, 1979.

Cardinali, D. P., & Wurtman, R. J. Hydroxyindole-O-Methyltransferase in rat pineal, retina, and Harderian gland. *Endocrinology*, 1972, *91*, 247–252.

Cohn, S. A. Histochemical observations on the Harderian gland of the albino mouse. *Journal of Histochemistry*, 1955, *3*, 342–358.

Davis, F. A. The anatomy and histology of the eye and orbit of the rabbit. *Transcripts of the American Ophthamological Society*, 1929, *27*, 401–441.

DeGhett, V. J. Developmental changes in the rate of ultrasonic vocalization in the Mongolian gerbil. *Developmental Psychobiology*, 1974, *7*, 267–273.

Derrien, E., & Turchini, J. Sur acculumation d'une porphyrine dans la glande de Harder des rongeurs du genre *Mus* et sur son mode d'excretion. *Compte Rendu des Séances de la Société de Biologie et de ses Filiales*, 1924, *91*, 637–639.

Ebling, F. J., Ebling, E., Randall, V., & Skinner, J. The effects of hypophysectomy and of bovine growth hormone on the responses to testosterone of prostate, preputial, Harderian and lachrymal glands and of brown adipose tissue in the rat. *Journal of Endocrinology*, 1975, *66*, 401–406. (a)

Elbing, F. J., Ebling, E., Randall, V., & Skinner, J. The synergistic action of α-melanocyte-stimulating hormone and testosterone on the sebaceous, prostate, preputial, Harderian and lachrymal glands, seminal vessicles and brown adipose tissue in the hypophysectomized-castrated rat. *Journal of Endocrinology*, 1975, *66*, 407–412. (b)

Elder, W. H. The oil gland of birds. *Wilson Bulletin*, 1954, *66*, 6–31.

Ellwood, R. W. Paternal and maternal behavior in the Mongolian gerbil. *Animal Behaviour*, 1975, *23*, 766–772.

Fentress, J. C. Development and patterning of movement sequences in inbred mice. In J. Kiger, (Ed.), *The biology of behavior*. Corvallis: Oregon State University Press, 1972, pp. 83–132.

Fentress, J. C. Specific and nonspecific factors in the causation of behavior. In P. P. G. Bateson & P. H. Klopfer (Eds.), *Perspectives in ethology*. New York: Plenum Press, 1973, pp. 155–224.

Fentress, J. C. Dynamic boundaries of patterned behavior: Interaction and self-organization. In P. P. G. Bateson, & R. A. Hinde (Eds.), *Growing points in ethology*. New York: Cambridge University Press, 1976, pp. 135–169.

Figge, F. H. J., Strong, L. C., Strong, L. C., Jr., & Shanbrom, A. Fluorescent porphyrins in Harderian glands and susceptibility to spontaneous mammary tumors. *Cancer Research*, 1942, *2*, 335–342.

Fourman, J., & Ballantyne, B. Cholinesterase activity in the Harderian gland of Anas domesticus. *Anatomy Records*, 1967, *159*, 17–26.

Gale, B. G., Jr. Social transmission of acquired behavior: A discussion of tradition and social learning in vertebrates. In J. S., Rosenblatt, R. A. Hinde, E. Shaw, & C. Beer (Eds.), *Advances in the study of behavior.* New York: Academic Press, 1976, pp. 77–100.

Gerling, S., & Yahr, P. Maternal and paternal pheromes in gerbils. *Physiology and Behavior,* 1982, *28,* 667–673.

Goodwin, M., & Regnier, F. Unpublished research, 1981.

Gottlieb, G. Conception of prenatal development: Behavioral embryology. *Psychological Review,* 1976, *83,* 215–234.

Gould, S. J. *Ontogeny and phylogeny.* Cambridge, Mass.: The Belknap Press of Harvard University Press, 1977.

Gulotta, E. F. Mammalian species (*Meriones unguiculatus*). *The American Society of Mammalogists,* 1971, No. 3, 1–5.

Harder, J. J. Glandula Nova Lachrymalis. *Acta Eruditorum,* Leipzig, Germany: 1694, 49–52.

Hart, J. S. Rodents. In G. C. Whittow (Ed.), *Comparative physiology of thermoregulation, Vol. 2: Mammals.* New York: Academic Press, 1971, pp. 1–149.

Hofer, M. A. *The roots of human behavior.* San Francisco: W. H. Freeman, 1981.

Humphrey, T. Postnatal repetition of human prenatal activity sequences with some suggestions of their neuroanatomical basis. In R. J. Robinson (Ed.), *Brain and early behavior.* New York: Academic Press, 1969, pp. 43–84.

Jacob, J., & Poltz, J. Composition of uropygial gland secretions of birds of prey. *Lipids,* 1975, *10,* 1–8.

Jost, U. 1-Alkyl-2, 3-diacyl-sn-glycerol, the major lipid in the Harderian gland of rabbits. *Hoppe-Seyler's Zeitschrift für Physiological Chemistry,* 1974, *335,* 422–426.

Jost, U., Kühnel, W., & Schimassek, H. A morphological and biochemical analysis of the Harderian gland in the rabbit. *Cytobiologie,* 1974, *8*(3), 440–456.

Kanwar, K. C. Morphological and cytochemical studies on the Harderian glands of rats. *Cellule,* 1960, *61,* 129–143.

Kennedy, G. Y. Harderoporphyrin: A new porphyrin from the Harderian gland of the rat. *Comparative Biochemical Physiology,* 1970, *36,* 21–36.

Kittrell, E. M. W. *The Harderian gland and thermoregulation.* Dissertation, University of Texas at Austin, May 1981.

Kittrell, E. M. W., & Thiessen, D. D. Does removal of the Harderian gland affect the physiology of the Mongolian gerbil (*Meriones unguiculatus*). *Physiological Psychology,* 1981, *9,* 299–304.

Kühnel, W. Structure and cytochemistry of the Harderian gland in rabbits. *Zeitschrift für Zellforschung und Mikroscopische Anatomie,* 1971, *119,* 384–404.

Kuo, Z. *The dynamics of behavior development.* New York: Random House, 1967.

Leon, M. Mother–young reunions. In J. M. Sprague & A. N. Epstein (Eds.), *Progress in psychobiology and physiological psychology.* New York: Academic Press, 1979, pp. 301–304.

Leubbert, S. J., McGregor, L. E., & Roberts, J. C. Temperature acclimation in the Mongolian gerbil (*Meriones unguiculates*): Changes in metabolic rate and the response to norepinephrine. *Comparative Biochemistry and Physiology,* 1979, *63A,* 169–175.

Loewenthal, N. Beitrag zur Kenntnis der Harderischen Drüssen bei den Säugetieren. *Anatomischer Anzeiger,* 1892, *7,* 546–556.

McKinney, F. Oiling preening (Einolen). *Behaviour,* 1965, *25,* 120–220.

McManus, J. J., & Mele, J. A. Temperature regulation in the Mongolian gerbil, *Meriones unguiculates. New Jersey Academy of Science,* 1969, *14,* 21–22.

Mele, J. A. Temperature regulation and bioenergetics of the Mongolian gerbil *Meriones unguiculatues. American Midlands Naturalist,* 1972, *87,* 272–282.

Moltz, H., & Lee, T. M. The maternal pheromone of the rat: Identity and functional significance. *Physiology and Behavior,* 1981, *26,*(2), 301–306.

Mueller, A. P., Sato, K., & Glick, B. The chicken lachrimal gland, gland of Harder, caecal tonsil, and accessory spleen as sources of antibody producing cells. *Cell Immunology,* 1971, *2,* 140–152.

Orten, J. M., & Keller, J. M. Dietary protein and protoporphyrin formation in the rat. *Journal of Biological Chemistry,* 1946, *165,* 163–167.

Payne, A. P. Pheromonal effects of Harderian gland homogenates on aggressive behavior in the hamster. *Journal of Endocrinology,* 1977, *73,* 191–192.

Payne, A. P. Attractant properties of the Harderian gland and its products on male golden hamsters of differing sexual experience. *Proceedings of the Society for Endocrinology,* 1978, 8/30–9/2.

Payne, A. P. The attractiveness of Harderian gland smears to sexually naive male golden hamsters. *Animal Behavior,* 1979, *27,* 897–904.

Payne, A. P., McGadey, J., Moore, M. R., & Thompson, G. Cyclic and seasonal changes in Harderian gland activity in the female golden hamster. *Proceedings of the Society for Endocrinology,* 1976, 6/9–10/9.

Payne, A. P., McGadey, J., Moore, M. R., & Thompson, G. Androgenic control of the Harderian gland in the male golden hamster. *Journal of Endocrinology,* 1977, *75,* 73–82.

Pendergrass, M. L., & Thiessen, D. D. Body temperature and autogrooming in the Mongolian gerbil, *Meriones unguiculatus. Behavior and Neural Biology,* 1981, *33,* 524–528.

Prosser, C. L., & Nelson, D. O. The role of nervous systems in temperature adaptation of poikilotherms. *Annual Review of Physiology,* 1981, *43,* 281–300.

Randall, J. Unpublished research, 1981.

Randall, J. A., & Thiessen, D. D. Seasonal activity and thermoregulation in *Meriones unguiculatus:* A gerbil's choice. *Behavioral Ecology and Sociobiology,* 1980, *7,* 267–272.

Randall, W., Elbin, J., & Swenson, R. Biochemical changes involved in a lesion-induced behavior in the cat. *Journal of Comparative and Physiological Psychology,* 1974, *86,* 747–750.

Reiter, R. J., & Klein, D. C. Observations on the pineal gland, the Harderian glands, the retina, and the productive organs of adult female rats exposed to continuous light. *Journal of Endocrinology,* 1971, *51,* 117–125.

Richard, G. Ontogenesis and phylogenesis: Mutual constraints. *Advances in the Study of Behavior,* 1979, *9,* 229–278.

Richmond, G., & Sachs, B. D. Grooming in Norway rats: The development of adult expression of a complex motor pattern. *Behaviour,* 1981, *75,* 82–95.

Roberts, W. W., Bergquist, E. H., & Robinson, T. C. L. Thermoregulatory grooming and sleep-like relaxation induced by local warming of preoptic area and anterior hypothalamus in opposum. *Journal of Comparative and Physiological Psychology,* 1969, *67,*(2), 182–188.

Rosenblatt, J. S. Stages in the early behavioural development of altricial young of selected species of non-primate mammals. In P. P. G., Bateson, & R. A. Hinde (Eds.), *Growing points in ethology.* New York: Cambridge University Press, 1976, pp. 345–383.

Schmidt-Nielsen, K. *Animal physiology.* London: Cambridge University Press, 1979.

Stokes, D. Personal communication, July 1982.

Stricker, E. M., Everett, J. C., & Porter, E. A. The regulation of body temperature by rats and mice in the heat: Effects of desalivation and the presence of a water bath. *Communications in Behavioral Biology,* 1968, Part A, *2,* 113–119.

Teitelbaum, P., & Epstein, A. The lateral hypothalamic syndrome: Recovery of feeding and drinking after lateral hypothalamic lesions. *Psychological Review,* 1962, *69,* 74–90.

Thiessen, D. D. Thermoenergetics and the evolution of pheromone communication. In J. M. Sprague, & A. N. Epstein (Eds.), *Progress in psychobiology and physiological psychology.* (Vol. 7). New York: Academic Press, 1977.

Thiessen, D. Effects of water deprivation on the Mongolian gerbil, *Meriones unguiculatus:* Absence of Harderian gland involvement. *Physiological Psychology,* 1980, *8*(3), 379–382.

Thiessen, D. Unpublished research, 1983.

Thiessen, D. D., & Clancy, A. Unpublished research, 1980.

Thiessen, D. D., & Kittrell, M. W. The Harderian gland and thermoregulation in the gerbil (*Meriones unguiculatus*). *Physiology and Behavior,* 1980, *24,* 417–424.

Thiessen, D. D., & Rice, M. Mammalian scent gland marking and social behavior. *Psychological Bulletin,* 1976, *83,* 505–539.

Thiessen, D. D., Clancy, A., & Goodwin, M. Harderian gland pheromone in the Mongolian gerbil *Meriones unguiculatus. Journal of Chemical Ecology,* 1976, *2*(2), 231–238.

Thiessen, D. D.. Graham, M., Perkins, J., & Marcks, S. Temperature regulation and social grooming in the Mongolian gerbil (*Meriones unguiculatus*). *Behavioral Biology,* 1977, *19,* 279–288.

Thiessen, D. D., Pendergrass, M., & Harriman, A. E. The thermoenergetics of coat color maintenance by the Mongolian gerbil, *Meriones unguiculatus. Thermal Biology,* 1982, *7,* 51–56.

Waring, A., & Perper, T. Parental behaviour in the Mongolian gerbil (*Meriones unguiculatus*): I. Retrieval. *Animal Behaviour,* 1979, *27,* 1091–1097.

Wetterberg, L., Geller, E., & Yuwiler, A. Harderian gland: An extraretinal photoreceptor influencing the pineal gland in neonatal rats? *Science,* 1970, *167,* 884–885.

Wetterberg, L., Yuwiler, A., Geller, E., & Shapiro, S. Harderian gland: Development and influence of early hormonal treatment on porphyrin content. *Science,* 1970, *168,* 996–998.

Wetterberg, L., Yuwiler, A., Ulrich, R., Geller, E., & Wallace, R. Harderian gland: Influence on pineal hydroxyindole-O-mehtyltransferase activity in neonatal rats. *Science,* 1970, *170,* 194–196.

Wight, P. A. L., Burns, R. B., Rothwell, B., & MacKenzie, G. M. The Harderian gland and the domestic fowl: I. Histology, with reference to the genesis of plasma cells and Russell bodies. *Journal of Anatomy,* 1971, *110,* 307–315.

Wilson, N. E., & Stricker, E. M. Thermal homeostasis in pregnant rats during heat stress. *Journal of Comparative and Physiological Psychology,* 1979, *93*(3), 585–594.

Woodhouse, M. A., & Rhodin, J. A. G. The ultrastructure of the Harderian gland of the mouse with particular reference to the formation of its secretory product. *Journal of Ultrastructure Research,* 1963, *9,* 76–98.

Wysocki, C. J. Neurobehavioral evidence for the involvement of the vomeronasal system in mammalian reproduction. *Neuroscience and Biobehavioral Reviews,* 1979, *3,* 301–341.

CHAPTER 7

Biparental Care

Hormonal and Nonhormonal Control Mechanisms

RAE SILVER

Introduction

Many observers have commented on the changing and complex interactions that must occur between the mother and her young in the period from birth to weaning (Galef, 1977; Hinde & Spencer-Booth, 1968; Hofer, 1978; Lehrman, 1961; Rosenblatt, 1965). The complexity increases by an order of magnitude when two parents share in the care of the offspring. Here, the mates must be coordinated with each other as well as with the needs of the developing young and the demands of the environment. Biparental care occurs in certain mammalian orders (Kleiman & Malcolm, 1981), and in birds 90% of the species are monogamous (Lack, 1968) and biparental care patterns predominate. The relative responsibilities of each parent range from equal sharing for the care of the young to total involvement by one parent (Skutch, 1957). Bisexual incubation predominates (54% of families). Generally, the eggs of species showing biparental care are attended at virtually all times by one or the other parent (White & Kinney, 1974). The demands of biparental care and the systems of male–female coordination are well exemplified in an analysis of doves. Such an analysis can proceed along several dimensions.

As Tinbergen (1963) noted, four kinds of questions must be answered if one is to understand a behavior pattern. The first two concern proximate causation and involve questions of development and mechanism. The second set of questions relates to ultimate causaton and to issues of survival value and

RAE SILVER • Department of Psychology, Barnard College, Columbia University, New York, New York 10027. The work described in this chapter was supported by NIMH grant 29380 and NSF grant BNS 7906282.

phylogeny. In the analysis of ultimate and proximate causes, it is to be expected that the four kinds of questions one might ask about parental behavior have different solutions in each of the sexes, though the end point of producing viable young is held in common.

Trivers (1972) has offered explanations for sex differences in the amount of parental care exerted in terms of "ultimate" causation. He suggested that in the absence of other factors, females are selected initially to show greater amounts of care because they contribute gametes that are more expensive in energy. The amount of care shown by monogamous species changes over the course of breeding as each parent's relative investment changes. Although "investment" has not been easy to measure, there have been several attempts to test Trivers's formulation (e.g., Burger, 1981; Howe, 1979; Weatherhead, 1979).

Answers to questions of proximate causation provide clues to ultimate causation and vice versa. Ethological theory emphasizes that in evolution, parental behavior systems have been shaped by the ordinarily expected environment and depend on that environment for adequate functioning. The discovery of inappropriate responses of animals in experimentally manipulated situations provides insight into the characteristics of the expected and the sufficient environmental cues. Again, it is anticipated that these cues differ for the sexes.

The Behavior of Doves

The present paper focuses on the parent–young interactions of ring doves (*Streptopelia risoria*). These pale beige birds breed very well in captivity and have been intensively studied by several investigators (Cheng, 1979; Lehrman, 1965; Hutchison, 1976; Vowles & Prewitt, 1971; Erickson & Martinez-Vargas, 1975). Research on ring doves provides as complete an analysis of biparental reproductive behavior as is available for any species. The ring dove has been domesticated for hundreds of years, and doves and other members of the pigeon family have served as subjects for experimental behavior analyses since the turn of the century (Craig, 1908, 1909; Whitman, 1919). Though there is some confusion on this point (Gaunt, 1980), *Streptopelia risoria* is descended from *Streptopelia roseogrisea*, the African collared dove (Goodwin, 1967; Murton & Westwood, 1975; Vaurie, 1961). Analysis of the calls of *S. roseogrisea* in Northern Cameroon and *S. decaocto* in Europe confirms that the vocalization of *S. risoria* is identical to the former and quite distinct from the latter (Cox, Andrews, Balsam, & Silver, 1983).

Male and female ring doves are morphologically identical. They can be distinguished by surgical exploration and visualization of the gonads, or by their behavior. In most laboratory studies, doves with previous experience of a breeding cycle are used as experimental subjects. Inexperienced birds are somewhat unpredictable in their breeding behavior in that they may take a long time to start building a nest, may lay infertile eggs, may break their eggs, or may fail to care adequately for newly hatched offspring. These problems arise less frequently in reproductively experienced animals.

Breeding Behavior

The principal activity that immediately follows the placement of a pair in a cage is an intense period of courtship lasting several hours. Thereafter, the level of courtship behaviors, such as strutting, bowing and cooing, hop-charging, and cackling, diminish. This initial intense level of courtship and aggressive behavior is probably a product of housing doves in visual isolation for a period prior to pairing, and of their confinement during testing to a small cage where they cannot avoid each other. After several hours have passed and for several consecutive days thereafter, courtship continues at a reduced level. The birds select a nest site by assuming a characteristic posture; they coo with head down and tail up in corners and in concave places in the cage. Eventually, they select a concave place, such as a provided nest bowl, in which to build their nest. They both participate in constructing the nest. Generally, the male carries the nest material to the female and she builds the nest. This phase of the breeding cycle lasts 7–11 days in the laboratory, but in feral doves in Florida, it can take weeks (personal observation). Feral doves often start to build a nest in more than one site prior to selecting the place where the eggs are finally laid. Though there are differences between feral and domestic doves in type of nest material selected and the time course of events during courtship, the particular behaviors displayed are not different.

After the female lays her two-egg clutch, both parents take turns incubating the eggs. The male sits for a block of time in the middle of the day, while the female sits the rest of the time. The eggs hatch in about 14 days. The parents feed their young by regurgitating crop milk and, later, crop milk mixed with seed. The squab begin to leave the nest at 8–10 days of age and make the transition to independent feeding at 12–14 days (Wortis, 1969). They continue to beg for food even after they are able to peck independently. When the young reach 18–21 days, the parents start to court anew. (For more detailed descriptions of the behaviors of breeding doves, see Erickson & Martinez-Vargas, 1975; Lehrman, 1965; Miller & Miller, 1958).

Experimental Analysis of Parental Care

During breeding, parental behavior is coordinated and intricately timed to meet the needs of the young. Parental responses appear to unfold. Each transition in the development of the young is matched by an adjustment in the behavior of the parents. This orderliness emphasizes the function of behavior and obscures underlying mechanisms. As noted above, the analysis of mechanisms of parental care should provide clues to how the environment has shaped behavior in evolution. In the following pages, the behavior of parents and young is described. Next, nonhormonal and hormonal mechanisms underlying behavioral transitions in breeding are analyzed. Finally, generalizable aspects of biparental care in doves are considered.

During incubation and brooding, parent doves sit on their nest 24 hours a day for about 20 days. They defend the nest from intruders by fluffing up and striking with their wings (Vowles & Harwood, 1966). Though this response serves to protect the young, that is not the immediate cause of the parent's behavior. Thus, if the eggs or newborn squab are removed from the nest and placed in clear view on the floor of the cage, they will be ignored (and will eventually die if not re-placed). Nevertheless, the parents will continue to defend the nest from intruders (unpublished observations). As Moore (1976) observed, the formation of a relationship to the nest site is a necessary prerequisite for the development of parental responsiveness to the young. It is the nest site that is defended. The expected environment is one in which the eggs and the young are in the nest.

A more dramatic illustration that incubation behavior involves responses to a complex stimulus network rather than to the young alone stems from studies of interactions between parent doves. If mates are separated from each other by a glass plate so that the female has the nest and the male is on the other side of the barrier, she continues to incubate the eggs by herself (Patel, 1936). However, if he is out of sight, she will stop sitting in a matter of days. If the nest is left with the male, he will not continue to sit even though the female is in full view. This result is impressive if one considers that once incubation begins, the mates are in contact for only a few minutes a day, at the time of nest exchange (Ball & Silver, in press; Lumpkin, Kessel, Zenone, & Erickson, 1982). Apparently, the male has to see his mate sitting in order to continue sitting himself. The parental incubation response is a response to the sight of the mate as well as a response to the nest.

Further proof that factors other than the young and the parents' internal state are important for the display of parental behavior comes from experiments in which mates were exchanged partway through incubation (Ball & Silver, in press). These birds had reached the fifth day in incubation and had undergone the accompanying physiological changes, when each bird was given a new partner at the same stage of the cycle. Even though they generally saw each other for only a few seconds at the time of nest exchange, many pairs failed to rear young (66%), and all showed a marked disruption of sex-typical sitting behavior. Given that doves are believed to form lifelong pair bonds, it is not surprising that the continued presence of the mate is an important aspect of the incubation response.

After the eggs hatch, the parents continue to brood and to feed the young squab. The thermal and nutritional needs of the young are provided for by both parents. Unlike the situation seen in other species (rats; Wiesner & Sheard, 1933; Selye, 1934; chickens: Collias, 1952), the duration of parental care cannot be extended by replacing the growing offspring with young squab (Hansen, 1966). Furthermore, if doves are sitting on infertile eggs, they will continue to sit for about as long as they would have if the eggs had hatched on schedule (Silver & Gibson, 1980). In these respects, the doves behave as though an internal timer determines the duration of parental care. Stimulus cues from the eggs as opposed to the young do not affect the duration of incubation.

Each of the foregoing studies (and the entire corpus of Lehrman's work: 1958, 1959, 1965) indicates that a highly synchronous set of stimuli and hormones operates to produce the successful rearing of young. Parental behavior has an elaborate support system in the sense that the response is not simply or even largely a response to the young—though young are certainly a necessary condition. The analysis of endocrine factors underlying parental behavior supports the notion that factors other than the young are important in maintaining parental responses.

Transitions in Parental Care during Breeding

Once the transition from nonbreeding to breeding is made, egg laying and fertilization, nest building, incubation of eggs, brooding, and feeding the young must occur in correct temporal sequence. The required synchrony between the parents, and among the parents and the young, is achieved by several mechanisms, none of which are predictable from observation of the behaviors of parent doves and their offspring. Some components involve responses to external stimuli, others to internal changes, and still others depend on an unfolding of a timed sequence. For each behavioral transition, one can tease out the underlying causes. In a biparental care system, it is important to regard each parent as a unique participant.

The first behavioral transition to consider is from nonbreeding to breeding. This analysis has been completed for many periodically breeding species. Farner and Follett (1979) observed that in general, the male comes into breeding condition sooner than the female, and he remains reproductively active longer. There are many mechanism for "fine-tuning" the time of breeding (Wingfield, 1980). In general, it is thought that the fine temporal adjustment of the onset of breeding is achieved by the female, who in turn can influence the male.

In doves held under a photoperiodic regimen of 8 hours' light and 16 hours darkness, the gonads regress. In photoperiods of 14 hours of light and 10 hours of darkenss, males show full gonadal development, while females have small ovarian follicles (2–3 mm in diameter) and show very slow follicular development (Cheng, 1979). The sight of a courting male, however, is enough to produce ovulation within 5–7 days (Erickson, 1970). Gonadal recrudescence in the male is hastened by exposure to females during the period of gonadal growth (Cheng, 1976). Thus, the transition from nonbreeding to breeding readiness is brought about by environmental factors that promote gonadal development in the male. Coordination of male and female is ensured by the interdependence of the endocrine and behavioral responses of the mates.

Once they are ready to breed, further coordination of the behavior of the mates is ensured by short-term and fine-grained tuning of their behavioral and endocrine systems. Thus, the male continues to bow-coo, chase the female, and nest-coo for days, until the female stays at the nest site. If the female is treated hormonally, so as to advance the occurrence of her attachment to the nest site (Martinez-Vargas & Erickson, 1973), or if this rapid attachment occurs spontaneously (Cheng, 1979), the male adjusts his behavior accordingly. The male's response is tuned to the female's behavior in that the duration of his courtship and nest-oriented displays is determined by her behavior, which is in turn affected by her endocrine state (Cheng, 1973b). Once she stays at the nest site and displays nest-cooing, he proceeds to gather nest material and carries it back to the female.

The male's endocrine system is also tuned to the events of the breeding cycle. Androgen levels in male ring doves rise within hours of exposure to a female and decline to baseline values by Day 1 of incubation, 7–9 days after pairing (Figure 1a; Feder, Story, Goodwin, Reboulleau, & Silver, 1977). Social stimuli affect the maintenance and decline of plasma androgens. In one experiment, males were paired with females and (1) were allowed to proceed uninterrupted to incubation, or (2) had their nest destroyed daily, or (3) were given no nest material (O'Connell, Reboulleau, Feder, & Silver, 1981). All males were bled on Day 8 after pairing. The males given nest material and left undisturbed exhibited the low androgen levels characteristic of the incubation phase. In contrast, the males whole nests were destroyed daily and those given no nest material had significantly higher androgen levels than the undisturbed males. It appears that interference with nest construction (and presumably incubation activity) prevents a decline in circulating androgens. This finding suggests that the beginning of incubation rather than the time since pairing regulates this decline. In another experiment, androgen levels were compared in males taken after two days of courtship with one female and exposed to either a novel incubating female or a novel courting female. Males exposed to incubating females exhibited the low androgen levels typical of incubation, while males exposed to novel courting females exhibited the high androgen levels typical of courtship (Figure 2). Evidently, the decline in the male's circulating androgens is strongly influenced by the behavior and the stimuli presented by the female partner and the nest.

Not suprisingly, each phase of breeding is a predecessor or "procomponent" for subsequent behavior in the cycle. The transition from courtship to incubation involves different processes in the sexes. Thus, as we have seen, courtship by the male is necessary for the ovarian development that leads to ovulation (Barfield, 1971). The male's courtship is effective even if he is separated from the female by a glass plate during the entire period of courtship (Patel, 1936; unpublished data). Such a female will build the nest by herself, nest-coo, lay (infertile) eggs, and begin to incubate as usual. However, if the glass barrier is removed once the eggs are laid, the male will not incubate. Instead, he will begin courtship anew (unpublished data). In this case, it is likely that the male has formed an attachment to the female, but not to the nest site.

The female's sexual behavior is closely linked to ovarian hormone secretion (Cheng, 1973b). Once the female starts to incubate (Figure 1b), she no longer secretes the ovarian hormones estrogen and progesterone (Silver, Reboulleau, Lehrman, & Feder, 1974; Korenbrot, Schomberg, & Erickson, 1974) and is no longer sexually responsive (Cheng, 1973a). the transition from nonincubation to incubation in the female is mediated by an increase in the secretion of ovarian hormones. Lehrman and his students showed that the courtship behavior of the mate stimulates the female to secrete gonadotropins and, subsequently, steroids (Lehrman, Wortis, & Brody, 1961; Lehrman, Brody, & Wortis, 1961). Radioimmunoassay of estradiol (Korenbrot et al., 1974) and progesterone (Silver et al., 1974) indicates that there is a gradual increase in these steroids from the beginning of courtship to the time of ovulation (Figure 1b). If a female is ovariectomized, she shows neither sexual nor parental behavior to the stimuli presented by the mate, the nest, and the eggs (Cheng & Silver, 1975). Though she shows sexual responsiveness when given estrogen alone (Cheng, 1973b), both estrogen and progesterone replacement are required for the onset of nest building and incubation (Chen & Silver, 1975). In summary, courtship by the male stimulates ovarian development and estrogen secretion, which bring about the transition to sexual responsiveness. Further ovarian stimulation results in progesterone secretion, which produces egg laying, the termination of sexual behavior, and the transition to parental behavior.

In males, there is no necessary change from sexual responsiveness to a lack thereof that accompanies the onset of incubation (Silver, Feder, & Lehrman, 1973). The male is capable of displaying the androgen-dependent courtship

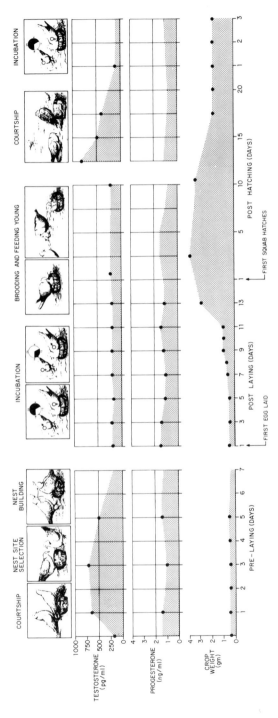

Figure 1a. Hormonal and behavioral changes of the reproductive cycle of the male ring dove. Secretion of testosterone and crop growth are related to behavioral stage, but progesterone levels do not change in a systematic manner.

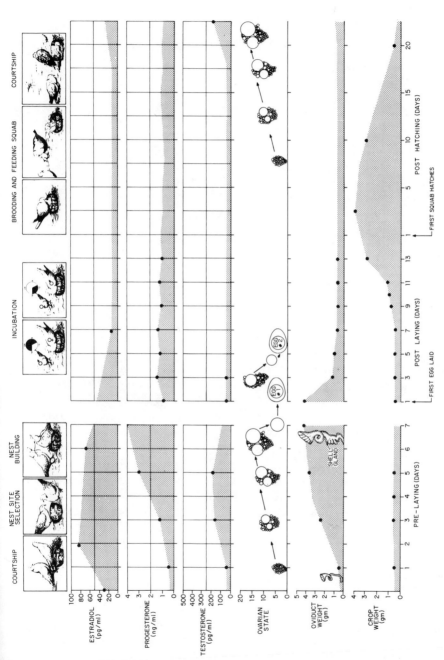

Figure 1b. Hormonal and behavioral changes of the reproductive cycle of the female ring dove. Ovarian growth and secretion of estrogen and progesterone indicates a clear relationship to crop development, oviduct size, and major behavioral events in the cycle. (After Silver, 1978.)

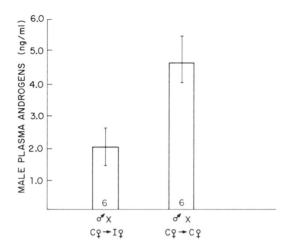

Figure 2. Mean plasma androgen levels in males taken from courtship with one female and exposed to either an incubating female (left side) or another courting female (right side). Values shown represent levels present two days after exposure to an incubating female or another courting female. (From O'Connell, Silver, Feder, & Reboulleau, 1981.)

behaviors of bow-cooing and nest-cooing throughout courtship and incubation. Thus, for him, the transition to caring for eggs does not necessarily bring with it a decline in sexual behavior (Silver & Barbiere, 1977). However, there is a transition from not incubating to incubating. One of the problems to which we and others have devoted a great deal of attention (see Silver, 1978; Cheng, 1979) is the search for the endogenous change that mediates the onset of male incubation. Although some solutions have been suggested, certain ambiguities remain. Cheng (1970) proposed that either environmental or hormonal factors are sufficient, and that the former were emphasized in Lehrman's (1965) experiments, while the latter were emphasized in my experiments (Silver & Buntin, 1973; Silver & Feder, 1973). This formulation is attractive in that it accounts for the fact that progesterone effectively induces incubation when administered exogenously to intact males (Lehrman, 1958). Also, pharmacological doses of testosterone induce progesterone receptors in male doves (Balthazart, Blaustein, Cheng, & Feder, 1980). This finding allows one to postulate that the courtship-induced elevation in testosterone seen at the onset of courtship (Feder *et al.,* 1977; O'Connell, Reboulleau, Feder, & Silver, 1981; O'Connell, Silver, Feder, & Reboulleau, 1981) renders circulating progesterone effective in inducing incubation (Cheng, 1979).

One problem with this interpretation is that there is no evidence that plasma progesterone levels change during courtship and incubation in male doves. Females do show elevated levels of progesterone preceding the onset of incubation. Furthermore, estrogen is more effective than testosterone in inducing progestin receptors (Balthazart et al., 1980). Nevertheless, females have large increases in plasma progesterone at the onset of incubation (Silver et al., 1974). Yet, it is not necessary to invoke a change in sensitivity to progesterone to explain the initiation of incubation in the female. Given the absence of evidence of changes in progestin receptors in males during a normal reproductive cycle, it seems worthwhile to continue to seek evidence of hormonal correlates of the transition from courtship to incubation.

Gonadectomy, which results in the disappearance of incubation behavior in females, is not effective in males. When known sources of progesterone are removed by castration (Silver & Feder, 1973) or by the pharmacological blockade of adrenal steroid secretion (Silver & Buntin, 1973), the male still displays incubation. Cheng (1979) argued that because progesterone is detectable (though unchanging) in breeding males, and because progesterone, along with testosterone, induces incubation in castrated males (Stern & Lehrman, 1969), the data can be interpreted to support the idea that this steroid combination normally induces male incubation. However, this interpretation is improbable, since males castrated three weeks previously and treated with either oil or high androgen (daily injections of 100 μg testosterone) continue to incubate. In this circumstance, neither gonadal steroid (testosterone, progesterone) is changing at the onset of incubation. Nevertheless, the males make the transition from nonincubating to incubating.

The transition from sitting on eggs (incubation) to sitting on young (brooding) is apparently not accompanied by a major behavioral transition. If squab are given to the parent earlier than the anticipated time of hatching, they will be brooded (Hansen, 1966). If young fail to hatch, the parents will continue to sit on the infertile eggs for about the same number of days, and with the same temporal pattern, as they would have sat on the young (Silver & Gibson, 1980). However, there are limits to using the form of a behavior pattern to draw inferences about behavior categories. Thus, Moore (1976) has shown that one does detect a transition from preference for eggs to preference for squab if incubating and brooding doves are given a choice between eggs and young. Also, if the eggs or young are removed altogether at any stage in the cycle, the parents stop sitting on the nest within a few days.

As the young grow, the parents start to court anew. Readiness to court is affected by the presence of eggs and young. If the nest is destroyed or the young are removed, the parents start to court within days. Parents rearing one squab start to court anew sooner than those rearing two (Silver, 1978). The underlying hormonal mechanism involves the suppression of luteinizing hormone (LH) and the concomitant enhancement of prolactin in the presence of young (Goldsmith et al., 1981; Goldsmith & Silver, 1982).

Plasma levels of LH have been analyzed throughout the breeding cycle

(Silver, Goldsmith, & Follett, 1981; Cheng & Follett, 1976). In males, LH levels are low in visually isolated animals, peak the day after pairing with a female, and decline to baseline levels during incubation and brooding (Figure 3). In females, an LH peak precedes ovulation. If eggs or squab are removed during the period of parental care, LH levels rise. The increase in LH following the removal of the eggs was more prolonged in late than in early incubation. It seems that the female enhances while the young (eggs or squab) suppress LH in male ring doves. Preliminary data in a study in which both LH and prolactin were measured in both sexes indicate that a similar sensitivity to the presence of the mate and the young occurs in females, and that during late incubation, LH levels fall in stimulus situations that produce rising prolactin levels, and vice versa (Goldsmith & Silver, 1982). Furthermore, we found that if the mates are separated in late incubation, they show a decline in plasma prolactin and an increase in plasma LH even though they continue to sit on the nest and the eggs. This result suggests that the presence of the partner is a necessary stimulus for the maintenance of prolactin secretion, even in incubating birds.

In summary, the behavioral transitions of the breeding cycle involve redundant behavioral processes and endocrine correlates that may differ in the sexes. These operate to ensure that the mates will be synchronized with each other and with the needs of the young. Some components of the reponses to the young are not finely tuned and are inflexible. There are mechanisms that ensure that parental behaviors and their associated endocrine responses

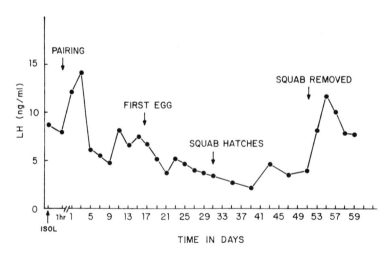

Figure 3. Plasma levels of LH during the breeding cycle in a male rearing two squab. (From Silver *et al.*, 1980.)

will not continue longer than the normal interval, and that readiness to start a new breeding cycle will occur soon after the removal or the loss of the young and/or the mate.

Daily Transitions in Parental Behavior

The foregoing studies emphasize the major behavioral transitions that bring about the initiation and the termination of each phase of parental care. If one focuses on another temporal level, a new class of demands for synchrony in the behavior of parents and young emerges. Dove parents keep their eggs covered at all times. To achieve this, complex coordination between the parents is required. That coordination of the behavior of mates is important can readily be gleaned from a consideration of avian nest-exchange display ceremonies. Nest exchange behavior often involves modified courtship displays or the presentation of nesting materials (see Armstrong, 1965). Many species have been reported to push a reluctant partner off the nest during nest exchange (Skutch, 1976).

In any species where the partners share in incubation, there must be a mechanism that determines when each partner will take its turn. In species where the eggs are incubated at all times, this can be a rather complex process. For example, gull parents keep their eggs covered at all times. They sit for irregular bouts, and at any particular time of day, they must choose whether to sit or not to sit. In gulls, the factors involved include tide, food quality and quantity, and temperature (McFarland, 1977). In contrast, dove parents have a much simpler and more rigid system, with each parent sitting for a single block at a fairly predictable time of day. Thus, on any day, only two behavioral transitions are made: once with the female-to-male exchange in the morning, and once with the male-to-female exchange in the afternoon. What are the factors influencing these daily bouts of parental care?

In an initial study, we analyzed in detail the pattern of incubation of 38 pairs of doves (Wallman, Grabon, & Silver, 1979). Even though the male incubates for a period of time in the middle of the day, there exist great interpair differences in the precise timing and frequency of nest exchanges and in the duration of sitting by each individual. In fact, pairs in which the male sits the least and the most differ by a factor of 3. Furthermore, pairs with nearly identical amounts of sitting over the cycle show substantial differences in the sitting pattern (Figure 4—compare Pairs 3, 4, and 5). Yet, despite this interpair variability, the incubatory patterns of paired doves develop so that the eggs are virtually never left uncovered. This pattern mandates fine tuning of the behavior synchronization of the mates.

Given these interpair differences, it is of interest to ask whether the amount and pattern of sitting are stable over consecutive breeding cycles. This

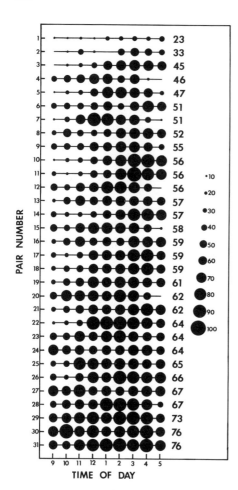

Figure 4. Daily patterns of sitting of 31 pairs of doves. Pairs are ranked from the pair with minimum male sitting (maximum female sitting) to the pair with maximum male sitting (minimum female sitting). The diameter of each dot is proportional to the percentage of observations at the time of day in which the male is sitting. The number to the right of each row is the overall percentage of observations in which the male was sitting. (From Wallman *et al.*, 1979).

question was explored by pairing birds with a given mate in breeding cycles 1, 2, and 4, and with a different mate in breeding cycle 3. There is a significant correlation between the amount of time a bird sits in a first and second breeding cycle with the same mate (cycle 1 vs. cycle 2). This correlation remains high even after a breeding cycle with a new partner (cycle 3) has been interposed (cycle 2 vs. cycle 4). In contrast, the correlation is much lower in pairs with unfamiliar mates of rather different sitting histories (cycle 3 vs. cycle 1 or cycle 2).

In addition to comparing the overall amount of sitting, one can determine whether the pattern of sitting over the course of the day is specific to each pair. To quantify the difference in the daily sitting pattern of an animal from one breeding cycle to the next, we developed a way to represent the amount of difference between two curves that plot the frequency distribution of sitting across the day. The results show that the pattern of sitting from cycle to cycle is consistent when the partner is the same (cycle 1 vs. cycle 2) and is less consistent after a period of separation (cycle 1 or 2 vs. cycle 4). The previous pattern of sitting provides no prediction about the sitting pattern with a new mate (cycles 1, 2, and 4 vs. cycle 3).

One can also ask whether the male, the female, or both partners change their amount of sitting when placed with a new mate. Birds were rank-ordered according to their incubating time in the first breeding cycle. In the third breeding cycle, the males that had sat the most were paired with the females that had sat the most (long-sitting males with long-sitting females), and the males that had sat the least were paired with the females that had sat the least (short-sitting males with short-sitting females). If one sex determines how much to incubate without reference to its mate, that sex would not be expected to show a significant correlation between the amount of sitting from cycle 1 and the change in amount of sitting from cycle 1 to cycle 3. Instead, our results show that there are significant correlations in both sexes (males, $r = .80$; females, $r = .67$; differences betweeen males and females not significant). Figure 5 shows that both partners adjust their responses, suggesting that cooperative interactions are the most important determining factor. The possibility that the female has the greater influence in determining the amount of sitting is supported, however, by the significant correlation ($p < .05$) in the amount of sitting in cycle 1 versus cycle 3 in females but not in males.

In another attempt to clarify the contribution of each partner to the sex-typical timing of incubation, we separated the partners from each other and gave each a nest bowl and eggs (Silver & Gibson, 1980). One might imagine that under these circumstances, each mate (sex) would sit only when its clock mechanism (whatever that might be) told it to sit. In fact, the results were not clear. When the mate was removed, each partner sat virtually all day long by itself until it stopped sitting altogether (Figure 6). It seems that the sex-typical diurnal rhythm of sitting is seen only in paired doves. If the partner does not appear, the operative rule is to keep the nest covered, at least for several days, and then to quit sitting.

Given that each pair establishes a stable pattern and amount of sitting, one can identify the optimal conditions for incubation and go on to ask further experimental questions about regulatory processes and mechanisms. Data showing the existence of a rhythmic sitting pattern in animals housed in a light–dark cycle tells us little about the nature of the underlying rhythmicity. Specifically, we would like to know whether the timing behavior of the parents involves an external start signal with a driven response to light, or whether the daily rhythm of parental care involves a self-sustaining oscillation or biological clock that persists in the absence of external environmental cues.

To explore these possibilities, we analyzed the effects of light on the

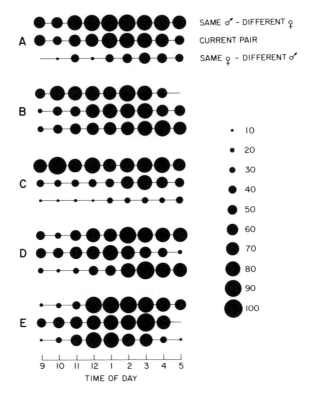

Figure 5. Comparison of pattern of sitting of birds with new mates (Cycle 3) and with original mates (Cycle 1). (The diameter of each dot represents the percentage of males sitting at each time of day, averaged over Days 1–25.) (From Wallman *et al.*, 1979.)

timing of sitting by dove parents (Silver & Nelson, 1982). In the first series, the light cycle was phase-shifted so that what had been the middle of the day (noon) now became the middle of the night (midnight). In response, dove parents adjusted their sitting time so that the male sat for a block of time toward the middle of the new light phase of the day. This result indicates that the cues for setting the timing of incubation are provided by the daily cycle of alternating light and dark.

   If there were a biological clock regulating the timing of sitting, one would expect it to measure time in the absence of light–dark cues, and to have a resetting mechanism so that it could adjust to local environmental cues. When parent doves are housed in constant dim light, they continue to sit for regular blocks of time, though sitting times are unentrained and are no longer synchronized to external time. As can be seen in Figure 7, the timing of sitting becomes free-running. These results indicate that an endogenous clock is involved in the timing of incubation bouts, but they do not clarify whether one or both mates have such a clock.

In another series of experiments we teased apart the doves' ability to measure time of day (presumably requiring a circadian clock) from the ability to measure duration of incubation (presumably requiring an interval timer). This study also addressed in a preliminary way the question of whether the male, the female, or both use a circadian clock to time their sitting bout. Doves were housed in a two-chambered breeding cage connected by an L-shaped hallway. The nest was located in one chamber, and food and water were located in the other. Movement between the chambers could be restricted by placing a gate in the hallway. The behavior of the doves was constantly monitored by 24-hour videotape recording.

Consider a male that usually incubates from about 10 A.M. until about 4 P.M. A gate can be placed in the hallway so that access to the nest is blocked

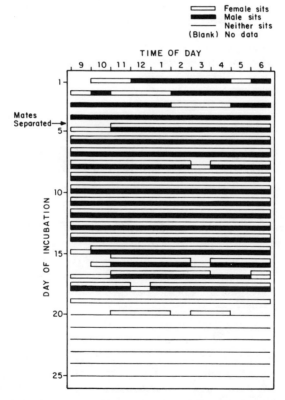

Figure 6. Sitting behavior of a representative pair of birds after separation from the mate on the fifth day of incubation. (From Silver & Gibson, 1980.)

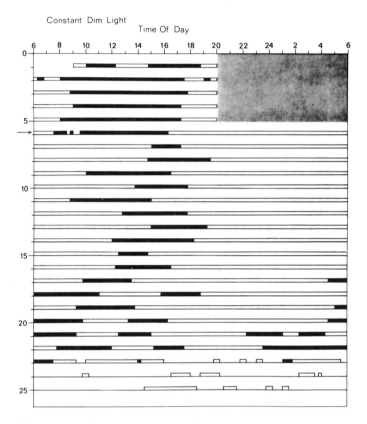

Figure 7. Daily timing of incubation during the 25 days after egg laying by representative pairs housed in constant dim illumination (.5 lux), starting on the sixth day of incubation.

until 1 P.M. We can now ask whether the male will incubate until 6 P.M. (suggesting that he measures duration on the nest) or until 4 P.M. (suggesting that he measures time of day), and whether the female will try to return to the nest at 4 P.M. (measures time of day) or at 6 P.M. (measures duration off the nest). The results (Figure 8) indicate that the female returns to the nest at the usual time of day for the male–female nest exchange, whereas the male is not prepared to leave the nest at this time. The result is that they vie for the nest each day for approximately two hours, from 4 P.M. to 6 P.M.

An analogous experiment, in which the female is kept off the nest for several hours at the beginning of her usual incubation period, indicates that she, too, measures duration on the nest to determine when to leave and that she measures time of day to determine when to start to sit. In summary, it seems that each sex uses the circadian clock to determine when to begin a bout of incubation. Although "social" rhythms are widespread and have been described previously (Regal & Connolly, 1980; Rusak, 1981), the sexually differentiated response of parent doves provides a unique opportunity to analyze the underlying mechanisms. In this context, it is most exciting to find that sex hormones can alter the timing of incubation, and we can study whether the interval and/or the circadian timer is affected by sex hormones.

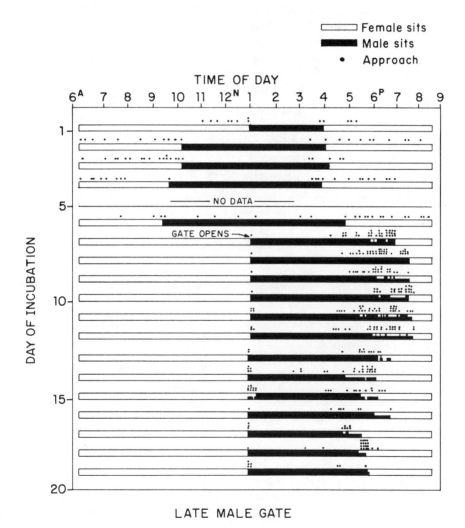

Figure 8. Timing of incubation by pairs in which the male is prevented from reaching the nest until 1 P.M., starting on Day 7 of incubation. Note the interactions between the mates at the time of the evening nest exchange.

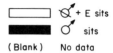

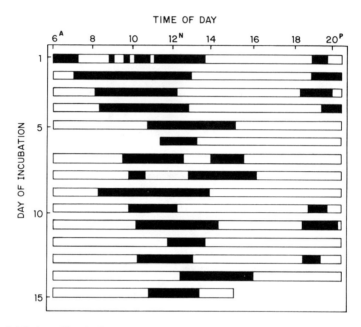

Figure 9. Timing of incubation by a pair of males of which one has been castrated and given estradiol and progesterone replacement therapy.

Role of Sex Hormones

If two intact males are paired in a breeding cage, they do not incubate. If two females are paired, they incubate, but the timing of sitting by each dove is irregular (Allen, 1978). However, if one male is castrated, is given estrogen, and is paired with an intact male, this "couple" show the characteristic timing of incubation, with the estrogen-treated male sitting at the female's time of day (Figure 9). Also, when a testosterone-treated ovariectomized female is paired with an intact female, the androgen-treated female sits in the middle of the day. These results indicate that sex hormones influence the way in which a circadian clock is used by parent doves. The mechanism might involve the coupling of the clock to neural mechanisms of parental behavior, or changes in sensory input or motor output mechanisms. Whatever the mechanism, the data show the important effects of the endocrine system in integrating the behavior of the mates.

Conclusions

The foregoing studies have uncovered a multitude of mechanisms that ensure the successful rearing of young. Interwoven behavioral and hormonal mechanisms result in a coordination of the behavior of the mates that guarantees that the young are protected from cold, heat, and aridity, and provided with food until they are weaned.

The Success of Columbiformes

It is worthy of note that the family Columbidae is tremendously successful. Approximately 1,000 species and subspecies of pigeons and doves are found everywhere in the world except the Arctic regions and some oceanic islands. The parental care system of Columbiformes is surprisingly uniform and seems at first glance exceedingly rigid. Both males and females participate in incubating the eggs and brooding the young, with the male sitting for a block of time during the middle of the day and the female sitting the rest of the time. This pattern is characteristic of the whole order of Columbiformes and is found in no other order of bires (Lorenz, 1937/1970). This claim has been verified in various field studies (Cox & Silver, 1977; Hoffman, 1969; Hock, 1963; Nice, 1938; Neff & Niedrach, 1946) and in reports on the passenger pigeon, *Ectopistes migratorius* (Halliday, 1978). Consider the fact that pigeons range in length from 6 to 33 inches (from the size of a skylark to that of a hen turkey). They live in regions that vary to the exteme in availability of water and food, in thermal demands on parents and their young, in photoperiods and breeding seasons, in predators, etc. Yet in all cases, both parents care for the young in a typical, highly stereotyped manner. It seems that there have been no pressures to vary this parental care pattern, or, alternatively, no variation has been successful. How or why does it work?

Parental behavior has been defined as responses that further the development of the young. This functional definition draws attention away from different levels at which parental behavior is organized. The story of the ring dove shows that many of the parental responses are unaffected, in the short run, by whether or not the needs of young are served. Parent doves continue to sit on and defend the nest when the eggs lie just outside the nest. This reaction is analogous to an animal's emitting an involuntary scream of fear that makes everyone flee. These responses have no associated intention. Following Grice (1969), some level of intention might be imputed if the behavior were more tuned to the needs of the egg, for example, if the parent tried to sit on the out-of-nest eggs. This is not the case. Possibly, one reason that Columbiformes, with their highly stereotyped pattern of parental care, have been successful is that the expected environment to which the behavioral and endocrine system is tuned is highly predictable. Even after pair bonding, nest site selection, and nest attachment have occurred, stimuli from the nest and the mate continue to play an important role in the behavioral and hormonal concomitants of parental behavior. In the short run (with a time scale of about 24 hours), the eggs and the young are not important in controlling incubation, brooding, and the associated hormones of reproduction. In a longer time scale (several days), the removal or loss of young results in endocrine changes and renewed breeding in both sexes. This system is stable and efficient in a wide range of environments. Whether the mate is necesary for the maintenance of responsiveness to the young in other species that show biparental care remains to be explored.

A Comparative Perspective

In humans, a different situation prevails. What does dove parental care have in common with that of other species, including humans? The contributors were asked, in writing these chapters, to "come naked." Here I shed some layers. Not only can humans be parents, as can doves, they can behave like parents in serving the needs of their young, as can doves, and they can behave like parents in order to serve the needs of their young, as doves do not. Take, for instance, the behavior of a lactating mother nursing her baby. She nurses the infant with the purpose of providing it with food so that it will grow. Nevertheless, there are mechanisms that ensure that she has milk and feeds the baby when it is born. The impact of these mechanisms hit home with the birth of my son. Because I am one of the few contributors to this volume who can tell this tale, I will take the liberty of doing so.

A casual reading of the literature on lactation had led me to believe that I would gradually become so sensitive to the stimuli presented by my own unique baby that eventually milk ejection would occur at the mere sight or sound of him. To my amazement, in the first few weeks of lactation, milk ejection occurred at a very high operant level and in response to any or no stimulus. The sight or cry of any baby, the thought of any child, the occurrence of a nursing time of day, the sight of a carriage—all triggered milk ejection. Sometimes I was sure that no thought or possible stimulus cue was present and milk ejection occurred. Each of these occurrences forced thoughts of the baby and interrupted any ongoing activities and ideas. At the time, these physiological responses felt as though the body was wired so that there was no possibility of my forgetting or neglecting that baby for more than an hour or a few hours at most. More formally, the physiological response served as cues that promoted maternal responses. Gradually, these milk ejection episodes came under discriminative control so that they occurred only when the baby was actually present and nursing. And I experienced greater freedom from physiologically imposed constraints on my thoughts and behavior. The physiological mechanisms associated with nursing and lactation seemed to provide a priming mechanism for parental behavior. It seemed that the hormonally induced stimulus and the motor responses of lactation produced a novel context in which a new set of behaviors was learned.

Formal analysis of the role of background or context in acquisition and performance has been carried out by learning theorists (Rescorla & Wagner, 1972; Gibbon & Balsam, 1981). Context cues refer to any aspects of the environment that are continuously present and nondifferentially associated with reinforcers. Context cues, such as those produced by changes in hormone secretions, can themselves act as stimuli to be learned, in addition to affecting response selection and sensory processing. As indicated by Balsam (1982), context learning occurs very rapidly, and thus, it can play a significant role in acquisition of new responses. This learning can be seen at the onset of maternal behavior in the postpartum animal (see Rosenblatt & Siegel, 1981, for review). A learning mechanism of this type would conceptually integrate behavioral changes thought to be produced by hormonal and by stimulus cues, primarily those from the young.

Previous research on mechanisms of the initiation and maintenance of maternal behavior has emphasized two main themes: the role of hormonal factors and the role of nonhormonal factors, or the transition between hormonal and nonhormonal control (Rosenblatt & Siegel, 1981). Our analysis of the parental behavior of ring doves has followed in the same tradition—with some new insights. In this biparental care system, the mate is a part of the necessary stimulus complex, supporting the hormonal and behavioral concomitants of parental behavior. Whether similar processes are involved in other species that show biparental care remains to be determined in future studies.

ACKNOWLEDGMENTS

I thank N. Ferleger, S. Ramsey, and N. Waks for assistance in the preparation of the manuscript and M. Cooper for comments on an earlier draft.

References

Allen, T. O. *Internal and external influences on the incubation behavior of ring doves (Streptopelia risoria).* Unpublished doctoral thesis, Duke University, 1978.

Armstrong, E. A. *The ethology of bird display and bird behaviour.* London: Dover, 1965.

Ball, G. F., & Silver, R. Timing of incubation bouts by ring doves. *Journal of Comparative Psychology,* in press.

Balsam, P. Bringing the background to the foreground: The role of contextual cues in autoshaping. In M. Commons, A. R. Wagner, & R. Herrnstein (Eds.), *The Harvard Symposium on the Quantitative Analysis of Behavior: Acquisition Process.* New York: Balinger, 1982.

Balthazart, J., Blaustein, J., Cheng, M. F., & Feder, H. H. Hormones modulate the concentration of cytoplasmic progestin receptors in the brain of male ring doves (*Streptopelia risoria*). *Journal of Endocrinology,* 1980, *86,* 251–261.

Barfield, R. J. Gonadotrophic hormone secretion in the female ring dove in response to visual and auditory stimulation by the male. *Journal of Endocrinology,* 1971, *49,* 305–310.

Burger, J. Sexual differences in parental activities of breeding black skimmers. *American Naturalist,* 1981, *117,* 975–984.

Cheng, M. F. Effects of ovariectomy on the reproductive behavior of female ring doves (*Streptopelia risoria*). *Journal of Comparative and Physiological Psychology,* 1973, *83,* 221–233. (a)

Cheng, M. F. Effects of estrogen on behavior of ovariectomized ring doves. *Journal of Comparative and Physiological Psychology,* 1973, *83,* 234–239. (b)

Cheng, M. F. Interaction of lighting and other environmental variables on activity of hypothalamo-hypophyseal-gonadal system. *Nature,* 1976, *263,* 138–149.

Cheng, M. F. Progress and prospect in ring dove research: A personal view. In J.S. Rosenblatt, R. A. Hinde, E. Shaw, & C. Beer (Eds.), *Advances in the study of behavior* (Vol. 9). New York: Academic Press, 1979, pp. 97–129.

Cheng, M. F., & Follett, B. Plasma luteinizing hormone during the breeding cycle of the female ring dove. *Hormones and Behavior,* 1976, *7,* 199–205.

Cheng, M. F., & Silver, R. Estrogen-progesterone regulation of nest building and incubation behavior in ovariectomized ring doves (*Streptopelia risoria*). *Journal of Comparative and Physiological Psychology,* 1975, *88,* 256–263.

Collias, N. E. The development of social behavior in birds. *Auk,* 1952, *69,* 127–159.

Cox, C., & Silver, R. The feral ring dove in Florida. *15th International Ethological Conference,* Bielefeld, West Germany (abstract), 1977.

Cox, C., Andrews, H., Balsam, P., & Silver, R. *Behavioral ecology of doves in northern Cameroon.* Manuscript submitted for publication, 1983.

Craig, W. The voices of pigeons regarded as a means of social control. *American Journal of Sociology,* 1908, *14,* 86–100.

Craig, W. The expression of emotion in the pigeons: I. The blond ring dove. *Journal of Comparative Neurology and Psychology,* 1909, *19,* 29–82.

Erickson, C. J. Induction of ovarian activity in female ring doves by androgen treatment of castrated males. *Journal of Comparative and Physiological Psychology,* 1970, *71,* 210–215.

Erickson, C. J., & Martinez-Vargas, M. C. The hormonal basis of co-operative nest building. In P. Caryl, P. Wright, & D. Vowles (Eds.), *Neural and endocrine aspects of behaviour in birds.* Amsterdam: Elsevier Press, 1975.

Farner, D. S., & Follett, B. K. Reproductive periodicity in birds. In E. J. W. Barrington (Ed.), *Hormones and evolution.* New York: Academic Press, 1979, pp. 827–872.

Feder, H. H., Storey, A., Goodwin, D., Reboulleau, C., & Silver, R. Testosterone and "5-α-dihydro-testosterone" levels in peripheral plasma of male and female ring doves (*Streptopelia risoria*) during the reproductive cycle. *Biology of Reproduction,* 1977, *16,* 666–677.

Galef, B. G., Jr. Mechanisms for the social transmission of food preferences from adult to weanling rats. In L. M. Barker, M. Best, & M. Domjan (Eds.), *Learning mechanisms in food selection.* Waco, Texas: Baylor University Press, 1977, pp. 123–148.

Gaunt, S. Thermoregulation in doves (Columbidae): A novel esophageal heat exchanger. *Science,* 1980, *210,* 445–447.

Gibbon, J. G., & Balsam, P. D. The spread of association in time. In C. M. Locurto, H. S. Terrace, & J. G. Gibbon (Eds.), *Autoshaping and conditioning theory.* New York: Academic Press, 1981.

Goldsmith, A. R., & Silver, R. Unpublished research, 1982.

Goldsmith, A. R., Edwards, C., Koprucu, M., & Silver, R. Concentrations of prolactin and luteinizing hormone in plasma of doves in relation to incubation and development of the crop gland. *Journal of Endocrinology,* 1981, *90,* 437–443.

Goodwin, D. Pigeons and doves of the world (1st ed.). London: British Museum (Natural History), 1967.

Grice, H. P. Utterer's meaning and intentions. *Philosophical Review,* 1969, *78,* 147–177.

Halliday, T. *Vanishing birds.* New York: Holt, Rinehart & Winston, 1978.

Hansen, E. W. Squab-induced crop growth in ring dove foster parents. *Journal of Comparative and Physiological Psychology,* 1966, *62,* 120–122.

Hinde, R. A., & Spencer-Booth, Y. The study of mother-infant interactions in captive group-living rhesus monkeys. *Proceedings of the Royal Society of London (Series B),* 1968, *169,* 177–201.

Hock, R. J. The influence of the nest site on incubation in mourning and ringed turtle doves. *Living Bird,* 1963, *2,* 41–46.

Hofer, M. A. Hidden regulatory processes in early social relationships. In P. P. G. Bateson & P. H. Klopfer (Eds.), *Perspectives in ethology* (Vol. 3). New York: Plenum Press, 1978, pp. 135–163.

Hoffmann, K. Zum Tagesrythmus der Brutablosung beim Kaptaubchen (*Oena capensis L.*) und bei anderen Tauben. *Journal of Ornithology,* 1969, *110,* 448–464.

Howe, H. F. Evolutionary aspects of parental care in the common grackle, *Quiscalus quiscula L. Evolution,* 1979, *33,* 41–51.

Hutchison, J. B. Hypothalamic mechanisms of sexual behavior with special reference to birds. In J. S. Rosenblatt, R. A. Hinde, E. Shaw, & C. Beer (Eds.), *Advances in the study of behavior.* New York, London: Academic Press, 1976.

Kleiman, D. G., & Malcolm, J. R. The evolution of male parental investment in mammals. In D. J. Gubernick & P. H. Klopfer (Eds.), *Parental care in mammals.* New York: Plenum Press, 1981, pp. 347–388.

Korenbrot, C. C., Schomberg, S. W., & Erickson, C. J. Radioimmunoassay of plasma estradiol during the breeding cycle of ring doves (*Streptopelia risoria*). *Endocrinology,* 1974, *94,* 1126–1232.

Lack, D. *Ecological adaptations for breeding in birds.* London: Methuen, 1968.

Lehrman, D. S. Effects of female sex hormones on incubation behavior in the ring dove (*Streptopelia risoria*). *Journal of Comparative and Physiological Psychology.* 1958, *51,* 142–145.

Lehrman, D. S. Hormonal response to external stimuli in birds. *Ibis,* 1959, *101,* 478–496.

Lehrman, D. S. Hormonal regulation of parental behavior in birds and infra-human mammals. In W. C. Young (Ed.), *Sex and internal secretions* (Vol. 2). Baltimore: Williams & Wilkins, 1961, pp. 1268–1382.

Lehrman, D. S. Interaction between internal and external environments in the regulation of the reproductive cycle of the ring dove. In F. A. Beach (Ed.), *Sex and behavior.* New York: Wiley, 1965, pp. 355–380.

Lehrman, D. S., Brody, P., & Wortis, R. P. The presence of the mate and of nesting material as stimuli for the development of incubation behavior and for gonadotropin secretion in the ring dove (*Streptopelia risoria*). *Endocrinology,* 1961, *68,* 507–516.

Lehrman, D. S., Wortis, R. P., & Brody, P. Gonadotropin secretion in response to external stimuli of varying duration in the ring dove (*Streptopelia risoria*). *Proceedings of the Society of Experimental Biology,* 1961, *95,* 373–375.

Lorenz, K. Über die Bildung des Instinktbegriffes. *Die Naturwissenschaften,* 1937, *25,* 289–300, 307–318, 325–331. (Translated in K. Lorenz, *Studies in animal and human behavior,* Vol. 1. Cambridge: Harvard University Press, 1970.)

Lumpkin, S., Kessel, K., Zenone, P. G., & Erickson, C. J. Proximity between the sexes in ring doves: Social bonds or surveillance? *Animal Behaviour,* 1982, *30,* 506–513.

Martinez-Vargas, M. C., & Erickson, C. J. Some social and hormonal determinants of nest building behaviour in the ring dove (*Streptopelia risoria*). *Behaviour*, 1973, *45*, 12–37.

McFarland, D. J. Decision making in animals. *Nature*, 1977, *269*, 15–21.

Miller, W. J., & Miller, L. S. Synopsis of behaviour traits of the ring dove. *Animal Behavior*, 1958, *6*, 3–8.

Moore, C. L. The transition from sitting on eggs to sitting on young in ring doves, *Streptopelia risoria:* Squab-egg preferences during the normal cycle. *Animal Behavior*, 1976, *24*, 36–45.

Murton, R. K., & Westwood, N. J. Integration of gonadotropin and steroid secretion, spermatogenesis and behaviour in the reproductive cycle of male pigeon species. In P. Wright, P. G. Caryl, & D. M. Vowles (Eds.), *Neural and endocrine aspects of behaviour in birds*. Amsterdam: Elsevier, 1975, pp. 51–89.

Neff, J. A., & Niedrach, R. J. Nesting of the band-tailed pigeon in Colorado. *Condor*, 1946, *48*, 72–72.

Nice, M. M., Notes on two nests of the Easter Morning Dove. *Auk*, 1938, *55*, 95–97.

O'Connell, M. E., Reboulleau, C., Feder, H. H., & Silver, R. Social interactions and androgen levels in birds: I. Female characteristics associated with increased plasma androgen levels in the male ring dove (*Streptopelia risoria*). *General and Comparative Endocrinology*, 1981, *44*, 454–463.

O'Connell, M. E., Silver, R., Feder, H. H., & Reboulleau, C. Social interactions and androgen levels in birds: II. Social factors associated with a decline in plasma androgen levels in male ring doves (*Streptopelia risoria*). *General and Comparative Endocrinology*, 1981, *44*, 464–469.

Patel, M. D. The physiology of the formation of "pigeon's milk." *Physiological Zoology*, 1936, *9*, 129–152.

Regal, P. J., & Connolly, M. S. Social influences on biological rhythms. *Behaviour*, 1980, *72*, 171–197.

Rescorla, R. A., & Wagner, A. R. A theory of Pavlovian conditioning: Variations in the effectiveness of reinforcement and nonreinforcement. In A. H. Black & W. F. Procasy (Eds.), *Classical conditoning, Vol. 2: Current theory and research*. New York: Appleton-Century-Crofts, 1972, pp. 64–99.

Rosenblatt, J. S. The basis of synchrony in the behavioral interaction between the mother and her offspring in the laboratory rat. In B. M. Foss (Ed.), *Determinants of infant behaviour* (Vol. 3). London: Methuen, 1965, pp. 3–45.

Rosenblatt, J. S., & Siegel, H. I. Factors governing the onset and maintenance of maternal behavior among nonprimate mammals: The role of hormonal and nonhormonal factors. In D. J. Gubernick & P. H. Klopfer (Eds.), *Parental care in mammals*. New York: Plenum Press, 1981.

Rusak, B. Vertebrate behavioral rhythms. In J. Aschoff (Ed.), *Handbook of behavioral neurobiology, Vol. 4: Biological rhythms*. New York: Plenum Press, 1981, pp. 183–213.

Selye, H. On the nervous control of lactation. *American Journal of Physiology*, 1934, *107*, 535–538.

Silver, R. The parental behavior of ring doves. *American Scientist*, 1978, *66*, 209–215.

Silver, R., & Barbiere, C. Display of courtship and incubation behavior during the reproductive cycle of the male ring dove (*Streptopelia risoria*). *Hormones and Behavior*, 1977, *8*, 8–21.

Silver, R., & Buntin, J. Reproductive cycle of the male ring dove: I. Role of adrenal hormones in incubation behavior. *Journal of Comparative and Physiological Psychology*, 1973, *84*, 453–463.

Silver, R., & Feder, H. H. Role of gonadal hormones in incubation behavior of male ring doves (*Streptopelia risoria*). *Journal of Comparative and Physiological Psychology*, 1973, *84*, 464–471.

Silver, R., & Gibson, M. J. Termination of incubation in doves: Influence of egg fertility and absence of mate. *Hormones and Behavior*, 1980, *14*, 93–106.

Silver, R., & Nelson, S. Social factors influence circadian cycles in parental behavior of doves. *Physiology and Behavior*, in press.

Silver, R., Feder, H. H., & Lehrman, D. S., Situational and hormonal determinants of courtship, aggressive and incubation behavior in male ring doves (*Streptopelia risoria*). *Hormones and Behavior*, 1973, *4*, 163–172.

Silver, R., Reboulleau, C., Lehrman, D. S., & Feder, H. H., Radioimmunoassay of plasma progesterone during the reproductive cycle of male and female ring doves (*Streptopelia risoria*). *Endocrinology*, 1974, *94*, 1547–1554.

Silver, R., Goldsmith, A. R., & Follett, B. K., Plasma luteinizing hormone in male ring doves during the breeding cycle. *General and Comparative Endocrinology*, 1980, *42*, 19–24.

Skutch, A. F., The incubation patterns of birds. *Ibis*, 1975, *99*, 69–93.

Skutch, A. F. *Parent birds and their young*. Austin and London: University of Texas Press, 1976.

Stern, J. M., & Lehrman, D. S. Role of testosterone in progesterone-induced incubation behavior in castrated male ring doves (*Streptopelia ristoria*). *Journal of Endocrinology*, 1969, *44*, 13–22.

Tinbergen, N. On aims and methods in ethology. *Zeitschrift für Tierpsychologie*, 1963, *20*, 410–433.

Trivers, R. L. Parental investment and sexual selection. In Barnard Campbell (Ed.), *Sexual selection and the descent of man, 1871–1971*. Chicago: Aldine, 1972.

Vaurie, C. Systematic notes on palearctic birds, No. 49 Columbidae: The genus *Streptopelia*. *American Museum Novitates*, 1966, *29*, 1–25.

Vowles, D. M., & Harwood, D. The effect of exogenous hormones on agressive and defensive behaviour in the ring dove (*Streptopelia risoria*). *Journal of Endocrinology*, 1966, *36*, 35–51.

Vowles, D. M., & Prewitt, E. Stimulus and response specificity in the habituation of anti-predatory behaviour in the ring dove (*Streptopelia risoria*). *Animal Behavior*, 1971, *19*, 80–86.

Wallman, J., Grabon, M. B., & Silver, R. What determines the pattern of sharing of incubation and brooding in ring doves? *Journal of Comparative and Physiological Psychology*, 1979, *93*, 481–492.

Weatherhead, P. J. Do savannah sparrows commit the concorde fallacy? *Behavioral Ecology and Sociobiology*, 1979, *5*, 373–381.

White, F. N., & Kinney, J. L. Avian Incubation. *Science* 186, 107–115.

Whitman, C. O. *The behavior of pigeons*. (Posthumous work edited by H. A. Carr.) Washington: Carneigie Institute Publ. No. 257, 1919.

Wiesner, B. P., & Sheard, N. M. *Maternal behaviour in the rat*. Edinburgh: Oliver & Boyd, 1933.

Wingfield, J. L. Fine temporal adjustment of reproductive functions. In A. Epple and M. Stetson (Eds.), *Avian endocrinology*. New York: Academic Press, 1980, pp. 367–389.

Wortis, R. P. The transition from dependent to independent feeding in the young ring dove. *Animal Behavior Monographs*, 1969, *2*, Part 1, 3–54.

CHAPTER 8

Assessing Caregiver Sensitivity to Infants

Toward a Multidimensional Approach

ALAN R. WIESENFELD and CAROL ZANDER MALATESTA

Over the past 15 years, there has been a proliferation of research on parent–infant attachment. This work has generated a lively exchange of ideas among researchers of various theoretical persuasions (cf. Rajecki, Lamb, & Obmascher, 1978; Lamb & Easterbrooks, 1981). We are now faced with the challenging task of evaluating and integrating this field. In this chapter, we discuss parental sensitivity to infant cues in an expanded context of caregiver sensitivity and development. We also trace the development and application of a psychophysiological paradigm for the study of parental responsiveness to infants and present recent research in this area from our own laboratory. We then explore some of the methodological issues in the study of parental sensitivity.

Background

The Concept of Sensitivity

Caregiver sensitivity has been hypothesized as being a prerequisite for a child's healthy social and emotional development. Lamb and Easterbrooks (1981) have defined sensitivity as "an adult's tendency to provide contingent, appropriate, and consistent responses to an infant's signals or needs" (p. 127).

ALAN R. WIESENFELD • Department of Psychology, Livingston College, Rutgers University, New Brunswick, New Jersey 08903.   *CAROL ZANDER MALATESTA* • The Graduate Faculty, New School for Social Research, New York, New York 10011.

In recent years, there has been increasing interest in the variables that affect parental responsivity to infants. This interest can be traced back to the original work of Bowlby and Ainsworth on mother–infant attachment and the quality of caregiving (Ainsworth, 1964, 1967; Bowlby, 1958, 1969). To summarize briefly, observations of hospitalized children in the United States and home-reared infants in Uganda led to the formulation of hypotheses on the relationship between caregiving practices and the development of infant attachment. These ideas were tested more formally in a Baltimore sample of mothers and infants (Ainsworth & Bell, 1969; Ainsworth, Bell, & Stayton, 1972; Ainsworth & Wittig, 1969). Twenty-six mother–infant pairs were observed during feeding sessions in the home during the first three months of life. The mother's sensitivity to her infant's cues was assessed. Maternal sensitivity was evaluated by coding and scoring such variables as the mother's attention to the infant, her timing of responses to the infant's signals, the pacing of feeding, and the degree of *en face* orientation. When 23 of these same infants were 12 months old they were observed in a laboratory setting, and their attachment behavior toward the mother was assessed. Differences in quality of attachment were found to correlate with variations in maternal sensitivity. Infants who were "ambivalent" or "avoidant" on reunion following a separation tended to have mothers who had received low sensitivity ratings, while more "securely attached" infants had mothers who had received higher sensitivity ratings. Using the classification scheme developed by Ainsworth on the quality of infant attachment, subsequent investigators have found that differences in attachment style (secure, ambivalent, or avoidant), as assessed in the Ainsworth–Wittig Strange Situation paradigm, are correlated with later patterns of development. For example, these styles of attachment correlate with the child's behavior with strangers, with behavioral interactions with mothers in problem-solving situations, and in relations with other children in a nursery setting (Sroufe & Waters, 1977; Ainsworth, Blehar, Waters, & Wall, 1978).

Over the years, the concept of maternal sensitivity has become theoretically important in the field of child development. The Strange Situation paradigm for assessing infant–mother attachment has been equally influential. However, it is important to remember that the original theoretical link between attachment and maternal sensitivity was based on a study of only 23 mother–infant pairs. In addition, there are problems in inferring a direct casual link between maternal behavior and attachment patterns:

> Theoretical considerations alone . . . make it clear that the different patterns of behavior in the strange situation cannot be attributed simply to variations in maternal sensitivity, as some have argued, and an extensive investigation of the antecedents of the behavior patterns is clearly needed. (Lamb, 1979, p. 69)

In the original Ugandan study, Ainsworth herself acknowledged that both infant constitutional factors and familial situational factors could affect the mother–infant relationship. However, she has ignored these factors in her more recent work. Ainsworth has also stressed that "sensitivity" is a complex, multidetermined psychological factor, a point to which we will return later.

Bowlby and Ainsworth do not stand alone in their emphasis on linkages between maternal responsivity to infant signals and developmental outcome. Other workers have also proposed that the child's social and emotional development is based on the extent of maternal responsivity, contingency, and reciprocity (Sroufe, 1979; Brazelton, Tronick, Adamson, Als, & Wise, 1975; Lewis & Rosenblum, 1974).

With this as background, let us take a look at another way in which investigators have sought to construe and measure sensitivity.

The Psychophysiological Assessment of Responsivity to Infant Signals

The psychophysiological approach to assessing parental responsivity originated with the work of Lewis Leavitt, Wilberta Donovan, and J. D. Balling at the University of Wisconsin (Leavitt & Donovan, 1975; Donovan, Leavitt, & Balling, 1978). Their experimental paradigm consisted of having mothers view previously prepared videotapes of smiling and crying infants while physiological measures such as heart rate and skin conductance response were recorded concurrently.

The above paradigm has been used subsequently in a number of related investigations and has provided interesting findings about parental responses to their young. Individual differences in adult responsivity to infants have now been demonstrated repeatedly. However, these variations have not yet been linked systematically to different developmental outcomes. Nor has there emerged a theoretical framework for integrating this work.

In the original Donovan, Leavitt, and Balling study, the physiological responses evoked by different infant expressions were viewed within an orienting and defensive-response framework. Evoked deceleratory cardiac changes were interpreted as reflecting parental *receptivity* to the signal (i.e., an orienting response), and acceleratory changes as indicating *rejection* of the signal (i.e., a defensive response). This investigation demonstrated that adults had differing physiological response patterns to videotapes of infant affect, which depended on the emotional valence of the child's signal. It was reported that infant cry signals consistently elicited cardiac accelerations in mothers. The smile, on the other hand, evoked little measurable autonomic change when viewed after a crying episode, but it resulted in a cardiac response when seen *before* a crying stimulus. It was argued by Donovan *et al.* that the order effect in their data actually reflected the existence of reduced parental receptivity to the positive signal for interaction (i.e., the smile) because of the immediately preceding aversive experience with the cry signal. Although the concept of reduced versus enhanced receptivity resulting from one's immediate experience with infants has not been pursued as actively in later work, it is clear that Leavitt and Donovan's laboratory work put the physiological approach to assessing caregiver receptivity to infants "on the map." They were the first investigators to design and establish a workable and controlled experimental paradigm for studying individual differences in parental responsivity, and they promoted the orienting–defensive-response framework as a means of interpreting elicited physiological changes as reflections of individual variations in sensitivity. In later studies, response patterns to infant signals were related to concurrent behavioral differences observed during feeding. Donovan and colleagues' general assumption has been that the patterns of evoked parental physiological response observed in the laboratory are analogue measures of *precursors to caregiving response behaviors* in parents, which are appropriate to the affective infant signals employed as stimuli. The idea that physiological responses observed in the laboratory are related to actual caregiving patterns outside the laboratory finds repeated expression in several later studies by other investigators.

This notion of a physiological-behavioral connection lends interpretive meaning to physiological results (obtained within the laboratory analogue of a caregiving situation), despite very limited data linking physiological and behavioral responsivity. Two follow-up studies, using a similar paradigm, were published by Ann Frodi and Michael Lamb (Frodi, Lamb, Leavitt, & Donovan, 1978; Frodi & Lamb, 1980). These studies also yielded some provocative findings on variations in parental responsivity. Adult responsivity and receptivity to infants varied according to differing characteristics of the signaling child (e.g., the child's status as premature or full term) and to parental characteristics as well, such as status as an identified child abuser. Recently, Donovan (1981) has extended this physiological paradigm to demonstrate that experiential factors, such as an experimentally induced feeling of helplessness, may modify subsequent maternal receptivity and efficacy in terminating the crying of infants in a simulated caregiving situation.

Our own involvement in the area of parental responsivity is traceable to a first study conducted by the senior author (Wiesenfeld & Klorman, 1978) that was designed to assess how the mother's *relatedness* to the signaling infant influenced her pattern of physiological and subjective emotional responses. While Donovan, Leavitt, and Balling's research appeared to comprise a successful working measure of parental responsivity to infants, these researchers chose not to use the subjects' own children as stimuli. Instead, the emotional displays of *unfamiliar* infants of the same age as the mother's own child served as the stimuli. It is worth noting that a similar strategy has been employed consistently in this area of research. In contrast, the direction of our own work has been to examine the responsiveness of parents to their own infants. Attachment implies a very specific kind of parent–child bond (Ainsworth, 1972) and should be preceded by an equally specific pattern of receptivity and response from the primary caregiver. Thus, a more appropriate responsivity paradigm should involve signals from the caregiver's own child, and this has been the course that we have pursued.

The first study (Wiesenfeld & Klorman, 1978) used videotaped smiling and crying episodes, depicting the subject's *own* child, as well as another 5-month-old infant unfamiliar to the subject. Two landscape videotapes served as neutral control stimuli: the taped episodes were briefer than those employed by Donovan *et al.,* so that monitoring of phasic physiological changes and habituation of responses over the course of repeated trials was possible. The stimulus tapes were not accompanied by a sound track, as they were in the Donovan *et al.* study. In line with the original hypothesis, the results indicated that the subject's physiological and subjective reactions to the infant emotional displays differed markedly depending on her relationship to the signaling child. In reponses to her *own* child's displays, the mother's physiological pattern was characterized by cardiac accelerations and large skin conductance responses. On the other hand, responses to the two unfamiliar children's expressions were nonsignificant deceleratory cardiac trends and smaller electrodermal reactions. It was crucial methodologically to ask whether a subject's responsivity to infants in general could be considered equivalent to her responsivity to her own child. The patterns of physiological results were quite different from those reported by Donovan *et al.,* in which unfamiliar infant crying scenes had evoked acceleratory cardiac responses. In the Wiesenfeld and Klorman investigation, similarly valanced scenes elicited cardiac decelerations, and thus, the responses were not as readily interpretable as indications of specific caregiving patterns. The mother's response to her own child (heart rate acceleration) was instead interpreted as reflecting the occurrence of an *affective* response process in the mother (i.e., in this instance, excitement over viewing her child's expressions), rather than as a precursor to caregiving behaviors. The results strongly suggested that without concurrent measures of behavior, one must use caution in interpreting the meaning of physiological response data in assessing individual differences in caregiver sensitivity. It appears that relatively minor modifications of laboratory test procedures, such as changing stimulus duration and the presence of a sound track, significantly affect the response pattern to infant signals. A major inferential leap is involved in the assumption that these laboratory observations are representative of actual caregiving dispositions and behaviors *in vivo.*

Two later investigations in our laboratory (Wiesenfeld & Malatesta,

1982; Wiesenfeld, Malatesta, & DeLoach, 1981), concerning parental response to and recognition of the sounds of familiar and unfamiliar infant distress cries, also indicated that the mothers responded differentially to the distress signals of their own child (vs. those of an unfamiliar infant), and furthermore, that the mothers' physiological and emotional responsivity to their children's distress cries significantly surpassed that of the fathers. We also observed that the mothers were superior to the fathers in their ability to identify and differentiate between the cries of familiar and unfamiliar 5-month-old children, and that the fathers displayed no evidence of a specific response pattern to their own children's signals. It is quite possible that the male and female responses and differential discriminatory abilities resulted from different experiences in caregiving and only reflected a learning phenomenon. (Our records indicated that all of the mothers in the sample were the primary caregivers in their families and that all the fathers worked away from the home.) Alternatively, it is possible that the observed differences in female physiological response and discrimination accuracy represented a different symbiotic involvement, which caused a stronger identification with the child. It should also be noted that although the mothers were, as a group, more sensitive in their ability to differentiate types of cries and in recognizing their own infant's cry versus that of an unfamiliar infant, this general trend obscures great individual differences. Some individual fathers were as accurate as the most accurate of mothers.

Since we had speculated that some of the differential sensitivity displayed by mothers could be explained by different amounts of experience in direct caregiving, we set out to investigate the experience factor in child care in a study of maternal responsiveness to infant emotional signals, using the mother's *parity* status as an independent variable. Here we made the assumption that parity was a readily applied measure of caregiving experience. We were also interested in examining the possible impact that the mother's feeding status might have on maternal sensitivity to signals, since *post hoc* inspection of the cardiac curves suggested that as a group, breast-feeders responded differently from bottle-feeders. In addition, the comparative literature on animals had suggested that lactation has significant effects on maternal behavior, possibly enhancing the mother's responsivity to infant signals, especially to infant distress cries (see Wiesenfeld & Malatesta, 1982, for a discussion of this literature).

In our more recent study (Wiesenfeld, Malatesta, Whitman, Granrose, & Uili, 1983), 48 mothers and their 5-month-old infants were recruited; half of the mothers were breast-feeders, half bottle-feeders, with an equal number of primipara and multipara in both groups, and an equal balance of male and female infants. There were two visits to the laboratory. During the first visit, we videotaped the infant in order to capture smiling, crying, and neutral expressions. We then edited the tapes so that we had similar stimulus tapes of each infant's expressions to present to each subject on the following visit. When the mothers returned, they viewed these videotapes as we monitored their heart rate, skin conductance, and facial expressions. After completion of the stimulus sequence, the subject was shown each of the three scenes again and was asked to rate her own *subjective* emotional reactions on a 10-point scale while viewing the episodes. These subjective self-assessments included ratings of happiness, sadness, anxiousness, irritation, and helplessness, as well as a rating of how much the subject wanted to "go and pick up the baby." At the conclusion of the session, the mothers went home with questionnaires to fill out and return. The questionnaires asked about the reasons that the subject had chosen that particular method of feeding and her degree of current satisfaction with the method. These questions were embedded in the questionnaire with other buffer items.

We had hypothesized, on the basis of prior comparative data, that the breast-feeders and the more experienced (multiparous) mothers would show greater receptivity to their children's signals (as indicated by their greater physiological and emotional reactions) than the bottle-feeders and the less experienced primipara. Figure 1 depicts the cardiac responses of breast- and bottle-feeding subjects averaged across the three infant stimuli. At first glance, it appeared that our hypotheses were disconfirmed. We found that it was the *bottle-feeders* who evinced the greatest cardiac acceleration in response to the videotapes of their infants. They thus appeared to be *more* responsive to their infants' signals as a group, at least in the absolute magnitude of the cardiac response (see Figure 1). However, this interpretation is constrained by the observation that the nursing mothers showed a trend toward initial heart-rate deceleration, a trend that did not appear in the waveform of the bottle-feeders. In prior studies, a deceleratory phase has been considered indicative of receptivity, when interpreted within an orienting–defensive-response framework.

This conflict in interpretation of the cardiac curves illustrates an inherent problem often encountered in this investigative area, that of interpreting meaning of physiological response data. Greater absolute physiological responsivity to infant signals does not necessarily reflect the existence of an underlying disposition toward greater parental sensitivity. Our results may be a case in point. Nonetheless, we do note that there are different maternal patterns of physiological response to infants depending on their status as breast- or bottle-feeders. Fortunately, our concurrent measures of subjective response shed some light on the meaning of these differing patterns. In response to stimulus tapes of their own infants' affective signals, the *multiparous* bottle-feeders rated themselves as significantly *less* inclined to pick up their infants than either group of breast-feeding mothers, and bottle-feeding

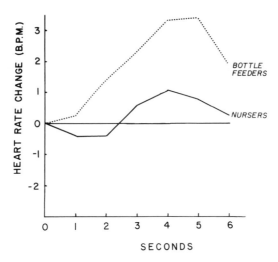

Figure 1. Breast versus bottle-feeding mothers' cardiac responses to their 5-month-olds' emotional expressions (Wiesenfeld, Malatesta, Whitman, Granrose, & Uili, 1983).

mothers in general assigned less overall developmental importance to the act of feeding their child (as measured by their responses to the questionnaire about why the mode of feeding was chosen).

The questionnaire responses revealed that the breast- and bottle-feeders held markedly different conceptions of their own specific role in providing care for the child. Bottle-feeders assigned *other* family members greater care-taking responsibility than nursing mothers. This finding suggests that the groups of mothers may have different priorities regarding their own involvement in caregiving.

The most significant finding of our research involved different physiological and subjective response patterns in breast-feeding and bottle-feeding subjects. Both groups showed accelerated heart rate response to the affective signals of their own infants, but the bottle-feeders showed a greater amplitude of cardiac response overall. The breast-feeders evidenced a slight trend toward a biphasic cardiac response pattern, with a slight initial deceleratory component. The response pattern suggested that the bottle-feeders may have been more physiologically aroused by the infant stimuli and more responsive to the affective signals. On the other hand, the extremity of their acceleratory cardiac response could indicate greater general excitability (i.e., more anxiety than the breast-feeders in the recording situation). In fact, measures of skin conductance response indicated that the bottle-feeders had higher resting electrodermal levels *before* stimulus presentation, but they showed no differential skin conductance response when the stimuli were actually presented. In terms of the reasons cited for having chosen one mode of feeding over the other, breast-feeders more commonly indicated baby-centered reasons versus mother-centered or family-centered reasons than the bottle-feeders. At present, we are still analyzing some of the data, and more definitive conclusions await completion of this analysis. However, we may begin to speculate about the meaning of certain patterns. As a first interpretation, it occurred to us that the observed responsivity differences might reflect individual personality differences that antedate a subjects's choice of feeding mode or, as suggested earlier, that these differences reflect different priorities. Another possibility, based on animal comparative literature, is that the hormones associated with breast-feeding may act to modify or inhibit the breast-feeding subjects' general arousal. Although one must be cautious in making comparisons, especially across such markedly different species, it is worth nothing that lactation has been associated with a reduced responsivity to environmental stressors in rodents (Stern & Levine, 1974; Stern, Goldman, & Levine, 1973; Thoman, Conner, & Levine, 1970). However, lactating mice, at least, remain especially responsive to the distress cries of their offspring—even more responsive than their nonlactating counterparts (Newton, Peeler, & Rawlins, 1968; Beach, 1977).

Contrary to our expectations, the present study did not disclose different maternal responses to the three types of infant affective stimuli of smiling, crying, and quiescence from the breast- and bottle-feeding mothers. This result ran contrary to our expectations, because sensitivity constructs imply an ability of the sensitive individual to discriminate nuances among emotional stimuli. The lack of a discernible "types" effect, however, does not necessarily indicate that there is no differential responsiveness to cries and smiles under routine caregiving conditions in a more naturalistic setting. With the exception of the "precry face" (Oster, 1978), there is normally an auditory component in infant distress, and there is reason to believe that the influence of the cry on the caregiver may reside largely in its acoustic properties (Murray, 1979). In an earlier report (Wiesenfeld & Malatesta, 1981), we did note differences between breast-feeders and bottle-feeders in their cardiac response to audiotapes of infant cries. In that study, breast-feeders showed greater cardiac acceleration. However, this was a *post hoc* observation and further study is required. In the present study, all infant stimulus tapes were silent, and it is perhaps not wise to compare the results across sensory modalities. We believe that it will be important to evaluate this methodological question further with a suitable factorial design.

Despite the possibility that the physiology of the lactating mother may have contributed to the variance in heart rate observed in the present study, we have recently begun to explore the additional possibility that certain enduring dispositional personality variables might be even more influential in accounting for individual variation. In the previous study, individual differences within feeding groups were noted. It is quite possible that the mother's personality makeup could comprise a common source of variance; personality factors could also account for a mother's ordering of priorities with regard to caregiving. Conceivably, such dispositional differences could substantially affect the mother's general conception of the defining properties and responsibilities of the maternal role. For example, the subject might believe that the feeding experience is a most crucial aspect of interaction and care during the early months and would therefore be motivated to attend to it closely. The existing literature on individual differences in parental sensitivity indicates that sensitivity has been conceptualized as a trait that varies from mother to mother but remains a relatively invariant attribute within individual mothers (Lamb & Easterbrooks, 1981).

Reasoning that sensitivity to an infants' emotional signals should also be related to adult receptivity to emotional experiences in general, we investigated female adults' responsivity to infants as a function of the personality trait of empathy (Wiesenfeld, Whitman, & Malatesta, in press). We hypothesized that highly empathic individuals, who are generally affectively responsive, would also be *specifically* more responsive to infant affective communication. Subsamples of adults—in this case, adult (nulliparous) women, who had been selected for their extremely high or low scores on the Mehrabian and Epstein (1972) empathy questionnaire—participated in our study (Figure 2). Their psychophysiological and emotional responses to infant affective

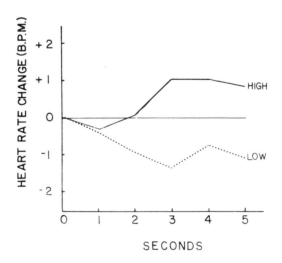

Figure 2. High versus low-empathy women's cardiac response to infant emotional expressions (Wiesenfeld, Whitman, & Malatesta, in press).

displays were recorded, as well as their attitudes toward the developmental importance of responding to infant communications. This time, our dependent measures included measures of cardiac and electrodermal response, facial expressions of emotion, and self-reported subjective emotional reactions. The infant stimuli included silent facial displays of smiles, cries, and quiescent expressions by two male and two female 5-month-old infants. The results were strongly supportive of our initial hypothesis. Although the high- and low-empathy subjects had comparable amounts of prior caregiving experience, the high-empathy women evinced significantly greater self-reported emotional reactions than their lower-empathy counterparts. They were also more responsive autonomically and reported a greater inclination to go and pick up the stimulus infant. Furthermore, the self-ratings of the high-empathy subjects indicated more acceptance of specific attitudinal items regarding the value assigned to caregiver response to infant communications, and greater rejection of the idea that caregivers could become "overinvolved" with a child. It seems that the highly empathic subjects were more likely to assign developmental importance to responding to infant signals and, in fact, did exhibit greater emotional response to the signals than did low-empathy women.

On the basis of our recent work and that of others, we conclude that the study of individual differences in parents' sensitivity toward their young can help us understand how variations in parental care quality affect early development. Responsivity to infants comprises a basic building block for the provision of adequate care and stimulating psychological environments for infants. There have been several demonstrations, from a number of laboratories, that variations in parental responsivity may be reliably measured and quantified, yet no universally accepted framework exists for the interpretation of these variables, nor do we yet understand how subtle variations in parental sensitivity affect the child's later personality development. Furthermore, we do not yet adequately understand how responsivity to infants affects, or is affected by, other skills in caregiving and by support from the family and the larger social environment. Nonetheless, on the basis of our most recent work, we propose that parental sensitivity be conceptualized as closely related to empathy, and that a subject's receptivity to infant signals varies with other caregiver characteristics such as feeding status.

Although we feel that parental sensitivity is one crucial element in the quality of early caregiving, we need to learn a great deal more about how such variations in sensitivity affect the child's psychological and social development within the broad "middle range." Investigators have tended to depend on extreme parental individual differences in their studies (e.g., normal care vs. child abuse) and on correlational findings and have underplayed the proviso originally cited by Ainsworth that differences in sensitivity toward infants may be accompanied by many other potentially important individual differences. Some significant intervening factors may be the parents' intelligence, personal maturity, empathy, and social competence, and the family's social integration. At the present time, we have extremely limited information about how parental sensitivity is regulated by other variables such as parental personality makeup and by child attributes such as temperamental variation, yet these variables may be especially important. A recent study by Crockenberg (1981) has indicated that the influence of variations in maternal responsiveness can be overridden by the amount of social support available and that relationships among individual differences and developmental outcomes may depend on the specific temperamental demands of individual infants.

By definition, sensitivity to infants is comprised of a multidimensional and complex set of skills and attributes; it includes several behavioral, physiological, cognitive-attitudinal, and dispositional components. Although there is considerable *theoretical* support for the notion that all of these components may be found to interrelate, we have very little theoretical or empirical information about the degree to which one response modality relates to another, and about which dimension is to be considered most crucial with respect to the child's later development. Investigators in this area have relied on measures of only one or two dimensions of responsivity, thereby rendering it difficult to equate the findings of studies using diverse measures of parental sensitivity. It is obvious that we will need to undertake further research that seeks to validate the reliability and the predictive, concurrent validity of the psychological *construct* of parental sensitivity. Along these same lines, we will need to undertake more longitudinal investigations so that we may learn how early influences, such as very *insensitive* parenting, is affected by other, potentially compensating factors, such as peer relationships. Another kind of useful information to be derived from such longitudinal effort concerns the question of whether parental sensitivity is an enduring quality or trait of parents, or whether its existence may depend on the specific demands of the situation observed and/or the particular developmental tasks to be found in each phase of a child's development.

Symbiosis implies mutual benefit to mother and infant. In the human infant, a gradual process of individualization occurs, involving both physiological and psychological change, and this process may be enhanced or retarded by the nature or quality of the caregiving environment. Developmental work on human infancy has focused on the benefits that the child derives from its mother's care, yet we know little about the reciprocal benefits that the mother derives from her efforts, beyond the obvious fact of reproduction. We hope that our work, focused on parents' responses to their young, may give further insight into the psychosocial benefits of parenting.

Our work suggests that affective benefits regularly accrue to mothers from the care that they provide their infants. For example, responding effectively to the crying infant not only terminates an unpleasant stimulus, but relieves the mother's empathic distress. Mothers consistently report that responding is an exciting and stimulating experience and, particularly in the instance of responding to smiling, an extremely pleasurable one. Informal accounts also suggest that mothers regularly experience pleasure in providing the routine child care during activities involving social interaction, such as feeding and changing.

At a more general motivational level, it is not unreasonable to assume that the mother experiences a greater general sense of mastery as she learns to provide better care for her child and acquires greater competence in the role of parent. In terms of the mother's own feelings of well-being as an adult, a greater personal sense of relatedness and closeness to family members and perhaps society as a whole is a beneficial by-product of parenting. This interpersonal benefit undoubtedly provides the mother with greater social support, a variable increasingly related to better psychological and physical health. Although these speculations need to be supported by continued investigation, we have been impressed by the nearly complete absence of regret reported by subjects about having become a parent.

The early symbiotic infant–mother relationship implies a sharing, and the sharing of affect (or empathy) has been considered a major component of parental sensitivity. However, as we have pointed out in this chapter, sensitive parenting requires a good deal more than the ability to share in an infant's emotional experience. As the child's psychological individuation progresses over the first two years, the mother's response to the child needs to change concurrently if she is to continue to provide sensitive care. Beyond the earliest physical needs, communicated nonverbally in infancy, the child develops new needs: for social response, for limits and the freedom to explore the environment, and for experience as an individual. Thus, sensitive parenting involves a process, and it requires that the mother's early symbiotic relationship with the child yield progressively to the child's growing individual identity and independence.

It is quite possible that this parental adaptation process is regulated, in part, by the emergence of developmental landmarks during the first 18 months (for example, changes in feeding and sleep patterns, the appearance of the social smile, weaning, stranger apprehension, and speech). These events serve as overt cues to the mother to readjust her conception of the child and its needs, and to regulate her caregiving accordingly. The mother's ability to receive and process these developmental signals is a major component of sensitivity. Nonetheless, it appears that this parental quality (i.e., adaptability) has largely been neglected as a component of parental sensitivity, because there has been a tendency to view caregiver sensitivity as a static quality that is measurable simply and at a single point in time, rather than viewing it as a process that occurs in a specific dyad over time. In addition, because this process occurs in a specific infant–mother pair, one must assume that the existence of sensitivity depends, in good part, on the "goodness of fit" of the mother's and the child's temperamental characteristics. We believe that sensitive caregiving is the ability of both the mother and the infant to "tune in" to each other and also to "remain in tune" over time.

Since sensitivity involves adaptation and change, it is unlikely that a single measure of parental sensitivity is appropriate across all phases of the child's development. Latency of parental response to the infant's distress crying may be a viable measure during the earliest symbiotic phase but may not be as valuable at a later time. The notion of "receptivity" to the child's signals, as employed in the psychophysiological studies reviewed in this chapter, is a promising conceptual scheme for studying parental sensitivity, yet methodological problems remain. In isolation, physiological measurements of receptivity tell little about other aspects of early care, such as the parent's behavioral skills and child-rearing values. We need to develop a multidimensional measurement system that assesses the multiple facets of caregiving and information about how the measures interrelate at different phases, in accordance with the differing demands placed on the parent. A large number of studies of parental sensitivity have relied on theoretical work based on Ainsworth's original 23 dyads (Ainsworth & Bell, 1969; Ainsworth *et al.*, 1972; Ainsworth & Wittig, 1969). However, the amount of empirical evidence that supports the idea that parental sensitivity is a major influence on the child's social development is limited. Little information exists on the reliability of the sensitivity ratings used by investigators, and there are virtually no cross-situational data on the concurrent validity of the construct. In sum, we need more information to validate the construct *sensitivity* before it can be measured reliably and used to predict the scope of its influence on child development.

References

Ainsworth, M. D. Patterns of attachment behavior shown by the infant in interaction with his mother. *Merrill-Palmer Quarterly*, 1964, *10*, 51–58.

Ainsworth, M. D. S. *Infancy in Uganda: Infant care and the growth of love.* Baltimore: Johns Hopkins Press, 1967.

Ainsworth, M. D. S. Attachment and dependency: A comparison. In J. L. Gewirtz (Ed.), *Attachment and dependency.* Washington, D.C.: V. H. Winston, 1972.

Ainsworth, M. D. S., & Bell, S. M. Some contemporary patterns of mother-infant interaction in the feeding situation. In A. Ambrose (Ed.), *Stimulation in early infancy.* London: Academic Press, 1969.

Ainsworth, M. D. S., & Wittig, B. A. Attachment and exploratory behavior of one-year-olds in a strange situation. In B. M. Foss (Ed.), *Determinants of infant behavior* (Vol. 4). London: Methuen, 1969.

Ainsworth, M. D. S., Bell, S. M., & Stayton, D. J. Individual differences in the development of some attachment behaviors. *Merrill-Palmer Quarterly*, 1972, *18*, 123–143.

Ainsworth, M. D., Blehar, M. C., Waters, E., & Wall, S. *Patterns of attachment*. Hillsdale, N. J.: Erlbaum Associates, 1978.

Beach, F. A. Hormonal control of sex-related behavior. In F. A. Beach (Ed.), *Human sexuality in four perspectives*. Baltimore: Johns Hopkins University Press, 1977.

Bowlby, J. The nature of the child's tie to his mother. *International Journal of Psycho-Analysis*, 1958, *39*, 350–373.

Bowlby, J. *Attachment and loss, Vol. 1: Attachment*. London: Hogarth, 1969.

Brazelton, T. B., Tronick, E., Adamson, L., Als, H., & Wise, S. Early mother-infant reciprocity. In *Parent–infant interaction*, Ciba Foundation Symposium 33. Amsterdam: A.A.P., 1975.

Crockenberg, S. B. Infant irritability, mother responsiveness, and social support influences of infant–mother attachment. *Child Development*, 1981, *52*, 857–865.

Donovan, W. L. Maternal learned helplessness and physiologic response to infant crying. *Journal of Personality and Social Psychology*, 1981, *40*, 919–926.

Donovan, W. L., Leavitt, L. A., & Balling, J. D. Maternal physiological response to infant signals *Psychophysiology*, 1978, *15*, 68–74.

Frodi, A. M., & Lamb, M. E. Child abusers responses to infant smiles and cries. *Child Development*, 1980, *51*, 238–241.

Frodi, A. M., Lamb, M. E., Leavitt, L. A., & Donovan, W. L. Fathers and mothers responses to infant smiles and cries. *Infant Behavior and Development*, 1978, *1*, 187–198.

Lamb, M. Social development in infancy: Reflections on a theme. *Human Development*, 1979, *22*, 68–72.

Lamb, M. E., & Easterbrooks, M. A. Individual differences in parental sensitivity: Origins, components, and consequences. In M. E. Lamb & S. R. Sherrod (Eds.), *Infant social cognition*. Hillside, N.J.: Erlbaum, 1981.

Leavitt, L. A., & Donovan, W. *Maternal physiological response to infant gaze*. Paper presented at a meeting of the Society for Psychophysiological Research, Toronto, October 1975.

Lewis, M., & Rosenblum, L. (Eds.). *The effect of the infant on its caregiver: The origins of behavior* (Vol. 1). New York: Wiley, 1974.

Mehrabian, A., & Epstein, N. A measure of emotional empathy *Journal of Personality*, 1972, *40*, 525–543.

Murray, A. Infant crying as an elicitor of parental behavior: An examination of two models. *Psychological Bulletin*, 1979, *86*, 191–215.

Newton, N., Peeler, D., & Rawlins, C. Effect of lactation on maternal behavior in mice with comparative data on humans. *Lying-In: Journal of Reproductive Medicine*, 1968, *1*, 257–262.

Oster, H. Facial expression and affect development. In M. Lewis & L. A. Rosenblum (Eds.), *The development of affect*. New York: Plenum Press, 1978.

Rajecki, D. W., Lamb, M. E., & Obmascher, P. Toward a general theory of infantile attachment: A comprative review of aspects of the social bond. *Behavioral and Brain Sciences*, 1978, *1*, 417–464.

Sroufe, L. A. Socioemotional development. In J. D. Osofsky (Ed.), *Handbook of infant development*. New York: Wiley, 1979.

Sroufe, L., & Waters, E. Attachment as an organizational construct. *Child Development*, 1977, *48*, 1184–1199.

Stern, J. M., & Levine, S. Psychobiological aspects of lactation in rats. In D. F. Swaab & J. P. Schade (Eds.), *Integrative hypothalamic activity: Progress in brain research* (Vol. 41). Amsterdam: Elsevier, 1974.

Stern, J. M., Goldman, L., & Levine, S. Pituitary-adrenal responsiveness during lactation in rats. *Neuroendocrinology*, 1973, *12*, 179–191.

Thoman, E. B., Conner, R. L., & Levine S. Lactation suppresses adrenal corticosteroid activity and aggressiveness in rats. *Journal of Comparative and Physiology and Psychology*, 1970, *70*, 363–369.

Wiesenfeld, A. R., & Klorman, R. The mothers' psychophysiological reactions to contrasting expressions by her own and an unfamiliar infant. *Developmental Psychology*, 1978, *14*, 294–304.

Wiesenfeld, A. R., & Malatesta, C. Z. Infant distress: Variables affecting responses of caregivers and others. In L. W. Hoffman, R. J. Gandelman, & H. R. Schiffman (Eds.), *Parenting: Its causes and consequences.* Hillsdale, N.J.: Erlbaum, 1982.

Wiesenfeld, A. R., Malatesta, C. Z., & DeLoach, L. L. Differential parental response to familiar and unfamiliar infant distress signals. *Infant Behavior and Development*, 1981, *4*, 305–320.

Wiesenfeld, A. R., Malatesta, C. Z., Whitman, P., Granrose, C. & Uili, R. *Feeding mode and responsivity to infant signals.* Unpublished manuscript, 1983.

Wiesenfeld, A. R., Whitman, P. B., & Malatesta, C. Z. Individual differences in adult women in responsivity to infants: Evidence in support of an empathy concept. *Journal of Personality and Social Psychology*, in press.

Psychoendocrine Responses of Mother and Infant Monkeys to Disturbance and Separation

CHRISTOPHER L. COE, SANDRA G. WIENER, and SEYMOUR LEVINE

In mammalian and avian species, it is essential that the young maintain at least periodic contact with their mother in order to obtain nurturance and warmth. This contact is ensured through the development of emotional dependency or attachment, as well as by the complementary distress reaction that occurs following sudden or forced separation of mother and infant. During the last several years, our laboratory has investigated this response as a way of evaluating how mother and infant primates cope with stressful situations. This research not only has generated new information on the nature of attachment processes in nonhuman primates but has also provided a unique way of determining how young organisms cope with stress. In addition to demonstrating that social relationships are important in the mediation of stress and coping, we have found that the concepts developed in the stress literature have a surprising degree of applicability to an understanding of the dynamics of mother–infant relationships.

Two of the most important factors in determining how well an organism copes with stress are the degree of *control* and *predictability* that it has in a stressful situation. Control can be broadly defined as the ability to make active responses during aversive stimulation. These responses are frequently effective

CHRISTOPHER L. COE, SANDRA G. WIENER, and SEYMOUR LEVINE • Department of Psychiatry and Behavioral Sciences, Stanford University School of Medicine, Stanford, California 94305. This research was funded by the following grants to S. Levine: MH-23645 from NIMH, HD-02881 from NICH&HD, and Research Scientist Award MH-19936 from NIMH.

in allowing the individual to avoid or escape the aversive stimulus, but they may also reduce stress simply by allowing a change from one set of stimulus conditions to another. Thus, rats that can press a lever to avoid shock, for example, show less severe physiological disturbance than do yoked controls that cannot respond, even though both groups receive the same number of shocks (Weiss, 1968). Providing information that enhances the predictability of the stressful events can also modify the aversiveness of the situation. In studies on stress, animals that receive a predictable shock typically show less stress-induced pathology than animals receiving the same amount of unpredictable shock (Gliner, 1972; Weiss, 1970). The effect of predictability can be complex, however, and it appears to be most effective when the organism can also exert control; that is, predictable aversive stimulation may be preferred over unpredictable stimuli only when accompanied by control (Weinberg & Levine, 1980).

These concepts are extremely helpful in elucidating the response of mothers and infants to separation, since this kind of disturbance represents a major loss of control. In previous research our laboratory has demonstrated that the separation of mother and infant monkeys elicits the typical array of physiological responses that occur following other physical and psychological stressors (for reviews of earlier work, see Coe & Levine, 1981; Mendoza, Coe, Smotherman, Kaplan, & Levine, 1980). These responses include marked elevations in plasma levels of adrenocorticoids (Mendoza, Smotherman, Miner, Kaplan, & Levine, 1978), as well as alterations in heart rate and body temperature regulation (Reite, Short, & Seiler, 1978; Reite, Short, Kaufman, Stynes, & Pauley, 1978). In addition to helping us to understand separation trauma, the concepts of control and predictability have been useful in explaining how an infant deals with stressful stimuli in the mother's presence. The major thesis of our chapter is that the infant, through a variety of behaviors that include auditory and motoric responses, can modulate its response to stress by achieving proximity and contact with its mother. The severe trauma induced by separation may result in large measure from a loss of this control. Moreover, early interactions between infant and mother provide opportunities for learning the contingencies and experiencing the control that may be the basis for coping patterns in adulthood.

It has been amply demonstrated that primate infants reared apart from their mothers show marked behavioral deficits in adulthood (Harlow & Harlow, 1969). A close examination of these deficits leads to the conclusion that these infants are incapable of dealing with dynamic environments and are therefore unable to cope with even normal environmental changes (Mason, 1971). Indeed, one of the most critical functions of the caregiving figure may be to provide a secure base from which to explore the environment. Harlow *et al.*'s classic studies showed that when surrogate-reared infants were placed in a novel environment, they initially clung fearfully to their surrogates. After a while, they were able to venture off and explore the environment, but when tested without their surrogates, they were entirely overwhelmed by the novel environment. Similarly, it is a common observation in developmental studies that the infant uses the mother as a secure vantage point from which to begin exploring the environment and relies heavily on her reactions to determine the potential danger of a new situation. In those species that carry their young continously after birth (including all anthropoid primates), the mother may actually be the infant's entire environment for the first several months of life. We hypothesize, therefore, that it is through initial interactions with the mother that the infant develops a behavior pattern that becomes the basis for subsequent social relations, as well as for coping with environmental perturbations. Although alterable in later life, this pattern of interaction with the environment may markedly constrain subsequent behavior and learning.

Given the importance of mother–infant interactions, it is not surprising that there are several motivational processes designed to ensure continuance of this emotional bond. Most prominent is the severe disturbance that occurs following sudden or forced separation. The distress responses of infants to involuntary separation from their mothers has been known for a long time, but the general significance of this reaction was not appreciated until Bowlby (1969) pointed out the parallels between human and animal responses. Since then, numerous studies have been conducted describing the biphasic nature of the response: a period of agitation or "protest" followed by a phase of adaptation that may include depression (Mineka & Suomi, 1978; Rosenblum & Plimpton, 1981). In addition, what was once thought to be an invariant response has now proved to be extremely susceptible to environmental influence. Of particular significance are the ways in which separation is induced (e.g., voluntary or forced—Robertson & Robertson, 1971) and the nature of the separation environment (e.g., novel or familiar, with or without social support—Rosenblum, 1971a; Weinraub & Lewis, 1977; Coe, Mendoza, Smotherman, & Levine, 1978).

Despite the plethora of studies, however, the literature on the effects of mother–infant separation is still difficult to synthesize, primarily because of the wide variety of experimental paradigms and diverse behavioral measures used by different investigators. To provide a means of systematically evaluating important issues involved in the separation response, we began a programmatic study of the behavioral and hormonal consequences of separation in mother and infant monkeys. Our primary measure of stress has been plasma levels of adrenocorticoids, since these hormones have been reliably used as an index of stress in other situations (Mason, 1968; Rose, 1980; Hennessy & Levine, 1979). This assessment of physiological activity offered us the unique opportunity to evaluate how well behavioral responses reflected the internal state. In the following pages, we describe our findings on the concomitant behavioral and hormonal responses during separation, and we show how efficacious our approach has been in evaluating the nature of the infant's response to different kinds of separation.

In earlier studies we demonstrated that the pituitary-adrenal system of mother and infant squirrel monkeys became highly activated following separation. At 30 min after the onset of separation, circulating levels of cortisol typically increased 75–150 $\mu g/100$ ml of plasma ($\mu g\%$), whether the separated member of the dyad was left in the home environment or placed in a novel cage (Coe *et al.*, 1978; Mendoza, Smotherman, Miner, Kaplan, & Levine, 1978). The occurrence of an adrenal response concurs with findings in other species (Hill, McCormack, & Mason, 1973), but the unusually large magnitude of the increases appears to be due primarily to the high level of corticosteroid secretion in the squirrel monkey. It is premature to speculate on the functional significance of the high hormone levels; suffice it to say for the present discussion that high adrenal and gonadal output is a taxonomic characteristic of many New World monkeys (Abbott & Hearn, 1978; Dixson, Martin, Bonney, & Fleming, 1980; Nagle, Denari, Riarte, Quiroga, Zárate, Germino, Merlo, & Rosner, 1980).

Response to Prolonged Separation

In order to determine a temporal pattern of the cortisol response and to establish the ultimate capactiy of the adrenal system, we decided to evaluate mother and infant squirrel monkeys during longer separations. The first experiment in this series assessed the behavioral and physiological responses of mother and infant squirrel monkeys at 1, 3, and 6 hr after separation. Five infants were reared with their mothers until 3 months of age, the point at which the infants become increasingly independent of their mothers. A blood sample was then taken under nondisturbed conditions to ascertain basal cortisol levels. Thereafter, the dyads were separated for either 1, 3, or 6 hr, with the order of the experimental conditions balanced across subjects at weekly intervals. Blood samples were always collected at 1600 hr to control for the diurnal decline in hormone levels; thus, the onset of the separation was 1500, 1300, and 1000 hr for the 1-, 3-, and 6-hr conditions, respectively. During the separation, mothers and infants were kept in adjacent small novel cages ($46 \times 46 \times 51$ cm), which permitted auditory and olfactory, but not visual, contact. Behavioral observations were collected during the 30 min preceding the termination of the separation.

As can be seen in the upper graph of Figure 1, we observed that the infants emitted distress vocalizations at the highest rate during the first hour after separation; calling declined significantly by the end of the 6-hr separation [$F(2,8) = 4.94$, $p < .05$]. The infants also showed more agitated movement during the first hour than at the end of the 6-hr separation (moving 72% of the time as compared with 48%), although the continued high activity levels in some infants prevented this difference from reaching statistical significance. In contrast to the decline in behavioral response, the plasma cortisol levels of the infants increased progressively during the separation (see lower graph of Figure 1). Both mothers and infants showed significant elevations over basal levels during all three separations [$F(3,12) = 16.84$, $p < .001$; $F(3,12) = 27.05$, $p < .001$, respectively]. However, whereas cortisol titers in the mothers peaked at 1 hr and thereafter plateaued, the infants' increased further at 6 hr.

This prolonged adrenal response led us to extend the time evaluation in another experiment on hormonal and behavioral responses during the first 24

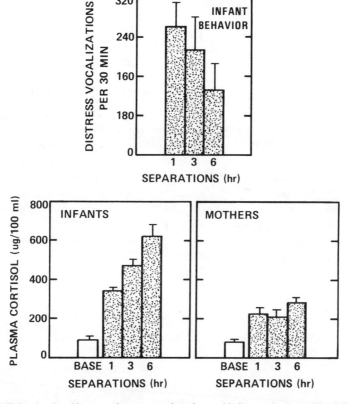

Figure 1. Behavioral and hormonal responses of mother and infant squirrel monkeys following 1-, 3-, 6-hr separations in adjacent cages. Infant distress vocalizations ($\overline{X} \pm$ SE) during the 30 min prior to the end of separation are portrayed in the upper graph.

hr after separation. We also examined the effect of two different separation environments: (1) *adjacent separation*—as before, the separated mother and infant were placed in adjacent cages with visual access blocked by an opaque barrier, and (2) *total separation*—the separated infant was placed in a sound-attenuated room in another building to prevent any dyadic communication. Because of the longer time of separation, the infants were reared undisturbed with their mothers until 4 months of age before manipulations commenced. Data were collected from the eight dyads under the following four separation conditions: (1) 6 hr adjacent separation; (2) 24 hr adjacent separation; (3) 6 hr total separation; and (4) 24 hr total separation. Separations occurred at weekly intervals in a counterbalanced design across subjects. Blood samples were also collected to ascertain basal cortisol levels at this age. As in the previous experiment, all separations were designed to end at 1600 hr to minimize the effect of diurnal hormone variation. Behavioral observations were recorded during the 30 min prior to the end of the separation, after which blood samples were taken from both mother and infant.

The hormonal findings from this experiment are portrayed in the lower graph of Figure 2. Cortisol levels continued to be significantly elevated over basal values at 24 hr in both mothers [$F(4,28) = 8.59$, $p < .01$] and infants [$F(4,28) = 22.31$, $p < .001$]. Particularly striking was the infants' adrenal response after 24 hr of total separation: plasma cortisol levels averaged 981 μg%, significantly above that in all other conditions ($p < .05$). These heightened levels were in marked contrast to those in the adjacent separation condition, which did not evoke further increases between 6 and 24 hr. The influence of the environment on the response to separation was also evident in some of the behavioral measures. Infants emitted significantly more distress vocalizations during both 6 and 24 hr of the adjacent separation [$F(1,7) = 16.54$, $p < .01$]. Similarly, the mothers showed more signs of behavioral disturbance when the infant was proximal, and they engaged in significantly higher levels of agitated movement after 6 hr of adjacent separation than after 6 hr of total separation [$F(1,7) = 5.80$, $p < .05$]. It should be mentioned, however, that behavioral observations of the mothers were of limited value in this experimental paradigm when the mother was housed alone. Given the limited behavioral options available, the mothers engaged in only four types of disturbance behavior, often in an idiosyncratic manner: (1) pacing; (2) sleeping excessively; (3) agitated eating or drinking; and (4) periodically vocalizing in response to the distress calls of their infants. Thus, the assessment of plasma cortisol levels has been particularly useful in the evaluation of the degree of maternal distress in this situation, which does not facilitate the expression of more sophisticated seeking or compensatory behaviors that have been observed in other settings (Rosenblum & Youngstein, 1974; Rosenblum & Plimpton, 1981).

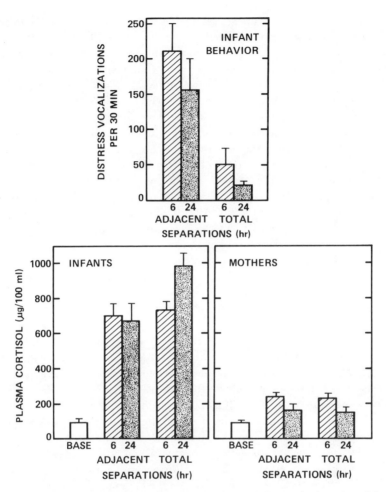

Figure 2. Behavioral and hormonal responses of mother and infant squirrel monkeys following 6- or 24-hr separations in either adjacent or totally isolated cages. Infant distress vocalizations ($\overline{X}$ ± SE) during the 30 min prior to the end of separation are portrayed in the upper graph.

Modulation of the Separation Response by Environment Familiarity

The strong influence of environmental factors on the separation response, which was found in the previous experiment, has also been reported in a number of studies of children (for review, see Weinraub & Lewis, 1977). The disturbance of separation appears to be reduced in the home environment and, conversely, is accentuated in unfamiliar places and when strangers are present (Kagan, 1974; Sroufe, Waters, & Matas, 1974). In fact, some theorists have suggested that the separation response is due primarily to the fear evoked by the manner of separation, rather than to the actual breaking of contact between mother and infant (Robertson & Robertson, 1971). One critical variable in separation studies on two species of nonhuman primates has been the presence of familiar, supportive individuals (bonnet macaques—Rosenblum & Kaufman, 1968; langurs—Dolhinow, 1980). While the mother's presence in an adjacent cage was highly stressful for the separated infant in the previous experiment, possibly because she was inaccessible, we have found familiarity with the separation environment is indeed an important factor in modulating the response of both mothers and infants.

In our early work on the possible benefits of the familiar environment, we looked at the effect of providing a caregiving adult female during the separation (Coe *et al.*, 1978). Four mother–infant pairs were housed in a small social group with a pregnant female to serve as a potential "aunt." The separation conditions consisted either of removing the mother for 30 min and allowing the separated infant to be aunted or of removing the infant alone to a novel cage. As Rosenblum (1971a) had reported previously, pregnant females are very apt to care for distressed infants, and the maintenance of contact with the aunt did ameliorate the overt behavioral signs of disturbance, such as distress calling. Assessment of plasma cortisol levels after both types of separation, however, revealed that the infants underwent equivalent activation of the pituitary-adrenal system in each condition. Thus, it appeared that the external appearance of behavioral quiescence was misleading, and we found the same results in a folllow-up study on the putative benefits of aunting.

Given the importance of this issue, we recently conducted another study to examine more systematically the effects of the familiar social environment on the separation response. We felt that the 30-min time point we had used previously might be insufficient for distinguishing the possible long-term benefits of social support. Indeed, our feelings were justified, since we found clear effects of the familiar environment on the behavioral and physiological responses when we extended our evaluations to 4-hr separations. In this study, 10 infants were subjected to 1-, 2-, or 4-hr separations in either their home environment or a novel, isolated cage. The home environment consisted of 1–3 mother–infant dyads with 2–4 other adult females present. The social membership of these groups was constant from the infants' birth, and each of the five social groups lived permanently in their own cage (1.6 × 1.8 × 1.8 m). When each infant reached 3 months of age, it was subjected to six separations at 10-day intervals. In three conditions, the mother was removed and the infant was left in the home environment for either 1, 2, or 4 hr; in the other three conditions, the infant was removed and isolated for either 1, 2, or 4 hrs. The order of the conditions was counterbalanced across subjects, with all separations terminating at 1200 hr. Infants were observed through one-way glass for the last 30 min of each separation, and a blood sample was collected from both mother and infant for subsequent analysis of plasma cortisol. We obtained an additional sample from both dyad members under nondisturbed conditions to determine basal cortisol levels.

In order to fully explore the potential effect of aunting, we also took advantage of a unique opportunity to examine the differential influence of prior experiences with aunting. Squirrel monkey populations have tended to speciate across their large range in South America (Napier & Napier, 1967), and some varieties show clear behavioral differences (e.g., Mendoza, Lowe, & Levine, 1978). One difference is the greater propensity of Peruvian squirrel monkeys to show aunting behavior when compared with Bolivian squirrel monkeys, a difference that may be due in part to the lower locomotor activity of Bolivian neonates (Kaplan, 1979). Thus, in our current experiment on aunting, we used six Peruvian infants from three social groups and four Bolivian infants from two social groups to assess the possible effects of different aunting propensities.

Concurring with our casual observations, the records collected on the normative behavior of these groups indicated that the Peruvian infants moved off their mothers more rapidly than did the Bolivian infants. The Peruvian infants spent significantly less time in the dorsal carry positon, especially between 7 and 11 weeks of age $[F(5,40) = 2.63, p < .05]$. In turn, the Peruvian infants spent significantly more time in contact with the nonmaternal females in the cage across their first three months of life $[F(1,8) = 7.29, p < .05]$. However, this circumstance proved to have little effect on the response to separation, because both types of infants showed a similar behavioral and hormonal reaction to the two kinds of separation (Figure 3). All 10 infants always showed significant elevations over basal levels during the separations $[F(6,48) = 45.65, p < .001]$, although the length and type of separation significantly influenced the magnitude of the adrenal response. Cortisol levels rose progressively with time during both types of separation $[F(2,16) = 72.40, p < .001]$, and the cortisol levels following infant removal were always significantly higher than after separation in the home cage $[F(1,8) = 35.48, p < .001]$. For both Peruvian and Bolivian infants, 4 hr of total separation evoked the greatest adrenal reponse, although the cortisol levels of the Bolivian infants that averaged 1029 μg% were significantly above the values obtained in all other conditions.[1]

Our assessment of the infants' plasma cortisol levels during separations longer than 30 min indicated that the home environment was clearly effective

---

[1] The issue of subspecies differences goes beyond the scope of the present paper, but the difference in cortisol output of Peruvian and Bolivian infants may reflect the greater adrenal capacity of Bolivian squirrel monkeys observed in adulthood.

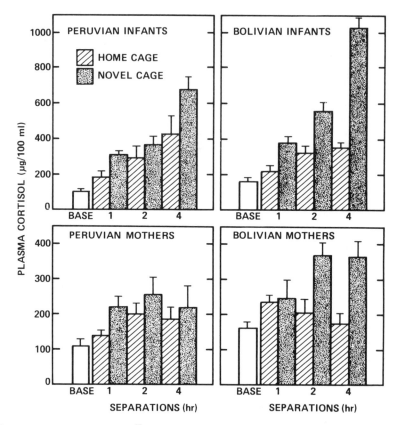

Figure 3. Plasma cortisol levels ($\overline{X} \pm SE$) following 1-, 2-, or 4-hr separations in home or totally isolated cages. Responses of squirrel monkeys of the Peruvian and Bolivian varieties are illustrated.

in reducing the aversiveness of separation. In keeping with the hormonal data, observations of the infants' behavior also suggested that they were less distressed in the home environment. Distress vocalizations were emitted during only 20% of the 30-sec intervals as compared with 58% in the novel environment. This variation in distress calling is actually much greater than the percentage values indicate, because the infants in the novel environment called at a more rapid rate, averaging 116 calls per 30 min. Moreover, when isolated in the novel environment, they exhibited the agitated and stereotyped movement patterns much more frequently than when left in the home cage. The reduced disturbance in the home cage may have been attributable to the time spent in contact with other adult females, which averaged 20% of the observation. Of interest in this regard was our finding that Bolivian females spent an equivalent amount of time in caregiving behavior directed toward the separated infants. Thus, despite a subspecies difference in the propensity to aunt under nondisturbed conditions, both Peruvian and Bolivian females engage in equal amounts of compensatory behavior toward a distressed infant.

The effect of the home environment was not only apparent for the separated infants. Assessment of the mothers' plasma cortisol levels following the two types of separation, either in the home cage or following removal to an unfamiliar cage, indicated that their degree of adrenocortical activation was also affected by environmental factors (Figure 3). All experimental conditions resulted in significant cortisol elevations over basal levels [$F(6,48) = 6.98, p < .001$], but the increments were significantly greater when the mothers were removed alone from the social group [$F(1,8) = 11.19, p < .01$]. This reduction of stress in the home environment has now proved to be an important factor in several other stress studies conducted on adults in different situations. For example, when the adrenocortical responses to fear-eliciting stimuli, such as a snake, are evaluated in the home cage, the stress responses may be entirely buffered as compared to striking elevations when tested alone (Vogt, Coe, & Levine, 1981). Conversely, we have found that testing of subjects in an unfamiliar environment may compound the trauma of aversive stimuli, such as a snake, and the effect of novelty may entirely overwhelm the salience of the variable that we, the investigators, seek to evaluate.

This issue had particularly important consequences in several studies that our laboratory conducted in collaboration with Dr. Joel Kaplan (SRI International) comparing the separation responses of mother-reared and surrogate-reared squirrel monkeys. In the initial experiment comparing the separation responses of mother-reared infants and surrogate-reared infants, both types of infants were removed from their home cage for 30 min (Mendoza, Smotherman, Miner, Kaplan, & Levine, 1978). Separation of the infant from the mother or the cloth surrogate in this manner evoked striking cortisol responses in all subjects, suggesting that the emotional attachment to a cloth surrogate was similar to that between infants and their biological mothers. However, in a subsequent evaluation, we showed that surrogate-reared infants were reacting primarily to the novel environment (Hennessy, Kaplan, Mendoza, Lowe, & Levine, 1979). Separation of surrogate-reared infants in the home cage, by simply removing the surrogate, did not elicit an adrenal response. Thus, their response differed greatly from that of mother-reared infants, which even in the home cage showed marked behavioral disturbance and adrenal activation following separation, albeit not as great as in a novel environment. The absence of a stress response on the part of the surrogate-reared infants in the latter study suggested the development of a more diffuse emotional bond, due to the absence of contingent interaction with a responsive mother.

This interpretation has received support from other sources (Reite, Short,

Kaufman, Stynes, Pauley, 1978), although it differs significantly from the general view presented in the lay literature. While attempting to show the potency of the bond between infant rhesus monkeys and their surrogates (Harlow & Zimmerman, 1959), early laboratory studies inadvertently de-emphasized the importance of mother–infant interactions. In addition, studies on surrogate-reared monkeys indicated that juvenile peer interactions, rather than formative experiences with the mother, provided the primary basis for socialization (Harlow, 1969). As we have become increasingly cognizant of the complex nature of primate behavior, more deficiencies in the performance of surrogate-reared infants have been reported. Monkeys deprived of social contact early in life tend to have inadequate communication skills (Miller, Ranelli, & Levine, 1977), to form simpler social relations (Anderson & Mason, 1974), and to be more aggressive at a lower social rank (Ruppenthal & Sackett, 1979). Additionally, males are often inadequate sexually (Wallen, Bielert, & Slimp, 1977), and females are less proficient mothers (Ruppenthal & Sackett, 1979). When these deficiencies are viewed in conjunction with the findings from learning studies, it is apparent that the absence of mothering in surrogate-reared infants can also have a general influence on emotionality. Early rearing without social partners results in performance difficulties on learning tasks involving variable stimuli and response inhibition (Sackett, 1970; Gluck, 1979), excessive eating and drinking even under nondisturbed conditions (Miller, Caul, & Mirsky, 1971), and alterations in adrenal responses to novel situations (Ruppenthal & Sackett, 1979). Although these studies amply demonstrate the importance of mother–infant interactions, it should be mentioned that some primate species, such as the squirrel monkey and the pigtail macaque, appear to be less severely affected than the rhesus macaque when reared without mothers (Kaplan, 1977).

Modulation of the Separation Response by Reunion

The specificity and uniqueness of the mother–infant bond have also been apparent in several of our studies on the beneficial effects of reunion after brief separations. We demonstrated that immediate reunion with the mother following momentary separation buffers the adrenal response to disturbance (Levine, Coe, Smotherman, & Kaplan, 1978). Typically, when an adult monkey is caught and then returned to its cage, elevated cortisol levels are still apparent 30 min later (Mendoza, Smotherman, Miner, Kaplan, & Levine, 1978). However, when a mother–infant dyad is similarly caught and returned to the home cage, only moderate adrenal activation occurs at 5, 15, or 30 min after capture and separation (Figure 4). Thus, contact between mother and infant appears to buffer the response to environmental perturbations in a way that comparable contact with an aunt does not.

Once the adrenocortical activation has occurred, however, the effect of reunion is not as rapid. We have evaluated the effect of a 30-min reunion after a 30-min separation and have found that mothers, but not their infants, returned to basal levels (Levine *et al.,* 1978). This difference between mothers and infants may reflect an important ability of mothers to return to psychological equilibrium at a more rapid rate, or it may indicate that adults can return to physiological homeostasis quicker because of more efficient hormone clearance. These alternative hypotheses are now being explored in ongoing experiments conducted in our laboratory.

Influence of Repeated Separation

In addition to the effects of reunion, one of the factors that has been shown to significantly influence the separation response is previous separation experience. Several studies have reported that a series of repeated separations results in successively greater behavioral trauma (Mineka & Suomi, 1978; Mineka, Suomi, & DeLizio, 1981). This occurs in spite of the normal maturational progression toward greater independence, and despite the greater predictability for the infant inherent in repeating the separations. Thus, the findings appear to concur with Weinberg and Levine's views (1980) that the predictability of an aversive event does not provide much benefit if it is uncontrollable and, in fact, that repeated exposure may enhance its aversiveness. During the last year, we have started systematically evaluating the response to repeated separations and have found that the effect is quite complex, depending largely on the nature of the prior separation experience.

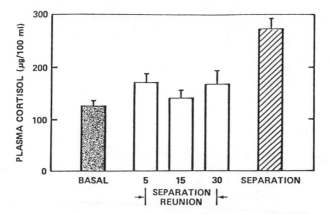

Figure 4. Comparison of plasma cortisol levels in squirrel monkeys at three different times after momentary separation and reunion and after a 30-min separation. Values of mothers and infants were averaged since they showed a similar pattern of response.

In this chapter, we discuss two studies: one that showed clear evidence of adaptation across separations, and another that indicated that repetition augmented the amount of the infant's behavioral trauma.

In the former study, five squirrel monkey infants were subjected to six identical 1-hr separations at 10-day intervals. These infants were reared undisturbed in small mother–infant groups, each containing 3–4 dyads, until they were 3 months of age. At this point, each infant was subjected to a series of six separations, which consisted of removing and isolating the infant in a sound-attenuated room for 1 hr. The separated infant was observed for the last 30 min of the separation, and then blood samples were collected from both mother and infant before reuniting them in the home cage. To control for the effect of repeated blood sampling, samples were also collected from five mother–infant pairs that lived in the same social groups. These samples were obtained at equivalent 10-day intervals, six times at 0900 hr prior to any disturbances.

As can be seen in Figure 5, each of the six separations resulted in a consistent cortisol elevation. Plasma cortisol levels were significantly higher after separation in both mothers [$F(1,8) = 18.89, p < .01$] and infants [$F(1,8) = 21.59, p < .01$], as compared with the levels in the dyads from which only basal blood samples were collected. Although the adrenal response was constant across the six separations, the infants' behavioral response changed dramatically (see Figure 6). The frequency of distress calling decreased

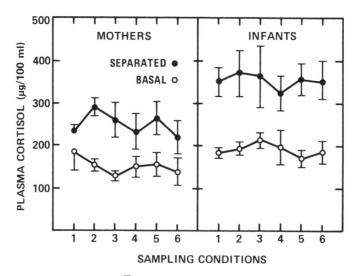

Figure 5. Plasma cortisol levels ($\overline{X} \pm SE$) following six 1-hr separations at 10-day intervals, compared with levels of dyads sampled only for basal levels at 10-day intervals.

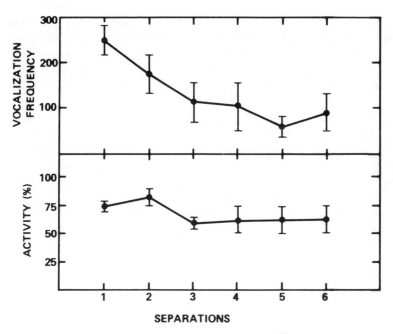

Figure 6. Infant distress vocalization and percentage of time active ($\overline{X} \pm$ SE) during 30 min prior to end of six 1-hr separations at 10-day intervals.

significantly from the first to the third separation, from an average of 250 to 144 calls per 30 min [$F(5,20) = 13.38 \, p < .001$] and then continued to decline at a slower rate. The infants' level of agitated movement also decreased somewhat, but as in previous studies, the continued occurrence of high activity prevented this measure from being statistically significant. In keeping with the decline in the behavioral response to separation, observations of the infants' behavior in the home cage on undisturbed days indicated that there was no overt effect of the separations on normative behavior. These observations consisted of 30-min records obtained on each dyad during the 9-day intervals between separations. Detailed analysis of mother–infant interactions, such as play and exploratory behavior, failed to reveal any long-term consequences of the separation trauma as compared with the behavior of those infants that experienced only the disturbance of blood sampling.

These data yield a radically different interpretation from prior studies on juvenile rhesus monkeys, which suggested increasing degrees of disturbance with repeated separations (Mineka, 1981; Suomi, Harlow, & Domek, 1970). In part, the observed adaptation may have been due to the acute nature of the separation (1 hr as compared to 4 days) and the longer intervals between separations (10 days as compared to 3 days). Moreover, our more benign separation procedures may also have accounted for the absence of a carry-over effect into the ongoing behavior between mothers and infants. In contrast, widely cited studies by Hinde and co-workers have indicated that separations lasting 7–14 days have protracted effects on the dynamics of the mother–infant relationship for many months (McGinnis, 1980; Hinde & Spencer-Booth, 1971; Hinde, Leighton-Shapiro, & McGinnis, 1978).

We have found that some types of separations do cause infants to evince increasing amounts of behavioral trauma when the separations are repeated (Jordan, Patterson, Coe, & Levine, 1983). The exacerbated response observed in this second study may have been due to two important differences in methodology: the separations occurred at 2-day intervals, and six infants were separated from their mothers simultaneously. These procedural differences were chosen because the experiment had a different focus, which was to assess the effects of the predictability of separation duration. In this experiment, we examined fixed-length versus variable-length separations in order to evaluate some issues involved in the theoretical framework of coping. For one group of infants, the separation condition involved being separated from their mothers for a fixed interval of 30 min with a signal (light flashes) presented 5 min prior to reunion. Another group of infants were separated for varying lengths of time, ranging from 6 to 60 min with an average of 30 min, and the signal was presented randomly during the separation. Both groups were tested every other day for a total of 20 separations.

Separations of both types elicited the typical adrenal activation observed in previous research, but the behavioral data from this experiment indicated that specific aspects of the separation paradigm can have a profound influence on the behavioral response that occurs. In contrast to the finding of the preceding study, neither group showed a decline in distress calling or agitated activity across the repeated separations (Figure 7). Infants separated for varying lengths of time showed relatively constant levels of calling and activity, while infants that were separated for fixed amounts of time showed significant increases in calling and activity. The fixed-interval group became increasingly more agitated than the variable-interval group as the separations were repeated; although both groups showed similar patterns of behavior on the first day of separation, their calling rate and activity levels were significantly different on Day 20 ($t = 2.73$, $p < .05$; $t = 2.48$, $p < .02$, respectively.).

The finding that separations of a fixed duration evoke a greater response appears on initial reflection to be somewhat surprising. In general, studies on stress have shown that predictable situations are less aversive than unpredictable ones (for reviews, see Hymowitz, 1979; Seligman, 1975; Badia, Harsh, & Abbott, 1979). However, when an individual is unable to exert control over the situation, the converse may be true: events that are not controllable may

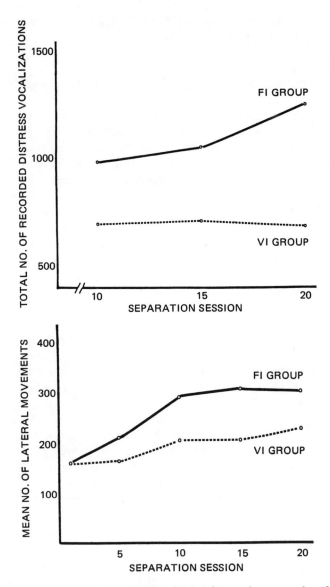

Figure 7. Total number of distress vocalizations for six infants and mean number of movements per 30-min session during repeated separations. FI infants were always separated for 30 min, whereas VI infants were separated for separations of variable length every 2 days.

be made more stressful by predictability (Weinberg & Levine, 1980). The separation paradigm clearly falls in the latter category, since reunion is controlled completely by the experimenter.

Further Support for Environmental Influences on the Separation Response

Regardless of the specific interpretation, the most important point is that the behavioral and physiological response to separation can be extremely malleable and are highly dependent on environmental circumstances. We have derived further support for this view from a series of comparable studies on mother–infant dyads of another primate species, the rhesus monkey. It was essential to evaluate the responses of this species for several important reasons. First, the rhesus monkey has been the traditional subject of studies on attachment and separation in nonhuman primates for over 20 years (Harlow & Zimmerman, 1959; Seay, Hansen, & Harlow, 1962). In addition, the rhesus monkey produces much lower circulating levels of adrenal hormones that are more comparable to those of humans (basal values typically range between 7 and 25 μg%). There are also several differences in the dynamics of the mother–infant relationship related to the ventral support of the infant as opposed to the dorsal carrying of the squirrel moneky, even though the developmental time course across the first six months is similar (Rosenblum, 1971b).

The conclusions from our rhesus monkey studies are quite similar to those on the squirrel monkey, but several significant differences must be mentioned. While the rhesus monkey infant undergoes marked adrenal activation following separation, the plasma levels of cortisol after 3-hr separations average only 39 μg% (Smotherman et al. 1979). Moreover, in a study conducted by Gunnar et al., (1981), adrenal response tended to subside after 24 hr (Figure 8). In this study, nine mother–infant pairs were removed from their social group when the infants were between 5 and 11 months of age. Each dyad was housed in a separate cage for 5 days in order to habituate the animals to being away from the social group. Five of the mother–infant pairs were then separated by removing the mothers and housing them in a different room, while the other four pairs served as controls. The changes in the infants' behavior and plasma cortisol levels over the next 12 days are shown in Figure 8, with the cortisol data presented with respect to the basal levels obtained on the fifth day of habituation ($\bar{X}$ = 19–29 μg%). Large increases in plasma cortisol levels occurred in the separated infants at 30 min after the removal of the mothers. Cortisol levels were still significantly elevated at 3 hr after separation, averaging 19 μg% over basal levels, but by 24 hr and thereafter, the levels were not significantly above those obtained on the last day of habituation.

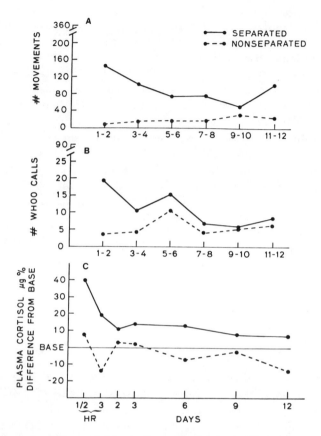

Figure 8. Changes in plasma cortisol levels, distress vocalizations, and movements of separated and nonseparated infant rhesus monkeys across a 12-day period. The cortisol levels reflect the deviation from basal levels determined prior to separation, and the behavioral frequencies were assessed during 30-min daily observations (Gunnar *et al.*, 1981).

The plasma cortisol reduction that occurred in separated infants during the 24 hr after removal paralleled the more extreme signs of behavioral disturbance, including plaintive "whoo" calls and agitated movements (Figure 8). The behavioral changes across the 12 days of separation suggested an adaptation to the separation condition, although the infants remained agitated and vigilant, and did not show overt signs of a depressive phase. In more recent studies[2], however, we observed that the behavioral response pattern in rhesus infants is extremely dependent on environmental factors, as

[2] In addition to S. Levine, these studies were conducted by C. Gonzalez, D. Franklin, and D. Johnson.

discussed previously for the squirrel monkey. While the cortisol response appears to be similar during various prolonged separations in the rhesus monkey, declining by 24 hr after separation onset, the level of calling and agitated movement may vary considerably. When separated rhesus infants were totally isolated instead of maintained in the same room with other separated infants, the level of calling and activity was much lower. In this situation, whoo calls were emitted only infrequently after several days of separation. In contrast, when the separated infants were kept within sight of their social group, calling and agitated movement were maintained at a significantly higher rate. This higher level of behavioral agitation occurred whether or not the separated mother remained within the social group. Thus, as in the studies on the squirrel monkey, the behavioral responses proved to be extremely contingent on environmental factors.

General Discussion

Taken as a whole, these studies provide substantial support for the view that mother–infant separation is a potent source of both behavioral disturbance and physiological stress. The pituitary-adrenal system has responded in almost all types of separation that we have studied, a finding that agrees with the work of Reite, Short, and Seiler (1978) and Reite, Short, Kaufman, Stynes, and Pauley (1978) on other physiological systems. In the rhesus monkey, the more circumscribed adrenal response has limited its effectiveness for distinguishing different experimental procedures after 24 hr, whereas the squirrel monkey's high adrenal output has been extremely valuable in evaluating the differential degree of trauma caused by different types of separation. In the case of separations lasting 4–24 hr in the squirrel monkey, we can clearly differentiate the effects of different separation environments and, specifically, the beneficial influence of the home environment. Moreover, the absence of an adrenal response following certain experimental manipulations was also extremely valuable in delineating important functions of mother–infant interactions. It appears that resumption of contact between mother and infant can entirely buffer the endocrine response that typically follows some disturbances.

In the case of immediate reunion following momentary separation, resumption of contact between mother and infant appears to inhibit the typical adrenal response to handling. This finding provides a unique demonstration of the specificity of the infant's attachment bond, since contact with a familiar female does not produce the same effect. This finding also reveals the important role that the maternal figure may have in modulating the infant's arousal levels. Perhaps one of the most significant functions that the mother has for the infant is to serve as a stable emotional base from which to begin exploring the environment and interacting with other conspecifics. In this regard, it is of interest that the mother appears to return to resting cortisol levels more quickly than the infant following adrenal activation (Levine *et al.*, 1978), and the infant appears to be more indiscriminate in its responses (Vogt & Levine, 1980). The mother clearly provides opportunities for the learning of contingencies that cannot possibly be fulfilled by an inanimate surrogate. It is not surprising, therefore, that surrogate-reared infants do not show the typical adrenal response to separation when left in the home cage. Hennessy and Kaplan (1981) have also reported that the cloth surrogate does not reduce the squirrel monkey infant's response to novelty, although this assertion differs from earlier work on rhesus monkeys indicating that the presence of a surrogate does decrease the cortisol response to an unfamiliar environment (Hill *et al.*, 1973).

These studies bring up an important issue concerning the general sensitivity of the pituitary-adrenal system to nonsocial variables related to novelty and stimulus change. As shown in numerous studies on rodents, novelty, uncertainty, and conflict are potent stimulators of corticoid release, and this response is often resistant to habituation (Mason, 1968; Hennessy & Levine, 1979). Over the years, the sensitivity of the adrenal response has created numerous problems for investigators, who have found it troubling that there are so many salient and potentially confounding factors (Natelson, Tapp, Adamus, Mittler, & Levin, 1981). When working with physiological measures, one must be cognizant of experimental procedures that may override the variables of interest. Similarly, time parameters are of the utmost importance. Not only have we found time of day to be important, but the duration of experimental conditions can also alter the findings and interpretations. In our initial studies, we utilized 30-min separations (Coe *et al.*, 1978; Levine *et al.*, 1978; Mendoza, Smotherman, Miner, Kaplan, & Levine, 1978b), and this time point has proved to be less reflective of environmental factors than separations of longer duration. We have now found that the sustained adrenal response during separations of 4–6 hr more accurately reflects the degree of disturbance. Especially in the rhesus monkey, which returns toward basal cortisol levels by 24 hr after the onset of stress, it is critical to choose the appropriate time parameters for investigation.

These variables not only influence endocrine responses, but as we have attempted to show in this chapter, they can affect the behavioral responses as well. The behavioral response to separation is not as invariant as is typically described. The traditional measures of distress calling and agitated movement used in most studies (Rosenblum & Plimpton, 1981), vary considerably depending on the circumstances of separation. Thus, a separated infant when left in the home cage emitted calls only infrequently; an infant separated from, but adjacent to, its mother called much more often than a totally isolated infant. Distress vocalizations also decreased across prolonged separations, being highest during the first hour and dramatically lower after 24 hr of separation. These data, therefore, bring into serious question the heavy reliance on calling frequency as the primary agitation measure in most studies on mother–infant separation. Clearly, one cannot assume that vocalization frequency is an adequte measure of internal state. Moreover, as we are now investigating, calling appears to be an instrumental response that the infant can utilize both to effect reunion after separation and to manipulate ongoing interactions with the mother. In a very real sense, distress calling allows the infant to exert control over its mother and, thus, may play a critical role in the learning of causal relationships and the initial exercise of power that provides the foundation for subsequent coping strategies.

The variability in the separation response also has a particular bearing on the use of mother–infant separation as an animal model of human depression. Under certain circumstances, it has been possible to provoke a depressionlike syndrome in separated monkey infants (Mineka, 1981; Kaufman & Rosenblum, 1967), and this finding has been the impetus for numerous studies. However, it must be emphasized that the depressive response is not a universal one in nonhuman primates. In species where there is social support following mother removal, depression does not occur (Kaufman & Rosenblum, 1967; Coe *et al.*, 1978); nor does it usually occur when the infant is totally isolated from the social group (Coe & Levine, 1981; Gunnar *et al.*, 1981). In the latter case, we have typically observed continued agitation and the maintenance of vigilance.

It appears that depression occurs only when the infant is entirely overwhelmed—in the terminology of Lazarus (1966), when continued "appraisal" of the situation indicates that further behavioral responses will not alter the aversive situation. This response pattern is probably analogous to the "learned helplessness" syndrome (Seligman, 1975). However, emotional withdrawal to this degree is not a typical response, and as Rosenblum and Plimpton (1981) have suggested, the protest phase of the separation response is probably the more adaptive component since it is more likely to facilitate survival. Even under extremely adverse circumstances, the organism usually tries to adapt and cope. The adrenocortical response, while reflecting stress, also initiates this adaptational phase. It remains for future studies to determine how the adrenal response influences the adaptational process, and to establish what aspects of the parent–offspring interaction facilitate the infant's ability to cope with stressful situations.

ACKNOWLEDGMENTS

We would like to acknowledge the invaluable collaboration with J. Kaplan at the Stanford Research Institute International and the contributions of past and present members of the laboratory: D. Franklin, J. Glass, C. Gonzalez, B. Goodlin, M. Gunnar, M. Hennessy, E. Lowe, S. Mendoza, W. Smotherman, and A. Vickers.

References

Abbott, D. H., & Hearn, J. P. Physical, hormonal and behavioral aspects of sexual development in the marmoset monkey, *Callithrix jacchus*. *Journal of Reproduction and Fertility*, 1978, *53*, 155–166.

Anderson, C. O., & Mason, W. A. Early experience and complexity of social organization in groups of young rhesus macaques (*Macaca mulatta*). *Journal of Comparative Physiology and Psychology*, 1974, *87*, 681–690.

Badia, P., Harsh, J., & Abbott, B. Choosing between predictable and unpredictable shock conditions: Data and theory. *Psychological Bulletin*, 1979, *86*, 1107–1131.

Bowlby, J. *Attachment and loss: Attachment*. New York: Basic Books, 1969.

Coe, C. L., & Levine, S. Normal responses to mother-infant separation in nonhuman primates. In D. F. Klein & J. Rabkin (Eds.), *Anxiety: New research and changing concepts*. New York: Raven Press, 1981, pp. 155–177.

Coe, C. L., Mendoza, S. P., Smotherman, W. P., & Levine, S. Mother-infant attachment in the squirrel monkey: Adrenal response to separation. *Behavioral Biology*, 1978, *22*, 256–263.

Dixson, A. F., Martin, R. D., Bonney, R. C., & Fleming, D. Reproductive biology of the owl monkey, *Aotus frivirgatus griseimembra*. In T. C. Anand Kumar (Ed.), *Non-human primate models for study of human reproduction*. Basel: Karger, 1980, pp. 61–68.

Dolhinow, P. An experimental study of mother loss in the Indian langur monkey (*Presbytis entellus*). *Folia Primatologica*, 1980, *33*, 77–128.

Gliner, J. A. Predictable vs. unpredictable shock: Preference behavior and stomach ulceration. *Physiology and Behavior*, 1972, *9*, 693–698.

Gluck, J. P. The intellectual consequences of early social restriction in rhesus monkeys (*Macaca mulatta*). In G. C. Ruppenthal & D. T. Reese (Eds.), *Nursery care of nonhuman primates*. New York: Plenum Press, 1979, pp. 253–268.

Gunnar, M. R., Gonzalez, C. A., Goodlin, B. L., & Levine, S. Behavioral and pituitary-adrenal responses during a prolonged separation period in infant rhesus macaques. *Psychoneuroendocrinology*, 1981, *6*, 65–75.

Harlow, H. F. Age-mate or peer affectional systems. *Advances in the Study of Behavior*, 1969, *2*, 333–383.

Harlow, H. F., & Harlow, M. K. Effects of various mother-infant relationships on rhesus monkey behaviors. In B. M. Foss (Ed.), *Determinants of infant behaviour* (Vol. 4). London: Methuen, 1969, pp. 15–36.

Harlow, H. F., & Zimmerman, R. R. Affectional responses in the infant monkey. *Science*, 1959, *130*, 421–432.

Hennessy, J. W., & Levine, S. Stress, arousal and the pituitary-adrenal system: A psychoneuroendocrine hypothesis. In J. Sprague & A. Epstein (Eds.), *Progress in psychobiology and physiological psychology* (Vol. 8). New York: Academic Press, 1979, pp. 133–178.

Hennessy, M. B., & Kaplan, J. N. *The effects of separation and novelty on the behavior and cortisol levels in surrogate-reared infant squirrel monkeys.* Paper presented at the Developmental Psychobiology meetings, November 1981, New Orleans.

Hennessy, M. B., Kaplan, J. N., Mendoza, S. P., Lowe, E. L., & Levine, S. Separation distress and attachment in surrogate-reared squirrel monkeys. *Physiology and Behavior,* 1979, *23,* 1017–1023.

Hill, S. D., McCormack, S. A., & Mason, W. A. Effects of artificial mothers and visual experience on adrenal responsiveness of infant monkeys. *Developmental Psychobiology,* 1973, *6,* 421–429.

Hinde, R. A., & Spencer-Booth, Y. Effects of brief separation from mother on rhesus monkeys. *Science,* 1971, *173,* 111–118.

Hinde, R. A., Leighton-Shapiro, M., & McGinnis, L. Effects of various types of separation experience on rhesus monkeys 5 months later. *Journal of Child Psychology and Psychiatry,* 1978, *19,* 199–211.

Hymowitz, N. Suppression of responding during signaled and unsignaled shock. *Psychological Bulletin,* 1979, *86,* 175–190.

Jordan, T. C., Patterson, J., Coe, C. L., & Levine, S. *Predictability and coping with separation in infant squirrel monkeys.* Manuscript in preparation, 1983.

Kagan, J. Discrepancy, temperament and infant distress. In M. Lewis & L. A. Rosenblum (Eds.), *The origins of fear.* New York: Wiley, 1974, pp. 229–248.

Kaplan, J. Growth and development of infant squirrel monkeys during the first six months of life. In G. C. Ruppenthal & D. J. Reese (Eds.), *Nursery care of nonhuman primates.* New York: Plenum Press, 1979, pp. 153–164.

Kaufman, I. C., & Rosenblum, L. A. The reaction to separation in infant monkeys: Anaclitic depression and conservation withdrawal. *Psychosomatic Medicine,* 1967, *29,* 648–675.

Lazarus, R. S. *Psychological stress and the coping process.* New York: McGraw-Hill, 1966.

Levine, S., Coe, C. L., Smotherman, W. P., & Kaplan, J. N. Prolonged cortisol elevation in the infant squirrel monkey after reunion with mother. *Physiology and Behavior,* 1978, *20,* 7–10.

Mason, J. W. A review of psychoendocrine research on the pituitary-adrenal cortical system. *Psychosomatic Medicine,* 1968, *30,* 576–607.

Mason, W. A. Motivational factors in psychosocial development. In W. J. Arnold & M. M. Page (Eds.), *Nebraska Symposium on Motivation, 1970.* Lincoln: University of Nebraska Press, 1971, pp. 35–67.

McGinnis, L. M. Maternal separation studies in children and nonhuman primates. In R. W. Bell & W. P. Smotherman (Eds.), *Maternal influences and early behavior.* New York: Spectrum, 1980, pp. 311–336.

Mendoza, S. P., Lowe, E. L., & Levine, S. Social organization and social behavior in two subspecies of squirrel monkeys (*Saimiri sciureus*). *Folia Primatologica,* 1978, *30,* 126–144.

Mendoza, S. P., Smotherman, W. P., Miner, M. T., Kaplan, J. & Levine, S. Pituitary-adrenal response to separation in mother and infant squirrel monkeys. *Developmental Psychobiology,* 1978, *11,* 169–175.

Mendoza, S. P., Coe, C. L., Smotherman, W. P., Kaplan, J., & Levine, S. Functional consequences of attachment: A comparison of two species. In R. W. Bell & W. P. Smotherman (Eds.), *Maternal influences and early behavior,* New York: Spectrum, 1980, pp. 235–252.

Miller, R. E., Caul, W. F., & Mirsky, I. A. Patterns of eating and drinking in socially-isolated rhesus monkeys. *Physiology and Behavior,* 1971, *7,* 127–134.

Miller, R. E., Ranelli, C. J., & Levine, J. M. Nonverbal communication as an index of disturbance. In I. Hanin & E. Usdin (Eds.), *Animal models in psychiatry and neurology.* Oxford: Pergamon, 1977, pp. 171–180.

Mineka, S. Depression and helplessness in primates. In H. Fitzgerald, J. Mullins, & P. Gage (Eds.), *Primate behavior and child nurturance* (Vol. 3). New York: Plenum Press, 1981.

Mineka, S., & Suomi, S. J. Social separation in monkeys. *Psychological Bulletin,* 1978, *85,* 1376–1400.

Mineka, S., Suomi, S. J., & DeLizio, R. Multiple separations in adolescent monkeys: An opponent-process interpretation. *Journal of Experimental Psychology, General,* 1981, *110,* 56–85.

Nagle, C. A., Denari, J. H., Riarte, A., Quiroga, S., Zárate, R., Germino, N. I., Merlo, A., & Rosner, J. M. Endocrine and morphological aspects of the menstrual cycle in the cebus monkey (*Cebus appela*). In T. C. Anand Kumar (Ed.), *Non-human primate models for study of human reproduction.* Basel: Karger, 1980, pp. 69–81.

Napier, J. R., & Napier, P. H. *A handbook of living primates.* New York: Academic Press, 1967.

Natelson, B. H., Tapp, W. N., Adamus, J. E., Mittler, J. C., & Levin, B. E. Humoral indices of stress in rats. *Physiology and Behavior,* 1981, *26,* 1049–1054.

Reite, M., Short, R., Kaufman, I. C., Stynes, A. J., & Pauley, J. D. Heart rate and body temperature in separated monkey infants. *Biological Psychiatry,* 1978, *13,* 91–105.

Reite, M., Short, R., & Seiler, C. Physiological correlates of maternal separation in surrogate-reared infants: A study in altered attachment bonds. *Developmental Psychobiology,* 1978, *11,* 427–435.

Robertson, J., & Robertson, J. Young children in brief separation: A fresh look. *Psychoanalytic Study of the Child,* 1971, *26,* 264–315.

Rose, R. M. Endocrine responses to stressful psychological events. *Psychiatric Clinics of North America,* 1980, *3,* 251–275.

Rosenblum, L. A. Infant attachment in monkeys. In R. Schaffer, (Ed.), *The origins of human social relations.* New York: Academic Press, 1971, pp. 85–113. (a)

Rosenblum, L. A. The ontogeny of mother-infant relations in macaques. In H. Moltz (Ed.), *The ontogeny of vertebrate behavior.* New York: Academic Press, 1971, pp. 315–367. (b)

Rosenblum, L. A., & Kaufman, I. C. Variations in infant development and response to maternal loss in monkeys. *American Journal of Orthopsychiatry,* 1968, *38,* 418–426.

Rosenblum, L. A., & Plimpton, E. H. Adaption to separation: The infant's effort to cope with an altered environment. In M. Lewis & L. A. Rosenblum (Eds.), *The uncommon child: Genesis of behavior* (Vol. 3). New York: Plenum Press, 1981.

Rosenblum, L. A., & Youngstein, K. P. Developmental changes in compensatory dyadic response in mother and infant monkeys. In J. Lewis & L. A. Rosenblum (Eds.), *The influence of the infant on its caregiver.* New York: Wiley, 1974, pp. 141–161.

Ruppenthal, G. C., & Sackett, G. A. Experimental and husbandry procedures: Their impact on development. In G. C. Ruppenthal & G. A. Sackett (Eds.), *Nursery care of nonhuman primates.* New York: Plenum Press, 1979, pp. 269–287.

Sackett, G. A. Innate mechanisms, rearing conditions and a theory of early experience effects in primates. In M. R. Jones (Ed.), *Miami Symposium on the Prediction of Behavior: Early Experience.* Miami: Miami University Press, 1970, pp. 11–53.

Seay, B., Hansen, E., & Harlow, H. F. Mother-infant separation in monkeys. *Journal of Child Psychology and Psychiatry,* 1962, *3,* 123–132.

Seligman, M. E. P. *Learned helplessness: On depression, development and death.* San Francisco: W. H. Freeman, 1975.

Smotherman, W. P., Hunt, L. E., McGinnis, L. M., & Levine, S. Mother–infant separation in group-living rhesus macaques.: A hormonal analysis. *Developmental Psychobiology,* 1979, *12,* 211–217.

Sroufe, L. A., Waters, E., & Matas, L. Contextual determinants of infant affective response. In M. Lewis & L. A. Rosenblum (Eds.), *The origins of fear.* New York: Wiley, 1974, pp. 49–72.

Suomi, S., Harlow, H., & Domek, C. Effect of repetitive infant-infant separation of young monkeys. *Journal of Abnormal Psychology,* 1970, *76,* 161–172.

Vogt, J. L, & Levine, S. Response of mother-infant squirrel monkeys to separation and distur-
    bance. *Physiology and Behavior,* 1980, *24,* 829–832.
Vogt, J. L., Coe, C. L. & Levine, S. Behavioral and adrenocorticoid responsiveness of squirrel
    monkeys to a live snake: Is flight necessarily stressful? *Behavioral and Neural Biology,* 1981, *32,*
    391–405.
Wallen, K., Bielert, C., & Slimp, J. Foot clasp mounting in the prepubertal rhesus monkey: Social
    and hormonal influences. In S. Chevalier-Skolnikoff and F. E. Poirier (Eds.), *Primate bio-social
    development.* New York: Garland, 1977, pp. 439–462.
Weinberg, J., & Levine, S. Psychobiology of coping in animals: The effects of predictability. In S.
    Levine & H. Ursin (Eds.), *Coping and health.* New York: Plenum Press, 1980, pp. 39–59.
Weinraub, M., & Lewis, M. The determinants of children's responses to separation. *Monographs of
    the Society for Research in Child Development,* 1977, *42,* Serial No. 172.
Weiss, J. M. Effects of coping responses on stress. *Journal of Comparative Physiology and Psychology,*
    1968, *65,* 251–260.
Weiss, J. M. Somatic effects of predictable and unpredictable shock. *Psychosomatic Medicine,* 1970,
    32, 397–408.

CHAPTER 10

Allometric Influences on Primate Mothers and Infants

GARY G. SCHWARTZ and LEONARD A. ROSENBLUM

In his 1874 address before the British Association, "On the Hypothesis That Animals Are Automata," Thomas Huxley employed a small deceit: "my intention," he revealed at last, "is to apply the doctrine to man." Huxley's position was essentially Descartes's, but with one critical emendation. Huxley's canon of evolutionary continuity ("that great doctrine . . . which forbids that any natural phenomena can come into existence suddenly or without some precedent") was irreconcilable with Descartes's view that animals are senseless—mere machines tht "eat without pleasure, cry out without pain, and grow without knowing." "But," Huxley rejoined, "it does not in the slightest degree follow that they are not sensitive and *conscious* automata." We may be cerebral, the message ran, but we are cybernetic nonetheless.

Our intention in this paper is to extend the hypothesis that primates are *thermal* automata and to suggest that many facets of infant growth and development may be accounted for by this view. We emphasize at the outset that despite Lavoisier's belief that life is combustion, we do not hold that "everything is thermal" (nor, incidentally, that primates are really machines). Rather, our hypothesis is a heuristic fiction: we treat primates as thermal machines in the hope of sparking fresh hypotheses about the way primates work.

In order to make our case, we must invoke a scientific variant of evolu-

GARY G. SCHWARTZ and LEONARD A. ROSENBLUM • Department of Psychiatry and Primate Behavior Laboratory, State University of New York, Downstate Medical Center, Brooklyn, New York 11203. Preparation of this chapter was supported by Grant #MH15965 (USPHS) and by funds provided by the State University of New York.

tionary continuity; much of the material we adduce has been drawn freely from the work of others. Even our approach, allometry, is largely the brain-child of Thomas Huxley's grandson, Sir Julian. Indeed, if we have any legitimate claim to originality, it is a perverse one: many of the data we borrow were never intended for the purposes to which we put them.

To introduce the notion that primates are thermal automata we begin by introducing the perspective of "scaling," using (superficially at least) an un-likely example: the allometry of primate hair. Smaller primate species, in essence, are systematically furrier than larger ones. The tailoring of insulation to body size represents one solution to the architectural problems faced by primates of similar shape but dissimilar scale. The thermal problems illus-trated by this static comparison are essentially those confronting primate neonates, only *writ large.*

The effects of size are more than skin deep: allometry exerts a pervasive influence on primate life histories. In smaller species, for example, infants themselves are proportionately larger—and so, we suggest, are the metabolic costs of rearing them.

Finally (following Huxley), we consider the implications of this perspec-tive for humans. In humans, thermal constraints may influence patterns of neonatal growth and mortality. Many such observations could be predicted by the geometry of the newborn.

On Comparing Great with Small

"For we can demonstrate by geometry," observed Galileo, "that the large machine is not proportionately stronger than the small." Galileo's disquisi-tions on the necessary effects of size upon shape (written while Galileo was under arrest by the Holy Office) mark the historical foundations of allometry. Allometry, in short, is the general study of size and its consequences (Gould, 1966); it explains (among many other things) why gorillas have such big bones, why small primates have disproportionately enormous infants, and why marmosets are furrier than men.[1]

The heart of allometry is that physical factors (particularly the most ubiquitous one, body mass) set limits on the possible sizes, shapes, and even sorts of organisms. Consider, for example, why giants exist only in the

---

[1] Though correct, this definition hardly packs the same punch as, allometry "explains why any fly can walk up a wall, but only Jesus could walk on water" (Gould, 1971, p. 239). The laws of physics govern all objects, but their effects are not the same at all sizes: a *Drosophila* can scale walls because the gravitational forces acting on its tiny mass are overcome by electrostatic attaction (Went, 1968). Humans may ignore the effects of molecular attraction; they cannot fly in the face of gravity.

imagination: Were a giant 10 times the height of a human, he would be 10 times as wide and 10 times as thick; thus his weight would be increased by 1,000. Yet the cross section of his bones would be increased only by 100, and as a result, each square centimeter of giant bone would have to support a weight 10 times that of its human counterpart. As human bones break under 10 times their normal weight, a colossus would collapse under his own mass. Giants are found only in fairy tales because they would fracture in reality (Haldane, 1946; cf. Galileo, 1954).

To be self-supporting, a giant has two choices: switch to a material with greater compressive strength than bone, or increase the size (and hence modify the shape) of his limbs. Terrestrial vertebrates (the problem of support does not arise for aquatic ones, whose weights are supported by bouyancy) have adopted the second: the mass of their bones increases faster than body mass as a whole; larger animals have relatively thicker legs (Barr, 1899; Schmidt-Nielsen, 1977). Like Alice in *Through the Looking Glass*, who had to run merely to stay in one place, isomorphic animals of dissimilar size must change structurally if they are to remain functionally the same.

Huxley's Equation

The relationship between bone mass and total body mass (or between any two variables) can be expressed by Julian Huxley's equation of simple allometry[2]:

$$y = bx^a \text{ or in logarithmic terms, } \log y = \log b + a \log x$$

where y is one part of the organism (say, bone weight) and x is another, commonly body size (e.g., body weight). Plotted on logarithmic coordinates, a (the allometric exponent) is the slope of the relationship between y and x, and the constant b (the allometric coefficient) describes the y-intercept. If y increases more slowly with increasing values of x, then a will be less than 1; if more rapidly a will be greater than 1. For example, in a plot of skeletal mass versus body mass in vertebrates from shrews to elephants, $a = 1.13$ (Schmidt-Nielsen, 1977). Differential limb thickening is one of the "classics" of allometry; it occurs intraspecifically during ontogeny (Jolicoeur, 1963, in humans) and interspecifically among adults of different vertebrate species (Günther, 1975). Such structural compensations are not restricted to animals;

[2] After his initial report on relative growth in 1924, and particularly after 1932, the power function became widely known as *Huxley's equation*. In fact, Snell (among others) used this equation for the interspecific scaling of brain size in 1891, six years before Huxley's birth. For a history of primate brain allometry, see Jerison (1973), Holt, Check, Mellits, and Hill (1975), and Martin (1981).

even the cross section of a mushrooms stem broadens differentially in proportion to the cap weight it must support (Ingold, 1946).

Although Huxley's equation may have theoretical disadvantages in some instances (see Smith, 1980, for a useful critique), it has three simple advantages in practice: First, the power function admits ready visual interpretation; when plotted logarithmically, the results are often straight lines. Second, the slope of the log-log plot indicates proportional size changes that are "scale-independent"; that is, they are unaffected by the actual unit of measurement. Third, a Pearson product–moment correlation coefficient can be used to indicate the strength of the bivariate relationship. The signal advantage of the allometric approach, however, is more conceptual than statistical: it is the power that allometry offers us to extract empirical generalizations from mountains of otherwise unscalable data. (For the theoretical and statistical justifications of Huxley's equation, see Cock, 1966; Gould, 1966; Jungers & German, 1981; Mosimann & James, 1979; Platt & Silvert, 1981.)

One case in which Huxley's equation can help distinguish the forest from the trees is in the scaling of primate hair.

Of Marmosets and Men

"The loss of hair is an inconvenience and probably an injury to man even under a hot climate" (Charles Darwin, *The Descent of Man, and Selection in Relation to Sex*, 1871/1981).

After counting nearly a quarter of a million hairs from the preserved skins of scores of primate species, Adolph Schultz (1969), the renowned Swiss anthropologist, despaired: "We have as yet no plausible explanation for these surprisingly wide discrepancies in the density of hair of wild simian primates" (p. 119).

A celebrated puzzle since *The Descent*, the relatively glabrous skin of humans (in contrast to monkeys) had, by the 1930s, inspired some ingenious and improbable solutions: "disuse-atrophy" and "gravitational attraction" were once popular explanations (Kidd, 1903; see Figure 1) as was (later), "domestication-induced degeneracy," the thesis that human hairlessness was the stigma of civilization—the toll of tweedy trousers and tight-fitting hats (Miller, 1931).[3]

---

[3] Droll as this conceit may initially appear, "domestication-induced degeneracy," in more ominous garb, was to become a propagandist's catchword in support of the racial "purification" programs of Nazi Germany (cf. Lorenz, who in 1940 could write: "The selection for toughness, heroism, social utility . . . must be accomplished by some human institution if mankind, in default of selective factors, is not to be ruined by domestication-induced degeneracy"; translated by Eisenberg, 1972, p. 124).

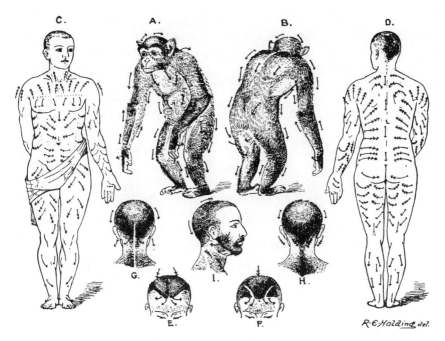

Figure 1. Hypothetical derivation of human hairlessness from the pilose condition of the assumed prototype of human beings. According to Kidd (1903): "Primitive tracts of hair shown by arrows with single heads; those acquired by morphological changes marked by arrows with two heads; those acquired by use and habit marked by arrows with three heads." (From Kidd, 1903.)

Hoping to quash such idle Darwinizing, Adolph Schultz meticulously counted all the hairs within 1-cm² samples from 72 primate skins. The resultant data deflated notions like degeneration (the great apes, for example, turned out nearly as naked as humans, though they are hardly domesticated), but uncondensed and only barely analyzed, they suggested no clear interpretation, and Schultz commended his tabulations to an appendix (1931), to await the wistful legacy of "future research."

But are Schultz's data really so baffling?

The density of hair in anthropoid primates ranges over a thousand fold: from greater than 4000 hairs/cm² between the shoulder blades of some marmosets, to fewer than 4 hairs/cm² on the backs of some men. Yet body weight—from the 200-g *Cebuella* to the nearly 200-kg *Gorilla*—shows a similar range. To compare the density of hair from primates of different sizes, we must examine the effects due to the one variable that Schultz overlooked, *body size*.

For organisms of similar shape (isometry), surface areas are proportional to the 2/3 power of their volumes, and we calculated these values from published means of species weights. Hair density at each of Schultz's 1-cm^2 samples (he took three: one from the vertex, one from the lower angles of the shoulder blades, and one from a distance overlying the breastbone) was plotted against surface area by the power function $y = bx^a$. Regression lines were fitted by means of least squares.

The relationship between hair density (y) and surface area (x) in adults of 23 anthropoid species are described by the following equations:

For the scalp, $y = 4.96x^{-.553}(r = -.709)$;
back, $y = 6.06x^{-.789}(r = -.807)$;
and chest, $y = 5.87x^{-1.00}(r = -.794)$.

For all cases, correlations were significant beyond the .001 level ($df = 22$). The pronounced negative slopes indicate that hair density decreases with increasing surface area; increasingly massive primates have systematically sparser coats. Figure 2 depicts the best fit line for hair density (chest) versus surface area.

When scaled in relation to the largest organ of the body, the skin, the

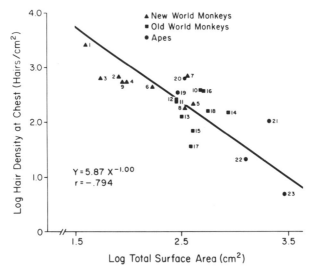

Figure 2. Negative allometry of hair density measured at chest versus body surface area in 23 anthropoid primate species (data from Schwartz & Rosenblum, 1981). 1. *Callithrix jucchus;* 2. *Saguinus bicolor;* 3. *Saguinus geoffroyi;* 4. *Aotus trivirgatus;* 5. *Aloutta villosa;* 6. *Cebus capuchinus;* 7. *Lagothrix lagothrica;* 8. *Ateles geoffroyi;* 9. *Saimiri sciureus;* 10. *Macaca maurus;* 11. *Cercopithecus pygerthrus;* 12. *Cercopithecus aethiops;* 13. *Erythrocebus patas;* 14. *Pygathrix nemaeus;* 15. *Macaca mulatta;* 16. *Nasalis larvatus;* 17. *Macaca speciosa;* 18. *Papio anubis;* 19. *Hylobates lar;* 20. *Hylobates moloch;* 21. *Pongo pygmaeus;* 22. *Pan (sp);* 23. *Gorilla gorilla.*

relationship between hair density and body surface area appears embarrass-ingly linear. We proposed that the negative allometry of hair density and body surface area represents an architectural adaptation to the thermal constraints of decreasing ratios of surface area to volume (Schwartz & Rosenblum, 1981). This follows from the fundamental principle of allometric growth, what D'Arcy Thompson (1917) called the "Principle of Similitude": If geometrical similarity is maintained with size increase, any series of objects will exhibit progressively decreasing ratios of surface area to volume. Thus, a 200-kg gorilla, with a mass 1,000 times that of a marmoset, has an exposed surface only 100 times as great. Since heat dissipation is limited by free surface, the disproportionate scaling of surfaces and volumes poses contrasting problems for primates differing in body mass. Small primates, because of their relatively enorm us ratios of surface to mass (and consequent high rates of heat loss), must counter their tendency to lose internal heat to the environment. More massive primates face the opposite problem: without effective mechanisms for evaporative cooling (Montagna, 1972), they must dispel vast quantities of core-generated heat through a comparatively tiny shell. Since they cannot sweat, most primates are greatly troubled by radiant heat: if left in the sun unprotected, a gorilla simply bakes (Guilloud & Fitz-Gerald, 1967); its situa-tion is paralleled in humans with hereditary ectodermal dysplasia. Afflicted individuals (a family of which was described by Darwin, 1887) lack sweat glands and must douse themselves with water in order to prevent hyperther-mia from exercise or high temperatures (Sunderman, 1941).[4]

As the ratio of surface to volume decreases in a static series of adult primates, the advantage of an insulating coat diminishes as well; this rela-tionship is reflected in Fourier's Law of Heat Conduction. With the temperature differential between an animal's core and the environment constant, Fourier's Law states that heat flows from an animal's core in direct proportion to the animal's surface area and in inverse proportion to its insulation. Since hair density is the most important factor determining the insulation of animal

---

[4] The gorilla's inability to withstand the thermal stresses of the savannah is typical. As a gruesome but compelling example, Gibbs (1912) compared the responses of monkeys (taxon unspecified, but very likely Taiwan macaques) that were tied to boards and placed in the tropical sunlight, versus those of restrained but shaded controls. Two of the three radiant-exposed animals died within an hour. Similarly, Sherrington (1924), who opined that African monkeys (*Cercopithecus, sp.*), "being from a tropical climate . . . should rather like than dislike the heat," raised the temperature of their quarters to 47°C, with fatal results. Nakayama, Hori, Nagasaka, Tokura, and Tadaki (1971), reporting similar data for the Japanese macaque, concluded: "Although the tropical origin of the primate is well accepted, any effective devices for dissipating heat, such as profuse sweating or vigorous panting observed in other animals, have never been observed in the monkey" (p. 332). Nakayama *et al.*'s generalization requires some revision: the patas monkey (*Erythrocebus*), a savannah primate, seems to be an accomplished sweater (Mahoney, 1980), and the night monkey (*Aotus*) pants (LeMaho, Goffert, Rochas, Felbabel, & Chatonnet, 1981).

coats (Tregear, 1965), the reciprocal relationship of hair density to body surface apparently represents an "appreciation" of Fourier's Law by natural selection. Although numerous factors influence the insulational value of mammalian coats (e.g., hair length and coat depth; Cena & Clark, 1979), hair density is the most critical—particularly for smaller mammals, in which even tiny increments in hair length or coat thickness would drastically impede locomotion (Tracy, 1977; cf. Bergmann, 1847, translated in Kleiber, 1975, p. 222).

Do these allometric trends betray the solution to the puzzle of human hairlessness? Skeletal remains of the earliest hominids, the australopithecines, indicate a probable body weight between 45 and 70 kg (Pilbeam & Gould, 1974). Estimation of hair density from these weights suggest that a substantial depilation probably occurred on the basis of body mass sometime *prior* to the human migration from a forest to a grassland habitat during the Pliocene. The ecological shift from shaded forest to open savannah entailed (among other things) a dramatic increase in exposure to high levels of solar heat (Barnicot, 1959).

In addition to its function as an insulator, a dense coat of hair is the principal mammalian defense against solar heat, as a dense pelage can reflect 50% of incident radiation (Schmidt-Nielsen, 1964). Yet, once reduced in proportion to body mass, the sparse coat of the australopithecines could afford little radiant protection. This was Darwin's dilemma in *The Descent:* hairlessness *would* be an injury to humans under a hot climate. The only alternative to reducing a high radiant heat load by reflective means was to guarantee a high relative heat loss through evaporative cooling. We suggested that thermal sweating evolved as a compensation for the human loss of body hair under the high radiant heat loads of the Pliocene savannah—a conclusion reached independently by Newman (1970) and by Montagna (1972). With the evolution of active, eccrine sweating (from glands that are curiously present but thermally inoperative in most nonhuman primates), natural selection would permit the further reduction of the remnant human coat to its present vestigial condition.

In short, humans have not lost their hair "in order to" sweat (Pilbeam, 1972); that idea is pure Lamarkism. Hair, by the way, is no impediment to evaporation (Cena & Monteith, 1975). Humans sweat *because* they have lost their hair.[5]

[5] Our hypothesis purports to explain differences in pilosity among species; it says little about differences between the sexes (e.g., between human males and females). Women may be less hirsute than men for reasons of sexual selection, as Darwin (1871/1981) suggested. But the problems of interspecific and intersexual pilosity are distinct, despite the appeal of solving one through the other (although see Hamilton, 1973, for several ingenious attempts). Earlier in *The Descent,* Darwin thought that differences in the hair of primate species were the result of correlated growth (p. 194), only to reject this view in favor of sexual selection in *Selection in Relation to Sex* (p. 376).

Coda

In his well-known book *The Life of Primates* (1969), Adolph Schultz projected that the *aperçu* into human hairlessness would be discovered in the field. Ironically, the answer was uncovered in the library—concealed amidst the dense underbrush of his own data. But it would be unfair to leave the story there. Why did Schultz end up so far from the discovery? It would be easy to dismiss him as a mere cataloguer—an empiric who expected that, like Botticelli's *Venus,* the explanation would emerge from a sea of data, fully formed. Besides, Julian Huxley's *magnum opus,* his classic *Problems of Relative Growth,* appeared in 1932, a year after Schultz's paper; maybe Schultz simply missed the allometric approach.

Nothing could be further from the truth. Not only was Schultz's labor motivated by theory (one he scotched, that of the degenerationists), but Schultz himself was the foremost authority on relative growth in primates; many of the "standard" techniques in studies of human growth were pioneered by him (e.g., Schultz, 1929). Schultz's failure to recognize the relationship between hair density and body size stemmed from one assumption—an assumption that was provisional and anatomically perfectly natural, but one that, physiologically, proved surprisingly mistaken. "The countless minute glands in the skin of all primates," Schultz wrote on reviewing his data in 1969, "have as yet been investigated in only a few species. Lacking systematic information . . . it can merely be stated that apparently most primates can and do sweat over at least many parts of their body surface" (p. 114). Here was where Schultz miscounted: save for physiologically minute quantities (mostly on the palms and soles), most primates *cannot* and *do not* sweat over their general body surface (Montagna, 1971; Myers, 1971). If primates could make effective use of evaporative cooling, as Schultz mistakenly assumed, then the flow of radiant and convective heat through their coats would be of only trivial importance—their fur could stay. But like the giant who could not withstand the force of his own mass, if insulated isometrically over a 1,000-fold range in size, nonhuman primates could not withstand the heat generated by theirs. Instead, primates have compensated for the negative allometry of surface/mass in thermal kind: by a negative allometry of hair density/surface.

The Principle of Similitude

The consequences of D'Arcy Thompson's "Principle of Similitude" are not limited to animal surfaces, although strictly speaking, they depend on them. Since the body's surface area determines an animal's heat loss, and progressively smaller animals have proportionately larger surfaces, it follows that smaller animals face disproportionate heat losses. Small mammals can respond by increasing their insulation, but this solution has obvious limits.[6] To remain in thermal equilibrium, small endotherms (birds and mammals) must compensate for their tremendous heat losses by prodigious heat production. The famous "mouse to elephant curve," first fitted by Kleiber (1932) to Huxley's power function, showed that metabolic rate in mammals is proportional to body mass to the .75 power. Viewing Kleiber's regression on a log scale, it is easy to overlook the immensity of the range in metabolism that it encompasses: the metabolic rate of a 5-ton elephant, for example, is .07 ml O_2 per gram per hour; that of a 5-g. shrew, 7.40 (Schmidt-Nielsen, 1975). It is not easy to overlook its consequences.

Many life history traits, particularly in small taxa, are simply sequents of the "iron law" of body surfaces and metabolism (Eisenberg, 1981). For example, to fuel their metabolic machines, small endotherms eat constantly (the voraciousness of shrews is legendary); even the six-times-larger mouse consumes its own weight in food in four days (Schmidt-Nielsen, 1975). At night, the tiniest endotherms, hummingbirds, and shrews, must undergo torpor—they would starve to death if they slept (Brown, Calder, & Kodric-Brown, 1978).

Some energetic effects of size may be relatively easy to predict. For instance, an endotherm's food requirements are reflected in the area that must be searched in order to obtain them (assuming that resources are evenly dispersed). Thus, the finding that home range size in primates is proportional to metabolic body size (body mass .75; Harvey & Clutton-Brock, 1981) is not all that surprising (or all that new; cf. McNab, 1963, 1980); in balancing its energy budget, a primate's degrees of freedom are limited. (For an excellent introduction to the energetics of endotherms, see McNab, 1974; also Bartholomew, 1977; King & Farner, 1961; Bourlière, 1975).

However, many life history consequences of size may be less intuitively apparent. These include the effects of adult size on neonatal size and the effects of size on growth and developmental rates. In the material that follows, we consider some life history consequences of maternal body size for primates. Ideally, the tool for this task is multivariate allometry, which would permit us to ask how much residual variance between two life history variables is accountable by a third, and so on. Gaps in the available data preclude this, and we rely instead on separate bivariate plots. These plots are only illustrative; they serve, in C. H. Waddington's characterization of allometry (1950, p. 513), "as a rough-and-ready shorthand method of description."

[6] For a 60-g mouse to have the same per-gram metabolic rate as a 600-kg steer, given the same heat conductivity of hair cover, the mouse would require a coat 20 cm thick. In fact, the per-gram metabolic rate of the mouse is 20 times that of the steer (Kleiber, 1932).

Regressions were calculated by the method of least squares and lines fitted by hand. (For an impressive synthesis of mammalian life history data, see Eisenberg, 1981; for an illustration of multivariate allometry, see Bekoff, Diamond, & Mitton, 1981.)

Allometry of Neonatal Size

"The use of logarithmic grid paper," Julian Huxley observed in 1927, "is insufficiently known to most biologists. Much labour can, however, often be saved by its use." The occasion for Huxley's remark was Oskar Heinroth's (1922) monumental paper on the relation between egg weight and body weight in birds. Heinroth's tabulations were presented *in extenso,* and for 432 species; that was precisely the problem: Uncondensed data, Huxley stated, "give on the whole a somewhat confused impression. . . . I have, therefore, been through his facts and have analyzed them in a rather more radical way."

Huxley's "more radical way" was the now-familiar allometric plot. When logarithmically reorganized, Heinroth's data on the relationship between egg weight (y) and body weight (x) showed an intriguing pattern: for small values of x, across diverse taxonomic groups, the value of a (the slope) approached 1, but with increasing maternal weight, a eventually decreased to the limiting value of $2/3$. Huxley (1927) envisioned that two antagonistic processes were at work:

> It may be suggested that the linear relation, the weight of the egg increasing in direct proportion to the weight of the bird, would be that which would be most advantageous [in the struggle for existence]; but that physical difficulties stand in the way of its realization. The egg is an enormous cell, and each successive increase in size will presumably be achieved with proportionately greater difficulty. Nourishment for the growth of the egg must come through the egg's surface; and therefore, an increase proportional to surface-increase may give the lower limiting value for our curve. (p. 460)

Thus, the relationship between egg and maternal mass reflected a compromise between the evolutionary advantage of maximizing the egg mass and the physiological difficulty of supporting it. "Whether this be the correct interpretation or no," Huxley mused, "the general regularity of the curves is of considerable interest." Subsequent research not only has confirmed his interpretation, but has shown the phenomenon to be far more general than Huxley imagined (see Millar, 1981; Kaplan & Salthe, 1979; Blueweiss, Fox, Kudzman, Nakashima, Peters, & Sams, 1978).

A double logarithmic plot of maternal weight versus neonatal weight in the two primate suborders Haplorhini (tarsier, monkeys, apes, and humans) and Strepsirhini (lemurs and lorises) (Figure 3) immediately reveals two things:

1. In both suborders, neonatal weight increases with negative allometry;
2. At any given maternal weight, haplorhine neonates are two to three times larger than strepsirhine newborns (Leutenegger, 1973).

The slope of the logarithmic plot ($a = .67$) indicates that primate neonates, like Heinroth's eggs, are not scaled isometrically to maternal mass; their relative mass suggests a surface-dependent physiological constraint. (The slope of both regression lines lies outside the confidence limits of the universal metabolic exponent, .75). Leutenegger (1976) reasonably concluded that the physiological limiting factor determining the relative size of primate fetuses may be the surface area of the maternal placenta. Differences in absolute neonatal size between the two suborders (as reflected in the different values of b, the allometric coefficient) may reflect their characteristic types of placentation (strepsirhines have a noninvasive, epitheliochorial placenta, haplorhines an invasive, hemochorial one; Luckett, 1975).

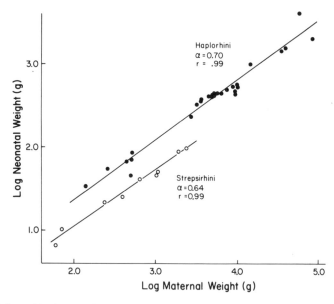

Figure 3. Logarithmic plot of neonatal weight (g) versus maternal weight (g) in two primate suborders, Strepsirhini (lemurs and lorises) and Haplorhini (tarsier, monkeys, apes, and humans). For species with multiple births, "neonatal weight" represents the weight of the entire litter. Data from Leutenegger (1979), with additional material.

Yet the most "obvious" thing about the negative allometry of neonatal size is that smaller mothers have proportionately larger offspring. As a consequence, maternal size constraints should be most conspicuous at the smallest (absolute) sizes, where offspring are (relatively) largest. Leutenegger (1979) has proposed an intriguing hypothesis to suggest that such size constraints may have influenced the evolution of primate litter size. Leutenegger's hypothesis conjoins two patterns of allometric growth. The first of these is a classic observation: within a related series, smaller animals have relatively larger crania; the second is the negative allometry of neonatal-maternal weight (Leutenegger, 1973; Figure 3). The intersection of these trends results in small primates giving birth to infants with disproportionately large crania—so large, in fact, that they exceed the dimensions of the mother's birth canal. In the 6000-g howler monkey (*Aloutta*), for example, the diameter of the female's pelvic canal is comfortably in excess of that of the neonate's head, and the 300-g infant is easily delivered. By contrast, in giving birth to a 100-g infant, the 600-g squirrel monkey (*Saimiri*) delivers a neonate that represents 17% of her nonpregnant weight and whose cranial diameter exceeds that of her pelvic outlet. The strenuous delivery in *Saimiri* (Takeshita, 1961) is accomplished only through dilation of pelvic ligaments (Bowden, Winter, & Ploog, 1967).

Apparently, the squirrel monkey represents the lower critical size for the production of the usual sngle offspring in anthropoid primates.[7] At a smaller maternal size, the cranial dimensions of a single neonate would so exceed the dimensions of the birth canal as to render delivery impossible. Leutenegger suggested that anthropoids smaller than *Saimiri*, the Callitrichidae (marmosets and tamarins), have "solved" this problem via the mechanical expedient of smaller, multiple births. By producing twins and occasionally triplets, callitrichids reduce the size of an individual newborn to a size commensurate with maternal architecture. Despite the production of twins, newborn cranial dimensions in the common marmoset (*Callithrix jacchus*) still exceed pelvic dimensions by about 4%—demonstrating even more emphatically the selective advantage of smaller, multiple births.

It is intriguing in this regard that callitrichid males exhibit an exceptional degree of parental care. Within the first few weeks of infant life, the male carries the twin newborns on his back, returning them to the mother only intermittently for nursing. This unusual male parental investment may represent a compensation for the female's high energetic costs of twinning, costs that are evident in the relative composition of maternal milk.

---

[7] Eberhart (1981) correctly pointed out that the similarly sized talapoin monkey (*Miopithecus*), which can deliver an infant 20% of its own mass, may represent the size-limiting case for singleton births.

Mother's Milk

Comparing the composition of the milk of different species is a little like comparing intelligence (Gould, 1981): it is not always clear which measurements to use or what the measures actually mean. The first to attempt such an interspecies comparison was Gustov von Bunge (1902), who found a negative correlation between the percentage of protein and ash in the milk of nine species (dog, cat, rabbit, goat, sheep, horse, cow, pig, and human) and the time it took for the young to double their birth weight. Since then, others have studied the relationship between milk composition and growth rate, with conflicting results. Powers (1933) suggested that the comparison should be made, not with the percentage of protein in the milk, but with the fraction of total energy content of the milk attributable to protein. Adding a few species and recalculating Bunge's data in this way, Powers reported no correlation between growth rate and energy content. Bernhart (1961) on the other hand, endorsing Powers's fractional energy approach, recalculated Powers's recalculations against the *logarithm* of the days required to double the birth weight, and reported a strong negative correlation between the two.

Bunge's approach has been criticized often. Blaxter (1961), for example, argued that one must measure milk quantity as well as quality. Similarly, Jenness and Sloan (1970) questioned the generality of Bernhart's findings on the grounds that Arctic and/or aquatic mammals (whose heat loss problems, by the way, are enormous; Ronald & Dougan, 1982) fail to observe these trends: the fat content of the milk of these mammals is too high. (The percentage of fat in the milk of the 52-kg goat, *Capra ibex*, for example, is 7%; at 53% fat, the milk of the similarly sized Northern fur seal, *Callorhinus ursinus*, is practically butter.)

The factors governing the composition of a species' milk are admittedly complex (Jenness, 1974), but the logical basis for Bunge's original hypothesis is unimpeached: granting a selective advantage in nurturing offspring as efficiently as possible, a species' milk should be adapted to the growth and maintenance requirements of its young. Growth and maintenance generally depend on different energy substrates: protein for the former, fat and lactose for the latter. (Some protein is used to cover obligatory nitrogen losses, but unless fat is deposited—as it is in Arctic and aquatic mammals—for insulation, fat and lactose are used principally for maintenance.) Thus, for most terrestrial mammals, the quotient: protein (g)/(fat + lactose) (g) represents a biologically meaningful measure of the relative growth potency of milk. This ratio is equivalent to the one used by Powers (1933); it differs only in emphasizing that protein and energy are different means for different ends. (For a summary of postnatal growth and milk composition, see Björnhag, Knutsson, & Sperber, 1979; their conclusions for 20 nonprimate species confirm Bernhart's.)

Data on the relative composition of maternal milk were obtained from Jenness (1974) and were regressed logarithmically against maternal weight (Clutton-Brock & Harvey, 1977). The relationship between "relative milk protein" (protein (g)/(fat + lactose) (g)) for the 12 primate species for which data are available is depicted in Figure 4. For this sample, mothers in smaller primate species have milk that, relative to fat and lactose, is disproportionately high in protein. Since protein is used to promote relatively rapid growth, the milk of smaller primates appears "designed" to favor rapid growth at the expense of maintenance.

As these data are not directly comparable to Bernhart's (his data compared milk composition to growth rates), we next address the question of whether smaller primate species actually do grow faster, as their milk composition would suggest.

Infant Growth

Comparing the growth rates of primates is simpler than comparing their milk composition, since endothermic vertebrates exhibit characteristic sigmoidal growth curves to which growth-rate constants can be readily cal-

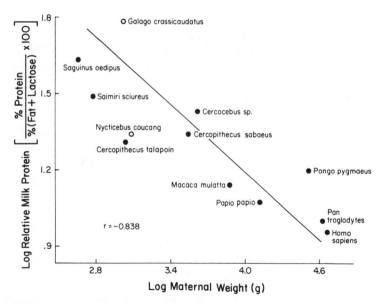

Figure 4. Allometric plot of relative protein content of mother's milk (% protein/% [fat + lactose]) versus maternal weight (g) in 12 primate species. Data on milk content from Jenness (1974); weights from Clutton-Brock and Harvey (1977).

culated (Taylor, 1968). Relative growth rates (g/day/neonatal weight (g)) were fitted over the comparatively linear phase of growth: the interval between the achievement of 5% and 30%-50% of the adult weight (cf. the relative growth rate of Björnhag *et al.*, 1979). Relative growth rates were calculated from Case (1978b), from Willes, Kressler, and Truelove (1977), and from corresponding neonatal weights. Differences in relative growth rates that stem from differences in rearing (e.g., laboratory versus wild) introduce variance into the correlation but should not bias the results. Where possible, growth rates were calculated by sex, and all were regressed against maternal weight in the standard fashion.

The relationship between relative growth rate and maternal weight in 15 primate species is shown in Figure 5. In general, infants in smaller primate species grow relatively faster than infants in larger species. This relationship, of course, is not independent of the negative allometry of neonatal weight

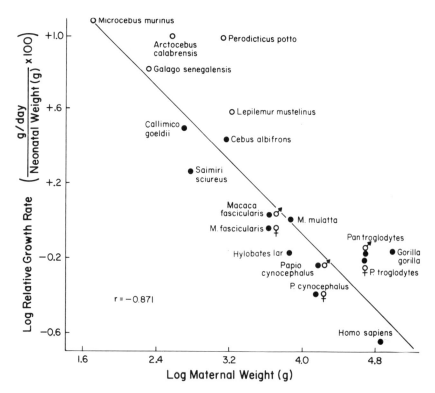

Figure 5. Allometric plot of relative growth rate (g/day/neonatal weight (g)) versus maternal weight (g) in 15 primate species. Relative growth rates computed from Case (1978b), plus additional material.

(Figure 3). The regression of growth rate (g/day) versus maternal weight (g), however, yields similar results (*a*, in this case, is approximately .35 and considerably less than the expected .75; see Case, 1978b); smaller species still grow faster. These results are scarcely surprising; small size and relatively rapid growth are usually coadapted traits (Stearns, 1976; Eisenberg, 1981). The rapid growth and high energy demands of the small infants, however, must place disproportionate demands on the small mother. These demands are offset, in part, by the infants' relative age at weaning.

Weaning Age

Considering the scientific interest that has been accorded comparative lactation (see Blaxter, 1961; Jenness & Sloan, 1970; Lincoln, Chapter 5), initially, it seems surprising that little attention has been devoted to comparative weaning. The surprise vanishes with the realization that there is considerable economic interest in the first and mostly psychological interest in the second. Yet weaning as a subject suffers less from lack of interest than from lack of a useful metric; it is very difficult, for example, to measure "weaning" in free-living primates (see Altmann, 1980, for a pioneering attempt), or even to determine the precise ages at which weaning begins and ends. For instance, in macaques, weaning behaviors (e.g., the mother pushing her infant's head from her nipple) may begin as early as 4 months, although weaning is probably not "complete" (i.e., daytime suckling rates do not drop to near zero) until about 8 months of age (Rosenblum, 1971). Faced with the problem of determining a precise weaning age, we rely on a sort of "upper critical limit": we define "weaning age" as that infant age by which an author reports that weaning is complete.

Data on weaning age were extracted from the literature. Prosimian data are from Doyle (1979); data for anthropoid primates, where possible, are taken from naturalistic studies. A comparable datum for humans was obtained from Konner's (1975) ethnography of the !Kung, a preindustrial society of the Kalahari Desert.

The allometric relationship between weaning age (months) and maternal weight is shown in Figure 6.

In order to interpret Figure 6 it is necessary first to recognize that physiological time—the "rate of living" for any organism—is itself not isometric with body mass (Hill, 1950). That physiological time scales allometrically is readily seen by considering such time in its grossest expression: lifespan. A logarithmic regression of maximum observed lifespan against body mass in 35 species of primates reveals that lifespan is approximately proportional to mass$^{.25}$ (Economos, 1980). In fact, .25 is an exponent characteristic of the basal

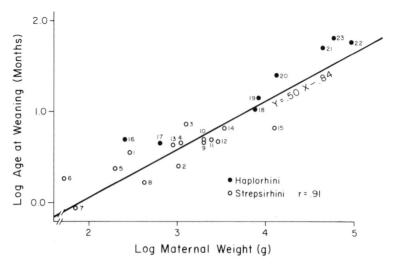

Figure 6. Allometric plot of weaning age (months) versus maternal weight (g) in 23 primate taxa. Data for prosimians are from Doyle (1979) and from additional material. 1. *Arctocebus calabrensis.* 2. *Nycticebus coucang.* 3. *Perodictus potto.* 4. *Galago crassicaudatus.* 5. *Galago senagalensis moholi.* 6. *Galago demidovii.* 7. *Microcebus murinus.* 8. *Cheirogaleus major.* 9. *Lemur macaco.* 10. *Lemur fulvus.* 11. *Lemur catta.* 12. *Lemur variegata.* 13. *Lemur mustilenus.* 14. *Propithecus verreauxi.* 15. *Indri indri.* 16. *Callithrix jacchus.* 17. *Saimiri sciureus.* 18. *Macaca nemestrina* 19. *Presbytis* sp. 20. *Papio anubis.* 21. *Pan troglodytes.* 22. *Gorilla gorilla.* 23. *Homo sapiens.*

rates of cyclic phenomena in general; among other things, it describes the relationship between body mass and cardiac cycle time in endotherms and the time from birth to fledging in birds (Lindstedt & Calder, 1981).

Inspection of Figure 6, however, reveals that time to weaning in primates scales not to the quarter power of mass, but to the square. One interpretation of this finding is that it is simply a sophisticated expression of the anthropological commonplace that, as a whole, primates mature very slowly; this group of phenomena is often termed *neoteny* (Gould, 1977).

There is, however, more information here than that. Relative to physiological time (mass$^{.25}$), a slope of .50 for time to weaning indicates that smaller primate species are weaning their infants disproportionately faster than larger species (or, equivalently, larger species are taking a disproportionately long time to wean theirs). These differences are not simply the result of variation in gestation times. A regression of gestation time versus maternal mass in 53 species of primates yields an exponent of approximately .11 (Schwartz, unpublished observations). A ratio of weaning time to gestation time expressed as common allometric powers of body mass yields:

$$\text{Mass}^{.50}/\text{Mass}^{.11} \propto \text{Mass}^{.39}$$

Even adjusted for differences in gestation time, smaller primates wean earlier.[8]

Galileo, it seems, was right: the large machine is *not* proportionately stronger than the small. Not only are the infants of smaller species relatively enormous, but the milk they consume is disproportionately proteinaceous. Although they are weaned relatively earlier, smaller infants still "milk" their mothers—literally and figuratively—far more than infants of larger species do theirs. If "small is beautiful" (so the maxim goes, Schumacher, 1975), it certainly is not cheap.

One advantage of studying these relationships allometrically, apart from the shorthand summary of information, is that although interspecific allometry cannot reveal causal connections (Gould, 1975; Martin, 1981), it can suggest working hypotheses concerning functional constraints. For known physical reasons, a .5-kg endotherm (other things being equal) could not be built with the metabolic rate of a 50-kg one. For reasons that are less obvious, mothers in small primate species apparently must nurse their young with richer milk, but for a shorter time.

Why should this be the case? Two possibilities come immediately to mind. One is that by reducing the absolute amount of time spent nursing, mothers could curtail the tremendous metabolic cost of lactation, which, in other mammals at least, scales to the .75 power of body mass (Linzell, 1972). A second possibility, suggested by Ricklefs (1969) for birds, is that a strategy of relatively accelerated growth would reduce the period the young spend at small sizes, when newborn mortality is greatest. Clearly, these possibilities are neither mutually exclusive nor exhaustive, and while we may be unable to choose among them at present, we can appreciate Galileo's dictum that "for every machine and structure, there is a necessary limit beyond which neither art nor nature can pass; it is here understood, of course, that the material is the same and the proportion preserved" (1954, p. 3).

On Philology

At this point it may be helpful to introduce a linguistic example. The English word *monkey* stems from the proper name *Moneke,* the son of Martin the Ape in the medieval beast epic *Reynard the Fox* (1498). Thus, with respect to etymology, *monkey* is a descendent of *ape;* with respect to current usage, the opposite is true. (The apes, families *Hylobatidae* and *Pongidae,* are descendents

---

[8] Since allometric equations are not algebraic identities, their manipulation cannot produce empirical equations. When the correlation coefficients are high, however, such approximations are often very good (Stahl, 1962).

of Miocene monkeys.) To suppose that apes really gave rise to monkeys would be an obvious conflation of philology and phylogeny—of the genesis of terms with the genesis of taxa. The fact is that the origin of structures—whether anatomical, behavioral, or linguistic—is essentially independent of their eventual utility (Mayr, 1976; Gould & Lewontin, 1979).

Now consider the observation that infant rhesus monkeys cling avidly (and later, exhibit strong emotional attachments) to nonfeeding terry cloth surrogates in favor of nutritive "mothers" constructed of bare wire—a behavior considered evidence of an innate need for "contact comfort," and heralded as the prototype of "love" (Harlow, 1958).[9] Just as the modern use of *monkey* is a poor guide to the original, the emotional bond of an infant to its terry-cloth surrogate reveals little about the *genesis* of contact clinging. Harlow's explanation conflates the initial physical attachment with a subsequent emotional one and concludes that a "need" for the latter is somehow the cause of the former. Even a tyro recognizes that the explanation "M clings because M has a need for clinging" is no explanation at all (Craik, 1967; Hempel, 1965).

We contend (and we are scarcely the first: see Blaxter, 1961; Jeddi, 1972, 1977; cf. Wallace, 1869/1972, p. 33) that the origins of contact comfort are *thermal*. Thermotaxis is an innate response of nearly all mammalian neonates (Rosenblatt, 1976), and considering Thomas Huxley's "canon of continuity," we should suspect it of primate newborn as well. One hint can be found in Harlow's own data: up to the age of 15 days (when the preference reverses), newborn rhesus monkeys prefer a heated, wire surrogate to a room-temperature cloth one (Harlow & Suomi, 1970). So do newborn rabbits, dogs, and cynomolgus macaques (Jeddi, 1970, 1972, 1977). In thermal terms, these (and a great many other) newborn mammals are "obligate parasites" (Galef, 1981); the costs of thermoregulation simply outstrip the neonates' resources. The thermal netural zone of the newborn macaque (the temperature range at which metabolism is at a minimum), is high ($35\,°C$) and extremely narrow ($\pm 1.5\,°C$). Although the infant is capable of doubling its metabolic rate on cold exposure (Dawes, Jacobson, Mott, & Shelley, 1960), this temporary thermogenesis would be insufficient to forestall hypothermia even under relatively favorable climatic conditions (e.g., $25\,°C$; Hull, 1973).

These data prompt a rekindling of the received doctrine on contact comfort: the newborn's incentives for clinging are mainly metabolic; in any case, they seem far less lofty than "love." The infant monkey later may "love" its mother (surrogate or other), but the newborn clings for *life*. The concept of *contact comfort* thus needs redress, but we should beware of throwing

[9] Since the term *contact comfort* has been applied, *inter alia*, both to the infant's behavior and to its presumed motivation, we prefer *contact clinging* for the behavior (Schwartz & Rosenblum, 1982).

out the baby with the bathtowel. The fact that infant monkeys develop emotional attachments to "cuddly" objects—the phenomenon of contact comfort—is of uncontested importance to comparative psychology. Perhaps the capacity to form such elaborate attachments is unique to primates. But the claim that the psychological aspects of contact comfort betray the biological basis of contact clinging is an evident error; it is the mistake of confusing a logical idea for a psychological one (Ghiselin, 1966). Similar semantic confusions have long plagued the study of form and function.

The problem of untangling the origin of anything from its present use is exacerbated by language: we tend to name things after some function, usually anthropocentric ones. Since sweating is a conspicuous function of human eccrine glands, we christen these structures "sweat glands" and assume that eccrine glands evolved "for" this end. Yet the realization that eccrine glands are present in the integument of virtually all mammals (Whittow, 1971) but function in sweating in only a few (and only in those beyond a certain critical mass; Schmidt-Nielsen, 1964) completely topples this modern "argument from design." We may call eccrine glands "sweat glands" if we wish, although they could hardly have evolved for that purpose.[10]

As Darwin (1886) recognized, the issue is one of linguistic convention:

> Although an organ may not have been originally formed for some special purpose, if it now serves for this end, we are justified in saying that it is specially adapted for it. On the same principle, if a man were to make a machine for some special purpose, but were to use old wheels, springs and pulleys only slightly altered, the whole machine, with all its parts, might be said to be specially contrived for its present purpose. Thus throughout nature almost every part of each living being has probably served, in a slightly modified condition, for diverse purposes, and has acted in the living machinery of many ancient and distinct living forms. (pp. 283–284)

Darwin's exegesis is a fitting conclusion here—but better still is the injunction of Germany's keenest philologist, Friedrich Nietzsche:

> For every kind of historiography there is no more important proposition than this, which has been discovered with so much effort, but now also ought to be discovered once and for all: the cause of the origin of a thing and its eventual usefulness, its actual employment and incorporation in a system of aims, lie worlds apart. (Kaufmann, 1968, p. 452)

---

[10] Unless, of course, one argues that such "nonfunctional" glands are vestigial—precisely the claim of several eminent physiologists on the status of eccrine glands in primates (e.g., Folk, 1974). Proponents of the "vestigial" view have yet to explain why the vast majority of these (tropical) taxa have independently foregone the "necessity" of sweating. "Adaptationists," on the other hand, have still to suggest a plausible origin for such structures, for just as the psychological utility of contact clinging is no proof of "psychological" design, the present thermoregulatory role of eccrine glands admits few clues to their primitive function.

Neonatal Thermoregulation

"The baby, human or monkey, if it is to survive, must clutch at more than a straw" (Harlow, 1958).

Louis Agassiz, Darwin's great American opponent, once proclaimed that God's resources were not so meager than He must make men from monkeys (Pfeifer, 1972). The resources of newborn humans, however, are strikingly like those of newborn monkeys: both are strictly circumscribed by size. In the following section, we highlight some research on the pediatric implications of size for neonatal growth and thermoregulation.

Like most mammalian newborn, human neonates face immediate geometric and metabolic disadvantages: at birth we are small, wet, physiologically immature (at least by adult standards; see Galef, 1981), and insulated even more poorly than other primates. Ironically, these problems are aggravated by the thermal environment in which most "civilized" women give birth: the ambient conditions of hospital delivery rooms are well below the thermoneutral zone of a naked full-term infant (Hey & Katz, 1970; Miller & Oliver, 1966). Under normal delivery room conditions, the newborn's core temperature commonly falls 2-3°C (Adamson, 1966), and hospital staff traditionally employ a variety of procedures to counter the infant's initial hypothermia. For example, drying babies immediately after birth (especially their heads) reduces heat lost through evaporation, as does oropharyngeal suctioning (heat losses due to evaporation of amniotic fluid from the respiratory tract can be considerable; Nalepka, 1976). Blankets and heating pads minimize conductive losses; incubators, mostly convectional ones; and radiant losses are combated with radiant heaters. Curiously, this array of hospital technology may have overshadowed a more fundamental heat source: the mother's body.

Recently, Färdig (1980) questioned whether current hospital procedures are actually more effective than maternal heat in promoting neonatal thermoregulation. She compared the skin and core temperatures of infants given skin-to-skin contact immediately following delivery (infants were dried, blanketed, and placed on the mothers' bare chests) with the temperatures of infants similarly treated but placed immediately in radiant-heated cribs. The results for these two groups (17 mothers and babies in each) are replotted in Figure 7. The infants given direct skin-to-skin contact had significantly higher skin temperatures than the infants given radiant heat and were significantly less likely to have rectal temperatures below the thermoneutral zone.

Little wonder that newborn monkeys cling!

Not only is infant thermoregulation optimized by the selection of a warm microenvironment, infant growth rates are as well. One advantage of raising a newborn mammal in a thermoneutral environment is that calories

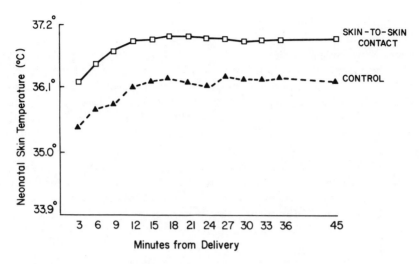

Figure 7. Mean skin temperature (abdomen) of human neonates given immediate maternal-infant contact (placed on mother's bare chest after cutting the umbilicus) and control neonates (placed in a radiant-heated Kreiselman crib) as a function of time after delivery. Data are replotted from Färdig (1980).

otherwise expended for maintenance can be channeled into growth (Brody, 1945). Thus, in a study of healthy infants of low birth weight, Glass and colleagues (1968) reared two groups of infants for two weeks in incubators that maintained skin temperature at either 35.0°C ("cool") or 36.5°C ("warm"). Both groups received 120 Kcal of food per kilogram of body weight per day. During the experimental period, "warm" infants showed significantly greater gains in body weight and length than did "cool" infants. ("Cool" infants, of course, were hardly cool but were well within their thermoneutral zone.) Interestingly, these temperature differences in growth could be offset by adjusting the calories supplied by the milk. In a subsequent study, "cool" infants given a dietary supplement of 8 Kcal showed weight and length gains comparable to those of the unsupplemented "warm" infants. "Cool" infants without dietary supplementation showed a slight growth retardation. Apparently, the retarded growth of the unsupplemented "cool" infants reflected a diversion of nutrients from growth to heat production.

However, the accelerated growth of the "warm" infants was costly in another way: without experience with cooler temperatures, "warm" infants were less able to defend themselves againt a drop in core temperature during a standard cold-stress test administered at the end of the two-week period. The authors concluded that an optimum environment for small asymptomatic neonates may be a slightly "cool" one augmented with a hypercaloric diet;

such infants have the advantage of both a rapid gain in weight and an increaed ability to resist an acute cold stress (Glass, Silverman, & Sinclair, 1969).[11]

The diversion of calories from growth to maintenance may help to explain the intriguing findings of Scott and Richards (1979). In their study, month-old babies "fidgeted" less and gained weight more rapidly on the days when they were placed in incubators in which lambswool pads were substituted for cotton bedding. The striking gain in weight (as much as 10 g/day extra) could not be explained solely by a reduction of oxygen consumption or radiant heat loss, since at the temperatures used ($33.5\,^\circ$C incubator, $27.1\,^\circ$C room), month-old babies are already within their thermoneutral zone, where a reduction in heat loss is not necessarily associated with decreased energy expenditure (Hey, 1975). Scott and Richards hypothesized that the tactile qualities of the lambswool may have exerted an indirect effect on growth by reducing infant stress and, consequently, decreasing infant metabolic rate (stress hormones like thyroxine and catecholamines typically increase metabolic rate). Such "calming" effects of physical contact may underlie the soothing effects of Harlow's terry-cloth surrogates and may contribute to the greater thermal stability Färdig observed in neonates given immediate skin-to-skin contact.

Similar findings on infant metabolism were summarized by Cross, who reported that infants' rates of oxygen consumption and normal postpartum fall in deep body temperature could both be diminished—merely by placing a thick woolen hat over the newborn's wet head! This expedient takes advantage of the fact that nearly 70% of the neonate's metabolic activity is concentrated in the brain (Cross, Stothers, & Stratton, 1975) and thus can be partially conserved by insulating the cranium. (The same amount of material wrapped around the infant's abdomen has little effect; Cross, 1979.) Although hardly as charming, a decrease in oxygen consumption and an increase in infant skin temperature also can be achieved via the simple addition of a second wall to a traditional convection-heated incubator (Marks, Lee, Bolan, & Maisels, 1981; unlike Cross's hat, which conserves heat by several avenues, the decrease in heat loss caused by the incubator wall is due principally to radiant savings).

The recognition of climate's indirect effects on patterns of human growth is not new (cf. Roberts, 1973), and we conclude this section with one of the

[11] A phenomenon remarkably similar to Glass's "cool"-supplemented infants occurs in mice, apparently produced through artificial selection: wild mice (*Mus musculus*) that are bred for several generations in refrigerators near $0\,^\circ$C (so-called Eskimo mice) produce milk that, compared with that of controls, is significantly higher in both protein and fat. Eskimo mice are heavier than control mice at all ages as well (Barnett, 1979). Endotherms seem to have very limited degrees of freedom indeed!

early demonstrations of climatic effects on the newborn. In a fascinating but neglected paper, Villermé and Milne-Edwards (1829) compiled data on the mortality of neonates in two provinces of France, one at 49° latitutde ("Nord"), and the other more southerly, at 45° latitude ("Midi") during the period 1818–1819. The results of their census, they urged, demonstrated "a remarkable coincidence between the lowering of the general temperature and the increase in the mortality of the newborn" (translation, p. 303). (Their paper also includes much sound advice, e.g., that priests should be sure that infants are carefully dried after baptism.)

As their tabulations predated the use of descriptive statistics, we have calculated the percentage of mortality for the two provinces and have analyzed these, by month, againt the monthly low temperatures of Paris. (At practically 49° latitude, Paris gives a good estimate of the climate of Nord and is conservative for Midi.) The results are shown in Figure 8. Neonatal mortality is significantly greater in the north and, even with our estimated temperatures, shows a marked peak during the winter months. More recent reports on the effects of temperature on neonatal mortality (e.g., Bonser & West, 1979) and, particularly, on the disadvantages of small size (Day, Caliguiri, Kamenski, & Ehrlich, 1964) attest to the importance of geography and geometry on the survival of the newborn.

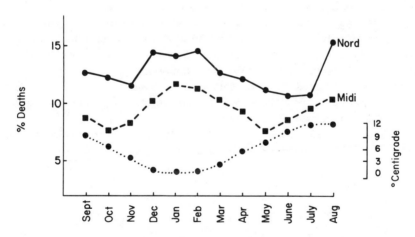

Figure 8. Monthly percentage of mortality (death/births) for live-born infants 3 months or older as a function of latitude and temperature in the provinces "Nord" (49° latitude) and "Midi" (45° latitude), France, during 1818–1819. Data on infant mortality calculated from Villermé and Milne-Edwards (1829), temperatures are the monthly lows in Paris and are from the Air Ministry, Meterological Office, London (1960).

Conclusion

In this chapter we have had two goals: first, to stress the thermal significance of body size for our understanding of primate adaptation, and second, to illustrate possible metabolic constraints on primate mothers and infants. We conclude with a few remarks about each.

The obvious reason for studying the thermal effects of size is that these are so ubiquitous (Swan, 1974). Since primates exhibit an essentially similar body plan constructed at dissimilar sizes, primate design should "automatically" reflect the effects of scale. The effects of scaling on behavior, however, may be far from obvious. For example, in "opting" for chronic insurance against hypothermia, small, densely furred primates face acute hyperthermia during periods of intense activity or heat stress. Since they can barely sweat, many small primates have evolved "unusual" acute thermoregulatory behaviors, including the "opportunisitc" use of urinary (Robinson, 1980) and respiratory (Schwartz, 1981, 1983) fluids.

A second reason for studying allometric relationships is that functional explanations for one group of endotherms (e.g., primates) may be tested by comparison with similar trends identified in another (birds, for instance). As a result, we may discover some entirely unsuspected adaptations in one group of animals and eliminate claims of spurious adaptation in others. For example, consider the champion of modern "just so" stories, Sir Alistair Hardy's (1960) "aquatic ape" hypothesis. Caricaturized for simplicity, it runs essentially as follows: Since humans are relatively hairless, and hairlessness is a trait shared by aquatic mammals, human nudity is the watermark of a previously aquatic existence. (Hardy supposed that the transitional man-apes, about whom the fossil record is notoriously silent, spent the Miocene by the sea; hence the absence of a [savannah] record.) This is a remarkable bit of woolly reasoning: on the evidence of the naked mole rat (*Heterocephalus*), we might as well conclude that early humans were subterranean or, as bipedality is found in birds, that our ancestors were feathered.[12]

Hardy's hypothesis is not erected here as a straw man; it has recently been resuscitated (in the pages of the Royal Society's *Philosophical Transactions*, no less) as a ground for the archaeological exploration of the Danakil Alps—a Pliocene island formation where the supposed remains of our "aquatic" ancestors may presumably be found (La Lumiere, 1981).

With the aid of appropriate allometric comparisons, many subtler "just

---

[12] Current wisdom holds that nudity in *Heterocephalus* is a thermoregulatory specialization: fossorial rodents face great difficulties in the dissipation of metabolic heat while burrowing (McNab, 1966). The covariation of characters is a classic taxonomic problem; even Plato once defined man as a "featherless biped."

so" stories can be cut to size. For example, our hypothesis concerning the evolution of hair density is not peculiar to primates; if it is correct, then among isometric endotherms with broadly similar physiology and geographic distribution, insulation should decrease with increasing body mass. In avian species, the quantity of feathers per unit of body mass shows the expected negative allometry: bigger birds have relatively fewer feathers (Turček, 1966). Similar phenomena should obtain for the coats of mammals. The Felidae are isometric endotherms with a large range in size and would provide a good test of this hypothesis. If smaller cats are not furrier than larger ones, then our explanation for primates will require rethinking.

The energetics of primate mothers and infants are similarly influenced by size constraints. Smaller primate mothers bear the brunt of several interrelated trends: the negative allometries of neonatal weight, milk protein, and infant growth; in small species, infants are relatively heavier and hungrier; they grow faster and are weaned earlier. The net result is that motherhood is far more expensive in smaller endotherms (Case, 1978a; Trivers, 1974). This conclusion is scarcely surprising. The smallest mammalian endotherms, shrews, may not survive beyond the weaning of their first litter (Forsyth, 1976), and semelparity (breeding only once) may be a life history trait of other small mammals (Braithwaite & Lee, 1979; Eisenberg, 1981).

Yet these analyses raise more questions than they answer. Why, for example, do mothers in small primate species compound their tremendous energy costs by producing milk so high in protein? One explanation may lie in reducing the mortality risks attendant on absolute neonatal size—by minimizing the absolute time the young spend at small sizes.

Selective forces acting to minimize the lactational drain on the small mother should favor a milk composition that meets but does not exceed the maximum growth capabilities of the newborn (Oftedal, 1980). In 1945, Brody suggested that the speed of infant growth was the evolutionary factor determining a species' milk composition, rather than the milk composition's influencing the growth rate. Recent studies have confirmed his insight; increasing the protein content of the milk does not increase the growth rate: humans fed breast milk grow at rates virtually identical to those fed cow's milk containing two to three times as much protein (Svenningsen, Lindroth, & Lindquist, 1982; Räihä, Heinomen, Rassin, & Gaull, 1976). The relatively high-protein milk of small mothers, favoring growth at the expense of maintenance, implies that the infant's maintenance requirements are met elsewhere—perhaps from physical contact with the mother's body.

Data reviewed for humans indicate that the mother's body may be the opitmal thermal environment for the neonate (Färdig, 1980), and that small absolute size is the best predictor of neonatal mortality (Day et al., 1964). If these trends obtained in smaller primate species (Huxley's canon in reverse!), then by channeling the majority of calories into growth, small mothers could reduce neonatal mortality indirectly, by reducing the absolute time in which neonatal mortality is greatest—effectively speeding their infants through a risky period. Just such a coadapted relationship between neonatal mortality, growth rates, and adult body size occurs among altricial birds (Ricklefs, 1969; cf. Williams, 1966). Whether a similar relationship occurs among primates is (at present) only speculation. But that, after all, is one of the fascinating advantages of allometry: the discovery of comparative trends that invite further exploration.

ACKNOWLEDGMENTS

We thank Drs. Jeanne Altmann and Jerry Eberhart for helpful comments on the manuscript and Ms. Susan Woldenberg for mathematical assistance. We are especially grateful to Ms. Ellen Tanner, Director of Interlibrary Loans at the Downstate Medical Center, for her tireless pursuit of manuscripts *in occultis locis.*

References

Adamson, K., Jr. The role of thermal factors in fetal and neonatal life. *The Pediatric Clinics of North America,* 1966, *13,* 599–619.
Altmann, J. *Baboon mothers and infants.* Cambridge, Mass.: Harvard University Press, 1980.
Barnett, S. A. Comportement, croissance et influences maternelles et génétiques dans l'adaptation de la souris au froid, *Bulletin et Mémoirs de la Societé d'Anthropologie de Paris,* 1979, *13,* 146–160.
Barnicot, N. A. Climatic factors in the evolution of human populations. *Cold Spring Harbor Symposium on Quantitative Biology,* 1959, *29,* 115–129.
Barr, A. Comparisons of similar structures and machines. *Transactions of the Institution of Engineers & Shipbuilders in Scotland,* 1899, *42,* 322–360.
Bartholomew, G. A. Body temperature and energy metabolism. In M. S. Gordon (Ed.), *Animal physiology: Principles and adaptations.* New York: Macmillan, 1977, pp. 364–449.
Bekoff, M., Diamond, J., & Mitton, J. Life history patterns and sociality in canids: Body size, reproduction, and behavior. *Oecologia,* 1981, *50,* 386–390.
Bernhart, F. W. Correlation between growth-rate of the suckling of various species and the percentage of total calories in the milk. *Nature,* 1961, *191,* 358–360.
Björnhag, G., Knutsson, P., & Sperber, I. Postnatal growth and milk composition. *Swedish Journal of Agricultural Reserach,* 1979, *9,* 65–74.
Blaxter, K. L. Lactation and the growth of the young. In S. K. Kon & A. T. Cowie (Eds.), *Milk: The mammary gland and its secretion* (Vol. 2). New York: Academic Press, 1961, pp. 305–361.
Blueweiss, L., Fox, H., Kudzma, V., Nakashima, D., Peters, R., & Sams, S. Relationships between body size and some life history parameters. *Oecologia,* 1978, *37,* 257–272.
Bonser, R., & West, R. Sudden infant death and low temperature. *Lancet,* December 22/29, 1979, p. 1379.
Bourlière, F. Mammals, small and large: The ecological implications of size. In F. B. Golley, K. Petrusewicz, & L. Rsyzkowski (Eds.), *Small mammals: Their productivity and population dynamics.* Cambridge: Cabmridge University Press, 1975, pp. 1–8.

Bowden, D., Winter, P., & Ploog, D. Pregnancy and delivery behavior in the squirrel monkey (*Saimiri siureus*) and other primates. *Folia primatologica,* 1967, *5,* 1-42.

Braithwaite, R. W., & Lee, A. K. A mammalian example of semelparity. *American Naturalist,* 1979, *113,* 151-155.

Brody, S. *Bioenergetics and growth.* New York: Reinhold, 1945.

Brown, J. H., Calder, W. A., III, & Kodric-Brown, A. Correlates and consequences of body size in nectar-feeding birds. *American Zoologist,* 1978, *18,* 687-700.

Bunge, G. V. *Text-book of physiological and pathological chemistry.* Philadelphia: Blakiston, 1902.

Case, T. J. Endothermy and parental care in the terrestrial vertebrates. *American Naturalist,* 1978. *112,* 861-874. (a)

Case, T. J. On the evolution and adaptive significance of postnatal growth rates in the terrestrial vertebrates. *Quarterly Review of Biology,* 1978, *53,* 243-282. (b)

Cena, K., & Clark, J. A. Transfer of heat through animal coats and clothing. In D. Robertshaw (Ed.), *Environmental physiology III* (Vol. 20). Baltimore: University Park Press, 1979, pp. 1-42.

Cena, K., & Monteith, J. L. Transfer processes in animal coats III. Water vapour diffusion. *Proceedings of the Royal Society of London,* 1975, *188B,* 413-423.

Clutton-Brock, T. H., & Harvey, P. H. Primate ecology and social organization. *Journal of Zoology (London),* 1977, *183,* 1-39.

Cock, A. G. Genetical aspects of metrical growth and form in animals. *Quarterly Review of Biology,* 1966, *41,* 131-190.

Craik, K. *The nature of explanation.* Cambridge: Cambridge University Press, 1967.

Cross, K. W. *La chaleur animale* and the infant brain. *Journal of Physiology (London),* 1979, *294,* 1-21.

Cross, K. W., Stothers, J. K., & Stratton, D. An indirect estimate of total brain energy metabolism in the new-born infant. *Journal of Physiology,* 1975, *250,* 15P.

Darwin, C. *On the origin of species: A facsimile of the first edition.* Cambridge, Mass.: Harvard University Press, 1981. (Originally published, 1859.)

Darwin, C. *The descent of man, and selection in relation to sex. A facsimile of the 1871 edition.* Princeton, N.J.: Princeton University Press, 1981.

Darwin, C. *The various contrivances by which orchids are fertilized by insects* (2nd ed.). New York: Appleton, 1886.

Darwin, C. *The variation of animals and plants under domestication* (2nd ed.). New York: Appleton, 1887.

Dawes, G. S., Jacobson, H. N., Mott, J. C., & Shelley, H. J. Some observatons on foetal and new-born rhesus monkeys. *Journal of Physiology (London),* 1960, *152,* 271-298.

Day, R. L., Caliguiri, L., Kamenski, C., & Erlich, F. Body temperature and survival of premature infants. *Pediatrics,* 1964, *34,* 171-181.

Doyle, G. A. Development of behavior in prosimians with special reference to the lesser bushbaby, *Galago senegalensis moholi.* In G. A. Doyle & R. D. Martin (Eds.), *The study of prosimian behavior.* New York: Academic Press, 1979, pp. 157-207.

Eberhart, J. A. *Relationships between hormones and behavior in a social group of talapoin monkeys.* Unpublished doctoral dissertation, University of Cambridge, 1981.

Economos, A. C. Taxonomic differences in the mammalian life-span body weight relationship and the problem of brain weight. *Gerontology,* 1980, *26,* 90-98.

Eisenberg, J. F. *The mammalian radiations.* Chicago: University of Chicago Press, 1981.

Eisenberg, L. The *human* nature of human nature. *Science,* 1972, *176,* 123-128.

Färdig, J. A. A comparison of skin-to-skin contact and radiant heaters in promoting neonatal thermoregulation. *Journal of Nurse-Midwifery,* 1980, *25,* 19-28.

Folk, G. E., Jr. *Textbook of environmental physiology.* Philadelphia: Lea & Febiger, 1974.

Forsyth, D. J. A field study of growth and development of nestling masked shrews (*Sorex cinereus*). *Journal of Mammalogy,* 1976, *57,* 708-721.

Galef, B. G., Jr. The ecology of weaning: Parasitism and the achievement of independence by altricial mammals. In D. J. Gubernick & P. H. Klopfer (Eds.), *Parental care in mammals.* New York: Plenum Press, 1981, pp. 211–241.

Galilei, G. *Dialogues concerning two new sciences* (H. Crew & A. de Salvio, trans.). New York: Dover, 1954.

Ghiselin, M. T. On psychologism in the logic of taxonomic controversies. *Systematic Zoology,* 1966, *15,* 207–215.

Gibbs, H. D. *Phillipine Journal of Science,* 1912, *137,* 91.

Glass, L., Silverman, W. A., & Sinclair, J. C. Effect of the thermal environment on cold resistance and growth of small infants after the first week of life. *Pediatrics,* 1968, *41,* 1033–1046.

Glass, L., Silverman, W. A., & Sinclair, J. C. Relationship of thermal environment and caloric intake to growth and resting metabolism in the late neonatal period. *Biologia Neonatorium,* 1969, *14,* 324–340.

Gould, S. J. Allometry and size in ontogeny and phylogeny. *Biological Reviews,* 1966, *41,* 587–640.

Gould, S. J. D'Arcy Thompson and the science of form. *New Literary History,* 1971, *2,* 229–258.

Gould, S. J. Allometry in primates with emphasis on scaling and the evolution of the brain. *Contributions to Primatology,* 1975, *5,* 244–292.

Gould, S. J. *Ontogeny and phylogeny.* Cambridge, Mass.: Harvard University Press, 1977.

Gould, S. J. *The mismeasure of man.* New York: Norton, 1981.

Gould, S. J., & Lewontin, R. C. The sprandrels of San Marco and the Panglossian paradigm: A critique of the adaptationist programme. *Proceedings of the Royal Society of London B,* 1979, *205,* 581–598.

Guilloud, N. B., & Fitz-Gerald, F. L. Spontaneous hyperthermia in the gorilla. *Folia Primatologica,* 1967, *6,* 177–179.

Günther, B. Dimensional analysis and theory of biological similarity. *Physiological Reviews,* 1975, *55,* 659–699.

Haldane, J. B. S. On being the right size. In H. Shapley, S. Rapport, & H. Wright (Eds.), *A treasury of science.* New York: Harper & Brothers, 1946, pp. 321–325.

Hamilton, W. J., III. *Life's color code.* New York: McGraw-Hill, 1973.

Hardy, A. Was man more aquatic in the past? *New Scientist,* 1960, *17,* 642–645.

Harlow, H. F. The nature of love. *American Psychologist,* 1958, *13,* 673–685.

Harlow, H. F., & Suomi, S. J. Nature of love—simplified. *American Psychologist,* 1970, *25,* 161–168.

Harvey, P. H., & Clutton-Brock, T. H. Primate home-range size and metabolic needs. *Behavioral Ecology and Sociobiology,* 1981, *8,* 151–155.

Heinroth, O. Die Beziehungen zwischen Vogelgewicht, Eiergewicht, Gelegegewicht, und Brutdauer. *Journal für Ornithologie,* 1922, *70,* 172–249.

Hempel, C. G. *Aspects of scientific explanation.* New York: Free Press, 1965.

Hey, E. N. Thermal neutrality. *British Medical Bulletin,* 1975, *1,* 69–74.

Hey, E. N., & Katz, G. The optimum thermal environment for naked babies. *Archives of the Diseases of Childhood,* 1970, *45,* 328–334.

Hill, A. V. The dimensions of animals and their muscular dynamics. *Science Progress,* 1950, *38,* 209–230.

Holt, A. B., Cheek, D. B., Mellits, E. D., & Hill, D. E. Brain size and the relation of the primate to the nonprimate. In D. B. Cheek (Ed.), *Fetal and postnatal cellular growth: Hormones and nutrition.* New York: Wiley, 1975, pp. 23–44.

Hull, D. Thermoregulation in young mammals. In G. C. Whittow (Ed.), *Comparative physiology of thermoregulation* (Vol. 3). New York: Academic Press, 1973, pp. 167–200.

Huxley, J. S. Constant differential growth-ratios and their significance. *Nature,* 1924, *114,* 895–896.

Huxley, J. S. On the relation between egg-weight and body-weight in birds. *Journal of the Linnean Society of London (Zoology),* 1927, *36,* 457–466.

Huxley, J. S. *Problems of relative growth.* New York: Dover, 1972. Reprint of the 1932 edition (Methuen & Co., London).

Huxley, T. H. On the hypothesis that animals are automata, and its history. *Nature,* 1874, *10,* 362–366.

Ingold, C. T. Size and form in agarics. *Transactions of the British Mycological Society,* 1946, *29,* 108–113.

Jeddi, E. Comfort du contact et thermoregulation comportementale. *Physiology and Behavior,* 1970, *5,* 1487–1493.

Jeddi, E. Thermoregulatory efficiency of neonatal rabbit search for fur contact comfort. *International Journal of Biometeorology,* 1972, *15,* 105.

Jeddi, E. Ontogenese du confort thermique et hypothese theorique sur sa place dans le developpement affectif. *Inserm,* 1977, *75,* 101–144.

Jenness, R. The composition of milk. In B. L. Larson & K. R. Smith (Eds.), *Lactation, a comprehensive treatise* (Vol. 3). New York: Academic Press, 1974, pp. 3–107.

Jenness, R., & Sloan, R. E. The composition of milks of various species: A review. *Dairy Science Abstracts,* 1970, *32,* 599–612.

Jerison, H. J. *Evolution of the brain and intelligence.* New York: Academic Press, 1973.

Jolicoeur, P. The multivariate generalization of the allometry equation. *Bioemetrics,* 1963, *19,* 497–499.

Jungers, W. L., & German, R. Z. Ontogenetic and interspecific skeletal allometry in nonhuman primates. *American Journal of Physical Anthropology,* 1981, *55,* 195–202.

Kaplan, R. H., & Salthe, S. N. The allometry of reproduction: An empirical view in salamanders. *American Naturalist,* 1979, *113,* 671–688.

Kaufmann, W. (Ed.). *The portable Nietzsche.* New York: Penguin Books, 1968.

Kidd, W. *The direction of hair in animals and man.* London: Adam and Charles Black, 1903.

King, J. R., & Farner, D. S. Energy metabolism, thermoregulation and body temperature. In A. J. Marshall (Ed.), *Biology and comparative physiology of birds.* (Vol. 2). New York: Academic Press, 1961, pp. 215–288.

Kleiber, M. Body size and metabolism. *Hilgardia,* 1932, *6,* 315–353.

Kleiber, M. *The fire of life.* Huntington, N.Y.: Krieger, 1975.

Koner, M. Relationships among infants and juveniles in comparative perspective. In M. Lewis & L. Rosenblum (Eds.), *Friendship and peer relations.* New York: Wiley, 1975.

La Lumiere, L. P. Evolution of human bipedalism: A hypothesis about where it happened. *Philosophical Transactions of the Royal Society of London,* 1981, *B292,* 103–107.

LeMaho, Y., Goffart, M., Rochas, A., Felbabel, H., & Chatonnet, J. Thermoregulation in the only nocturnal simian: The night monkey *Aotus trivirgatus. American Journal of Physiology,* 1981, *240,* R156–R165.

Leutenegger, W. Maternal-fetal weight relationships in primates. *Folia Primatologica,* 1973, *20,* 280–293.

Leutenegger, W. Allometry of neonatal size in eutherian mammals. *Nature,* 1976, *263,* 229–230.

Leutenegger, W. Evolution of litter size in primates. *American Naturalist,* 1979, *114,* 525–531.

Lindstedt, S. L., & Calder, W. A., III. Body size, physiological time and longevity of homeothermic animals. *Quarterly Review of Biology,* 1981, *56,* 1–16.

Linzell, J. L. Milk yield, energy loss in milk, and mammary gland weight in different species. *Dairy Science Abstracts,* 1972, *34,* 351–360.

Lorenz, K. Durch Domestikation verusachte Störungen arteigenen Verhaltens. *Zeitschrift für angewandte Psychologie und Characterkunde,* 1940, *59,* 2–81.

Luckett, W. P. Ontogeny of the fetal membranes and placenta, their bearing on primate phylogeny. In W. P. Luckett & F. S. Szalay (Eds.), *Phylogeny of the primates.* New York: Plenum Press, 1975, pp. 157–182.

Mahoney, S. A. Cost of locomotion and heat balance during rest and running from 0 to 55°C in a patus monkey. *Journal of Applied Physiology: Respiratory, Environmental and Exercise Physiology,* 1980, *49,* 789–800.

Marks, K. H., Lee, C. A., Bolan, C. D., & Maisels, M. J. Oxygen consumption and temperature control of premature infants in a double-wall incubator. *Pediatrics,* 1981, *68,* 93–98.

Martin, R. D. Relative brain size and basal metabolic rate in terrestrial vertebrates. *Nature,* 1981, *293,* 57–60.

Mayr, E. The emergence of evolutionary novelties. In E. Mayr, *Evolution and the diversity of life.* Cambridge, Mass.: Harvard University Press, 1976, pp. 88–113.

McNab, B. K. Bioenergetics and the determination of home range size. *American Naturalist,* 1963, *97,* 133–140.

McNab, B. K. The metabolism of fossorial rodents: A study in convergence. *Ecology,* 1966, *47,* 712–733.

McNab, B. K. The energetics of endotherms. *Ohio Journal of Science,* 1974, *74,* 370–380.

McNab, B. K. Food habits, energetics, and the population biology of mammals. *American Naturalist,* 1980, *116,* 106–124.

Millar, J. S. Pre-partum reproductive characteristics of eutherian mammals. *Evolution,* 1981, *35,* 1149–1163.

Miller, D. L., & Oliver, T. K. Body temperature in the immediate neonatal period: The effect of reducing thermal loss. *American Journal of Obstetrics and Gynecology,* 1966, *94,* 964–969.

Miller, G. S., Jr. Human hair and primate patterning. *Smithsonian Miscellaneous Collections,* 1931, *85,* 1–13.

Montagna, W. Cutaneous comparative biology. *Archives of Dermatology,* 1971, *104,* 577–591.

Motnagna, W. The skin of nonhuman primates. *American Zoologist,* 1972, *12,* 109–121.

Mosimann, J. E., & James, F. C. New statistical methods of allometry with application to Florida red-winged blackbirds. *Evolution,* 1979, 33, 444–459.

Myers, R. D. Primates. In G. C. Whittow (Ed.), *Comparative physiology of thermoregulation* (Vol. 2). New York: Academic Press, 1971, pp. 283–326.

Nakayama, T., Hori, T., Nagasaka, T., Tokura, H., & Tadaki, E. Thermal and metabolic responses in the Japanese monkey at temperatures of 5–38°C. *Journal of Applied Physiology,* 1971, *31,* 332–337.

Nalepka, C. D. Understanding thermoregulation in newborns. *Journal of Obstetrical, Gynecological and Neonatal Nursing,* 1976, *5,* 17–19.

Newman, R. W. Why man is such a sweaty and thirsty naked mammal: A speculative review. *Human Biology,* 1970, *42,* 12–27.

Oftedal, O. T. Milk and mammalian evolution. In K. Schmidt-Nielsen, L. Bolis, & R. Taylor (Eds.), *Comparative physiology: Primitive mammals.* Cambridge: Cambridge University Press, 1980, pp. 31–42.

Pfeifer, E. J. United States. In T. F. Glick (Ed.), *The comparative reception of Darwinism.* Austin: University of Texas Press, 1972, pp. 168–226.

Pilbeam, D. *The ascent of man.* New York: Macmillan, 1972.

Pilbeam, D., & Gould, S. J. Size and scaling in human evolution. *Science,* 1974, *186,* 892–901.

Platt, T., & Silvert, W. Ecology, physiology, allometry and dimensionality. *Journal of Theoretical Biology,* 1981, *93,* 855–860.

Powers, G. F. The alleged correlation between the rate of growth of the suckling and the composition of the milk of the species. *Journal of Pediatrics,* 1933, *3,* 201–216.

Räihä, N.C., Heinomen, K., Rassin, D. K., & Gaull, G. E. Milk protein quantity and quality in low-birth-weight infants: I. Metabolic responses and effects on growth. *Pediatrics,* 1976, *57,* 659–674.

Ricklefs, R. E. Preliminary models for growth rates in altricial birds. *Ecology,* 1969, *50,* 1031–1039.

Roberts, D. F. Climate and human variability: An Addison-Wesley module in anthropology. No. 34, 1973, 1–38.

Robinson, J. G. Correlates of urine washing in the wedge-capped capuchin *Cebus nigrivattatus*. In J. F. Eisenberg (Ed.), *Vertebrate ecology in the northern neotropics*. Washington, D.C.: Smithsonian Institution Press, 1980, pp. 137–143.

Ronald, K., & Dougan, J. L. The ice lover: Biology of the harp seal (*Phoca groenlandica*). *Science*, 1982, *215*, 928–933.

Rosenblatt, J. S. Stages in the early behavioural development of altricial young of selected species of non-primate mammals. In P. P. G. Bateson & R. A. Hinde (Eds.), *Growing points in ethology*. Cambidge: Cambridge University Press, 1976, pp. 345–383.

Rosenblum, L. A. The ontogeny of mother-infant relations in macaques. In H. Moltz (Ed.), *The ontogeny of vertebrate behavior* New York: Academic Press, 1971.

Schmidt-Nielsen, K. *Desert animals: Physiological problems of heat and water*. Fair Lawn, N.J.: Oxford University Press, 1964.

Schmidt-Nielsen, K. *Animal physiology, adaptation and environment*. London: Cambridge University Press, 1975.

Schmidt-Nielsen, K. Problems of scaling: Locomotion and physiological correlates. In T. J. Pedley (Ed.), *Scale effects in animal locomotion*. New York: Academic Press, 1977, pp. 1–21.

Schultz, A. H. The technique of measuring the outer body of human fetuses and of primates in general. *Contributions to embryology* #117 (Carnegie Institute of Washington #394), 1929, *20*, 213–257.

Schultz, A. H. The density of hair in primates. *Human Biology*, 1931, *3*, 303–321.

Schultz, A. H. *The life of primates*. New York: Universe Books, 1969.

Schumacher, E. F. *Small is beautiful: Economics as if people mattered*. New York: Harper & Row, 1975.

Schwartz, G. G. *Thermal influences on the behavior of squirrel monkeys* (Samiri sciureus): *Does Samiri origins of platyrrhine sneezing*. *American Journal of Primatology*, 1981, *1*, 325–326.

Schwartz, G. G. *Thermal influences on the behavior of squirrel monkeys* (Samiri Scuireus): *Does Samiri sneeze to thermoregulate?* Unpublished doctoral thesis, Downstate Medical Center of the State University of New York, 1983.

Schwartz, G. G., & Rosenblum, L. A. Allometry of primate hair density and the evolution of human hairlessness. *American Journal of Physical Anthropology*, 1981, *55*, 9–12.

Schwartz, G. G., & Rosenblum, L. A. Primate infancy: Problems and developmental strategies, In B. B. Wolman (Ed.), *Handbook of developmental psychology*. Englewood Cliffs, N.J.: Prentice-Hall, 1982, pp. 63–75.

Scott, S., & Richards, M. Nursing low birthweight infants on lambswool. *Lancet*, May 12, 1979, p. 1028.

Sherrington, C. S. *Journal of Physiology (London)*, 1924, *58*, 405.

Smith, R. J. Rethinking allometry. *Journal of Theoretical Biology*, 1980, *87*, 97–111.

Snell, O. Die Abhängigkeit des Hirngewichts von dem Körpergewicht und den geistigen Fähigkeiten. *Archiv für Psychiatrie und Nervenkrankheiten*, 1891, *23*, 436–446.

Stahl, W. R. Similarity and dimensional models in biology. *Science*, 1962, *137*, 205–212.

Stearns, S. C. Life history tactics: A review of the ideas. *Quarterly Review of Biology*, 1976, *51*, 3–47.

Sunderman, F. W. Persons lacking sweat glands. *Archives of Internal Medicine*, 1941, *67*, 846–854.

Svenningsen, N. W., Lindroth, M., & Lindquist, B. Growth in relation to protein intake of low birth weight infants. *Early Human Development*, 1982, *6*, 47–58.

Swan, H. *Thermoregulation and bioenergetics: Patterns for vertebrate survival*. New York: American Elsevier, 1974.

Takeshita, H. On the delivery behavior of squirrel monkeys (*Saimiri sciurea*) and a mona monkey (*Cercopithecus mona*). *Primates*, 1961, *3*, 59–72.

Taylor, St., C. S. Time taken to mature in relation to mature weight for sexes, strains and species of domesticated mammals and birds. *Animal Production,* 1968, *10,* 157–169.

Thompson D'Arcy, W. *On growth and form.* Cambridge: Cambridge University Press, 1917.

Tracy, C. R. Minimum size of mammalian homeotherms: Role of the thermal environment. *Science,* 1977, *198,* 1034–1035.

Tregear, R. T. Hair density, wind speed, and heat loss in mammals. *Journal of Applied Physiology, 1965, 20,* 796–801.

Trivers, R. L. Parent-offspring conflict. *American Zoologist, 1974, 14,* 249–264.

Turček, F. J. On plumage quantity in birds. *Ekologia Polska—Seria A,* 1966, *14,* 617–634.

Villermé, M., & Milne-Edwards, H. De l'influence de la température sur la mortalité des enfans nouves-nés. *Annales d'Hygiène Publique et de Medicine Légale,* Part 1, 1829, *2,* 291–307.

Waddington, C. H. The biological foundations of measures of growth and form. *Proceedings of the Royal Society of London B,* 1950, *137,* 509–514.

Wallace, A. R. *The Malay Archipelago.* New York: Dover, 1972 (Reprint of the 1869 edition, Macmillan, London.)

Went, F. W. The size of man. *American Scientist,* 1968, *56,* 400–413

Whittow, G. C. (Ed.). *Comparative physiology of thermoregulation.* New York: Academic Press, 1971.

Willes, R. F., Kressler, P. L., & Truelove, J. F. Nursery rearing of infant monkeys (*Macaca fascicularis*) for toxicity studies. *Laboratory Animal Science,* 1977, *27,* 90–98.

Williams, G. C. *Adaptation and natural selection. A critique of current evolutionary thought.* Princeton, N.J.: Princeton University Press, 1966.

Costs and Benefits of Mammalian Reproduction

BENNETT G. GALEF, JR.

Parisitism and Symbiosis: Metaphors of Mammalian Mother–Young Interaction

The relationship between parent and offspring is only one type of intimate association between living organisms observed in nature. Infants, parasites, symbiotes: all participate in relationships characterized by metabolic dependence between participants. This multiplicity of naturally occurring dependent relationships is useful in the study of parental behavior because an analysis of one type of intimate association can provide insight into others. For example, viewing the developing mammal as a parasite of its mother[1], as a metabolically dependent active exploiter of its dam, can suggest ways of analyzing parent–offspring relationships not apparent from more traditional perspectives (Galef, 1981).

Parasitism is only one type of intimate association which could serve as a metaphor for the association between mother and young (see Alberts & Gubernick, Chapter 2). The defining characteristics of a parasitic relationship

---

[1] The relationship between dam and young is analagous to that between host and parasite only at a somatic or phenotypic level of analysis. The presence of maternal genes in a dam's offspring and the absence of a host's genes in its parasite makes the analogy unworkable at the genetic level (see Galef, 1981, for further discussion). As I am concerned in the present chapter with the effects of reproduction on the soma of dams, the analogy may be useful.

BENNETT G. GALEF, JR. • Department of Psychology, McMaster University, Hamilton, Ontario L8S 4K1, Canada. Preparation of this chapter was greatly facilitated by grants from the National Science and Engineering Research Council of Canada and the McMaster University Research Board.

are injury inflicted by the parasite on its host and absence of benefits returned to the host by its dependent (LaPage, 1963). In other types of intimate association such as symbiosis[2] or mutualism, each participant provides the other with benefits. Thus the appropriateness of the terms *symbiosis* or *parasitism* as metaphors of the phenotypic relationships between mammalian mothers and altricial young depends on whether the dam suffers somatic costs in bearing and rearing offspring and whether the young return benefits to their dam. If juveniles deplete their dam or place their dam at risk, reducing her chances of subsequent reproduction, a parasitic metaphor of the mother–young relationship would seem approapriate. If on the contrary, rearing a litter enhances or leaves unchanged a parent's future reproductive potential, the interaction between mother and young is more akin to a symbiotic than a parasitic relationship.

For reasons both theoretical (see below) and intuitive, I and many others have assumed that the demands made on a dam by a litter considerably reduced her future fecundity. The pertinent literature search convinced me that this matter is not as straightforward as I had thought. Reproductively active mammals have behavioral and physiological strategies that may negate the potential costs and risks associated with reproduction. Further, reproductively active individuals can garner phenotypic benefits from their grown offspring, benefits that may outweigh any residual reproductive costs. Consequently, young mammals may act as phenotypic symbiotes rather than phenotypic parasites of their dams.

Parental Investment and Life History Tactics: Theories and Data

Trivers (1972) has defined parental investment as "any investment by the parent in an individual offspring that increases the offspring's chance of surviving (and hence reproductive success) at the expense of the parent's ability to invest in other offspring" (p. 139). The "other offspring" in Trivers's definition could be either contemporaries of the individual receiving parental investment or products of reproductive episodes subsequent to that in which the individual under consideration was born. Trivers's model is clearly suitable for discussing the relationship among individuals born in a single reproductive episode. However, even if resources can be provided to one

---

[2] There is some inconsistency in the biological literature concerning the use of the term *symbiosis* (Whitfield, 1979). Some authors employ *symbiosis* as a generic term to refer to any intimate association of animals or plants of different species regardless of whether the metabolic dependence is unilaterally or mutually beneficial. In this case *mutualism* is used to specify an association in which the interactants benefit one another. I have used *symbiosis* in the dictionary or ordinary sense to refer to an association advantageous to both participants and not harmful to either.

member of a litter only by denying resources to others, engaging in a reproductive episode does not necessarily lessen the ability of reproducers to provide resources for future offspring.

It is frequently postulated that engaging in a reproductive episode compromises an individual's probability of future successful reproduction. Bell (1980, p. 47), for example, suggested that any increase in fecundity is attained only at the expense of adding to the mortality risk. Similarly, Schaffer (1974) and Charlesworth and Leon (1976) hypothesized that reproduction is costly because it involves a commitment of available resources to reproduction, rather than to self-maintenance and growth. Assertions that reallocation of resources or increased mortality are phenotypic costs of reproduction are useful because they raise significant empirical issues. Is it the case, as Bell suggested, that reproductively active females have a reduced probability of survival? Do females, in fact, allocate resources necessary for their own growth and maintenance to their young?

While answers to these questions may seem obvious, they are not. For example, the hypothesis that reproduction necessarily involves allocation by a dam to her young of resources that she would otherwise utilize for self-maintenance or growth assumes that the resources exploited by an individual are environmentally limited. If, to the contrary, resource acquisition by reproductively inactive individuals living in adequate environments is self-limited rather than environmentally limited, then it would not be necessary for reproductively active individuals to sacrifice growth or self-maintenance to reproductive activity. Reproductively active individuals might simply devote more time to resource acquisition than reproductively inactive individuals. There is no *a priori* reason that the reproductively active individual need make phenotypic sacrifices during reproduction.

The need for empirical verification of hypotheses concerning the somatic costs of reproduction has been recognized, but the confirming evidence is surprisingly weak. Bell (1980) referred readers to Stearns (1976) and Calow (1977) for examples of reproduction increasing mortality. Examination of Stearns's original sources regarding increased mortality in reproductively active female mammals generally either provides no support for the hypothesis that fertility increases mortality or is irrelevant to it. Among those cited in Stearns (1976, p. 17) or Calow (1977, p. 569), Geist (1971, p. 300) only suggested that barren female mountain sheep may have a better chance of survival than those pregnant or suckling. He called for empirical investigation of that hypothesis, rather than presenting evidence to support it. Berger (1972, p. 162) suggested that increased mortality in olive baboon females at the "assumed" beginning of the adult stage (47–52 months) "may represent mortality incurred during the first pregnancy or birth," but he provided no evidence that this is so.[3] Numerous studies showing that "half-starved domestic animals are relatively infertile" (Maynard & Loosi, 1962, p. 434) do not directly support the hypothesis that fertility increases mortality. In fact, such evidence suggests that animals do not attempt to reproduce if reproduction would be phenotypically costly.

In subsequent sections, I have reviewed literature relevant to the costs and benefits resulting from female mammalian reproduction, particularly in rodents. The questions I have addressed are whether and how reproductive episodes affect future fecundity. I have focused attention on rodents because of the wealth of laboratory data on reproduction in that order and the necessity of experimentation under controlled conditions to evaluate the costs of engaging in many reproductive activities.

It might be argued that data collected in the laboratory are inadequate for appraising the effects of reproduction on survival or fecundity, because laboratory-maintained subjects are protected from a variety of factors that affect the costs and risks incurred by females engaging in reproduction in natural circumstances. Unfortunately, studies in nature can rarely be sufficiently well controlled to permit unequivocal determination of the causes of any observed changes in mortality or fecundity associated with reproduction. Reproductively active and inactive members of free-living populations surely differ prior to self-assignment to the two reproductive states. In consequence, interpretation of field studies of reproductive effects on future fitness is difficult. For example, Richdale (1957) found that 3-year-old penguins that had previously reproduced (in their second year) lost only 18% of their eggs prior to hatching, while penguins reproducing for the first time in their third year lost 30% of their eggs during incubation. While these data have been interpreted as demonstrating a "negative cost" of reproduction in 2-year-old

---

[3] I have not had the opportunity to examine in detail all the references cited by Calow and Stearns regarding the cost of reproduction in iteroparous species. However, in each case that I have examined, the data have not carried the message attributed to them. Two further examples will suffice: (1) Clough (1965) found no effects of reproductive activity on resistance to starvation in voles (*Microtus pennsylvanicus*) but did find that reproducing females had a significant "slightly lower resistance," as measured by survival time in 9.5°C water, than nonbreeding females of similar weight; (2) barnacles lose weight following reproduction, either as the result of expulsion of egg masses (Crisp & Patel, 1961) or as the result of a reduction of feeding activity (Barnes, 1962). However, the effects of loss of weight on future fecundity are not established. Williams (1962) stated that curtailed growth "would mean lowered fecundity in the next breeding season" (p. 172). Daly and Wilson (1978) suggested that "reproducers are more apt to be squeezed out by their neighbors and to lose the chance to reproduce again" (p. 129). Neither cited any reference to support these notions. The inconsistency in interpretation suggests that these are hypotheses concerning, not empirical observations of, effects of reproduction on future fecundity.

penguins (Bell, 1980), they are also consistent with the hypothesis that only the most reproductively capable penguins breed in their second year. Such confounds, while unavoidable, are the curse of unobtrusive field studies.

On the other hand, the generality of laboratory findings is open to question. They may provide an accurate description and a causal analysis of events unique to the laboratory itself and of little relevance to more general issues. Furthermore, in standard laboratory situations, many of the factors are absent that might differentially affect reproductively active and inactive individuals (e.g., predators, disease-bearing organisms, fluctuations in food supply and temperature, and social interaction with conspecifics). While it might be possible to introduce such variables into controlled settings, there will always be uncertainty about whether any controlled situation adequately reflects the challenges that organisms face in natural habitats.

In ideal circumstances, it would be possible to determine under controlled conditions both the magnitude of each cost and benefit (in terms of future fecundity) associated with reproduction, and the environmental range in which those costs and benefits influence reproducers. Such laboratory data could be used to model reproductive histories of natural populations subject to particular environnmental pressures. Field data could determine the adequacy of laboratory results to account for observed breeding histories in the natural environment. The data necessary even to approach the ideal situation are simply not available for any species.

Bioenergetics of Pregnancy and Lactation

Potential Costs of Pregnancy and Lactation

The demand for nutrients that embryos and suckling young make on their dam certainly has the potential to reduce her capacity for self-maintenance. Individual offspring may grow to more than one-third their adult weight while still dependent on their dam for nutrition (guinea pigs; Paterson, 1967), and litters of suckling young may approach twice the weight of their dam before they wean (bank voles; Kaczmarski, 1966).

To provide for the growth of young, reproducing rodents require from 166% to 234% of the calories needed by reproductively inactive controls (Millar, 1979). Lactating rats and mice, respectively, contribute the equivalent of 44% and 110% of the calcium in their skeletons to their offspring (Simkiss, 1967). More generally, the requirements of lactating rats for the majority of essential dietary components are from 2 to 10 times the amounts needed by nonlactating individuals (Nelson & Evans, 1961).

Reducing Costs of Reproduction

The demand for nutrients that young place on their dam can be met in either of two ways: (1) the dam can increase her rate of ingestion and alter her selection of nutrients to meet the needs of her young, or (2) she can catabolize her own tissues for substances needed by her young (e.g., elephant seals). Some mammals (e.g., humans—Hytten & Thompson, 1961; cotton rats—Randolph, Randolph, Mattingly, & Foster, 1977) employ a mixed strategy, increasing nutrient intake during pregnancy beyond the immediate needs of developing fetuses and self-maintenance, storing the surplus, and then catabolizing that surplus and passing it on to neonates during the nursing period, when the nutrient needs of the mother–young aggregate are greatest.

The first strategy, increasing nutrient intake, may be universal in rodents under laboratory conditions. It probably occurs whenever food is continuously available throughout pregnancy and lactation. Cotton rats (*Sigmodon hispidus*), for example, increase their food intake by 25% during pregnancy and 65% during lactation (Randolph *et al.*, 1977). In the laboratory rat, food intake increases 60% during pregnancy and from 180% to 250% during lactation (see Randolph *et al.*, 1977, p. 40, for further examples).

Reproductively active female rats (*Rattus norvegicus*) also increase their relative intake of specific nutrients, especially sources of protein, fat and calcium, if given the opportunity to do so (Richter, 1942). This increase mitigates the potential depletion of their reserves in meeting offspring demands.

Increased transduction of resources needed to meet nutrient requirements of a developing litter might appear to press a dam's capacity to process ingesta. However, reproductively active females are anatomically and physiologically quite different from nonreproductives. Pregnant or lactating laboratory rats, for example, exhibit increase in the length, weight, and absorptive capacity of their small intestine (Fell, Smith, & Campbell, 1963); increase in liver, kidney, stomach, and cecum weights (Fell *et al.*, 1963; Peter & Krynen, 1966; Souders & Morgan, 1957); and changes in blood hemoglobin (Bond, 1958; see Pond, 1978, and Widdowson, 1976, for further examples of reproduction-associated changes in morphology). Consequently, reproductively active females are able to process twice-normal quantities of food without sacrificing the efficiency with which they metabolize nutrients (Kaczmarski, 1966; Randolph *et al.*, 1977).

Some morphological alterations that accompany pregnancy and lactation are permanent. For example, the increase in liver size in rats results from increases in both the size and the number of liver cells. Following reproduction, the cell size returns to normal, while the cell number remains elevated, so rats that have reared litters have more cellular livers than those that have not lactated (Kennedy, Pearce, & Parrott, 1958). Other morphological alterations caused by reproduction are relatively temporary. For example, the bone erosion that occurs in all parts of the skeleton during lactation, irrespective of dietary calcium level, is repaired whether the female becomes pregnant again immediately or not (Ellinger, Duckworth, Dalgarno, & Quenouille, 1952). As Widdowson (1976) has stated, "whether permanent or temporary, there is no evidence that any of the changes [in the structure of the dam's body] do her any ultimate harm" (p. 11).

Evidence of Success

That rodent dams maintained in the laboratory with *ad libitum* access to food, nesting material, and warmth transduce to their young considerably more energy than is required for their growth and development, while continuing self-maintenace and normal growth, is strongly indicated by a variety of findings.

First, female laboratory rats allowed to reproduce continuously grow *more* rapidly than controls maintained without access to males, as indicated by reproductively induced increase in tibia length and body weight (the latter corrected for increased weight of uteri, ovaries, and mammary glands) (Bogart, Sperling, Barnes, & Asdell, 1939). Cotton rats in laboratory settings show positive energy balance throughout pregnancy and lactation (Randolph *et al.*, 1977).

Second, females of a variety of rodent species (rat, mouse, gerbil, old-field mouse, etc.) can become sexually receptive shortly following parturition and consequently (at least under laboratory conditions) nurse one litter while gestating a second. If either pregnancy or lactation pressed the females' capacity to transduce nutrients, one would expect females simultaneously pregnant and lactating to have difficulty in caring for both litters. To the contrary, Bruce and East (1956) found no difference between the weight of mouse pups weaned by female mice impregnated in a postpartum estrus and those weaned by nonpregnant females. Furthermore, and surprisingly if one assumes that reproduction stresses the energy transduction capacity of the mouse dam, impregnated lactating females reared a greater percentage of litters and as many pups per litter as nonpregnant individuals. Also, removal of the senior litter from a lactating and impregnated dam *decreased* her success with the litter initiated in postpartum estrus from an average of 8.0 to 6.5 pups per litter (Bruce & East, 1956).

The picture in rats is similar. Lactating and impregnated females produce litters of the same size and growth rate as females caring for only a single litter. Removal of the senior litter has no effect on either the number of young rats per junior litter at birth or the growth rate and weaning success of the junior litter (Babcock, Bogart, Sperling, & Asdell, 1940; Woodside, Wilson, Chee, & Leon, 1981). In the laboratory, lactating and nonlactating collared lemmings have litters of equal size (Hasler & Banks, 1975).

Such data do not suggest that laboratory reproduction is achieved at the expense of self-maintenance, and they are not consistent with the notion that reproductive females are pushed to the limits of their capacity to transduce nutrients. Rather, in supportive environments, females can both increase the resources they exploit, without sacrificing utilization efficiency, and select a modified spectrum of nutrients to meet the specific demands of reproduction. Thus, in energy-rich environments, they are able to maintain both themselves and a large number of offspring without deleterious consequences. Of course, females reproducing in natural circumstances may face environmentally imposed limits on resource transduction. (A discussion of strategies for coping with such environmental stress is on page 270.)

While field data on the effects of reproduction on survival in rodents are both difficult to collect and rare, Dapson(1979) has provided useful information on the old-field mouse (*Peromyscus polionotus*). He found, in general, that survival over two-month periods during the breeding season was independent of age even though the youngest age class was nulliparous, and the older classes contained many pregnant and many lactating females. The only exception was a disproportionate loss in the oldest age cohort in a population in which that cohort exhibited a high frequency of postpartum impregnation. While there is clearly a variety of interpretations of such correlational data, they do suggest that in free-living old-field mice, no cost is associated with simple reproduction, and some degree of risk is associated with simultaneous pregnancy and lactation.

Costs of Pregnancy and Lactation

Costs of Reproduction Per Se

Evidence that female rodents may be able to reproduce without incurring any obvious phenotypic cost by increasing both their capacity to transduce resources and their exploitation of external resources bears only indirectly on the question of the effects of one reproductive episode on subsequent ones.

If engaging in a reproductive episode reduces subsequent reproductive capacity in females, one would expect females to show decreased reproductive success with increasing parity. In the case of those mammalian species in which females deliver litters, loss of reproductive capacity might be reflected in either reduced litter size at birth or at weaning over successive parities.

Figure 1 presents data from a variety of sources (see figure caption for references) describing the mean size at birth of successive litters in Norway rats (both wild and domesticated), house mice, golden hamsters, old-field mice, Mongolian gerbils, bandicoots (*Perameles gunni*), and domestic sows. The data do not support the hypothesis that fecundity decreases with increasing parity. In every case, there was either a slight increase or no change in litter size at birth with successive reproductive episodes. It should be pointed out that if one extends such curves out to the tenth or fifteenth litter, a dramatic decrease in litter size is invariably observed. The difficulties in determining whether this decrease in number of young following 10 or more parturitions is the result of the effects of previous parturitions or of increasing age make data from older females difficult to interpret. For example, Porter (1967), in his experiment of most extreme outcome, found that laboratory rats that were first bred at 90, 120, and 200 days of age had, respectively, 7.2, 6.3, and 2.8 young per successfully breeding female. However, one might well expect that if participation in reproductive episodes *per se* reduced litter size, the cumulative effects of five or six reproductive acts should be perceptible. The

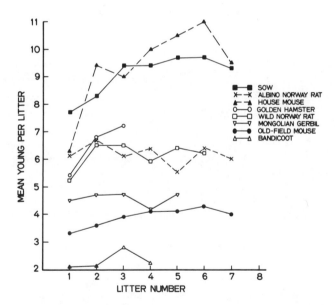

Figure 1. Number of young per litter at birth as a function of successive parturitions in the bandicoot (Heinshohn, 1966); the old-field mouse (Williams, Carmon, & Golley, 1965); the Mongolian gerbil (Marston & Chang, 1965; see also Tanimoto, 1943); the golden hamster (Day, 1976); the domesticated and wild Norway rat (King, 1924; see also Donaldson, 1924, p. 25); the house mouse (Biggers, Finn, & McClaren, 1962); and the domestic sow (Lush & Molln, 1942).

absence of such observable effect is not consistent with the hypothesis that reproductive effort reduces subsequent reproductive capacity.

It is interesting to note that in each case presented in Figure 1, as well as in a number of other data bases I have examined, the second litters were consistently larger than the first ones. It is also the case, at least in laboratory rats, that nearly 100% of females producing a first litter also produce a second (148 of 148; King, 1924), so the enhanced size of second litters cannot be due to differences in the sample of females producing first and second litters. The fact that increased size in second litters is found in female rats first bred at 306 days of age, as well as in those first bred shortly after puberty (Asdell, Bogart, & Sperling, 1941), indicates that the enhancing effects of a first parturition on a second are not simply the result of an age-related increase in litter size during the period immediately following the achievement of reproductive maturity. Taken together, the data suggest that first parturitions enhance second litter size and that subsequent parturitions have little effect on their successors.

In summarizing the results of what is, in my estimation, the most convincing study yet undertaken of breeding effects on future reproduction, Asdell *et al.* (1941) concluded that

1. Initiating breeding late in the life of a female rather than at the normal age *reduces* her reproductive ability by increasing the intervals between litters and reducing the size of litters.
2. The failure of females to give birth, with later resorption of fetuses, is *more* frequent in females first bred late in life than in those starting breeding early.
3. Virgin females show irregularities and cessation of estrus cycling earlier in life than do breeding females.
4. All females, regardless of their age at first breeding, produce more young and suckle them better after they have been reproducing "for a while" than they do in the first litter or two.

Such findings are consistent with the hypothesis that reproduction itself has a stimulative rather than an inhibitory effect on future reproduction. The only evidence presented by Asdell *et al.* (1941) of a reproductive cost involved females whose young were removed immediately following parturition. Females whose young were removed at birth produced subsequent larger litters than females suckling young. Unfortuantely, Asdell *et al.* bred the females in the former group every 28 days and those in the latter group every 42 days (Babcock *et al.*, 1940), so one cannot tell whether there is a cost associated with lactation or a benefit associated with brief interpartum intervals. In either case, both females breeding and suckling young and those breeding and not suckling from 100 days of age had litters at 280 days of age as large as or larger than those beginning breeding and suckling at 280 days of age, indicating that 180 days of reproduction (production of approximately four litters) had no adverse effect on future litter size.

The optimal, and rarely employed, experimental design for assessing the effects of previous reproduction on litter size involves matching females for breeding age and systematically varying their prior reproductive experience. I have been able to find only two studies using such a design, one by Day and Galef (unpublished observations), using golden hamsters as subjects, and one by Asdell *et al.* (1941), using rats. Both sets of data are presented in Figure 2. As is clear from an examination of the figure, in neither rats nor hamsters is there any sign of a previous breeding effect on the size of litters produced by females of a given age.

Data describing the effects of increasing parity on weaning success in rodents are far less common than those describing the effects of parity on litter size at birth. Asdell *et al.* (1941) found negligible effects of increasing parity in rats on either the percentage of young raised to 21 days of age or the weight of individual young at weaning. Marston and Chang (1965) reported no effect of successive litters on the number of pups weaned per litter by Mongolian gerbils, other than a tendency for mothers rearing first or second litters to be less successful in weaning young than those with greater reproductive experience.

Of course, parturitions could affect future fecundity not by reducing

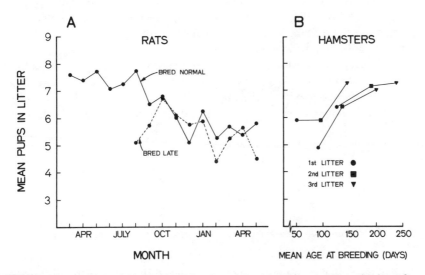

Figure 2. Panel A: Mean litter sizes of 50 female rats first bred either at 100 or 270 days of age (from Asdell, Bogart, & Sperling, 1941). Panel B: Mean litter sizes of 14 hamsters having first, second, and third litters at various ages (Day & Galef, unpublished observations).

litter size but by reducing the probability that a reproductively active female would survive or remain fertile. Babcock *et al.* (1940) determined the number of female rats either (1) first bred at the earliest possible date (approximately 65 days of age); (2) first bred at 100 days of age; or (3) first bred at 280 days of age still reproductively active after 365 days of age. They found no difference between the percentage of groups first bred at 100 and 280 days still breeding at 365 days, suggesting no effect of bearing from four to five additional litters on the survival or fertility in the goup first bred at 100 days. It is relevant to note that the females bred as soon as they reached puberty (at approximately 65 days of age) exhibited almost twice the infertility rate at one year as did the females first bred at 100 and 280 days (13.5%), even though the females first bred at 65 days bore only one more litter, on average, than did the females in the 100-day group. Further, the per-female lifetime production of offspring was 10% less in the females first bred as early as possible than in those females first bred at 100 days of age. Taken together, these data suggest that reproduction does impose a reduction in survival or fertility on those female rats breeding prior to reaching full maturity, but not on those breeding in their prime.

In mice, there appear to be more important effects of breeding on future survival and fecundity. Suntzeff, Cowdry, and Hixon (1962), for example, reported that the percentage of breeding female mice dying before 12 months of age (18%) is significantly greater than the percentage of breeding males or of virgin males or females dying in their first year (4%, 7%, and 6%, respectively). While providing clear evidence of a survival risk associated with reproduction, these data leave unresolved an important issue. It is, for example, possible that although engaging in a breeding episode carries a risk, that risk is reduced as a function of previous reproductive experience. Thus, although evidence of risk associated with reproduction is important, the effects of reproduction on that risk are equally so, and insofar as I know, there are no data available from which one can calculate the necessary conditional probabilities.

In sum, the extensive data available on rats suggest that the act of bearing and suckling a litter of young is more likely to augment than to reduce future fecundity. The limited data available on mice indicate an enhanced mortality resulting from reproductive effort *per se*.

Effects of Pregnancy and Lactation on Susceptibility to Infectious Disease

The data presented above, relevant to the question of the effects of reproductive episodes on their successors, offer relatively little support for the hypothesis that under laboratory conditions, each reproductive act carries an unavoidable cost in terms of future reproductive success. However, it is possible that a more focused examination of the specific potential costs associated with reproduction might provide a different picture. In the present section, I examine the possibility that reproductive activity increases the vulnerability of females to infectious disease.

A general review of the effects of pregnancy and lactation on immunological systems lies beyond both the scope of this chapter and the expertise of this author, and there is unfortunately no such review now available. However, even a superficial search of the literature reveals that changes in the endocrine system accompanying pregnancy and lactation have the potential to markedly alter the effectiveness of immunological defenses. Moderate levels of estrogen, for example, have been reported to increase body defenses by increasing phagocytic activity, raising serum γ-globulin levels, and increasing the rate of proliferation of antibody-producing cells (Kenny & Diamond, 1977; Nicol, Bilbey, Charles, Cordingly, & Vernon-Roberts, 1964). However, in large quantities estrogen is thymolyic and produces a depression in cellular immunity (Luz, Marques, Ayub, & Correa, 1975; Nelson, Hall, Manuel-Limson, Freidberg, & O'Brien, 1967). Thus, it is not easy to predict the net effects of reproductive activity on immunological defenses.

In those few studies in which the effects of pregnancy or lactation on response to artificially induced infection have been directly examined, the outcomes have been mixed. A number of investigators have reported increased susceptibility to disease in reproductively active animals. For example, both lactating and pregnant mice are more susceptible to foot and mouth disease than virgin controls (Campbell, 1960). There is also evidence of a pregnancy-associated depressed immunity to the rodent malarial parasite *Plasmodium berghei*, which results in a lethal recurrence of the disease during pregnancy in previously immunized mice (Van Zon & Eling, 1980).

The results of other studies indicate that susceptibility to disease varies as a function of the stage in pregnancy at which exposure to the infective agents occurs. Cotton rats (Weaver & Steiner, 1944) and possibly mice (Knox, 1950) are more resistant to murine poliomyelitic infection early in pregnancy than nonpregnant controls, but they are more susceptible to murine poliomyelitis and encephalomyocarditis virus late in pregnancy (Farber & Glasgow, 1968; Knox, 1950).

Pregnancy increases susceptiblity to some strains of a virus but not others. Dalldorf and Gifford (1954) reported that mice become progressively more susceptible to severe infection with the pancreatic line of Coxsackie B-1 virus as gestation advances, but that neither the A-strain nor the brain line of the B-1 strain induces illness in pregnant animals.

Pregnancy can also change susceptiblity to a disease by altering its portal of entry into the body. Thus, while pregnant mice are more susceptible to herpes simplex Type-2 virus introduced intravaginally (the normal route of infection), they are less susceptible to the virus introduced intranasally (Overall, Kern, Schlitzer, Friedman, & Glasgow, 1975; Young & Gomez, 1979). Pregnant mice are less susceptible to influenza-A virus introduced intranasally (the normal route of infection) than nonpregnant controls (Young & Gomez, 1979).

Less direct tests of susceptibility to immunologically active agents than measures of survival in pregnant and nonpregnant mammals reveal evidence of no effects of pregnancy (Merritt & Galton, 1969); enhanced resistance in pregnant animals (Fabris, 1973; Kenny & Diamond, 1977; Mitchell, McRipley, Selvaraj, & Sbarra, 1966; Nicol *et al.*, 1964); and depressed resistance in pregnant subjects (Exon & Dixon, 1972; Rangnekar, Rao, Joshi, Virkar, Kora, & Dikshit, 1974). Such data are both contradictory and difficult to extrapolate to the effects on survival of exposure to disease-causing organisms.

Though there does seem to be a tendency for reproductively active females to be more susceptible than controls to viral agents, the effects of pregnancy on disease susceptibility seem to depend on the disease in question, the route of its entrance into the body, and the stage in pregnancy when exposure occurs. It should also be kept in mind that the selection of disease-causing agents for test in pregnant animals has been guided by clinical observations suggesting that pregnant human females suffer more severely from certain diseases than do nonpregnant women, for example, poliomyelitis (Pridelle, Lenz, Young, & Stevenson, 1952); pandemic influenza (Freeman & Barns, 1959); herpes simplex Type-2 (Young, Killam, & Greene, 1976); and malaria (Gilles, Lawson, Sibelas, Voller, & Allan, 1969). Evidence of enhanced resistance of pregnant women to other diseases, such as syphilis (Mitchell & Sbarra, 1965), is not of such practical importance and receives less mention in the literature and no experimental study.

The fact that experimental evidence of pregnancy-associated reduced resistance is mixed in a class of diseases generally selected for study on the basis of clinical indications that they are more virulent in pregnant than in nonpregnant women suggests that reduced resistance to disease during reproduction may not be a general phenomenon. However, available evidence does suggest a marginally enhanced susceptibility to disease in gravid animals.

In order for an organism to become ill, it must not only be susceptible to disease, but it must also be exposed to disease-causing agents. Even if reproductively active females are more susceptible to infection, they could reduce their probability of succumbing to illness by reducing their encounters with disease-bearing conspecifics. The tendency of pregnant or lactating females of many rodent species to isolate themselves and respond aggressively to the approach of conspecifics (Crowcroft, 1966; Gandelman, 1972; King, 1955; Hoogland, 1981a; Sherman, 1980a) might reduce exposure to contagious disease. While I do not think that there is any reason to suppose that the antisocial behaviors observed in pregnant or lactating mammals have evolved specifically in defense against infection, it is reasonable to suppose that behaviors that isolate reproductively active females serve such a secondary function. It is not known whether in natural circumstances the net effect of changes in susceptibility to disease and changes in exposure to disease resulting from reproductive activity is to increase or to decrease the probability of illness.

Risk of Predation during Pregnancy and Lactation

The data discussed in preceding sections were derived primarily from laboratory studies in which females were protected from the need to expose themselves to the increased risk of predation while attending their young or acquiring nutrients to be transduced to their young. It is not, however, necessarily the case that the behavioral changes associated with pregnancy and lactation involve enhanced predation risks. In the laboratory, domesticated female rats exhibit marked decrements in running wheel activity 24 hr after impregnation. Throughout pregnancy and lactation, they are less than one-third as active as they were prior to impregnation (Sloanaker, 1924). Such reduced activity is, perhaps, more likely to reduce predation risk than to enhance it. In a study of mouse killing in rats, Galef (unpublished observations) established colonies of wild *mus musculus* separated from colonies of wild *Rattus norvegicus* by semipermeable barriers through which mice, but not rats, could pass. In each of three replications, the order of capture of mice by rats was the same: males were killed before nonreproductive females, which were killed in turn before pregnant or lactating females. Attachment of lactating females to their nest sites reduced their rate of exploration and preserved many lactating females for some days after the last of their nonreproductive colony-mates had departed.

In the field, Madison (1978a,b) found no changes in the activity of pregnant voles, but a sharp reduction in activity during lactation. This reduction in activity was accompanied by enhanced predation on lactating voles by snakes, which took significantly more vole dams (together with their litters) than nonreproductively active females (Madison, 1978a). However, as snake predation accounted for only 20% of the total reported instances of predation on subjects during the three-year course of the study (Madison, 1979), the overall reproduction effects on predation susceptibility cannot be determined.

In other rodent species that have been intensively studied, the observed predation rates have generally been too low to permit an estimation of the predation impact on reproductively active females, as compared with inactive ones. During seven years of observation of prairie dog colonies, Hoogland (personal communication, 1980a) observed only eight instances of predator success: the capture of seven juveniles and one lactating female, which was also the most peripherally located animal in its colony. Sherman (1977, 1980a,b) similarly observed only one successful predatory attempt for each 347 hr of observation of Belding's ground squirrels. In the 14 instances in which adults were predation victims (of badger, coyote, and marten), 8 females and 6 males were taken. The data are simply too sparse to permit an assessment of the effects of prey reproduction on predator success. Because of the small size and the frequently nocturnal and fossorial habits of rodents, predation on them is not easily seen. There is, however, considerable discussion in the literature of factors enhancing predation on ungulate species in which predation is relatively easy to observe. These data are reviewed briefly below.

Mech (1970, pp. 246–263) devoted a chapter of his monograph on wolves to factors influencing prey selection: prey inexperience, prey malformation, illness, age, youth, injury, crippling, stupidity, abnormality in behavior, reduced sensory capacity, parasites, congenital disorders, diseases of the jawbone, rundown condition, infection with tape worm cysts, flesh wounds, bacterial infection, broken limbs, and a variety of other factors that may predispose deer, moose, and Dall sheep to fall prey to wolves. Pregnancy and lactation are conspicuous by their absence.

Schaller (1967, pp. 316–331) both reviewed the earlier literature on factors predisposing ungulates to predation (reaching conclusions similar to those of Mech) and reported his own findings on prey selection by tigers. The results varied markedly from one prey species to another. In the sambar, for example, yearling and adult males were taken four times more often than one would expect on the basis of their frequency in the population. On the other hand, female barashinha in late pregnancy were particularly susceptible to tigers.

Kruuk's (1972, pp 89–102) brief discussion of the characteristics of hyena prey shows that adult female wildebeests run the highest risk (and males the lowest) during the calving season, probably because of the female's reduced mobility prior to and while giving birth. However, hyenas, like wild dogs, leopards, and lions, take male gazelles more frequently than females. Although hyenas take female zebras more frequently than male zebras, Kruuk did not mention reproductive activity as significant in this differential mortality.

Schaller's monograph on prey selection (1972, pp. 221–232) in lions does not suggest that they are more likely to kill reproductively active female wildebeest, zebra, Thomson's gazelle, or buffalo. In fact, in each case, lions are more likely to kill adult males than females.

Considered together, the data are equivocal. Although in two cases, those of hyena predation on wildebeest and tiger predation on barasingha, pregnancy seems to be an important factor in vulnerability, pregnancy may not have the same deleterious effect on other ungulate prey. It is, of course, possible that the metabolic demands of pregnancy and lactation make reproductively active females more susceptible to starvation, disease, parasites, etc., and hence to predation. If this were the case, one might expect females to be more frequent prey than males, which, as indicated above, is not generally true.

Benefits of Reproduction

During the period in which altricial young are dependent on their dam, they acquire substantial resources from her, while she receives relatively little in return. Huddling with pups may save mothers some of the energy normally used for thermoregulation (Leon, Croskerry, & Smith, 1978), and mothers may recover some of the resources provided to their offspring by ingesting the placenta (Ewer, 1968) or the urine and feces of their young (Baverstock & Green, 1975; Friedman & Bruno, 1976). Still, there can be little question that if one restricts attention to the period prior to weaning, dams contribute far more to the well being of their young than they receive in return. However, if the time frame is expanded to include the total period of interaction between a dam and her young, the young of a given reproductive episode may eventually contribute substantial resources to their dam and her future offspring. Resources invested in offspring are frequently returned, possibly with interest.

Overt Benefits

Perhaps the clearest cases of return on parental energy transduced to offspring is to be found in social insect species, in which each new colony is founded by a solitary queen. To quickly summarize Oster and Wilson's (1978) description of the colony foundation process in such species; the solitary founding queen, inseminated during her nuptial flight, locates a suitable nest site, constructs the first nest cell, and then rears a first brood of workers herself, feeding larvae on her own tissue reserves. When the first workers eclose as adults, the queen reverts to egg laying, and the workers forage for food, feed and care for the young and the queen, enlarge the nest site, and provide all the resources required for continued colony growth. Once the colony reaches mature size, it begins to produce queens and males, thus continuing the cycle. Early brood production is essential for the production of later ones, and the energy that the queen invests in her first broods is returned many times.

If such a positive return on the maternal transduction of resources to offspring were limited to the social insects, it would be of little relevance to the energy exchange between mammalian mothers and young. There is, however, evidence of similar relationships in mammalian species, though in mammalian cases, early litter production facilitates future litter production, rather than being a necessary precursor to future reproduction.

Moehlman (1979), for example, has reported that the reproductive success of pairs of black-backed jackals in a given season can be significantly enhanced by the attendance of their young of a preceding year. Such "helpers" contribute food directly to the pups, regurgitate food to the lactating mother, guard the pups during periods of parental absence, groom the pups, etc. On average, each helper adds 1.5 surviving pups to the litter it attends. Thus, helper individuals increase their dam's success in future reproductive episodes well beyond the investment that the dam made in them. While it is true that only a small percentage of young produced by any pair return to help with subsequent litters, only previously reproductively active pairs have potential access to helpers, which increase later reproductive potential.

Black-backed jackals are not the only canid groups in which females can expect returns from their weaned offspring. Lactating Cape hunting dogs and their pups solicit regurgitated food from other closely related members of their pack (vanLawick & vanLawick-Goodall, 1971; Schaller, 1972, p. 325). That these older relatives of later young is suggested by the observation that following their mother's death, young can be successfully maintained by pack members from 5 weeks of age to weaning at 10 weeks (Schaller, 1972, p. 332).

Similarly, in dwarf mongoose packs, in which only the dominant female successfully produces young, the young are frequently suckled by the dominant female's grown daughters, whose own breeding is suppressed (Rood, 1980; see also Rasa, 1977; Ewer, 1973).

In wild house mice (*Mus musculus*) and, to a lesser extent, deer mice (*Peromyscus maniculatus bairdii*) females impregnated within a few days of one another may combine their young in a communal nest, often sharing the rearing with mature daughters from previous parturitions (Crowcroft & Row, 1963; King, 1963; Sayler & Salmon, 1969). Young house mice of a domesticated strain reared in a communal nest have been shown to exhibit enhanced rates of growth relative to young raised by individual females, when the number of young per dam is kept constant (Sayler & Salmon, 1969; Werboff, Steg, & Barnes, 1970). In the laboratory, wild rats (*Rattus norvegicus*) maintained in matrilineal groups similarly pool their litters (author's observation), though the effects of this communal rearing on the growth of the young is not known.

Covert Benefits

While the instances of return of maternal resources to the dam by her grown young described in the preceding section are particularly straightforward examples of ways in which engaging in open reproductive effort may increase future reproductive success, they may represent obvious cases of a commonly more subtle class of interactions between mothers and their grown offspring.

The potential for future return on maternal transduction of energy to young exists in those species in which (1) at least some grown young are matrilocal; (2) the dams are reproductively active over a sufficient period of time to allow a first litter to wean while the mother is still engaging in reproduction; and (3) individual species members gain reproductive potential from the presence of conspecifics.

While it is true that colonial lifestyles entail both costs and benefits (Hoogland & Sherman, 1976), it seems likely that in group-living species, the net benefits of social living outweigh the net costs (Bertram, 1978). In matrilocal species, an individual's own offspring obviously contribute their numbers to their dam's social groups and become potential sources of social benefits. Although the literature on the degree of consanguinity in rodent populations is far from complete, it does seem to be generally the case that in colonial rodents (for example, Norway rats, roof rats, Mongolian gerbils, prairie dogs, and Belding's ground squirrel), the basic social group consists of senior individuals and their offspring of several years (Crowcroft, 1966, p. 29; Gromov & Popov, 1979; Hoogland, 1981b; King, 1955; Sherman, 1977, 1980a; Telle, 1966). Thus, in many rodent species, a female's previous successful reproduction can increase the size of her group and thus increase her access to the benefits of group living. It is probably the case that the social benefits of reproduction are greater in small groups than in large ones, for as group size increases, the relative contribution of a single reproductive episode to group size decreases. Further, as population density or number increases beyond some optimum, the costs of group living may begin to outweigh the benefits.

Laboratory experiments on the effects of increasing population size on the reproducive success of female population members received considerable attention in the 1950s and 1960s. The study of the mechanisms underlying the regulation of population sizes in nature below the apparent carrying capacity of the environment focused attention on falling birthrates and infant survival rates in confined populations approaching asymptotic size. Data describing the typical results of such a study in house mice (Figure 3; Christian, Lloyd, & Davis, 1965) illustrate the well-known finding of decreased infant survival and

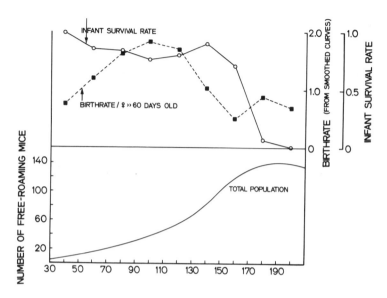

Figure 3. Demographic data from a freely growing confined population of house mice (*Mus musculus*) indicating the nursling survival rate and the birthrate per female over 60 days of age in two-day intervals. Also shown is the total population size over days. (From Christian, Lloyd, & Davis, 1965.)

female fecundity with increasing population size. The figure also reveals an equally robust, but generally ignored, phenomenon: an increase in individual female fecundity correlated with the growth of the population to moderate size. Unfortunately, the factors responsible for such an increase in reproductive efficiency have not been explored.

The clearest evidence of particular benefits of sociality in rodents is found in field studies of two highly matrilocal species, Belding's ground squirrel and the black-tailed prairie dog. In the latter species, Hoogland (1981b, p. 7) reported that he has not detected a single case in which a black-tailed female emigrated from her natal territory on her own apparent initiative. Similarly, "female Belding's ground squirrels mature and breed near their birth places until they die or disappear" (Sherman, 1977, p. 1248). Clearly, in such instances, daughters have the opportunity to provide social benefits to their dam and her subsequent offspring.

Both Belding's squirrels and black-tailed prairie dogs engage in complex antipredator behaviors, and the role of social life in predator defense has received the greatest attention. In black-tailed prairie dogs, increasing coterie size correlates with decreased latency in predator detection (Hoogland,

1981a); decreased time scanning for predators (Hoogland, 1979); and increased time feeding (Hoogland, 1981b). The fact that individuals living on the periphery of wards spend more time watching for predators than those living centrally, and that birth is synchronized in neighboring burrows, suggests that individuals living in groups may also benefit from "selfish herd" effects (Hamilton, 1971; Hoogland, 1979b) resulting from conspecific proximity.

Belding's ground squirrel adult females—and yearlings living near relatives—alarm-call in response to the appearance of predators, while juveniles do not, and juveniles frquently flee into burrows other than their home burrow (Sherman, 1977). There is thus a tendency for juveniles to gain protection from their older sisters, who provide both places of refuge and warning of potential danger.

Life in social groups may provide benefits other than enhanced protection from predation. Wild Norway rats, for example, eat foods brought to the home burrow by those conspecifics successful in foraging (Barnett & Spencer, 1951), and food caches are communally created and exploited resources (Calhoun, 1962, p. 109). Rats, both wild and domesticated, can also influence one another's food selection, providing some degree of protection against The ingestion of toxic foods, and reducing the time spent, especially by juveniles, in searching for food (Galef, 1976, 1977; Galef & Clark, 1971; Lavin, Freise, & Coombes, 1980; Steiniger, 1950). Trails from one place of safety to another and from refuges to feeding sites are cleared and maintained by the combined action of numerous animals (Calhoun, 1962, pp. 54–70; Telle, 1966). Matrilocal grown young provide food caches, refuges, trails, and information to their younger siblings and may thus increase their dams' reproductive success.

Similarly, nonbreeding adult and yearling black-tailed prairie dogs assist breeders in defense of the coterie territory, on which both they and the breeding adults and their young feed (Hoogland, 1981a; King, 1955). They also maintain the mounds around burrow entrances, carry nesting material into burrows other than those in which they sleep, and reduce the heat loss of conspecifics by huddling with them (Hoogland, 1981a,b).

While the data provide no unequivocal evidence of reproductive benefits to a dam resulting from the immediate presence of her sons or daughters, they are certainly consistent with such a view.

Discussion

The apparently straightforward argument that females engaging in reproduction must suffer reduced future reproductive potential ignores the fact that natural selection has been acting for millennia, both to weed out those phenotypes (and correlated genes) most adversely affected by reproductive effort, and to increase the frequency of genes promoting strategies circumventing potential reproductive costs. The question, and it is an empirical one, is whether members of some extant species have evolved behavioral and physiological mechanisms that allow them to overcome the potential costs and risks of reproductive effort. The capacities of the females of many rodent species to delay reproduction or implantation when severely stressed by environmental or reproductive demands, to resorb fetuses, and to cannibalize offspring that overtax capacity to transduce nutrients (Baevsky, 1963; Day & Galef, 1977; Hamilton, 1962; Russell, 1948; Woodside *et al.*, 1981; see, for review, Sadlier, 1969) suggest that the evolution of strategies that minimize the probability of incurring reproductive costs is far advanced. Furthermore, behavioral and anatomical adjustments exhibited by female rodents to meet the nutritive demands of their dependent young (see the sections on the bioenergetics of pregnancy and lactation) indicate that mechanisms can be evolved to reduce markedly the potential costs of reproduction. The issue is whether such strategies are sufficient to reduce realized costs to near zero. It may be as reasonable to assume that female mammals circumvent most of the potential deleterious effects of reproduction as it is to assume that they are invariably handicapped by previous reproductive success.

In this view, any failure of female mammals to circumvent potential reproductive costs is seen as a phenomenon requiring explanation. For example, Armitage and Downhower (1974) have found a significant positive correlation between mortality risk during hibernation and duration of snow cover in reproductively active female yellow-bellied marmots, but not in yearling females, adult males, or nonbreeding adult females. Further, reproducing females began to gain weight much later in the year than other marmots. Consequently, they may have failed to deposit fat stores sufficient to support prolonged hibernation in severe winters (Armitage & Downhower, 1974). Indirect evidence thus suggests that females rearing young may have an enhanced mortality during hibernation the subsequent winter (Harper, 1981, p. 118).[4]

If one adopts the view that reproduction inevitably has costs, the possible enhanced risk of mortality to be observed in reproductively active female marmots is easily accepted. If, to the contrary, one assumes that strategies for overcoming reproductive costs are available to female mammals, an explanation is required of the failure of reproductively active female marmots to

[4] The data on hibernation mortality collected by Armitage (1981) and his co-workers over a 20-year period, probably sufficient to determine directly the effects of reproduction on mortality, are now being analyzed.

compensate behaviorally for the enhanced energy demands of reproduction by increasing nutrient intake to forestall the mortality risk during severe winters subsequent to reproduction.[5]

The literature review presented above does not lead to the conclusion that reproduction in mammals is without costs or risks. Rather, it suggests that the general statement that reproduction invariably reduces future fecundity (Bell, 1980) cannot be adequately supported from available data. As indicated in this chapter, there is reason to believe that reproduction among rodents can enhance, reduce, or leave unchanged future fecundity, depending on the circumstances in which it occurs. Reproduction costs or benefits are not constant across species, environments, age classes, variations in population size, or successive parities. Adding members to one's social group may be beneficial in small populations but deleterious when numbers are great. The phenotypic costs of transducing energy to offspring may be negligible in resource-rich environments but severe in a marginal habitat. Susceptibility to predation may rise or fall during reproduction, depending on the hunting strategy of the major predators exploiting a population. The net effect of engaging in one reproductive episode on the probability of subsequent successful reproduction is determined by the interaction of a wide variety of factors, but there is no *a priori* reason to assume that such net effects are invariably, or even on average, negative.

Mammals are particularly difficult animals in which to determine the net cost of reproduction. Both the ability to increase nutrient intake when meeting the energy demands of developing young and the frequency of formation of matrilocal groups whose members may return parental investment introduce complexities absent elsewhere in the animal kingdom. For example, in a recent review of reproductive costs in reptiles, Shine (1980) provided strong evidence both of increased risk of predation in gravid females of several lizard species and reduced food intake in many gravid snakes, lizards, and crocodilians. Evidence of phenotypic costs of reproduction in reptiles is more

---

[5] One might suspect, given that during 4 or 5 summer months marmots must acquire sufficient nutrients to support life for all 12 months of the year, that even nonreproductively active marmots devote most of their time to feeding and therefore have no time to increase food intake during the reproductive phase of their life cycles. This is, however, not the case. Adult marmots feed only a few hours per day (at dawn and at dusk) and spend far more of the middle of the day "sitting" than feeding (Armitage, 1962).

Armitage (1981) has suggested that potential feeding time in marmots is far more restricted than simple observation suggests. Marmots may be incapable of activity during the warm part of the day because of the hyperthermia that such activity would entail. Thus, the failure of marmots to compensate for the energy demands of reproduction by increasing food intake may be the result of an absence of additional time in which high levels of activity are physiologically possible.

substantial than in mammals, and evidence of phenotypic benefits is lacking. The conclusion that reproduction is costly to reptiles is supported by the data; this is not the case for mammals.

There is, however, one sense in which reproduction cannot be cost-free, even to mammals. In all species whose reproductive histories I have examined, old animals are less reproductively capable than young ones: the sterility rates of the former are higher, and the litter sizes, when reproduction occurs, are smaller. Every reproductive episode takes time, and the time invested in a given litter moves a reproducer closer to senescence and reduced reproductive potential. Furthermore, there is the possibility of mortality during the time spent in a reproductive episode, which inevitably must reduce an individual's probability of future reproduction (see Williams, 1957, and Hamilton, 1966, for a discussion of related issues). Hence, the time invested in a reproductive effort, rather than the energy allocated to the young, may be the major cost to mammalian reproducers, especially those nearing the end of the reproductive period in their lives.

As mentioned in the introduction, I began the research for this chapter assuming that it would be a relatively simple matter to demonstrate that a juvenile mammal is a phenotypic parasite rather than a symbiote of its dam, that it reduces its dam's capacity to engage successfully in further reproduction. An examination of the literature reveals potential phenotypic benefits accruing to female mammals engaging in reproduction, as well as behavioral and physiological mechanisms that reduce substantially the potential costs of a reproductive effort.

Given that neither the relative magnitude nor the frequency of occurrence of the benefits and costs accruing to mammalian reproducers in natural circumstances is known, the net cost of reproduction cannot be calculated. The existence both of potential benefits accruing to reproducers and of strategies for minimizing reproductive costs requires abandonment of the *a priori* assumption that net costs are inevitably associated with reproductive effort. Greater attention to the acquisition of data is needed to determine the effects of reproduction of future fecundity.

ACKNOWLEDGMENTS

I sincerely thank Barbara Woodside, David Clark, Doris Jensen, Alison Fleming, Corinne Day, Dale Madison, Jack Hoogland, Paul Sherman, Mertice Clark, Jeff Alberts, and Martin Daley for their assistance in locating relevant references, and for providing reprints and preprints. Mertice Clark, Martin Daly, Paul Sherman, and Jeff Alberts contributed their time and energy in providing encouragement, insightful discussion, and most useful critical reviews of earlier drafts.

References

Armitage, K. B. Social behavior of a colony of the yellow-bellied marmot (*Marmota flaviventris*). *Animal Behavior*, 1962, *10*, 319–331.

Armitage, K. B. Personal communications 1981.

Armitage, K. B., & Downhower, J. F. Demography of yellow-bellied marmot populations. *Ecology*, 1974, *55*, 1233–1245.

Asdell, S. A., Bogart, R., & Sperling, G. The influence of age and rate of breeding upon the ability of the female rat to reproduce and raise young. *Cornell University Agricultural Experimental Station Memoires*, 1941, *238*, 3–26.

Babcock, M. J., Bogart, R., Sterling, G., & Asdell, S. A. The reproductive efficiency of the albino rat under different breeding conditions. *Journal of Agricultural Research*, 1940, *12*, 847–853.

Baevsky, U. B. The effects of embryonic diapause on the nuclei and mitotic activity of mink and rat blastocysts. In A. C. Enders (Ed.), *Delayed implantation*. Chicago: University of Chicago Press, 1963.

Barnes, H. So-called anecdysis in *Balanus balanoides* and the effect of breeding upon the growth of calcareous shell of some common barnacles. *Limnology and Oceanography*, 1962, *7*, 462–473.

Barnet, S. A., & Spencer, M. M. Feeding, social behavior, and interspecific competition in wild rats. *Behaviour*, 1951, *3*, 227–242.

Baverstock, P., & Green, B. Water recycling in lactation. *Science*, 1975, *187*, 657–658.

Bell, G. The costs of reproduction and their consequences. *American Naturalist*, 1980, *116*, 45–76.

Berger, M. E. Population structure of olive baboons (*Papio anubis* (J. P. Fisher)) in the Laikipia District of Kenya. *East African Wildlife Journal*, 1972, *10*, 159–164.

Bertram, B. C. R. Living in groups: Predators and prey. In J. R. Krebs & N. B. Davies (Eds.), *Behavioral ecology*. Sunderland, Mass.: Sinauer, 1978.

Biggers, J. D., Finn, C. A., & McClaren, A. Long-term reproductive performance of female mice: II. Variation of litter size with parity. *Journal of Reproduction and Fertility*, 1962, *3*, 313–330.

Bogart, R., Sterling, G., Barnes, I. C., & Asdell, S. A. The influence of reproductive condition upon growth in the female rat. *American Journal of Physiology*, 1939, *128*, 355–371.

Bond, C. F. Blood volume changes in the lactating rat. *Endocrinology*, 1958, *63*, 285–289.

Bruce, H. M., & East, J. Number and viability of young from pregnancies concurrent with lactation in the mouse. *Journal of Endocrinology*, 1956, *14*, 19–27.

Calhoun, J. B. *The ecology and sociology of the Norway rat.* Bethesda, Md.: U.S. Department of Health, Education and Welfare, 1962.

Calow, P. Ecology, evolution and energetics: A study of metabolic adaptation. In A. MacFadyen (Ed.), *Advances in ecological research*. London: Academic Press, 1977.

Campbell, C. H. The susceptibility of mother mice and pregnant mice to the virus of foot and mouth disease. *Journal of Immunology*, 1960, *84*, 469–474.

Charlesworth, B., & Leon, J. A. The relation of reproductive effort to age. *American Naturalist*, 1976, *107*, 303–311.

Christian, J. J., Lloyd, J. A., & Davis, D. E. The role of endocrines in the self regulation of mammalian populations. In G. Pincus, (Ed.), *Recent progress in hormone research* (Vol. 21). New York: Academic Press, 1965.

Clough, G. C. Viability in wild meadow voles under various conditions of population density, season, and reproductive activity. *Ecology*, 1965, *46*, 119–134.

Crisp, D. J., & Patel, B. The interaction between breeding and growth rate in the barnacle *Eliminius modestus* Darwin. *Limnology and Oceanography*, 1961, *6*, 105–115.

Crowcroft, P. *Mice all over.* London: Foulis, 1966.

Crowcroft, P., & Rowe, F. P. Social organization and territorial behavior in the wild house mouse (*Mus musculus* L.) *Proceedings of the Zoological Society of London*, 1963, *140*, 517–531.

Dalldorf, G., & Gifford, R. Susceptibility of gravid mice to Coxsackie virus infection. *Journal of Experimental Medicine,* 1954, *99,* 21–27.

Daly, M., & Wilson, M. *Sex, evolution, and behavior.* North Scituate, Mass.: Duxbury Press, 1978.

Dapson, R. W. Phenologic influences on cohort-specific reproductive strategies in mice (*Peromyscus polionotus*). *Ecology,* 1979, *60,* 1125–1131.

Day, C. S. D. *Pup cannibalism: A description and causal analysis of one aspect of maternal behavior of the golden hamster (Mesocricetus auratus).* Unpublished doctoral thesis, McMaster University, 1976.

Day, C. S. D., & Galef, B. G., Jr. Pup cannibalism: One aspect of maternal behavior in golden hamsters. *Journal of Comparative and Physiological Psychology,* 1977, *91,* 1179–1189.

Donaldson, H. H. *The rat: Data and reference tables.* Philadelphia: Wistar Institue of Anatomy, 1924.

Ellinger, G. M., Duckworth, J., Dalgarno, A. C., & Quenouille, M. H. Skeletal changes during pregnancy and lactation in the rat: Effect of different levels of dietary calcium. *British Journal of Nutrition,* 1952, *6,* 235–253.

Ewer, R. F. *Ethology of mammals.* New York: Plenum Press, 1968.

Ewer, R. F. *The carnivores.* Ithaca, N.Y.: Cornell University Press, 1973.

Exon, P. D., & Dixon, K. Immunological response in pregnancy. *British Medical Journal,* 1972, *4,* 361–362.

Fabis, N. Immunological reactivity during pregnancy in the mouse. *Experientia,* 1973, *29,* 610–612.

Farber, P. A., & Glasgow, L. A. Factors modifying host resistance to viral infection: II. Enhanced susceptibility of mice to encephalomyocarditis virus infection during pregnancy. *American Journal of Pathology,* 1968, *53,* 463–478.

Fell, B. F., Smith, K. A., & Campbell, R. M. Hypertrophic and hyperplastic changes in the alimentary canal of the lactating rat. *Journal of Pathology and Bacteriology,* 1963, *85,* 179–188.

Freeman, D. W., & Barnes, A. Deaths from Asian influenza associated with pregnancy. *American Journal of Obstetrics and Gynecology,* 1959, *78,* 1172–1175.

Friedman, M. I., & Bruno, J. P. Exchange of water during lactation. *Science,* 1976, *191,* 409–410.

Galef, B. G., Jr. Mechanisms for the social transmission of acquired food preferences from adult to weanling rats. In L. M. Barker, M. R. Best, & M. Domjan (Eds.), *Learning mechanisms in food selection.* Waco, Texas: Baylor University Press, 1976.

Galef, B. G., Jr. The social transmission of food preferences: An adaptation for weaning in rats. *Journal of Comparative and Physiological Psychology,* 1977, *91,* 1136–1140.

Galef, B. G., Jr. The ecology of weaning: Parasitism and the achievement of independence by altricial mammals. In D. J. Gubernick & P. H. Klopfer (Eds.), *Parental care in mammals.* New York: Plenum, 1981.

Galef, B. G., Jr., & Clark, M. M. Social factors in the poison avoidance and feeding behavior of wild and domesticated rat pups. *Journal of Comparative and Physiological Psychology,* 1971, *75,* 341–357.

Gandelman, R. Mice postpartum aggression elicited by the presence of an intruder. *Hormones and Behavior,* 1972, *3,* 23–38.

Geist, V. *Mountain sheep.* Chicago: University of Chicago Press, 1971.

Gilles, H. M., Lawson, J. B., Sibelas, M., Voller, A., & Allan, N. Malaria, anemia, and pregnancy. *Annals of Tropical Medicine and Parasitology,* 1969, *63,* 245–263.

Gromov, V. S., & Popov, V. S. Some features of the spatial-ethological structure of a Mongolian gerbil colony (*Meriones unguiculatus*) and attempts to influence it by pharmacological methods. *Zoological Journal,* 1979, *58,* 1528–1535.

Hamilton, W. J. Reproductive adaptations in the red tree mouse. *Journal of Mammalogy,* 1962, *43,* 486–504.

Hamilton, W. D. The moulding of senescence by natural selection. *Journal of Theoretical Biology,* 1966, *12,* 12–45.

Hamilton, W. D. Geometry for the selfish herd. *Journal of Theoretical Biology*, 1971, *31*, 295–311.

Harper, L. V. Offspring effects upon parents. In D. J. Gubernick & P. H. Klopfer (Eds.), *Parental care in mammals*. New York: Plenum Press, 1981.

Hasler, J. F., & Banks, E. M. Reproductive performance and growth in captive collared lemmings (*Dicrostonyx groenlandicus*). *Canadian Journal of Zoology*, 1975, *53*, 777–787.

Heinshohn, G. E. Ecology and reproduction of the Tasmanian bandicoots (*Perameles gunni* and *Isodon obesulus*). *University of California Publications in Zoology*, 1966, *80*, 1–96.

Hoogland, J. L. The effects of colony size on individual alertness of prairie dogs (Sciuridae: *Cynomys* spp.) *Animal Behavior*, 1979, *27*, 394–407.

Hoogland, J. L. Personal communication, 1980.

Hoogland, J. L. The evolution of coloniality in white-tailed and black-tailed prairie dogs (Scuridea: *Cynomys leucurus* and *C. ludovicianus*). *Ecology*, 1981, *62*, 252–272. (a)

Hoogland, J. L. Nepotism and cooperative breeding in the black-tailed prairie dog. (Scuridae: *Cynomys ludovicianus*). In R. D. Alexander & D. W. Tinkle (Eds.), *Natural selection and social behavior*. New York: Chiron Press, 1981. (b)

Hoogland, J. L., & Sherman, P. W. Advantages and disadvantages of bank swallow (*Riparia riparia*) coloniality. *Ecological Monographs*, 1976, *46*, 33–58.

Hytten, E. A., & Thompson, A. M. Nutrition of lactating women. In S. K. Kon & A. T. Cowie (Eds.), *Milk: The mammary gland and its secretion* (Vol. 2.) London: Academic Press, 1961.

Kaczmarski, F. Bioenergetics of pregnancy and lactation in the bank vole. *Acta Theriologica*, 1966, *11*, 409–417.

Kennedy, G. C., Pearce, W. M., & Parrott, D. M. V. Liver growth in the lactating rat. *Journal of Endocrinology*, 1958, *17*, 158–160.

Kenny, J. F., & Diamond, M. Immunological responsiveness to *Escherichia coli* during pregnancy. *Infection and Immunology*, 1977, *16*, 174–180.

King, H. D. Litter production and sex ratio in various strains of rats. *Anatomical Record*, 1924, *27*, 337–365.

King, J. A. Social behavior, social organization, and population dynamics in a black-tailed prairiedog town in the Black Hills of South Dakota. *Contributions from the Laboratory of Vertebrate Biology of the University of Michigan*, 1955, *27*, 1–123.

King, J. A. Maternal behavior in *Peromyscus*. In H. L. Rheingold, (Ed.), *Maternal behavior in mammals* New York: Wiley, 1963.

Knox, A. W. Influence of pregnancy in mice on the course of infection with murine poliomyelitis virus. *Procedings of the Society for Experimental Biology and Medicine* 1950, *73*, 520–523.

Kruuk, H. *The spotted hyena*. Chicago: University of Chicago Press, 1972.

LaPage, G. *Animals parasitic in man*. New York: Dover, 1963.

Lavin, M. J., Freise, B., & Coombes, S. Transferred flavor aversions in adult rats. *Behavioral and Neural Biology*, 1980, *28*, 15–33.

Leon, M., Croskerry, P. G., & Smith, G. K. Thermal control of mother-young contact in rats. *Physiology and Behavior*, 1978, *21*, 793–811.

Lush, J. L., & Molln, A. E. Litter size and weight as permanent characteristics of sows. *Technical Bulletin, U.S. Department of Agriculture, No. 836*, 1942.

Luz, N. P., Marques, M., Ayub, A. C., & Correa, P. R. Effects of estradiol upon the thymus and lymphoid organs of immature female rats. *American Journal of Obstetrics and Gynecology*, 1975, *122*, 561–564.

Madison, D. M. Behavioral and sociochemical susceptibility of meadow voles (*Microtus pennsylvanicus*) to snake predation. *American Midland Naturalist*, 1978, *100*, 23–28. (a)

Madison, D. M. Movement indicators of reproductive events among female meadow voles as revealed by radio-telemetry. *Journal of Mammalogy*, 1978, *59*, 835–843. (b)

Madison, D. M. Impact of spacing behavior and predation on population growth in meadow voles. In R. E. Byers (Ed.), *Proceedings of the third eastern pine and meadow vole symposium.* New Paltz, N.Y., Feb. 14–15, 1979, pp.20–29.

Marston, J. H., & Chang, M. C. The breeding, management, and reproductive physiology of the Mongolian gerbil. *Laboratory Animal Care,* 1965, *15,* 34–48.

Maynard, L. A., & Loosi, J. K. *Animal nutrition.* New York: McGraw-Hill, 1962.

Mech, D. C. *The wolf.* Garden City, N.Y.: Natural History Press, 1970.

Merritt, K., & Galton, M. Antibody formation during pregnancy. *Transplantation,* 1969, *7,* 562–566.

Millar, J. S. Energetics of lactation in *Peromyscus maniculatus. Canadian Journal of Zoology,* 1979, *57,* 1015–1019.

Mitchell, G. W., & Sbarra, A. J. The role of the phagocyte in host parasite interactions: II. The phagocytic capabilities of leukocytes in pregnant women. *American Journal of Obstetrics and Gynecology,* 1965, *91,* 755–762.

Mitchell, G. W., McRipley, R. J., Selvaraj, R. J., & Sbarra, A. J. The role of the phagocyte in host-parasite interactions: IV. The phagocytic activity of leukocytes in pregnancy and its relationship to urinary tract infections. *American Journal of Obstetrics and Gynecology,* 1966, *96,* 687–697.

Moehlman, P. D. Jackal helpers and pup survival. *Nature,* 1979, *277,* 382–383.

Nelson, J. H., Hall, E. J., Manuel-Limson, G., Freidberg, H., & O'Brien, F. J. Effects of pregnancy on the thymolymphatic system: I. Changes in the intact rat after exogenous HCG, estrogen, and progesterone administration. *American Journal of Obstetrics and Gynecology,* 1967, *98,* 895–899.

Nelson, M. M., & Evans, H. M. Dietary requirements for lactation in the rat and other laboratory mammals. In S. K. Kon & A. T. Cowie (Eds.), *Milk: The mammary gland and its secretion* (Vol. 2). New York: Academic Press, 1961.

Nicol, T., Bilbey, D. L. J., Charles, L. M., Cordingley, J. L., & Vernon-Roberts, B. Oestrogen: The natural stimulant of body defence. *Journal of Endocrinology,* 1964, *30,* 277–291.

Oster, G. F., & Wilson, E. O. *Caste and ecology in the social insects.* Princeton, N.J.: Princeton University Press, 1978.

Overall, J. C., Jr., Kern, E. R., Schlitzer, R. L., Friedman, S. B., & Glasgow, L. A. Genital *Herpesvirus hominis* infection in mice: I. Development of an experimental model. *Infection and Immunity,* 1975, *11,* 476–480.

Paterson, J. S. The guinea pig or cavy. In W. Lane-Peter (Ed.), *The UFAW handbook on the care and management of laboratory animals.* Edinburgh: E & S Livingstone, 1967.

Peter, J. M., & Krynen, C. H. Organ weights and water content of lactating rats. *Growth,* 1966, *30,* 295–303.

Pond, C. M. The significance of lactation in the evolution of mammals. *Evolution,* 1978, *31,* 177–199.

Porter, G. The Norway rat (*Rattus norvegicus*). In W. Lane-Petter (Ed.), *The UFAW handbook on the care and management of laboratory animals.* Edinburgh: E & S Livingstone, 1967.

Pridelle, H. D., Lenz, W. R., Young, D. C., & Stevenson, C. S. Poliomyelitis in pregnancy and the puerperium. *American Journal of Obstetrics and Gynecology,* 1952, *63,* 408–413.

Randolph, P. A., Randolph, J. C., Mattingly, K., & Foster, M. M. The energy costs of reproduction in the cotton rat (*Sigmodon hispidus*). *Ecology,* 1977, *58,* 31–45.

Rangnekar, K. N., Rao, S. S., Joshi, U. M., Virkar, K. D., Kora, S. J., & Dikshit, S. S. Humoral antibody formation during pregnancy. *Journal of Reproduction and Fertility,* 1974, *38,* 237–238.

Rasa, O. D. E. The ethology and sociology of the dwarf mongoose (*Helogale undulata rufula.* *Zeitschrift für Tierpsychologie,* 1977, *43,* 337–406.

Richdale, L. E. *A population study of penguins.* Oxford: Clarendon, 1957.

Richter, C. P. Total regulatory function in animals and human beings. *Harvey Lectures,* 1942, *38,* 63–103.

Rood, J. P. Mating relationships and breeding suppression in the dwarf mongoose. *Animal Behavior,* 1980, *28,* 143–150.

Russell, F. C. Diet in relation to reproduction and the viability of the young: I. Rats and other laboratory animals. *Commonwealth Bureau of Animal Nutrition Technical Communication,* 1948, *16,* 1–99.

Sadlier, R. M. F. S. *The ecology of reproduction in wild and domestic mammals.* London: Methuen, 1969.

Sayler, A., & Salmon, M. Communal nursing in mice: Influence of multiple mothers on the growth of the young. *Science,* 1969, *164,* 1309–1310.

Schaffer, W. M. Selection for optimal life histories: The effects of age structure. *Ecology,* 1974, *56,* 577–590.

Schaller, G. B. *The deer and the tiger.* Chicago: University of Chicago Press, 1967.

Schaller, G. B. *The Serengetti lion.* Chicago: University of Chicago Press, 1972.

Sherman, P. W. Nepotism and the evolution of alarm calls. *Science,* 1977, *197,* 1246–1253.

Sherman, P. W. The limits of ground squirrel nepotism. In G. W. Barlow & J. Silverberg (Eds.), *Sociobiology: Beyond nature/nurture?* Boulder, Colo.: Westview Press, 1980. (a)

Sherman, P. W. Personal communication, October 1980. (b)

Shine, R. *"Costs" of reproduction in reptiles. Oecologia,* 1980, *46,* 92–100.

Simkiss, K. *Calcium in reproductive physiology.* London: Chapman & Hall, 1967.

Sloanaker, J. R. The effects of copulation, pregnancy, pseudo-pregnancy and lactation on voluntary activity and food consumption of the albino rat. *American Journal of Physiology,* 1924, *71,* 362–394.

Souders, H. J., & Morgan, A. F. Weight and composition of organs during the reproductive cycle in the rat. *American Journal of Physiology,* 1957, *191,* 1–7.

Stearns, S. C. Life history tactics: A review of the ideas. *Quarterly Review of Biology,* 1976, *51,* 3–47.

Steiniger, von F. Beitrage zur Soziologie und sonstigen Biologie der Wanderratte. *Zeitschrift für Tierpsychologie,* 1950, *7,* 356–379.

Suntzeff, V., Cowdry, E. V., & Hixon, B. B. The influence of maternal age on offspring in mice. *Journal of Gerontology,* 1962, *17,* 2–8.

Tanimoto, K. Ecological research on animals in Manchuria carrying bubonic plague: Part III. *Zoological Journal,* 1943, *55,* 117–127.

Telle, H. J. Beitrag zur Kenntnis der Verhaltensweise von Ratten, vergleichend dargestellt bei *Rattus norvegicus* und *Rattus rattus. Zeitschrift für Angewandte Zoologie,* 1966, *53,* 129–196.

Trivers, R. L. Parental investment and sexual selection. In B. Campbell (Ed.), *Sexual selection and the descent of man.* New York: Aldine, 1972.

vanLawick-Goodall, H., & vanLawick-Goodall, J. *Innocent killers.* Boston: Houghton Mifflin, 1971.

van Zon, A. A. J. C., & Eling, W. M. Depressed malarial immunity in pregnant mice. *Infection and Immunity,* 1980, *28,* 630–632.

Weaver, H. M., & Steiner, G. Acute anterior poliomyelitis during pregnancy. *American Journal of Obstetrics and Gynecology,* 1944, *47,* 495–505.

Werboff, J. Steg, M., & Barnes, L. Communal nursing in mice: Strain specific effects of multiple mothers on growth and behavior. *Psychonomic Science,* 1970, *19,* 269–271.

Whitfield, P. J. *The biology of parasitism.* London: Edward Arnold, 1979.

Widdowson, E. M. Changes in the body and its organs during lactation: Nutritional implications. In *Breast feeding and the mother,* CIBA symposium, 1976.

Williams, G. C. Pleiotropy, natural selection and the evolution of senescence. *Evolution,* 1957, *11,* 398–411.

Williams, G. C. *Adaptation and natural selection.* Princeton, N.J.: Princeton University Press, 1962.

Williams, R. G., Carmon, J. L., & Golley, F. B. Effects of sequence of pregnancy on litter size and growth in *Peromyscus polionotus*. *Journal of Reproduction and Fertility,* 1965, *9,* 257–260.

Woodside, B., Wilson, R., Chee, P., & Leon, M. Resource partitioning during reproduction in the Norway rat. *Science,* 1981, *211,* 76–77.

Young, E. J., & Gomez, C. I. Enhancement of herpesvirus type 2 infection in pregnant mice. *Proceedings of the Society for Experimental Biology and Medicine,* 1979, *160,* 416–420.

Young, E. J., Killam, A. P., & Greene, J. F., Jr. Disseminated herpes virus infection. *Journal of the American Medical Association,* 1976, *235,* 2731–2733.

Index

Acetic acid, 53
Adrenals, 66
   adrenalectomy, 67–68
   adrenocorticoids, 18, 27, 67, 68, 155, 191
   cortisol, 192–210
   pituitary control, 192, 208
Agression, 18, 118
Allometry, 27, 215–248
   definition, 216–217
   Huxley's equation, 217–218
   neonatal size, 225–227
Alpha-adrenergic neurons, 66
Altricial species, 29
Alveolar tissue, 37, 77, 91, 108
Amenorrhea, 88
   lactational, 81
Amniotic fluid, 15
Amphibia, 116–117
Anogential stimulation, 12, 14, 22, 33, 69
Anosmia, 71
Antibodies, 24, 25. *See also* Milk
Approach behavior, 14–16. *See also*
   Maternal pheromone
Areolar region, 83, 85
Attachment style, 174
Auditory cues, 33, 37. *See also* Distress
   vocalizations
Aunting, 196, 197, 200
Autonomic regulation, 17, 64

Baboon, 251
Bandicoot, 257
Barasingha, 265
Baroreceptors, 66–67
Bat, 30
Beta-adrenergic neurons, 64, 66

Bile acids
   chenodeoxycholic, 48, 50, 54, 55
   cholic, 48–55
   deoxycholic, 2, 48, 50, 54–56, 58
   lithocholic, 48
Biparental care, 145–171. *See also* Birds
Birds, 117, 140
   bobwhite, 139
   chicken, 116
   duck, 118
   gull, 157
   magpie, 116
   pigeon, 165
   ring dove, 12, 145–171
   sparrow, 3
Blood pressure, 66
Bottle feeding, 178–180. *See also* Infant
Breast feeding, 178–181. *See also* Infant
Breeding cycle, 158. *See also* Incubation
Brucella, 25
Buffalo, 264

Cardiovascular system, 67. *See also* Heart
   rate
Caregiver sensitivity, 173–188
   psychophysiological assessment, 175–186.
      See also Infant
Catecholamines, 71, 72
   dopamine, 70
   norepinephrine, 67, 70
Caudate nucleus, 66
Cebuella, 219
Cecum, 48, 49, 51
Celiac ganglion, 66
Chemical cues, general, 14–16
Chemosensitivity, development of, 15

279

Child abuse, 183
Cholecystokinin, 66
Cholesterol, 52, 117
Clostridia, 53
Colostrum, 25. *See also* Milk
Columbiformes, 165–166. *See also* Birds
Contact comfort, 234, 235. *See also*
    Thermoregulation
Cooing
    nest-cooing, 150, 154
    bow-cooing, 154. *See also* Birds
Coprophagia, 23. *See also* Maternal
    pheromone
Cotton rat, 254–255, 257, 261
Courtship, 147, 151, 154, 155
Cow, 78, 82, 89, 92, 107
Crop growth, 152. *See also* Birds
Crying, 181, 183, 185, 188. *See also* Distress
    vocalizations; Infant

Deer, 79, 264
    red deer, 79
Diacyl glycerol ether, 116, 118
Diarrhea, 56
Dimethyl disulfide, 15
Distress vocalizations, 14, 178, 181, 183, 185,
    186, 193–195, 202, 203, 204–206,
    207–208, 209–210
Diving reflex, 55
DNA, 140
Dog
    cape hunting dog, 266
    wild dog, 264
Drinking, 194, 209
Dust-bathing, 139

Eccrine glands, 223, 235
Electroencephalographic patterns, 17.
    See also Sleep
Endocrine regulation, 17–18
Enteric immunocompetence, development
    of, 54
Enterohepatic circulation, 48. *See also*
    Prolactin
Ergocornine hydrogen maleate, 18, 46.
    See also Prolactin
Escherichia coli (E. coli), 52, 54–55
Estradiol, 151, 164, 261
Estrous cycle, 258
Exploration/exploratory behavior, 191, 203

Extension reflex, 17

Facial expressions, 179
Feces, 15, 23, 46, 52, 55. *See also* Copro-
    phagia; Maternal pheromone
Fetus, 37
Fish, 117
Food consumption, 19, 194, 200

Galactophore, 18, 83, 91, 93, 94, 108. *See also*
    Mammary gland
Gastrin, 66
Gastrointestinal tract, 53, 66, 67
    interoreceptors, 63
Gazelle, 264
Gender differentiation, 18
Gerbil, 113–143, 255, 257, 259, 267
    developmental schedule, 132
    development of grooming, 134–136
    hair growth and eye opening, 131. *See also*
    Sequeaction
Glucagon, 66
Goat, 82, 91, 95, 228
Gorilla, 31, 216, 219, 221, 225
Grooming, 4, 120, 121, 122, 124, 125,
    130–131, 134–136
Growth rates, interspecific differences,
    229–231
Guinea pig, 91, 103, 116, 117

Hair density
    allometry, 218–233
    monkey and humans, 218–223
    thermoregulation, 221–224
Hamster, 117, 118, 129, 257, 259
Harderian gland, 113–143
Harderian secretions
    autogrooming, 119, 135
    effects on behavior, 138
    infant development, 129–136
    parent–infant interactions, 129–136
    sensory and behavioral control, 119–124
    thermoregulation, 124–129, 130–136, 137,
    138
Heart rate, 61–69, 70, 72, 177, 179–182
    effect of maternal milk, 63–69
    effect of maternal separation, 64–65
Herring bodies, 97–98
Hibernation, 270
Histamine, 66

Homomorphy/heteromorphy, 4
Horse, 140
Huddling behavior of litter, 27, 28, 35, 69
Human, 140, 166, 173–188, 191, 254, 262
Hyena, 264, 265
Hyperactivity, 70–72
Hypothalamus, 86, 96, 103, 108
  magnocellular nuclei, 96, 100
  paraventricular nuclei, 96, 97
  septohippocampal inputs, 103
  supraoptic nuclei 96
Hypovolemia, 22

Ileum, 48
Incubation behavior, 147–157
  breeding cycles, 158
  castration, 155
  diurnal rhythm, 159–163
  gonadal hormones, 150–151, 154–155, 164
  nest defense, 165
  synchronization of mates, 157, 159
Infant, 29, 31, 173–188
  depression, 210
  head movements, 140
  plantar reflexes, 140
  signals, 175–186
  thermal interactions in, 29
Inquilinism,, 36
Insects, 265–266
  honeybee, 266
Insulin, 66
Intimate association, definition, 35–39
Intramammary pressure, 83, 86–88, 91–94,
  96–97, 99–100
Isovalency/contravalency, 4

Jackal, 266

!Kung Indians, 80, 91, 231

Lacrimal gland, 116, 117, 119, 136
Lactase, 24
Lactation, 4, 14, 15, 18, 19–24, 28, 34, 37,
  46, 47, 77, 78, 166, 167
  amenorrhea, 81
  concurrent asynchronous, 93–95
  hyperphagia, 18–19
  metabolic cost, 19, 253–254
  risk of predation, 263–265
  susceptibility to disease, 260–263

Lactobacillus/Bifidobacterium, 52, 54
Lactose, 24
Learned helplessness, 210
Lemming, 256
Lemur, 226
Leopard, 264
Lion, 264
Lipids, 24, 116, 117, 126, 132. *See also*
  Triglycerides
Litter size
  effects of maternal age, 272
  effects of successive parity, 256–260
Liver, 2, 48, 49, 50
  cystosol, 51, 52
  gender differences, 48–49
  receptors at, 48
  uptake of prolactin, 48–52
Loris, 226
Luteinizing hormone, 156

Macaque
  cynomolgus macaque, 234
  Japanese macaque, 221
  Taiwan macaque, 221. *See also* Monkey
Mammals
  eutherian, 81
  methatherian, 81
Mammary development, 37
Mammary gland, 21, 23, 25, 37, 77, 79, 81,
  83, 85, 94, 101, 108
  blood supply, 34
  contraction, 91–93
  ducts, 68, 72, 73
  engorgement, 79, 84
  innervation, 84
  mechanical stimulation, 92
  structure, 83–84, 91. *See also* Intramam-
    mary pressure; Mammary nerve;
    Myoepithelial cells
Mammary nerve, 84–85
Mammary receptors, 88
Marmoset, 218, 227
Marmot
  yellow-bellied marmot, 270
Marsupials, 81, 93
  agile wallaby, 81–83, 93–94
  red kangaroo, 81
Maternal pheromone, 45–60
  pheromonal bond, 45
  pheromonal symbiosis, 58

Maternal pheromone (*cont.*)
  prolactin, 46–52. *See also* Bile acids
Maternal body temperature, 27, 236–237
Maternal separation
  hyperactivity, 70–72
Metabolic rate, 27, 224
Methylatropine, 64
Micturition, 23
  reflex, 38, 89
Milk, 3, 17–18, 19–21, 24–25, 33–35, 37–38,
    52, 56, 63, 65–66, 68, 73–74, 77,
    228–229
  antibodies, 25
  caloric content, 20, 25–26
  composition, 241
  fatty acids, 56
  interspecific differences, 228–229
  nutritive components, 24–25, 78
  water content, 21
Milk ejection, 77–79, 80, 83–86, 90–91, 93,
    96–99, 102, 105, 108, 166
  definition, 108
  during anesthesia and sleep, 89–91, 92
  emotional factors, 108
  fornix, 105
  hippocamus, 105
  inhibition, 105–106
  locus ceruleus, 105
  paraventricular nucleus, 97
  patterns of, 86–89
  vasopressin, 95–96, 97
  women, 80–81, 83–86. *See also* Oxytocin
Milk transfer, 77–112
Mole, 117
Mongoose, 266
Monkey, 189–214, 215–248
  African monkey, 221
  howler monkey, 227
  rhesus monkey, 206–209
  squirrel monkey, 192, 197, 202, 208,
    227
  squirrel monkey, Peruvian and Bolivian,
    198
  talapoin monkey, 227. *See also* Macaque
Moose, 264
Mother–infant separation, 189–214
  as an animal model of human depression,
    210
  duration of interval, 209
  infant response to reunion, 200–201

Mother–infant separation (*cont.*)
  influence of repeated trials, 201–206
  modulation by environmental familiarity,
    195–196
  response of mother, 202
  types of, 194
  variable versus fixed interval, 204–206.
    See also Maternal separation
Mouse, 89, 117, 253, 255, 260, 261, 263,
    266–268
  deer mouse, 30, 266
  house mouse, 257, 266–268
  old-field mouse, 255–257
Myelin
  brain, 2, 54, 56, 58
Myoepithelial cells, 17, 84, 91–92, 99, 108.
    See also Milk ejection

Nasal-palatine duct, 116
Necrotizing enterocolitis (NEC), 54, 56.
    See also Bile acids
Neoteny, 232
Nest, 36, 70, 72, 126, 147, 148, 150
  attachment, 166
  site selection, 166. *See also* Nest building;
    Nest bout duration
Nest building, 12, 140, 150
Nest bout duration, 26–27
Nest defense, 148
Neurons
  magnocellular, 102, 104, 107–108
  oxytocin-producing, 96–100, 108
  oxytocinergic, 101
  paraventricular, 101
  supraoptic, 99
Nictitating membrane, 118–119
Nipple, 4, 15, 17, 36, 37, 82–83, 89
  attachment, 69, 81–83
  sensitivity, 85–86
  stimulation, 47
Novelty, 62, 64
Novel environment, 70
Nursing, 4, 12, 16, 18, 33, 35, 73–74, 179
  frequency, 80
  interval, 78–82
  k-strategists, 78
  r-strategists, 78
  strategies, 78
Nutrient interactions, 63
Nutritive resources, 19–21

Olfactory cues, 15–17, 33, 35, 38, 70, 71–72, 74. *See also* Maternal pheromone
Organ of Jacobson, 118
Ornithine decarboxylase (ODC), 68–69, 74
Oviduct, 153
Oxytocin, 17–18, 77–79, 81, 86–88, 91–96, 96–100, 105–107
  oxytocin-containing nerve fibers, 97
  oxytocin-producing neurons, 96–100, 108
  receptors, 95
  release, acetylcholine, 104
  release, carbochol, 104
  release, central pathways, 103–105
  release, conditioning, 106–108
  release, dopamine, 104
  release, electrical activity, 98–103
  release, noradrenaline, 104, 107
  release, number of suckling young, 101
  release, opioid peptides, 102
  release, serotomin, 107
  storage, transport, biosynthesis, 97–98. *See also* Milk ejection

Pair-bonding, 166
Parasympathetic blockade, 64
Parental investment, definition, 250
Parturition, 95
Pelage, 126, 128–129
Penguin, 252
Pentobarbitone, 94
Phenoxybenzamine (PBZ), 66
Pheromone, 47, 50–51, 53–54, 115–116, 118, 120, 124, 128, 131, 137. *See also* Maternal pheromone
Phospholipids, 117
Pig, 89, 92–93, 96, 117, 257
Pineal gland, 118
Pituitary stalk, 94
Population size, effects on fecundity, 267–269
Porphyrin pigments, 116
Posterior pituitary, 17, 81, 87–88, 91, 94, 96–97, 98, 100, 102. *See also* Oxytocin
Prairie dogs, 267
  black-tailed prairie dog, 268, 269
Precocial species, 29
Pregnancy, 34
  metabolic cost, 254–255
  postpartum, 255–256
  risk of predation, 263–265

Pregnancy (*cont.*)
  susceptibility to disease, 260–263
Progesterone, 151–152, 154–155
Prolactin, 18, 27, 37, 68, 77–78, 88, 107, 156
  receptors, 48
  release, serotonin and noradrenaline, 107
Propranalol, 64, 66
Protoporphyrin, 116–119, 135
Puberty, 18, 85

Rabbit, 79, 84, 89, 91, 98, 103, 105, 116, 118
Rickettsiae, 25
Reptiles, 117, 118
  crocodile, 271
  lizard, 271
  snake, 271
  turtle, 116
Reserpine, 71
Resource exchange, parent–young, 7–44
Roof rat, 267
Ruminants, 103

Saliva, 15, 124–126, 137
  human, 119
  salivary organ, 118
Salmonella, 25
Salt, 22, 37
  salt appetite, 22, 34–35, 37
Sand-bathing, 128
Scent gland, 137. *See also* Gerbil
Scent marking, 113, 122, 126, 133. *See also* Gerbil
Scorpion, 30
Sea otter, 30
Seahorse, 30
Seal
  elephant seal, 254
  fur seal, 228
  north Atlantic gray seal, 79
Secretin, 66
Self-licking, 15, 26, 36–37
Seminal vesicle, 137
Sequeaction, 136, 138–140
Sexual attraction, 118
Sheep, 89, 117
  Dall sheep, 264
  lambs, 92
  mountain sheep, 251
Skin conductance, 179
Sleep, 62, 72–74, 194

Small intestine, 48
Smiling, 181, 183, 185
Spinal cord, 65–66, 97, 103
Squirrel, 117
    Belding's ground squirrel, 264, 267–269
Streptococci, 53
Stress, 17–18, 181, 189–191, 199
Suckling, 17–18, 31, 33, 77
    suckling stimulation, 35, 38, 77, 82–85, 87
Surrogate rearing, 199–200, 209. *See also*
    Contact comfort
Symbiosis
    commensalism, 1–2, 8, 31, 45
    definition, 1–5, 9–11, 31–33, 45, 184,
        249–250
    mutualism, 1–2, 8, 31, 45
    parasitism, 1–2, 8, 31, 45, 249–250
    psychoanalytic meaning, 9
Sympathetic tone, 64–65
Sympathetic afferents, 66
Synchrony/asynchrony, 4

Tachycardia, 65
Tactile cues, 16, 33, 70
Tactile sensitivity, 15
Tactile stimulation, 16–17, 33, 37–38, 72, 74
Tamarin, 227
Tarsier, 225
Temperature regulation. *See*
    Thermoregulation.
Temperature zone, 126
Testosterone, 48, 49, 137, 152, 154–155, 164
Thermal balance, 25
Thermal cues, 16, 70
Thermal energy, 34, 37–38
Thermal interactions, 29, 63, 74
Thermal sensitivity, 15
Thermal stimulation, 16

Thermogenesis, 3, 26
Thermoregulation, 25–29, 72, 124–129,
    130–136, 137–138, 216, 234–235,
    236–240
Thyroid gland, 23, 66
    iodine uptake, 23
    thyroid stimulating hormone, 68
    thyroxine, 23, 238
Tiger, 264–265
Toxoplasma, 25
Transport of young, 12, 29–31, 191
Triglycerides, 56, 117. *See also* Lipids
Trypanosoma, 25

Ultrasonic cries, 122, 124, 131. *See also*
    Distress vocalizations
Urine, 3, 14–15, 18, 23, 33
    urine formation, 38. *See also* Resource
    exchange
Uterus, 37

Vagal tone, 65
Vagal afferents, 66
Ventral tegmentum, 103
Visual cues, 33, 37
Vole, 252, 253, 263

Water balance, 19
Weaning, 24, 34
Weaning age
    interspecific differences in primates,
        231–233
Wildebeest, 264–265
Wolf, 264
Women, 80, 85, 88, 91–93, 96, 98, 106–107,
    262

Zebra, 264